Struggles for Self-Determination

Katanga, Rhodesia, Transkei, and Bophuthatswana: Four African countries that, though existing in a literal sense, were, in each case, considered by the international community to be a component part of a larger sovereign state through which all official communications and interactions were still conducted. This book is concerned with the intertwined histories of these four right-wing secessionist states in Southern Africa as they fought for but ultimately failed to win sovereign recognition. Along the way, Katanga, Rhodesia, Transkei, and Bophuthatswana each invented new national symbols and traditions, created all the trappings of independent statehood, and proclaimed that their movements were legitimate expressions of national self-determination. Josiah Brownell provides a unique comparison between these states, viewed together as a common reaction to decolonization and the triumph of anti-colonial African nationalism. Describing the ideological stakes of their struggles for sovereignty, Brownell explores the international political controversies that their drives for independence initiated inside and outside Africa. By combining their stories, this book aims to draw out the relationships between the emergence of these four pseudo-states and the fragility of the entire postcolonial African state structure.

Josiah Brownell is Associate Professor of History in the Department of Social Science and Cultural Studies at the Pratt Institute in New York. He has written extensively on nationalism, decolonization, and white settlerism in Southern Africa, and is the author of *The Collapse of Rhodesia: Population Demographics and the Politics of Race* (2010).

Struggles for Self-Determination

The Denial of Reactionary Statehood in Africa

Josiah Brownell

Pratt Institute

CAMBRIDGE
UNIVERSITY PRESS

University Printing House, Cambridge CB2 8BS, United Kingdom

One Liberty Plaza, 20th Floor, New York, NY 10006, USA

477 Williamstown Road, Port Melbourne, VIC 3207, Australia

314–321, 3rd Floor, Plot 3, Splendor Forum, Jasola District Centre, New Delhi – 110025, India

103 Penang Road, #05–06/07, Visioncrest Commercial, Singapore 238467

Cambridge University Press is part of the University of Cambridge.

It furthers the University's mission by disseminating knowledge in the pursuit of education, learning, and research at the highest international levels of excellence.

www.cambridge.org
Information on this title: www.cambridge.org/9781108832649
DOI: 10.1017/9781108966825

First published 2022

A catalogue record for this publication is available from the British Library.

Library of Congress Cataloging-in-Publication Data
Names: Brownell, Josiah, author.
Title: Struggles for self-determination: the denial of reactionary statehood in Africa / Josiah Brownell, Pratt Institute, New York.
Description: Cambridge, United Kingdom; New York, NY: Cambridge University Press, 2022. | Includes bibliographical references and index.
Identifiers: LCCN 2021026858 (print) | LCCN 2021026859 (ebook) | ISBN 9781108832649 (hardback) | ISBN 9781108959971 (paperback) | ISBN 9781108966825 (epub)
Subjects: LCSH: Self-determination, National–Africa. | Recognition (International law) | Sovereignty. | Africa–History–Autonomy and independence movements. | Africa–Politics and government–1960– | Africa–Foreign relations–1960– | BISAC: HISTORY / Africa / General
Classification: LCC DT30.5 .B76 2022 (print) | LCC DT30.5 (ebook) | DDC 320.1/5096–dc23
LC record available at https://lccn.loc.gov/2021026858
LC ebook record available at https://lccn.loc.gov/2021026859

ISBN 978-1-108-83264-9 Hardback
ISBN 978-1-108-95997-1 Paperback

For my parents

Contents

Figures

Maps

Acknowledgments

This book project could not have been possible without the support, encouragement, patience, and good humor from so many people along the way. I cannot acknowledge them all, but there are some whom I must single out. First, I want to thank my wife, Bethany Sousa, who has been there for every twist and turn of this entire eight-year journey and has heard way too much about reactionary statehood than any women's rights lawyer should ever have to. I owe an enormous debt of gratitude to my brother, Reb Brownell, who read and made extensive comments on a late draft of this manuscript. My mother, Eleanor Brownell, and sister, Ginanne Brownell, have endured countless stories about this book's development, as have my two sons, Ryder and Cian, whom I would guess are the only two boys at their New York City schools who can correctly pronounce Bophuthatswana.

I did not realize I was writing *a book* until I was already deep into my research. In 2013, I gave a lecture as part of the Pratt Institute's School of Liberal Arts Lecture Series about what I thought was going to be a stand-alone article comparing Rhodesian and Katangese diplomacy. Afterward, it was my department chair at the time, Gregg Horowitz, who first encouraged me to extend what was then still a series of linked ideas into a book. And from there it grew, and its comparative scope became more ambitious. I owe much to those who volunteered their time to read and critique portions of this manuscript as it developed. In this regard, I need to make special mention of David Kenrick, who read and made incredibly helpful suggestions on two very different drafts of this book. It was David who nudged me early on to break free from my "rule of three" mental block and fully incorporate Bophuthatswana alongside Katanga, Rhodesia, and Transkei in this comparative study, which was crucial to the book's overall argument.

The ideas and arguments presented in this book have also greatly benefited from the questions, critiques, and criticisms from all the many attendees at various workshops, lectures, and academic conferences where I presented parts of this project as it took shape. I am especially grateful for the comments and questions raised by the participants in the Pratt Social Science and Cultural Studies department workshop where I presented two draft chapters. My colleague and fellow historian, Ann Holder, shared some very thoughtful and detailed feedback on these early chapters, and our conversation over a beer afterward convinced me to expand upon some of the comparative arguments I make in the book. I want to individually thank two other Pratt colleagues, Jennifer Telesca and Lisabeth During, for their good advice, great senses of humor, and solid support throughout. I owe a debt of gratitude to the chair of our department, Macarena Gomez-Barris, for carving out space and time for me to finish this book during a very challenging academic year for everyone. I am also grateful to John Aerni-Flessner, Barbara Cannady-Masimini, Frederick Cooper, Jeffrey Davidow, Denise Gamino, P. B. Gemma, Michael Hendershot, Robert Jackson, Diana Jeater, James Ker-Lindsay, Miles Larmer, Donal Lowry, Richard Mahoney, Nicole Martin, Rachel McLemore, Bernard Moore, C. J. Muller, Thomas Noer, Anthony Sousa, Brian Sousa, Katherine Sousa, Stevie Strauss, Lydia Walker, and Luise White, who all in different ways aided and supported me during this long project.

Various parts of this book have appeared in articles I wrote that were published in the *Journal of Southern African Studies*, *Journal of Imperial and Commonwealth History*, and *International Journal of African Historical Studies*, and in chapters in edited volumes published by Routledge and Palgrave Macmillan presses, and I want to thank these publishers for permitting me to use that content here. I wish to thank the editors and production staff at Cambridge University Press, in particular Maria Marsh and Atifa Jiwa, as well as the outside readers from Cambridge University Press, who provided me with invaluable suggestions and critiques of my draft chapters that greatly improved the final version of the book. Finally, this book would not have been possible without all the many knowledgeable and helpful archivists and librarians across the United States, Britain, and South Africa where I conducted my research.

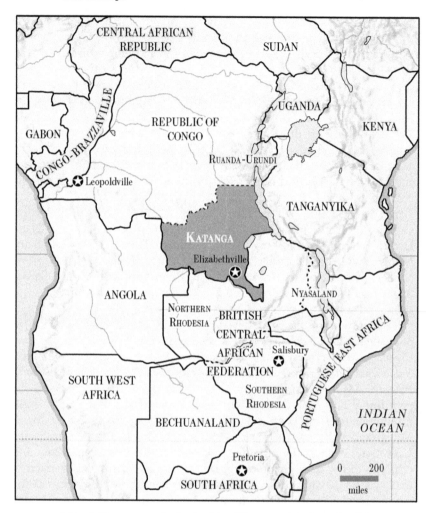

Map 1 Katanga at the beginning of its secession from the Congo in 1960

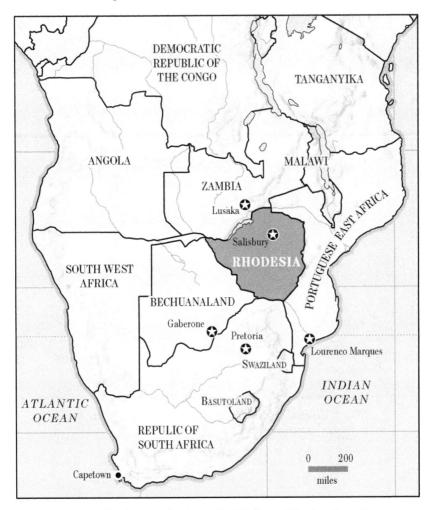

Map 2 Rhodesia at the time of its Unilateral Declaration of
Independence (UDI) in 1965

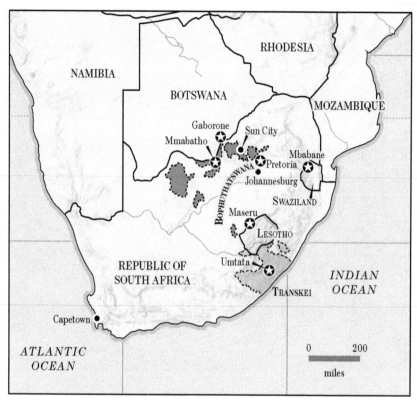

Map 3 Transkei and Bophuthatswana at the time of the latter's
purported independence in 1977

1 Introduction

The Nonexistence of Katanga, Rhodesia, Transkei, and Bophuthatswana

This is a book about four African countries that may not have ever existed.[1] No one denied that Katanga, Rhodesia, Transkei, and Bophuthatswana existed in a literal and physical sense: People could visit them, and many did.[2] Uniformed officials greeted visitors at border posts and airport passport controls, stamps and visas were impressed on travel documents, images of their political leaders hung on the walls of government offices, and they had functioning bureaucracies which produced all the requisite documents of legal statehood. They also created all of the universal trappings of statehood: designing new flags, currencies, postage stamps, and national anthems. In every possible way they held themselves out as independent countries, spoke the language of sovereignty,

---

[1] This opening sentence is a nod to John Sack's humorous travel log from the 1950s, *Report from Practically Nowhere: An Uproarious Account of Thirteen No-Account Countries – From Sark to Sikkim to Swat* (Harper & Bros., New York, 1955). Sack's book jacket reads: "This is a timely, authoritative assessment of thirteen of the most unimportant nations on the face of the earth ... The amazing fact is that all these countries exist."

[2] While there eventually would be four Bantustans that would declare their independence – Transkei (1976), Bophuthatswana (1977), Venda (1979), and Ciskei (1981) – this book only concerns the first two that declared independence, which were the only ones that made serious efforts to win international recognition. All four pseudo-states in this book were within the geographic and political region of "Southern Africa." Leroy Vail demarcates this region as "extending from Cape Town to south central Zaire [Congo] on a south-north axis, and from Namibia to Mozambique on a west-east axis, but with Angola largely excluded." Vail defined this region primarily in terms of the effects of the interconnected labor markets and related migrations to the economic hub of South Africa, writing "it has constituted a coherent regional unit over the past century or so." *The Creation of Tribalism in Southern Africa* (James Currey, London, 1989) p. 7. Filipe Ribiero de Meneses and Robert McNamara define Southern Africa in terms of the postcolonial white power structures remaining on the continent therough the 1970s, and as only constituting a distinct political concept from the mid-1960s onward. But they conceive of it as having similar geographic boundaries as did Vail, except that they include Angola "bounded at the south by the Cape of Good Hope, while its northern extent was a line that, by 1960, stretched westward from Luanda, Elizabethville (today's Lubumbashi) in Katanga ... Mufiliria, Ndola, Lusaka ... Kariba, Salisbury ... and Beira ..." Filipe Ribeiro de Meneses and Robert McNamara, *The White Redoubt, the Great Powers and the Struggle for Southern Africa* (Palgrave MacMillan, London, 2018) p. 4.

and in big and small ways they tried to assert their own individual international personalities. In terms of their actual state capacity and functionality, some of them were arguably more real than many of the legally recognized states to the north of them in Africa.[3] But while they existed in reality, Katanga, Rhodesia, Transkei, and Bophuthatswana did not exist in a legal sense. In each case, the international community considered them to be a component of a larger sovereign state through which all official communications and interactions were still conducted. This was because their many critics inside and outside Africa saw each of their claims for independence as little more than sleights of hand that coopted the language and distorted the values of anti-colonial nationalism as a means to preserve the structures of white power in postcolonial Africa.[4] As a consequence, these unrecognized regimes were not simply ignored, they were affirmatively shunned from the international community. So, while they imagined themselves to be sovereign states, the active rejections of their existences by the world community were perhaps greater acts of imagination. As detailed in this book, the stories of these reactionary pseudo-states were in part battles of competing illusions, with each one pretending to be a legal state, and the international community pretending that each one was not there at all.

In telling the stories of these four aspirant African states, this book aims to pull out the big from the small.[5] It is organized around a series of contests over the expressions of sovereignty made by these pseudo-states and their friends abroad, and their enemies' responses to those expressions. It unpacks the claims and counterclaims, representations and counter representations, and performances and counter performances, as a means to bring forward why the fates of these four reactionary

---

[3] On a visit to Bophuthatswana the Deputy Mayor of Paris, Pierre Bas, quoted the French writer Max Jalade in saying, "For a state whose existence is not recognised, Bophuthatswana seems strangely real!" Quoted in Peris Sean Jones, "Mmabatho, 'Mother of the People': Identity and Development in an 'Independent' Bantustan, Bophuthatswana, 1975–1994," PhD dissertation, Loughborough University (1997) p. 280.

[4] An editorial from *Sechaba*, the official organ of the ANC, described Bophuthatswana as "one of those racist tricks to fool the word that 'changes are taking place in South Africa.'" Editorial, "No to Bantustan Recognition!" *Sechaba* (October 1982).

[5] There are several terms that have been used to describe self-governing territories that claim sovereignty but which have not been accepted by the international community: contested states, de facto states, para-states, quasi-states, and unrecognized states. This book will refer to Katanga, Rhodesia, Transkei, and Bophuthatswana as contested states, aspirant states, would-be states, or pseudo-states, but sometimes will refer to their governments as regimes. For an overview of these various terms, see: J. Ker Lindsay, "Engagement without Recognition: The Limits of Diplomatic Interaction with Contested States," *International Affairs*, vol. 91, no. 2 (2015) fn. 6.

would-be states were seen to be so important at the time and why their precedents continue to matter to this day. It will concern both the symbolic and rhetorical contests over statehood in the realm of ideas and imagination, and the very tangible contests over their sovereign status. Among other things, this book will demonstrate that it was often in the outer extremities of these contested states, in the seemingly picayune legal details concerning the diplomatic statuses of foreign missions and the arcane minutia of passport visas or the rhetorical and propagandic significance of sending and receiving official visitors, where the international and domestic politics of nonrecognition were manifested. At times these were strange struggles, such as the controversies surrounding Rhodesia's issuance of postage stamps, or when herds of livestock wandered over the border from Lesotho into Transkei. Other times they could spark brightly, as with the uproar over Frank Sinatra performing at the Sun City Resort in Bophuthatswana. Simply put, this book examines the ways these four pseudo-states told themselves and the outside world that they were, and should rightly be, sovereign states, and the ways their opponents told them and the entire world that they were not and should never be.

All four would ultimately fail to win diplomatic recognition and gain acceptance in the family of nations. This book does not make any normative claims that these four should have been accepted into the international state system, nor does it argue that the international community treated them unfairly by denying them legal statehood.[6] Neither does it assert that they were fully without access to power, as in fact, each of them, in ways that will be discussed in detail below, had access to many resources – economic, political, and military – that in some respects made them much more powerful than their rival claimants to state control. As such, contrary to how they portrayed themselves in their propaganda campaigns, whether Katanga, Rhodesia, Transkei, and Bophuthatswana could rightly be described as underdogs depended upon what contextual frame was used: they were certainly underdogs in the United Nations in midtown Manhattan, but not in the financial canyons of lower Manhattan; underdogs in the Organization of African Unity (OAU) in Addis Ababa, but not on the streets of Elisabethville, Salisbury, Umtata, or Mmabatho; underdogs perhaps in the British

---

[6] This book aims, in part, to take up Frederick Cooper's broad challenge to look back on decolonization without "falling into the teleology of nation-building" and reexamine "the paths not taken, the dead ends of historical processes, the alternatives that appeared to people in their time." *Colonialism in Question: Theory, Knowledge, History* (University of California Press, Berkeley, 2005) pp. 12, 18.

Foreign and Commonwealth Office on Whitehall and the State Department in Foggy Bottom, but not always in the Houses of Parliament or up on Capitol Hill, and certainly not in the Union Buildings on Meintjieskop.

Pulling out these four would-be African states and analyzing them together has never been done before, and it is not intuitively obvious that they should be grouped together, nor that other would-be states should then be excluded. On the surface they appear to be quite different from one another, and those who have studied and written about these pseudo-states have taken them off on very different historiographical paths, grouping them with other movements and nations not included in this study.[7] Katanga, Rhodesia, Transkei, and Bophuthatswana were not exactly the same, and this book will not argue that they were. For what it is worth, when they existed these aspirant states often tried to distance themselves from each other – the short-lived Central African Federation (CAF), of which Rhodesia was the dominant member, did not publicly support the full independence of Katanga. Neither did Transkei nor Bophuthatswana recognize Rhodesia, and Rhodesia did not recognize either of them. Indeed, it was only after pressure was brought to bear on Transkei from South Africa that it decided to recognize Bophuthatswana and the other Bantustans. But it was partly because they *were* so similar that they tried to actively distance themselves from each other, since it was believed that each one's individual claims for statehood was weakened when it was associated with the others.[8] When

---

[7] There have been some notable transnational studies involving one or some of these four would-be states but never all four and only these four. See: de Meneses and McNamara, *White Redoubt*; Erik Kennes and Miles Larmer, *The Katangese Gendarmes and War in Central Africa: Fighting Their Way Home* (Indiana University Press, Bloomington, 2016); Lazlo Passemiers, "Safeguarding White Minority Power: The South African Government and the Secession of Katanga, 1960–1963," *South African History Journal*, vol. 68, no. 1 (2016); Donal Lowry, "The Ulster of South Africa," *Southern African-Irish Studies*, vol. 1 (1991); M. Rafiqul Islam, "Secessionist Self-Determination: Some Lessons from Katanga, Biafra, and Bangladesh," *Journal of Peace Research*, vol. 22, no. 3 (September 1985); M. Hughes, "Fighting for White Rule in Africa: The Central African Federation, Katanga, and the Congo Crisis, 1958–1965," *International History Review*, vol. 25, no. 3 (September 2003); James Ferguson, *Global Shadows: Africa in the Neoliberal World Order* (Duke University Press, Durham, NC, 2006); S. Williams, *Who Killed Hammarskjold? The UN, The Cold War, and White Supremacy* (Hurst, London, 2011); T. Scarnecchia, "The Congo Crisis, the United Nations, and Zimbabwean Nationalism, 1960–1963," *African Journal of Conflict Resolution*, vol. 11, no. 1 (2011).

[8] This matches with what Geldenhys also argued: "The fact, however, that Transkei's acceptance of independence was followed by Bophuthatswana and Venda inevitably strengthens the argument that Transkei is as much the product of Grand Apartheid as any other homeland. In short, Transkei's claims to international recognition have in effect been undermined by other homelands also opting for independence." Deon Geldenhuys,

these four are viewed together, however, over the tops of the walls of their respective national, regional, and linguistic historiographies, they reveal larger patterns and expose continuities through space and time that are hidden when each is seen only in its walled-off isolation.

While different in many ways, this book will show that these would-be states shared certain common elements that were of fundamental importance. All four emerged as reactions to the dramatic upheavals caused by the rise of pan-ethnic African nationalism and the rapid decolonization of the African continent. All of them harnessed important transnational right-wing networks across Africa, Europe, and North America that were energized by the dissolution of the European empires, the rise of the Afro-Asian Bloc, postcolonial migrations, and the international civil rights movements.[9] These four and only these four brought forth specific kinds of ideological, political, and symbolic contests with regard to the roles of ethnicity, race, and power in postcolonial Africa. It will be demonstrated below that they all presented related challenges to the dominant paradigm of postcolonial African statehood, and those with a stake in that vision of the African state system's success or failure viewed the successes or failures of these four would-be states as vitally important to their causes.[10]

There were certain resonances among all four independence bids that could be heard most clearly in the shared symbolic and rhetorical themes of their supporters and opponents. This can be partly explained by the allied aims behind their secessions and the similarly cold international receptions that welcomed each one, but they also reflected what typologies

---

"International Attitudes on the Recognition of Transkei," Occasional paper given to the South African Institute of International Affairs (October 1979), p. 7.

[9] For more on these white nationalist networks, see: Daniel Geary, Jennie Sutton, and Camilla Schofield (eds.), *Global White Nationalism: From Apartheid to Trump* (Manchester University Press, Manchester, 2020).

[10] Ryan Irwin makes the argument that it was the Katangese secession that "enlarged ongoing disagreements about the nature and meaning of postcolonial sovereignty." Among other things, this led to the creation of the Casablanca Group led by Ghana and Guinea, who united against a common understanding of neocolonialism. Ryan Irwin, "Sovereignty in the Congo Crisis," in Leslie James and Elisabeth Leake (eds.), *Decolonization and the Cold War: Negotiating Independence* (Bloomsbury, London, 2015) pp. 211–212. There were serious ideological, political disagreements between the Casablanca Group and the so-called Brazzaville Group led by the Ivory Coast. Additionally, there were ongoing tensions between African state leaders and leaders of liberation organizations. Nonetheless, from a wide perspective there were certain fundamental, shared ideological pillars that encompassed all these various individuals and groups. For a clear overview of some the tensions and divisions between the Brazzaville Group and the Casablanca Group, see: Anton Andereggen, *France's Relationship with Subsaharan Africa* (Praeger, Westport, 1994). For tensions between African state leaders and Southern African liberation groups, see: Ryan Irwin, *Gordian Knot: Apartheid and the Unmaking of the Liberal World Order* (Oxford University Press, Oxford, 2012).

their supporters and opponents overseas used to categorize them. It is important to note that while these would-be states were shaped in part by how others categorized them, they were also active subjects in these discourses, and they worked to associate their claims to self-determination as being like some and being unlike others, which played into the ideological predilections of potential overseas friends. There was also an important time element, and birth order mattered. Katanga's fate was well known to Rhodesia and all the Bantustans and provided their leaders with a template to follow or avoid, and overseas observers were also provided with a category into which Rhodesia and the Bantustans could be made to fit, or not. Likewise, Transkei and Bophuthatswana emerged a full decade after Rhodesia's declaration of independence from Britain, and while they overlapped for several years, Transkei and Bophuthatswana continued on long after Rhodesia collapsed. Bophuthatswana's independence was celebrated just over a year after Transkei's, an event which Transkeian regime strategists feared would indelibly stain Transkei's own independence movement by associating it with South Africa's wider Bantustan project. Comparisons over time such as this one, where the later subjects were intimately aware of the earlier ones, and some interacting with contemporary ones, necessarily complicates their objective comparisons, especially since there was a high degree of mimicry and purposeful repetition, avoidance, and rejection of earlier examples.

Katanga, Rhodesia, Transkei, and Bophuthatswana each made political decisions as to how they should present themselves to the outside world. The chapters below will pick through and separate out how these aspirant states saw themselves, how they wanted to be perceived overseas, and how important overseas constituencies projected what they wanted to see upon them. Attention will be given to the design and production of these pseudo-states' symbolic repertoires and their invented national traditions. As explained below, these four states looked the way they did partly to attach themselves to certain aesthetico-ideological lineages designed to generate the maximum sympathy and support from particular overseas constituencies. For example, this book will explain the significance of Katanga's ubiquitous copper crosses, why Rhodesia's founding moment and subsequent commemorations so closely mimicked American independence traditions and national symbols, and why the Bantustans' independence moments were closely scripted to follow the "freedoms at midnight" ceremonies elsewhere in Africa.[11]

---

[11] For Rhodesia's independence celebrations specifically, see: J. Brownell, "Out of Time: Global Settlerism, Nostalgia, and the Selling of the Rhodesian Rebellion Overseas," *The Journal of Southern African Studies*, vol. 43, no. 4 (Fall 2016) pp. 805–824.

One of the most intriguing elements that all four would-be states shared was that some of the same people played significant roles in each of them, and some bounced back and forth over their borders playing roles in two or more of these breakaway states. A common pivot point for many of these people was Rhodesia: first when it was still a colony of Britain and a component part of the CAF, then after 1965 when it attempted to secede from the British Empire, and finally even after the rebellion collapsed in 1980. Among this group were white mercenaries from Rhodesia and elsewhere who were drawn to the Katangese conflict to defend Moise Tshombe's secession from the Congolese National Army and United Nations troops. It was the federation that was one of the primary rallying points for mercenary recruitment and main entry point for mercenaries entering Katanga, and it was no accident that during the fighting against United Nations troops Katanga's leader, Moise Tshombe, briefly fled to the CAF for protection, before later returning to Katanga.[12] During the Rhodesian Liberation War, the white settler regime itself welcomed mercenaries from around Africa and the Western world to complement its regular forces in their fight against African guerrillas. Later still, many Rhodesian military men were invited to work for Transkei and Bophuthatswana.[13] The founder and leader of the elite Rhodesian special forces unit called the Selous Scouts was a man named Ron Reid Daly. After the end of the Rhodesian War, Reid Daly would go on to be the head of the Transkei Defense Forces for much of the 1980s, bringing along with him many of his former Rhodesian compatriots.

Not all of these Rhodesian men who bounced around were fighters, some were businessmen, economic or technical advisors, or seasoned politicians. Most famously there was Rowan Cronje, a South African-born Rhodesian who served as a minister in the Rhodesian cabinet throughout the entirety of the Rhodesian rebellion, holding such important posts as minister of health, labour and social welfare; manpower and social affairs; and education. In the mid-1980s, Cronje emigrated from Zimbabwe and quickly became Bophuthatswana's minister of defense, aviation, and foreign affairs. He would hold these portfolios until Bophuthatswana's reincorporation back into South Africa in 1994, a

---

[12] There were serious high-level talks between the Central African Federation Prime Minister, Roy Welensky, and Katangese leaders, including Tshombe, in the buildup to independence about Katanga possibly amalgamating into the CAF upon Congolese independence. See: Hughes, "Fighting for White Rule in Africa."

[13] See for example: Peris Sean Jones, "From 'Nationhood' to Regionalism to the North West Province: 'Bophuthatswananess' and the Birth of the 'New' South Africa," *African Affairs*, vol. 98, no. 393 (October 1999) p. 514.

process in which Cronje played an important role. These men included a man named Kenneth Towsey who was a Rhodesian official in the CAF's Department of External Affairs during the Katanga secession and was intimately involved in the formation of the federation's delicate policy toward Tshombe's regime. After Rhodesia's unilateral declaration of independence (UDI), he headed the Rhodesian Information Office (RIO) in Washington, DC for many years and served as the pseudo-ambassador to the United States. After the fall of Rhodesia, Towsey became a public relations officer for the Transkei government for much of the 1980s. This fluid network of white postimperials who used Rhodesia as a way station and a pivot point, all played important roles in bolstering, defending, and guiding these pseudo-states during their struggles for independence. It will be argued below that it was not simply a coincidence that these men with Rhodesian affiliations ended up playing significant roles in all of these breakaway states, and it was not that they were driven merely by better economic opportunities outside of Rhodesia. It will be shown that they identified these four independence movements, including Rhodesia, as all manifestations of the same ideological project. They were not alone in thinking this.

Others from further afield also saw in these four pseudo-states parts of a common project. Despite the uniform state-level rejection, each of these four could rely upon many powerful supporters inside and outside Africa. In the West it was often the very same people and institutions supporting all of them, and it was often the same people opposing them.[14] The degree to which the same characters reappear across each of these contested independence bids is remarkable. As a result, their struggles for recognition overseas, while different in some ways, still mapped along similar lines, featuring many of the same contestants, same sites of contest, and having the same general shape to their rhetorical exchanges. Even so, there was no single guiding hand behind this common project, no centralized cabal controlling its direction over the twenty-five years of this study. The reactionary project described below was largely given its shape by different people inside and outside Africa reacting to the same phenomena in similar ways.[15]

---

[14] See for example: J. Brownell, "Diplomatic Lepers: The Katangan and Rhodesian Foreign Missions in the United States and the Politics of Nonrecognition," *International Journal of African Historical Studies*, vol. 47, no. 2 (2014).

[15] This common ideological project was not the result of any formal agreement between political leaders. It was broader in terms of its scope of time and participants but also much more decentralized than the "unholy alliance" theory of an explicit conspiracy between South Africa, the federation, Portugal, and Katanga to halt African

This common ideological project took the specific form of what can be called reactionary statehood, though this was a term that no one used at the time, and one that the regime officials and their friends would have certainly disavowed. Nevertheless, it was reactionary because all were born in part as reactions to the decolonization of the continent under anti-colonial African nationalists, and in ways that will be described below, each represented an anathema to the ideological and structural pillars of African nationalism. While challenging this dominant anti-colonial African nationalist ideology, these four were still constrained by the radically changed international structure of postcolonial Africa, in particular the triumph of the nation-state model over competing forms of sovereignty, so each adopted the form and structure of statehood, and wrapped their causes in the clothing of national self-determination. It was their efforts to create new state forms and invent national traditions, to win international acceptance and create a foreign presence overseas, and the complex political contests this initiated inside and outside Africa that are the story lines around which this book is structured.

Struggles for Self-Determination focuses on a twenty-five-year period beginning in 1960 and ending in 1985. It begins just prior to the two-and-a-half-year Katangese secession from the Congo, through Rhodesia's fifteen-year rebellion against Britain, the declarations of independence of Transkei and Bophuthatswana, and ending in 1985 when, as a result of the anti-apartheid cultural boycott, Bophuthatswana's Sun City Resort effectively ceased to be a venue for world-class entertainment.

The Katangese secession from the Congo, which lasted from 1960 to 1963, was viewed at the time, and has been studied since, primarily through the lens of neocolonialism.[16] In a handful of days between the

---

independence and protect Western business interests. See: Rosalynde Ainslie, "The Unholy Alliance: Salazar, Verwoerd, Welensky" (AAM pamphlet, 1962). For the relationship between the federation and Katanga, see: Hughes, "Fighting for White Rule in Africa." Lazlo Pessemiers concludes in his study of South African and Katangese relations that the "unholy alliance" was not based upon any formal collusion between these leaders but was a product of a more "cautious and ad hoc" approach. Pessemiers, "Safeguarding White Minority Power." It was also related to but distinct from the "white redoubt" notion of the early to mid-1970s, which was actualized by a secret military and intelligence agreement between South Africa, Rhodesia, and Portugal between 1971 and 1974, called Exercise ALCORA. See: Filipe Ribeiro de Meneses and Robert McNamara, "The Last Throw of the Dice: Portugal, Rhodesia and South Africa, 1970–74," *Portuguese Studies*, vol. 28, no. 2 (2012) p. 205; de Meneses and McNamara, *White Redoubt.*

[16] "Conventional wisdom," Ryan Irwin writes, was that "Tshombe was merely a stooge of Belgian mining interests whose power stemmed from his willingness to pass along Katanga's riches to neocolonial overseers." Irwin goes on to argue that "up-close, the situation was less straightforward." Irwin, "Sovereignty in the Congo Crisis," p. 204.

Congo's independence from Belgium on June 30, 1960 and Katanga's secession from the Congo on July 11th, there was a mutiny of the Congolese army sparking widespread disorder throughout the country, and the reentry of Belgian troops into sovereign Congolese territory against the wishes of the Congolese central government headed by Prime Minister Patrice Lumumba. It was in this context, though not for that reason, that the provincial President of Katanga, Moise Tshombe, declared that his mineral rich province was "seceding from chaos," depriving the central government of a massive amount of its total tax revenue. Days after the secession, United Nations forces began to pour into the Congo. While Moise Tshombe was the head of the Katangese government, opponents of the secession pointed out that much of the workings of the state in the beginning were in the hands of his Belgian advisors, order was maintained by the Belgian-led security forces and foreign mercenaries, and the state was financed in large part by the giant Belgian and British company, Union Miniere du Haut Katanga (UMHK).[17] Despite aggressively making a case for sovereign recognition, no state, not even Belgium, ever officially recognized the Katangese regime's independence, even after the more overt links to Belgium were cut in 1961. Its secession was condemned by the Congo and the United Nations, and a series of UN resolutions created the legal foundations for the forcible reincorporation of the province back into the Congo. After complex political maneuverings in Leopoldville, Lumumba was forcibly removed from office in September 1960. In January 1961, Lumumba, who was then being detained at a Congolese military camp, was flown down to secessionist Katanga where he was beaten and then killed by a Katangese firing squad in the presence of Belgian officers and Katangese officials.[18] Though the precise details of Lumumba's death

---

A much welcome turn away from this conventional wisdom of Katanga which places the secession within wider regional context can be found in the excellent book by Kennes and Larmer, *Katangese Gendarmes*. See also: J. Brownell, "Book Review: Eric Kennes and Miles Larmer, *The Katangese Gendarmes and War in Central Africa*," *Journal of Modern African History*, vol. 55, no. 3 (2017).

[17] For arguments about the role of foreign interests in Katanga, see: D. N. Gibbs, *The Political Economy of Third World Intervention: Mines, Money, and US Policy in the Congo Crisis* (University of Chicago Press, Chicago, 1991); L. DeWitte, *The Assassination of Lumumba* (Verso, London, 2001); W. Minter, *King Solomon's Mines Revisited* (Basic Books, New York, 1986). For a compelling argument that the Katangese secession was in large part driven by local concerns and not external machinations, see: Kennes and Larmer, *Katangese Gendarmes*. They argue that had Katanga been entirely an external product, then it would have collapsed in mid-1961 when the bulk of the Belgian technicians, advisors, and military officers were forced to leave.

[18] See: Edouard Bustin, "Remembrance of Sins Past: Unraveling the Murder of Patrice Lumumba," *Review of African Political Economy*, vol. 29, no. 93/94, State Failure in the

are still a matter of some debate, Tshombe's direct involvement in the murder forever discredited him in the eyes of most of the world, and certainly among most African leaders.[19] After many months of diplomatic and political wrangling, and several inconclusive skirmishes between Katangese and UN forces, the United Nations forces finally crushed the secession in early 1963, and Katanga was reintegrated back into the Congo.

White settlers across the continent watched the events in the Congo with great trepidation, and none watched these events from a closer vantage point or with closer attention than Rhodesian settlers in the CAF. The colony of Rhodesia had been effectively self-governing within the British Empire since the early 1920s, and had come close to achieving independent Dominion status alongside other established settler societies of the British Empire, even though Rhodesia's white settler population never exceeded 5 percent of its total population. But while Rhodesia was nearly independent, it was never fully so. For a decade it had been one of the three component territories of the CAF, alongside Northern Rhodesia (Zambia) and Nyasaland (Malawi). But when the British dissolved the federation at the end of 1963, Zambia and Malawi were given full independence under African majority rule, while Rhodesia remained in its ambiguous quasi-independent status under white settler rule. This legal netherworld was a source of frustration and anxiety for many white Rhodesians who were unsure of their political future in a rapidly decolonizing continent.[20] On November 11, 1965, Prime Minister Ian Smith declared that his white settler government was unilaterally breaking away from Britain and was to be from that moment forward a fully sovereign state within the British Empire. This act was referred to at the time and since as UDI. Regime officials at home and overseas tried hard to win recognition of the white settler regime, but to no avail. Britain and the UN immediately declared that Rhodesia's independence was illegal, and the regime soon faced an escalating series of international sanctions. In 1970, Rhodesia declared itself to be a republic in the hope that clarifying its constitutional status might clear the path for international recognition. It did not have that effect. After 1972, the regime fought an increasingly bloody guerrilla war against black African liberation forces that put great

---

Congo: Perceptions and Realities (September–December 2002). See also: DeWitte, *The Assassination of Lumumba.*

[19] See: Irwin, "Sovereignty in the Congo Crisis," p. 211.

[20] For more on the bizarre legal status of Rhodesia and its practical effects, see: J. Brownell, "'A Sordid Tussle on the Strand:' Rhodesia House during the UDI Rebellion (1965–1980)," *The Journal of Imperial and Commonwealth History,* vol. 38, no. 3 (September 2010).

strains on its very limited manpower resources.[21] The Rhodesian regime finally collapsed in 1979, and after a brief transition back to British rule for the purpose of administering the independence election, the new state of Zimbabwe was created in 1980.

Of the aspirant states examined in this book, only Transkei and Bophuthatswana declared their independence with the approval of their mother country, and in fact their mother country was the only one ever to recognize their independence, just as South Africa was also the only state ever to recognize the other Bantustans of Venda in 1979 and Ciskei in 1981. In a 1976 ceremony that deliberately mimicked the "freedoms at midnight" flag-swapping ceremonies that occurred all across Africa a little over a decade before, South Africa purported to cede sovereignty over a southeastern portion of its territory bordering on the Indian Ocean to the new state of Transkei, one of the two established homelands of the Xhosa people (the other being Ciskei). As the first ethnic homeland to achieve pseudo-independence from South Africa, Transkei served as the flagship, but three other Bantustans would later follow this same path, the next being Bophuthatswana in 1977. The architects of apartheid envisioned their Bantustan strategy as a way to permanently disenfranchise and expatriate the African populations living in South Africa, thereby solving what they saw as the political problems of African nationalism and destabilizing demographic trends, without disrupting the republic's supply of cheap African labor – as Timothy Gibbs writes, it was "a strategy of shattering nationalist politics."[22] As critics of the Bantustan policy forcefully argued, despite their nominal independence they continued to be almost completely dependent upon South Africa.[23] In this way, the creation of Transkei and the other Bantustans can perhaps best be visualized not as the Bantustans breaking off from South Africa, but rather white South Africa breaking itself off from the Bantustans, leaving behind the political and moral burdens of their African populations.

On December 6, 1977, a little over a year after Transkei's independence celebration, South Africa purportedly ceded sovereignty to six enclaves (eventually adding another to make seven) spread across the Cape Province, Transvaal, and the Orange Free State that was purported

---

[21] See: J. Brownell, *Collapse of Rhodesia: Population Demographics and the Politics of Race* (I. B. Tauris, London, 2010).

[22] Timothy Gibbs, *Mandela's Kinsmen: Nationalist Elites and Apartheid's First Bantustan* (James Currey, London, 2017), p. 20. See also: R. Southall, *South Africa's Transkei* (Monthly Review Press, New York, 1983).

[23] B. Streek and R. Wicksteed, *Render unto Kaiser: A Transkei Dossier* (Ravan Press, Johannesburg, 1981).

to be the homeland of the Tswana peoples.[24] While it was absurd geographically, the pseudo-state Bophuthatswana was economically the most viable of the homelands, with extensive mining operations, and after 1979, a booming tourist destination called the Sun City Resort. Like Transkei, Bophuthatswana struggled in vain to win outside recognition. Neither Transkei nor Bophuthatswana found they could convince the outside world to evaluate their claims for statehood apart from the world community's strong opposition to South Africa's wider Bantustan system. In the case of Transkei, these efforts to create distance from apartheid included noisily breaking off diplomatic ties with South Africa for two years. But none of the Bantustans could ever escape their diplomatic isolation, and indeed Venda and Ciskei did not waste much energy trying to do so. When the apartheid regime finally collapsed in 1994, all the homelands were reincorporated back into South Africa.

A publicly unfriendly posture toward apartheid South Africa was for many years the sine qua non of state legitimacy in postcolonial Africa, and nothing was more damning in the eyes of independent Africa's state leaders than a close association with, or worse yet, a dependence upon South Africa.[25] As historian Jamie Miller points out: "The array of fledgling [African] states that emerged [after colonization] identified South Africa's apartheid system, with its entrenched racialism, as the symbolic antithesis to their emergent vision of what it meant to be a state in the postcolonial era."[26] For this reason, Katanga, Rhodesia, Transkei, and Bophuthatswana each had a conflicting push-and-pull relationship with their powerful ally, protector, and sometimes patron, the Republic of South Africa.[27] Unlike these four regimes, however, South Africa was always legally sovereign, and though it became increasingly isolated after

[24] Bophuthatswana would later add another enclave before it was reincorporated into South Africa.

[25] Ryan Irwin writes, "Just as anticommunism animated Washington's Cold War and anticapitalism oriented Moscow's stance abroad, the fight against apartheid gave form to the political project known as the Third World." Irwin, *Gordian Knot*, p. 5. Some African states did have limited diplomatic interactions with South Africa, but it was always domestically and internationally unpopular to do so. See J. Miller, *An African Volk: The Apartheid Regime and Its Search for Survival* (Oxford University Press, Oxford, 2016); Irwin, *Gordian Knot*; R. Pfister, *Apartheid South Africa and African States: From Pariah to Middle Power, 1961–1994* (I. B. Tauris, London, 2005).

[26] Miller, *An African Volk*, p. 7. By the late 1960s, however, this universal African state "militancy against white rule had run aground," p. 69. This provided the opportunity for Vorster to pursue his "outward policy" of African engagement in the 1970s, as Miller explains in his book.

[27] What the *New York Times* wrote in 1976 of Transkei was equally true of the other two, that the South African connection was "both a blessing and a curse." John Burns, "Transkei Approaches Nationhood Helped, and Burdened, by Its Ties to South Africa," *New York Times*, October 22, 1976.

the Sharpeville shooting of 1960, and even more so after the Soweto uprising in 1976, the republic continued to enjoy the fruits of being a functioning member of the international community. One of the many ironies running the length of the stories of these aspirant states is that while each of these four claims to sovereignty was in part tainted by their connections to South Africa, the republic's diplomatic status was unaffected. Diplomats from the republic still sipped cocktails at exclusive embassy functions in Washington, London, Paris, and elsewhere, its leaders met privately with other world leaders, its citizens traveled abroad on South African passports, largely without restriction, and the state conducted its international business and diplomacy with few obstructions.[28] All the while, Katanga, Rhodesia, Transkei, and Bophuthatswana were seen not to exist at all.

There is no conceptual space in the international system to fit pseudo-states. "Unrecognized states," Nina Caspersen writes, "are the places that do not exist in international relations; they are state-like entities that are not part of the international system of sovereign states; consequently they are shrouded in mystery and subject to myths and simplifications."[29] Typically, non-states are ignored by the international community, and there is an open collusion among legal states and international organizations to oppose secessionism. But Katanga, Rhodesia, Transkei, and Bophuthatswana were not simply ignored by the international community, even though at times they might have wished they had been. Instead, all four were despised as outcasts by the international community, and they were all despised for essentially the same reasons. Opponents wrote and spoke of these breakaway states in the language of epidemiology, characterizing them as dangerous contagions to be isolated and destroyed by the world community.[30] The recently decolonized African states to the north of them were particularly hostile, and the rest of the world community generally deferred to the pleas of those African states that called for their diplomatic quarantine, even though the applications of the quarantines in the West were uneven and sometimes half-hearted. In important ways, these four secessionist movements always transcended the regional politics of Southern Africa and were seen as global problems to be solved.

---

[28] It should be noted that this too began to change even for South Africa in the 1980s, as international sanctions regimes began to increasingly isolate the state. R. M. Price, *Apartheid State in Crisis: Political Transformation in South Africa, 1975–1990* (Oxford University Press, Oxford, 1991).

[29] N. Caspersen, *Unrecognized States* (Polity Press, Cambridge, 2012) p. 1.

[30] For an older, but still authoritative analysis of pariah states, see: D. Geldenhuys, *Isolated States: A Comparative Analysis* (Cambridge University Press, Cambridge, 1990).

As will be detailed in later chapters, in the years after the Second World War there was a marked change in the way new states were created and brought into the international community.[31] Older notions of sovereignty having to do with aspirant states meeting certain empirical standards gave way to a new paradigm that took no account of actual state capacity.[32] The realization of anti-colonial self-determination was the new frame of legal sovereignty. As Robert Jackson succinctly puts it: "To be a sovereign state today one needs only to have been a formal colony yesterday. All other considerations are irrelevant."[33] After decolonization from European control was completed, however, the right to self-determination expired. Under the new postwar paradigm, self-determination was characterized variously as a "one-shot" event, or a "closed chapter," and could not be invoked in the future to create newer ethno-national states.[34] As such, it was solely an anti-colonial principle that lost its moral power after alien European rule was eliminated, once, as Ali Mazrui coined it, "racial sovereignty" had been reestablished.[35] Thereafter the right of self-determination was subordinated to the bank vault-protected right of territorial integrity.[36] As a result, a new "moral language" of sovereignty was created wherein those making ethno-national claims against the newly decolonized states came to be disparaged as "separatists," "secessionists," or "irredentists," who threatened to "splinter" or "fragment" these fledgling states.[37] Unilateral secession

---

[31] For a good overview of the international law and state practice of secession, see chapters 1 and 2 in M. G. Kohen (ed.), *Secession: International Law Perspectives* (Cambridge University, Cambridge, 2006).

[32] R. Jackson, *Quasi-States: Sovereignty, International Relations, and the Third World* (Cambridge University Press, Cambridge, 1991) p. 34. See also: Barry Bartmann, "Political Realities and Legal Anomalies: Revisiting the Politics of International Recognition," in Tozun Bahcheli, Barry Bartmann, and Henry Srebrnik (eds.), *De Facto States: The Quest for Sovereignty* (Routledge, Oxfordshire, 2016) p. 12.

[33] Jackson, *Quasi-States*, p. 17.

[34] Linda Bishai, *Forgetting Ourselves: Secession and the (Im)possibility of Territorial Identity* (Lexington Books, Lanham, 2006) p. 33; R. Bereketeab, *Self-Determination and Secession in Africa: The Postcolonial State* (Routledge, Abingdon, 2016) p. 7; For a discussion of the dominance of the principle of territorial integrity over the principle of self-determination after Second World War, see M. Fabry, *Recognizing States: International Society and the Establishment of New States since 1776* (Oxford University Press, Oxford, 2010), pp. 147–178.

[35] A. Mazrui, *Towards a Pax Africana: A Study of Ideology and Ambition* (University of Chicago Press, Chicago, 1967).

[36] According to Caspersen, unrecognized states are those entities which "insist on their right to self-determination, but are faced with the stronger principle of territorial integrity," and thus are made to live in the "shadows of international relations." *Unrecognized States*, p. 1.

[37] Jackson, *Quasi-States*, p. 41. C. Young, *The Politics of Cultural Pluralism* (University of Wisconsin Press, Madison, 1976) p. 82.

on the basis of ethno-national claims for self-determination, and the establishment of de facto status, which used to be the primary mechanism for the creation of new states, had rather suddenly become illegitimate.[38]

Running contrary to this trend, all four pseudo-states in this study in part staked their claims for legitimacy upon the idea that cultural traditions and historical allegiances to ethnic and tribal configurations were superior to that of the newer concept of the pan-ethnic African nation within the bounds of the former colonial borders. In making this claim, all four emphasized their ethnic and tribal sources of support and legitimacy. Katanga's President, Moise Tshombe, was an urbane playboy and the son of a wealthy African businessman, but importantly he was also related by both birth and marriage to the Lunda paramount chief, a fact that he used to bolster his standing inside and outside Katanga as an authentic voice of the Katangese.[39] Kaiser Matanzima, the first President of Transkei, was a paramount chief of Emigrant Thembuland, and Bophuthatswana's President, Lucas Mangope, was a chief of the Bahurutshe.[40] Both Bantustan leaders used their statuses as "traditional leaders" to strengthen their claims to power, even though their positions as chiefs were "created and underwritten by the South African state."[41] In Rhodesia, Ian Smith's settler government disputed accusations that their regime lacked support among the African population, and repeatedly argued that the only true test of African opinion was through an Indaba, a gathering of the government-appointed African chiefs, rather than a statewide poll or a Western-style referendum.[42] One such Indaba was called in 1964 and it had delivered a unanimous vote in support of

---

[38] As Emerson humorously puts it: "*My* right to self-determination against those who oppress me is obviously unimpeachable, but *your* claim to exercise such a right against me is wholly inadmissible." Rupert Emerson, "The New Higher Law of Anti-Colonialism," in Karl Deutsch and Stanley Hoffmann (eds.), *The Relevance of International Law* (Schenkman Publishing, Cambridge, 1968) (emphasis in original) p. 162.

[39] See S. Hempstone, *Rebels, Mercenaries, and Dividends: The Katanga Story* (Praeger, Westport, 1962) pp. 68–72.

[40] For a critical assessment of Matanzima's claim to paramountcy, see: "The Making of a Puppet," *Mail & Guardian*, July 10, 2003. J. B. Peires referred to Kaiser Matanzima as "Dr. Verwoerd's most sincere black disciple." J. B. Pieres, "The Implosion of Transkei and Ciskei," *African Affairs*, vol. 91, no. 364 (July 1992) p. 366.

[41] The quote refers specifically to Mangope but is equally applicable to Matanzima. Michael Lawrence and Andrew Manson, "The 'Dog of the Boers': The Rise and Fall of Mangope in Bophuthatswana," *Journal of Southern African Studies*, vol. 20, no. 3, Special Issue: Ethnicity and Identity in Southern Africa (September 1994).

[42] For an excellent analysis of the Rhodesian Front's views on the unsuitability of one-man-one-vote systems, see chapter 3 in David Kenrick's *Decolonisation, Identity and Nation in Rhodesia, 1964–1979: A Race against Time* (Palgrave, London, 2019).

Rhodesia declaring its independence from Britain. All four argued that the African nationalists who opposed them were merely power-hungry political opportunists, with artificial and ephemeral constituencies, who were either dangerously naive to the communist threat or were themselves the puppets of foreign communist powers. According to these regimes, it was the socially conservative tribal hierarchies and village traditions that represented true African authenticity, not the newer ideologies of political liberation nor notions of pan-ethic civic nationalism.

It was not just that Katanga, Rhodesia, Transkei, and Bophuthatswana made ethno-national appeals to legitimacy that undercut the pan-ethnic African nationalism paradigm which accounted for such universal African hostility. It should be recalled that while Biafra's ethno-national secession from Nigeria, which lasted from 1967 to 1970, was officially condemned at the level of the OAU, it still won the support of several African leaders, most notably Tanzania's leader Julius Nyerere. What separated out these four from Biafra and other secessionist movements in Africa was that it was their ethnic, regional, or tribal claims to African political legitimacy in combination with the continued power and influence in the disputed territory of either their former colonizers or white settlers. In these four breakaway states, African nationalists saw the ghosts of old colonial divide and rule policies.[43] Even though each claimed support from the majority of "authentic" Africans, most African leaders viewed them as primarily securing white interests. Zambian President Kenneth Kaunda's memorable quote regarding the short-lived Zimbabwe Rhodesia government under Abel Muzorewa aptly characterizes African nationalists' views of all four breakaway states; that they were "… white power clad in black habiliments."[44] Just as pointedly, though less poetically, Oliver Tambo, the African National Congress (ANC) President, expressed this same notion of a black cover over white power in an interview from 1983: "… the Bantustans are a true injustice. And the people understand that the enemy is not even the group of administrators that have been appointed for the Bantustans. They are

---

[43] Leroy Vail describes several colonial administrative advantages for the creation and strengthening of "traditional authorities" in rural areas in Southern Africa. These included the lower administrative costs, the prevention of "potentially dangerous territory-wide political consciousness" as a counter to the "detribalized" Africans whom administrators were "deeply suspicious," and finally that operating through "traditional" forces in the villages helped to "counter the forces of social decay" associated with male migrant labor throughout Southern Africa. *Creation of Tribalism*, p. 13.

[44] Quoted in Jay Ross, "Britain Assails Nigerian Seizure of BP Interests," *Washington Post*, August 2, 1979.

obviously the regime's brutal agents, but the people understand that the enemy is the Pretoria regime."[45] It was therefore the double threat of the ethno-national centrifugal forces pushing out from the central state, combined with what was perceived as Western or white settler forces affirmatively pulling these pieces out, which made them so dangerous for African leaders. If these reactionary states survived, it was feared the entire African state system could fall apart.

Enemies of Katanga, Rhodesia, Transkei, and Bophuthatswana recognized that their successes or failures carried broader implications well beyond their own borders. All too aware of the vulnerabilities of their own individual fledgling states, anti-colonial African nationalists attempted to not just win independence for their particular colonial territory, but as Adom Getachew writes in a recent book, for them "decolonization was a project of rendering the world that sought to create a domination-free and egalitarian international order."[46] Articulating the interconnectedness of the anti-colonial project, Kwame Nkrumah pronounced on the occasion of Ghana's independence: "Our independence is meaningless unless it is linked up with the total liberation of the African continent."[47] This was a call for a new and more just international order without which these new African states "were constantly vulnerable to external encroachment and intervention."[48] Nkrumah, writing of the Congo crisis, elaborated on the connected fates of postcolonial African states: "If we allow the independence of the Congo to be compromised in any way by the imperialists and neo-colonialists, the whole of Africa will be exposed to grave risk."[49] Under this theory, the fates of all postcolonial African states were linked so that the dissolution of any new African state which could open it up to foreign "encroachment" was a threat to all other African states, recalling the famous quote from a much older anti-colonial nationalist, Benjamin Franklin: "We must all hang together, or, most assuredly, we shall all hang separately."

The importance of the fates of these four pseudo-states was felt on the other side of the ideological divide as well. Western friends of these four supported them and opposed the dominant form of anti-colonial African

---

[45] "Interview with Oliver Tambo by *Noticias*," August 5, 1983. Posted by South African History Online, accessed January 2, 2021, www.sahistory.org.za/archive/interview-oliver-tambo-noticias-05-august-1983-maputo.

[46] Adom Getachew, *Worldmaking after Empire: The Rise and Fall of Self-Determination* (Princeton University Press, Princeton, 2019) p. 2.

[47] Quoted in Getachew, *Worldmaking after Empire*, p. 1.

[48] Getachew, *Worldmaking after Empire*, p. 4.

[49] Kwame Nkrumah, *Challenge of the Congo: A Case Study of Foreign Pressures in an Independent State* (Panaf Books, London, 2002) p. xvi.

nationalism for a variety of different reasons. One important factor in determining how these four were treated in the West was their ideological anti-communism, as it provided a language to defend their causes that had an appeal across a wide political spectrum in the West. This did not mean that their anticommunism was merely a cynical marketing ploy for Western audiences. Neither should their anti-communist ideology be seen entirely as a safe cover for their Western friends' underlying racial motivations. The fear of communism animated the behaviors of many of the political actors in these dramas, even for some of the most vocal Western opponents of these regimes. For Western leaders, the fact that the Soviet Union, China, and the Eastern Bloc were hostile to all four regimes tested the outer limits of the maxim that "the enemy of my enemy is my friend." In addition, some Westerners had financial and business reasons to lobby their own governments to be more friendly to these breakaway states. Those with monetary interests in these territories – for instance, the lucrative mining industry in Katanga, or chrome extraction from Rhodesia, or one of a multitude of South African businesses – were often driven primarily by profit, not the politics of decolonization per se.

For many other supporters of these pseudo-states, however, the preservation of white supremacy and anticommunism were melded together as allied causes that were both crucial to saving Western Civilization. On a regional level, these conflicts were seen by some anxious white settlers in other territories as forward levees that must hold lest the swells of black African nationalism rush over and wash up on their own borders. So, white Rhodesians watched with horror the Katangese crisis, white South Africans anxiously watched the Rhodesian crisis, and white supremacists in the West watched with dread the slow demise of white settlerism in Africa ending with the fall of apartheid South Africa.[50] Not only were the fates of all four seen to be crucially important in the preservation of the

---

[50] See for example: South African Department of Foreign Affairs Archives, Box 1/156/1/19/1, "UDI Rhodesia's Position re: International Organizations and Agencies," Telegram from South African Ambassador H. L. Taswell Washington to Secretary DFA, Pretoria, November 18, 1965. Ambassador Taswell always saw the Rhodesian problem as a trial run for the looming battle over South Africa. Regarding sanctions he said, "To me it seems of primary importance that sanctions against Rhodesia should not succeed. If they succeed, the probabilities are that our enemies will make every effort to see that they are successfully applied against us. If sanctions fail against Rhodesia, the lesson to our enemies should be a very salutary one." South African Department of Foreign Affairs Archives, Box 1/156/1/19/1, "UDI Rhodesia's Position re: International Organizations and Agencies," Telegram from South African Ambassador H. L. Taswell Washington to Secretary DFA, Pretoria, "Rhodesia," January 7, 1966. This was not an uncontested argument, however. See Miller, *An African Volk.*

old order in Southern Africa, for some conservatives in the West these bids were seen as important contests in the parallel struggles over race relations at home. Under this mode of thinking, black civil rights struggles in the West and political liberation in Africa were simply cover for more sinister communistic motivations. These suspicions overlapped with deep-seated conservative fears of an activist UN dominated by newly decolonized countries. As one pro-Katanga organization in America breathlessly declared: "In resisting the UN aggression, the people of Katanga are the true Freedom Fighters not only for their own liberties, but for the cause of *world* freedom."[51] Defending Rhodesia's independence several years later, another American organization declared: "Should [Rhodesia] fail, all of Africa will suffer.... Chaos would inundate order, and Africa would not fail to read the message that Western Civilization has abdicated."[52] All sides therefore read the big in the small in the fates of these would-be states, and it was another scale of the big in the small that these independence bids were in part contested over the minutia of their sovereign expressions.

As diplomatic outcasts scrambling for any scrap of international legitimacy, Katanga, Rhodesia, Transkei, and Bophuthatswana were always sensitive to every rejection, slight, and snub, and were quick to tout any instance of a possible international breakthrough. At first glance, the sites of the contests over their sovereign expressions can appear small, bizarre, or even silly. But this apparent smallness hides the importance these contests had for both sides. Those rare instances of some sort of international acknowledgment, however miniscule, were widely celebrated by the countries, such as the 1961 Katangese International Fair, or Rhodesia hosting the 1968 World Ploughing Championship, when Transkei was allowed to participate in the 1977 World Tug of War Championship, or in 1980 and 1984 when World Boxing Association (WBA) heavyweight title fights were held at the Sun City Resort in Bophuthatswana. But these were exceptional leaks in the otherwise watertight barriers built around these regimes.

Each of these four was particularly vulnerable to exploitation by those offering promises of access and acceptance into the international community, and their illegal statuses left them especially vulnerable to scams

---

[51] ACAKFF advertisement (my emphasis), Folder ACAKFF, *The New York Times*, December 14, 1961, Box 6, Group Research Inc. Archives, Rare Book and Manuscript Library, Columbia University. See also "UN Secret Plan to Resume Military Operations in Katanga," Marvin Liebman Papers, Hoover Library, Stanford University, Box 56, Letter from Yergan to KFF friends and members, October 22, 1962.

[52] "Report from Rhodesia: Pointing the Way to a Multi-Racial Africa?" Liebman Papers, Box 2, Circular to AAAA members, January, 1966.

and fraud. As happened time and again for all four, some rumor of a diplomatic breakthrough would be leaked to the public in a fit of giddy exuberance and always the rising expectations of an end to their isolation turned quickly over to the dreaded realization of yet another rejection. By their very nature, the dealings of these unrecognized regimes were off the books and conducted outside of established state practices. Because of their illegal statuses they were forced to lurk in the demimonde of world society, maneuvering in the dark without the benefit of normal state-to-state communications, and without access to international legal recourse when they were tricked or defrauded by charlatans and conmen. Some of these scams were perpetrated by what one author termed "Uhuru Hoppers."[53] Matanzima's Transkei regime always seemed particularly gullible to the approaches of "Uhuru Hoppers," as shadowy foreigners made big promises and took state funds never to be heard from again, as happened when the government paid an Australian businessman up front to obtain Ecuador's recognition of Transkei. He never returned.[54] Katanga was the victim of a similar scam in an effort to win recognition from Costa Rica and later from Guatemala.[55] Lucas Mangope of Bophuthatswana was likewise the target of shysters and scam artists promising recognition in exchange for favors or money. But they were not merely passive actors in this illicit economy. As will be detailed in later chapters, Transkei and Bophuthatswana in particular were active and eager participants in the exchanges of official favors for money, and received bribes from private corporations for state favors. Like many other things in their histories, the line between bribery and official (pseudo) state business was a blurry one.

This book will tell the personal stories of those intimately involved with these failed independence bids inside and outside Africa. Being primarily a political history, this book does not set out to describe or relay what day-to-day life was like for the vast majority of Katangese, Rhodesians, Transkeians, and Bophuthatswanans living under these regimes. Neither does it focus primarily on Moise Tshombe, Ian Smith, Kaiser Matanzima, Lucas Mangope, and other notable regime officials whose stories have been recounted before and no doubt will be recounted again in the future. Instead, this book will look at those lesser-known semi-

---

[53] Peris Sean Jones defines "Uhuru Hoppers" as "individuals who promised the tantalizing prize of international recognition in return for personal power, prestige and economic benefit." He claims that Sol Kerzner of the Sun International Hotel Empire "was the archetypical example." Jones, PhD dissertation for Loughborough University, "Mmabatho, 'Mother of the People'," p. 284.

[54] See Streek and Wicksteed, *Render unto Kaiser*, p. 206.

[55] See Brownell, "Diplomatic Lepers."

public figures intimately involved with these struggles, those who were out there on the furthest extremities of these would-be states, fighting in the borderlands of contested sovereignty.

Supporters of these regimes overseas, whether nationals or not, ran in some rather small right-wing circles and many knew each other, worked with each other, and several operating from the United States even worked for more than one of these regimes. One of these personal stories concerned a Belgian, Michel Struelens, the head of the Katanga Information Service (KIS) in New York. Struelens was a charming and suave propagandist – one writer described him as a "Peter Lorre figure" – who was eventually deported on the direct orders of President John F. Kennedy.[56] An important American supporter of both Katanga and Rhodesia was Marvin Liebman, a former communist turned virulent anti-communist. He was a brilliant political organizer and a leading Barry Goldwater supporter who would go on to be one of the leaders of the New Right, and he was the major organizing force behind both the biggest pro-Katangese lobby and the biggest pro-Rhodesian lobby in the United States.[57] In his work defending these regimes, Liebman worked closely with the publisher of the influential conservative magazine, the *National Review*, William A. Rusher, as well as the magazine's founder William F. Buckley Jr. Kenneth Towsey, Rhodesia's pseudo-ambassador to the United States who was introduced above, was a phlegmatic and professional diplomat and public relations man, and someone whom one could easily imagine embedded deep into the mid-century corporate culture of a Ford Motor Company or an IBM. Towsey worked closely with Liebman and the *National Review* affiliated lobbying organizations.

Working for these independence movements was a wide cast of characters. The head of Rhodesia House in London, Sydney Brice, with his pomade part and lampshade moustache, was a master provocateur and a slippery dissembler whose activities were a constant thorn in the British government's side until his mission was finally shut down by British authorities. Another Rhodesian abroad was the accredited diplomatic

---

[56] Russell Warren Howe and Sarah Hays Trott, *The Power Peddlers: How Lobbyists Mold American Foreign Policy* (Doubleday, Garden City, NY, 1977) p. 176.

[57] Marvin Liebman, *Coming Out Conservative: An Autobiography* (Chronicle Books, San Francisco, 1992). The most famous champion of Rhodesia in the United States was not a public relations man at all, but the former Secretary of State under President Harry Truman, Dean Acheson. During the Congo Crisis and after, Acheson was outside the State Department lobbying the Kennedy and Johnson administrations against taking Africanist positions. It was in fighting for recognition of Ian Smith's regime in Rhodesia in particular which served as a somewhat odd addendum to Acheson's long and distinguished career. D. Brinkley, *Dean Acheson: The Cold War Years, 1953–71* (Yale University Press, New Haven, 1992) p. 305.

representative of Rhodesia in Lisbon, Harry Reedman, who was a manic, and almost delusional, bloviator and braggart, and his diplomatic status became a major international controversy for several years, one that briefly opened up a significant breach in Anglo-Portuguese relations. Also playing a role in this story was the "Sun King," Sol Kerzner, a fabulously wealthy and flamboyant South African hotel and casino magnate whose Sun City Resort would oddly serve as an important battleground over the legitimation of Bophuthatswana's statehood. But perhaps the most colorful and bizarre story associated with those defending these regimes was that of the former Tory backbencher and gay rights advocate, who later turned into a Labour Party candidate and a leading member of the Anti-Apartheid Movement: Humphry Berkeley. Berkeley arrived in Transkei in the late 1970s and somehow quickly convinced Kaiser Matanzima to appoint him as a roving ambassador and lead diplomatic advisor promising a plan to win recognition, in the process easing out the incumbent foreign minister. He failed to deliver on his promises, and left Transkei amid lurid tales of corruption, and a mind-boggling kidnapping.

Part of the interest in following these personal stories was that they sometimes contained surprising inversions of presumptive alignments of race and African politics. Some of these aspirant states' foreign representatives were black men acting as the faces of regimes widely perceived as being against the interests of black people. This optic was something which held out obvious appeal for the pseudo-states, but these appointments predictably drew outrage from certain quarters. For the men themselves, working on behalf for these regimes often meant profound social dislocation in their private lives.[58] Pointing out that in the historiography of African decolonization Europeans tended to remain central to narratives, Michael Collins notes that "[w]hen historians have emphasized African agency this has often (though not always) been within the framework of anti-colonial nationalism."[59] In contrast, this book explores agency as it concerns black individuals who pushed in opposite directions as that of the anti-colonial nationalists. These men included Tsepo "T. T." Letlaka, a man who went on a physical, political, and social journey from being a political exile from South Africa as a member of the banned Pan African Council (PAC) to working out of the South

---

[58] See: A. D. Dillard, *Guess Who's Coming to Dinner Now? Multicultural Conservatism in America* (New York University Press, New York, 2002).

[59] Michael Collins, "Nation, State and Agency: Evolving Historiographies of African Decolonization" in Andrew W. M. Smith and Chris Jeppensen (eds.), *Britain, France and the Decolonization of Africa: Future Imperfect?* (University College London Press, London, 2017) pp. 17–18.

African embassy as a diplomatic trainee reporting to his apartheid superiors, a journey that made him and his wife split from their closest friends and betray the cause they as a couple had dedicated much of their lives to. There was also the head of Transkei's Washington Bureau, Ngqondi "Leslie" Masimini, another former political exile from the PAC, who was, at least publicly, an unshakeable optimist, always tragically hopeful that Transkei's recognition was imminent and that it would eventually lead to the liberation of all of South African blacks.

The lines drawn between Katanga, Rhodesia, Transkei, and Bophuthatswana also ran through a small but disproportionately visible community of American blacks involved in the conservative movement. As Angela Dillard notes, "Whereas white conservatives focused primarily on the Eastern Bloc and on Latin America, black conservatives maintained similar positions on the need to keep Africa free of the communist menace."[60] These histories carry within them fascinating stories about black Americans who supported these pseudo-states, causes which made them ideological lepers to many of their American racial compatriots. These men included Max Yergan, Andrew Hatcher, and Jay Parker. Yergan was a civil rights activist and like Liebman was a former communist who became an anti-communist in his later years. He would go on to head the major pro-Katanga lobbying group in the United States and a major pro-Rhodesian lobbying group, both the creations of Marvin Liebman.[61] Andrew Hatcher was an associate Press Secretary for President John F. Kennedy, the first black man to serve in a White House Press Office, but by the 1970s he was doing public relations consulting for South Africa and Transkei. Jay Parker, who was a close friend of T. T. Letlaka, was an American public relations man who was hired to represent Transkei in Washington. After working for Transkei for several years, he went on to represent Venda, another Bantustan, and later worked for apartheid South Africa directly. Parker always saw Max Yergan as his ideological mentor, something he told the South Africans to show his bona fides.[62] Parker was a good friend of Jacob Motsi, Bophuthatswana's Washington representative, and when Motsi died in 1987, Parker's *Lincoln Review* journal wrote a glowing obituary for him, titled "Jacob Motsi: The Loss of a Friend."[63]

---

[60] Dillard, *Guess Who's Coming to Dinner Now?*, p. 45.

[61] D. H. Anthony III, *Max Yergan: Race Man, Internationalist, Cold Warrior* (New York University Press, New York, 2006).

[62] D. W. Tyson, *Courage to put Country over Color: The J.A. Parker Story* (unknown publisher, 2009).

[63] *Lincoln Review* (vol. 8, 1987).

There were other claims of racial and ideological incongruence going the other way. White liberals were regularly attacked in racialized terms by these aspirant states and their friends for their alleged pusillanimity and for displaying what regime supporters alleged was a sort of racial and cultural masochism for attacking white rule in Africa. White settlers in Africa long viewed UN General Secretary Dag Hammarskjold as public enemy "number one" because of his role in the Congo Crisis, and his plane crash and death in Northern Rhodesia is still an unsolved mystery.[64] Assistant Undersecretary of State for African Affairs G. Mennen "Soapy" Williams was one of the most vocal and spirited opponents of both Katanga and Rhodesia, something that drew the ire of the supporters of both regimes who labeled him variously as a hypocrite, an appeaser, and a race traitor.[65] When touring Africa, Soapy had famously declared that Africa should be for the Africans.[66] When Williams' tour took him to the CAF, one white settler let Soapy know exactly how he felt about him and his Africa-for-the-Africans quote by punching him in the face. Finally, musician, actor, and activist "Little Steven" Van Zandt, most famously of the E Street Band, is also central to this story. Van Zandt's "Sun City" music and video project in 1985 proved to be crucial in extending the application of the cultural boycott around South Africa to Bophuthatswana by specifically targeting and shaming musicians who performed at the Sun City Resort, musicians who were both white and black.

Nonexistent as they might have been in a legal sense, these regimes mattered in the real world, most acutely for those living under them and fighting against them. Though at times they appeared farcical, their sovereign claims were not merely the harmless proclamations of eccentric backyard monarchs.[67] In telling their stories, this book does not treat lightly the real-world impact of these secessions and the related violence connected with them. In the fighting associated with the Katangese secession alone it has been estimated that between 65,000 and 92,000 people died, in Rhodesia more than 20,000 deaths were attributed to the protracted guerilla war, and while it is harder to determine which deaths can be specifically pegged to Transkeian and Bophuthatswanan

---

[64] Williams, *Who Killed Hammarskjold?*.

[65] T. Noer, *Soapy: A Biography of G. Mennen Williams* (University of Michigan Press, Ann Arbor, 2006).

[66] In response, a letter writer to the *Rhodesia Herald* in 1961 wrote that perhaps America should be for the American Indians. "Reds in US Were First," *Rhodesia Herald*, Letter to the Editor, February 25, 1961.

[67] For a humorous look at micronations, see: J. Ryan, *Micro-nations: The Lonely Planet Guide to Home-Made Nations* (Lonely Planet, London, 2006).

independence, the overall struggle to end apartheid cost the lives of thousands.[68] The fates of these pseudo-states mattered whether they existed or not.

Struggles for Self-Determination is divided into six substantive chapters in addition to the Introduction and Conclusion. It is not structured to read like a conventional historical narrative, as only the penultimate chapter on the Sun City Resort is written as a traditional narrative history. Chapter 2, which analyzes the discursive web that marks off these four aspirant states as ideologically and politically distinct, is not chronological at all. The other four chapters are organized by themes: independence days and their commemorations, their quests for diplomatic recognition, their foreign missions in America, and their foreign missions in Europe. Each of these thematic chapters is further subdivided into sections that chronologically trace the individual narratives of Katanga, Rhodesia, Transkei, and Bophuthatswana's struggles for independence. Their stories will be retold in different ways across these chapters, every time bringing forward new aspects to the timeline and applying a different thematic focus. What follows in the chapters below takes up William Blake's famous call to see the world in a grain of sand. This granular study of all the various, small sovereign expressions of four failed independence bids aims to provide a view to the complexities of the relationship between individual states and the African state system as a whole. From these small grains it will inductively draw larger conclusions about the nature of postcolonial African statehood and the fragile and frayed cords that have bound and continue to bind the entire African state system together.

---

[68] See Passemiers, "Safeguarding White Minority Power," p. 72; P. Godwin and I. Hancock, *Rhodesians Never Die* (Oxford University Press, Oxford, 1993) p. 280.

2   Anti-nationalist Nationalisms
The Discursive Web of Reactionary Statehood in Africa

First, Katanga is the one part of the former Belgian Congo that, in general, managed to preserve law, order and decency. Second, Katanga, under President Tshombe, has kept its economy going. Third, Moise Tshombe is far and away the outstanding pro-Western and anti-communist leader of the former Belgian Congo. Fourth, the people of Katanga – black and white – support Tshombe overwhelmingly.[1]   *"Katanga Is the Hungary of 1961," American Committee for Aid to Katanga Freedom Fighters (ACAKFF) full-page advertisement, New York Times, December 14, 1961*

This has been the real tragedy of the Congo, Algeria, and Vietnam; tragedies that have benefited only the communists, who have made this false decolonization doctrine the cornerstone of their present policy of subversive "national liberation" wars of conquest. In these unhappy countries most Americans had difficulty in seeing the parallel with their own colonial past; in Rhodesia they can![2]   "We Hold These Truths to be Self-Evident ... But ..." Friends of Rhodesian Independence, flyer (no date)

Maybe we were too peaceful. Perhaps if we had killed some whites we would have gotten a lot of world publicity and everybody would recognize us now. Violence is the only thing that seems to get any attention.[3]   Leslie Masimini, Transkei's "Minister to North, Central, and South America," 1978

Katanga, Rhodesia, Transkei, and Bophuthatswana, and their friends abroad, all expended a great deal of their energies toward the goal of legitimating their independence movements and selling their worthiness for statehood to overseas audiences. Mirroring this exertion toward the opposite goal were their many enemies inside and outside Africa. These

---

[1] "Katanga Is the Hungary of 1961," ACAKFF full-page advertisement in the *New York Times*, December 14, 1961.
[2] Group Research, Inc., Box 146, Folder: Friends of Rhodesian Independence, FRI Flyer, "We Hold These Truths to Be Self-Evident ... But ..." (no date).
[3] "Minister for Transkei: 'Loneliest Diplomat'," *Sarasota Herald-Tribune*, UPI wire, June 4, 1978.

rhetorical and symbolic contests were waged over a series of media, some obviously political in nature, others less obviously so. In making their cases for sovereign recognition, these pseudo-states and their friends made several types of argument and made them for different audiences, with some crafted for ever more specific demographic and ideological slices of each. These arguments were made by the regime leaders in speeches, interviews, and press releases; through statements and literature distributed by their ministries responsible for information and foreign policy; sometimes via statements and materials produced by private public relations firms hired by these regimes; and also through rituals and symbolic performances of statehood and nationhood. Yet these various government-affiliated organs did not always coordinate smoothly. Friendly Western-based lobbying organizations also offered arguments, but they had their own agendas and reasons for advocating for these regimes that might or might not have lined up exactly with those of the regimes, and there were some notable conflicts among the different organizations.[4] Some of these types of argument were unique to the individual contested states, and some were, and are, common to every contested state. However, this chapter will only focus on those types of argument that these four states, and their friends, presented to international audiences that were exclusively shared by these four states, and the specific responses that these arguments elicited. Despite emerging from multiple sources with eliding, parallel, and sometimes contradictory agendas, coherent shapes can still be observed. When taken all together, these claims and counterclaims created a distinct discursive web that collectively marked out the unique ideological shape of Katanga, Rhodesia, Transkei, and Bophuthatswana as reactionary states that posed a unique and existential threat to the African state system.

The types of argument in support of their sovereign claims that were shared exclusively by these four states can be grouped into three broad argument families:[5] (1) arguments articulating their authentic natures and the inauthenticity of their nationalist rivals; (2) arguments trumpeting their pro-Western orientations; and finally (3) arguments about how these pseudo-states' sovereign claims favorably compared against legal

---

[4] In her study on Namibia's and Nagaland's independence movements, Lydia Walker delves into the tensions and occasional conflicts between aspirant nationalists and their advocates in the West. See "Decolonization in the 1960s: On Legitimate and Illegitimate Nationalist Claims-Making," *Past & Present*, vol. 242, no. 1 (February 2019).

[5] Perhaps the closest analogue to these four would-be states was Namibia's Transitional Government of National Unity, which existed from 1985 to 1989, but that government never asserted that it was a sovereign state. This Namibian comparison was provided to the author by Bernard Moore, a scholar of Namibian history.

states in Africa. The types of argument grouped into the authenticity family included that their independence claims were overwhelmingly supported by Africans in the villages, and that their nationalist opponents inside and outside their territories were inauthentic because of their adoption of imported ideologies and their reliance on artificial, colonially defined, pan-ethnic constituencies. Sometimes included among these arguments were that these aspirant states were political entities before European occupation and had precolonial proto-national identities. The argument family in regard to their pro-Western orientations included emphasizing their Christian values and social conservativism, fore-grounding that they were ideologically anti-communist and that their economies were capitalistic, but also that the modern West was degenerating and currently suffering from a form of masochistic self-defeatism. The final argument family compared these would-be states to independent African states and their nationalist rivals. Making generalizations about the nature of African nationalism and independent Africa, these arguments centered on the double standards of the international community in unfairly rejecting their legitimate independence bids while at the same time accepting, embracing, and making apologies for failed or failing African states.

At times these argument families blended together. Arguments that they were naturally Western-oriented were often accompanied by comparisons to other African states that were hostile to the West and more inclined to the Eastern Bloc. Arguments about the authentic nature of their support many times mixed with claims that postcolonial African leaders to their north were simply parroting foreign ideologies and were themselves the witting or unwitting puppets of foreign powers.[6] Arguments about the inauthenticity of their left-leaning nationalist rivals at times emphasized the natural ideological alliances and cultural affinities between their regimes and the West, including the harmony between traditional African market culture and free market capitalism, respect for socially conservative hierarchies, and their predominantly Christian faiths. Other times there were tensions between these arguments. For the purpose of analytical clarity, this chapter will pull these argument families apart and examine each of them separately, providing a few representative examples from each of the aspirant states. In doing so, this chapter will provide a broad framework to categorize the varied

---

[6] For a synopsis of South African officials' views of African nationalism in the 1950s and 1960s, especially their equation of African self-determination claims with corruptive foreign ideologies, see Miller, *An African Volk*, pp. 88–91.

rhetorical and symbolic contests described in more detail in the chapters that follow.

Across all their many personal rivalries, and political and ideological differences, the interests of all postcolonial African national leaders were aligned in confronting the general threat of fragmentation and in defending the territorial integrity of African states. This specter of ethnic fragmentation loomed over Africa and was often characterized as a reversion to atavistic tribalism. As early as the 1950s, Ghanaian independence leader Kwame Nkrumah expressed his concern about future African states dividing along ethno-regional and religious lines.[7] Decades later in an article in *The Guardian*, Ali Mazrui expressed his opposition to the creation of South Sudan in terms that mirrored Nkrumah's concern, asserting that African leaders rightly feared secessionism because of the domino effect. "After all," Mazrui writes, "there are more than 2,000 ethnic groups on the continent. If territorial self-determination was granted to even a tenth of them, it would be reduced to dozens of warring mini-states."[8] The fear was that a successful secession anywhere could open a Pandora's box everywhere. [9]

In secessionist movements elsewhere, leaders often saw their own homegrown secessionist movements. For instance, during the Biafran secession from Nigeria in the late 1960s, the federal government received support from the vast majority of African leaders, who often saw that conflict through the lens of their own separatist conflicts. Jomo Kenyatta of Kenya saw the Biafran secession and it reportedly reminded him of the Kenyan Shifta War.[10] Likewise, Emperor Haile Selassie wanted the Nigerian federal government to put down the secession quickly for fear that it would spread across Africa, which was likely an allusion to Ethiopia's struggle against Eritrean separatism.[11] It was not just African leaders who feared a secessionist chain reaction in Africa; Britain's support for Nigeria was in large part spurred by the fear of the wider effect of a Biafran victory across Africa.[12] It was partly out of a supposed effort to fend off this threat of fragmentation that African leaders defended their near-universal implementation of one-party rule and the maintenance of the apparatuses of state security and control inherited

---

[7] Kwame Botwe-Asamoah, *Kwame Nkrumah's Politico-Cultural Thought and Policies* (Routledge, New York, 2005).

[8] Ali Mazrui, "Is This Pakistanism in Sudan?" op-ed, *The Guardian*, February 9, 2011.

[9] Bereketeab, *Self-Determination and Secession in Africa*, p. 3.

[10] John L. Stremlau, *The International Politics of the Nigerian Civil War, 1967–1970* (Princeton University Press, Princeton, 1977) p. 346.

[11] Stremlau, *Politics of the Nigerian Civil War*, p. 346.

[12] Fabry, *Recognizing States*, p. 166.

from the colonial state to quell dissent. A dichotomy was therefore created and maintained publicly that the options facing postcolonial Africa could be either the maintenance of African sovereignty through the respect for each state's territorial integrity internationally (and perhaps the suffocation of dissent internally) or a disastrous disintegration into "chaos and civil wars."[13]

For many observers, in addition to being a reversion to atavistic tribalism, fragmentation seemed to signal a return of colonial control through the old concept of divide and rule. African nationalists viewed subnational ethnic claims to political authority as potential stalking horses for Western interests. This relationship between the size of the political unit and the threat of a return to Western dominance was expressed by Nkrumah in a speech in the early days of the Katangese secession:

The evil of balkanization, disunity and secessions is that the new Balkan states of Africa will not have the independence to shake off the economic colonial shackles which result in Africa being a source of riches to the outside world while grinding poverty continues at home. There is a real danger that the colonial powers will grant a nominal type of political independence to individual small units so as to ensure that the same old colonial type of economic organization continues long after independence has been achieved. This in itself is the source of the gravest potential for the world.[14]

In this construction, the threat of fragmentation was not just a political and economic threat but a moral one, and even a temporal one. Secession was seen as a move backward in time; a reversion to an earlier stage of development, and this drag backward happened not just to the seceding entity but also to the rump state left behind after the secession. Each successful secession also risked setting in motion a domino effect across Africa that threatened the entire postcolonial African state system.

Perhaps the most famous instance of a failed secessionist movement in Africa is not included among the four studied in this book: Biafra. At first glance, the attempted Biafran secession from Nigeria seemed to share many similarities with the four included in this study, in particular Katanga. Uneven resources across regions in these large and ethnically diverse states, including human capital in terms of educational

---

[13] This idea has been explicitly defended by many scholars. See, for example, Godfrey Mwakikagile, *Nyerere and Africa: End of an Era* (New Africa Press, Pretoria, 2010) p. 21.

[14] Nkrumah famously pushed for a larger United States of Africa, seeing even the inherited borders as being too small to be viable. Excerpted from the speech, "Africa's Challenge," delivered by Kwame Nkrumah to the Ghanaian Parliament in Accra on August 6, 1960. See also Ama Biney, *The Political and Social Thought of Kwame Nkrumah* (Palgrave Macmillan, New York, 2011).

attainment and labor markets, resulted in migrations across regions that exacerbated ethnic rivalries. While the Katangese secession was driven to a large extent by a nativist response to migration into Katanga from other parts of the Congo, Biafra's was spurred on by a defensive response to the killings of Ibos, who had migrated out from the eastern region across Nigeria. Both secessionist movements aimed to redraw their inherited colonial-era borders, and both primarily represented the interests of the dominant ethnic group in their regions. Both Tshombe and Emeka Ojukwu fought for and believed they had secured their regions' autonomy within a loose federal system through agreements with their central governments, but in both cases the central government moved away from the agreements.[15] Because Ibos are predominately Catholic, Biafra's cause resonated among many Catholics in the West, and much of Western aid support for Biafra was routed through Catholic organizations.[16] This was similar to the religious-based affinities that Tshombe had with fellow Methodists in the West. The secessions both lasted roughly the same length of time, with the eastern region of Nigeria declaring its independence from Nigeria on June 3, 1967, almost exactly seven years after Katanga seceded from the Congo, and Biafra collapsing in January 1970, again almost exactly seven years later.

Biafra pursued statehood using somewhat similar means as did Katanga, Rhodesia, Transkei, and Bophuthatswana. Like these four, Biafra created all the trappings of statehood including a flag, currency, and the issuing of postage stamps. Biafra supplemented its own pseudo-diplomatic envoys and domestic information ministries with the hiring of Western public relations experts who organized and customized the aspirant state's political messaging in host countries, and Biafra likewise also benefited from the creation of ad hoc domestic organizations formed to pressure their respective governments to recognize its statehood.[17] As it turned out, Biafra was more successful than any of the four in this book, ultimately winning recognition from Tanzania, Zambia, the Ivory Coast, Gabon, and Haiti.

[15] This was the Tananarive Conference in the Katangese case and the Aburi Agreement in the Biafran. For more on the Aburi Agreement, see Michael Gould, *The Biafran War: The Struggle for Modern Nigeria* (I. B. Tauris, London, 2013), pp. 48–55.

[16] Howe and Trott, *Power Peddlers*, p. 183.

[17] Morris Davis, *Interpreters for Nigeria: The Third World and International Public Relations* (University of Illinois Press, Urbana, 1977); Brian McNeil, "'And Starvation Is the Grim Reaper': The American Committee to Keep Biafra Alive and the Genocide Question during the Nigerian Civil War, 1968–70," *Journal of Genocide Research*, vol. 16, nos. 2–3 (2014). For a general overview of the Biafran secession, see Gould, *Biafran War*.

Biafra was not included in this study because despite the similarities noted above, it was different from Katanga, Rhodesia, Transkei, and Bophuthatswana in certain essential ways. For one, there was no clear affinity between Biafra and white settlerdom, or links between its secessionist movement and the foreign policy goals of apartheid South Africa. It had no clear neocolonial connections, it did not have strong ties to foreign capital, nor was it seen to be the tool of Western multinational corporations.[18] There was no obvious Cold War hook in the Nigerian Civil War, even though the Soviet Union supplied arms to the federal government during the conflict. Unlike the case of Patrice Lumumba's Congo just seven years before, no one made serious or sustained attempts to paint Nigerian leader Yakubu Gowon's federal government as communist leaning.[19] Finally, what Biafran supporters wanted, besides recognition, was not for the United Nations to stay out of the internal affairs of this civil conflict, as supporters of Katanga and Rhodesia and the Bantustans desperately wanted, but for the exact opposite: They called on the United Nations to intervene in the Nigerian conflict, not to put down Biafra but to save it.

Neither friends nor enemies of Biafra read it as a reactionary movement premised on salvaging white Western economic resources or white political influence, neither was it seen as a case of internationalist world government overreach, a last stand against world communism, or a reenergization of tribal structures that made such Western control inevitable. Not surprisingly, Biafra did not attract the same enemies or the same friends as the four movements studied in this book. Biafra came to be seen overwhelmingly as a humanitarian disaster, and much of the support for Biafra emerged from this wellspring rather than any of the ideological contests discussed in this chapter.[20] It is notable that the influential American conservative William F. Buckley, who was behind the biggest pro-Katanga and pro-Rhodesia lobbies, did not support the Biafran secession.[21] And quite a few American and British liberals were

---

[18] Nigeria's great oil reserves were only discovered by Shell Oil immediately prior to the war and were kept secret from both the Nigerian federal government and the Biafrans. The Biafrans, who had initially controlled the southern coastal areas where the oil fields were located, lost those areas early in the war. Gould, *Biafran War*, pp. 192–193.

[19] Gould, *Biafran War*, p. 68.

[20] The American ambassador to Nigeria, Elbert Matthews, jokingly recalled that the most powerful pro-Biafran lobby in the United States at the time was Pat, Tricia, and Julie Nixon. Howe and Trott, *Power Peddlers*, p. 183.

[21] Many conservatives did support Biafra, however, see Martin Staniland, *American Intellectuals and African Nationalists, 1955–1970* (Yale University Press, New Haven, 1991), pp. 256–264.

supportive of Biafra.[22] Conor Cruise O'Brien, who as the UN special representative of Secretary-General Dag Hammarskjold was behind the United Nations Operation in the Congo (ONUC's) Operation Morthor intended to crush Katanga's secession only six years before, offered that Biafra had the right to self-determination due to the humanitarian crisis and deserved "protective political sovereignty."[23] So, while it was similar in some respects with the other four aspirant states studied below, the Biafran secession from Nigeria was a bird of a different feather.[24]

Katanga, Rhodesia, Transkei, and Bophuthatswana all relied upon what they saw as an important distinction between authentic Africans and inauthentic Africans. It was vital to draw this distinction in order to counter accusations that the independence of all four was unpopular among their African populations, as well as to deflect from how all four were supported by the white settler and colonial power structure of Southern Africa, and by right-wing groups in the West. There was a symmetry among the contestants in these struggles in the use of the language of authenticity. And while the definitions and applications of this principle of authenticity were fought over, the field of rhetorical battle was agreed upon: Both supporters and opponents identified the foreignness and inauthenticity of their enemies and the indigeneity and authenticity of their own side.[25] On the ground, however, the sharp distinctions drawn between traditional elites and modern elites, ethno-regional identities and national identities, and rural people and urban people were blurred, and far from being fixed positions, these were fluid concepts, shifting and changing according to new situations.[26] But this was propaganda, and accordingly nuances were bleached out in favor of starker dichotomies, precision giving way to the power of an emotional punch.

---

[22] For example, Paul Connett, the founder of the American Committee to Keep Biafra Alive, the largest pro-Biafran organization in the United States, had worked on Democratic candidate Eugene McCarthy's presidential campaign. McNeil, "'And Starvation Is the Grim Reaper'."

[23] McNeil, "'And Starvation Is the Grim Reaper'," p. 322.

[24] See also Staniland, *American Intellectuals*, pp. 55–56.

[25] Mazrui posits a multitiered approach to foreign "interference" through his concept of racial sovereignty, which is allegedly a middle "level of externality" between the nation-state and the wider world. *Towards a Pax Africana*, chapter 2.

[26] See, for example, Vail's introduction, *Creation of Tribalism*. Larmer and Kennes make the point in regard to Katanga and Biafra that their ethno-regional basis of support was perhaps not so different from other modern African states. "[They] were commonly dismissed as the result of backward-looking 'tribalism' and contrasted to the supposedly pan-ethnic basis of African nationalism, overlooking the extent to which both ethnicity and ethnically based patronage networks commonly pervaded the supposedly modern institutions of the nation-state." Kennes and Larmer, *Katangese Gendarmes*, p. 7.

During much of the colonial period in Africa, power ran down and through the colonial state to the chiefs and the village headmen and back up in a mutually reinforcing relationship.[27] If tribal leaders were not compliant they would be replaced, if no tribal leaders (or tribes) could be identified, then the colonial state might help create them.[28] It was against the backdrop of this old alliance between the colonial state and local chiefs and headmen that African nationalists argued that the only way forward to true liberation was to move toward unified pan-ethnic nation-states within the former colonial borders, and anything other than that was normatively and temporally backward. Mozambique's liberation leader, Samora Machel, famously declared: "For the nation to live, the tribe must die."[29] In thinking this he was not alone. As Leroy Vail eloquently phrased it, "[in the 1950s and 1960s] most observers believed that parochial ethnic loyalties were merely cultural ghosts lingering on in the present, weakened anomalies from a fast receding past."[30] Yet the pulls of region and ethnicity did not die so easily. Even so, by the late 1950s there came to be a generalized agreement, or perhaps an acquiescence, on the part of the international community, aspirant African nationalists, and postcolonial leaders that the nation-state within the colonial borders was the only proper vessel for African self-determination. It was the African political elites who could speak this new language of pan-ethnic nationalism who were then poised to take control of the emerging states.[31] The Organisation of African Unity (OAU) would later explicitly endorse the maintenance of colonial borders in its charter, and civic notions of the nation would trump ethnic ones in Africa.[32] But not everyone was convinced that these pan-ethnic

---

[27] See Mahmood Mamdani, *Citizen and Subject: Contemporary Africa and the Legacy of Late Colonialism* (Princeton University Press, Princeton, 1996).

[28] See, for instance, Terence Ranger, "Missionaries, Migrants, and the Manyika: The Invention of Ethnicity in Zimbabwe," in Vail (ed.), *Creation of Tribalism*.

[29] Frantz Fanon wrote, "The elimination of the kaids and the chiefs is a prerequisite to the unification of the people." Fanon, *Wretched of the Earth* (Grove Press, New York, 2005) p. 51.

[30] Vail, *Creation of Tribalism*, p. 1.

[31] Toyin Falola writes, "[The modern educated intelligentsia] claimed nationality as the authentic voice of the 'natives.' The ultimate victory came with decolonization, when the Europeans who took over power from the traditional elite handed it over to the educated elite." Falola, *Nationalism and African Intellectuals* (University of Rochester Press, Rochester, 2001) p. 28. While the first part was undoubtedly the case, the actual division between educated elites and traditional elites was perhaps more blurred than Falola draws it. See, for example, Gibbs, *Mandela's Kinsmen*.

[32] Marco Zoppi, "The OAU and the Question of Borders," *Journal of African Union Studies*, vol. 2, nos. 1–2 (2013).

units were legitimate or that this new national political class was truly representative.[33]

Citing the large numbers of Belgian advisors and white mercenaries in Katanga's security forces, and its support from the white settlers and the large mining interests, Leopoldville portrayed Tshombe as nothing more than a stooge for white interests. Patrice Lumumba was asked in an interview about the Katanga secession on July 28, 1960, two weeks after Moise Tshombe's declaration, to which he replied,

There has never been a Katanga problem as such. The gist of the matter is that the imperialists want to lay their hands on our country's riches and to continue exploiting our people. The imperialists have always had their agents in the colonial countries. Tshombe, in particular, is an agent of the Belgian imperialists. Everything he says and writes is not his own. He merely mouths the words of the Belgian colonialists.[34]

Katanga's authentic roots were attacked by other opponents as well. In a press release for background from November 1961, the State Department presented their case that Tshombe's regime did not grow organically from the native soil, instead characterizing it as a foreign-created entity that Tshombe personally and selfishly benefitted from.

Mr Tshombe's Katanga is in no way a separate entity for which self-determination is relevant. It is and has been an integral part of the Congo which has existed as a territorial, political and economic unit for many decades ... It should be noted that Mr Tshombe's secessionist policies enjoy the support of only a minority, albeit a substantial minority of even the Katanga population ... The Congolese and most African and Asian states are persuaded that the Katanga is an artificial creation of local white settlers and European industrial interests and would collapse without their support.[35]

Supporters of all of these four aspirant states countered that the authentic African voice did not flow from the mouths of the Lumumbas or Mugabes, or Mandelas, but instead from the village chiefs and headmen, who allegedly spoke for real constituencies and ancient

[33] "Ethnic diversity," Timothy Gibbs explains, "proved a sore particular point for would-be nationalists. Ideas of African independence from colonial interference, which had been the dynamo of many protest movements were as likely to lead towards regionalist as towards nationalist politics." Gibbs, *Mandela's Kinsmen*, p. 19.

[34] Lumumba interview with TASS, July 28, 1960. Ryan Irwin makes the point that "Lumumba's instinctive desire was to internationalize the Congo Crisis – even as he lambasted Tshombe for reaching out to Western capitalists – merely underscored the contingent nature of Congolese sovereignty in 1960." Irwin, "Sovereignty in the Congo Crisis," p. 211.

[35] Kennedy Presidential Archives, Box 27A, National Security Files, Series: Countries: Congo, Folder: Congo, General 11/3/61–11/11/61, Department of State for the Press, "For Background Only," November 10, 1961.

interests.[36] They each made claims that they better reflected and protected precolonial culture and institutions than did the artificial colonial inheritance of the nation-state headed by "de-tribalized" African leaders.[37] Katanga and its friends abroad pointed out that its territory corresponded with a kingdom that preceded the formation of the Belgian Congo. Being related by both birth and marriage to the Lunda paramount chief was seen by Katangese propagandists to bolster Tshombe's claims to legitimacy.[38] He founded the Lunda Tribal Association which quickly grew into the CONAKAT party, and he can perhaps be most accurately described as a Lunda nationalist rather than a Katangese nationalist. But while dominated by Lundas, his party had the support of many smaller tribes, and his second-in-command was a Bayeke, Godefroid Munongo. At its core, CONAKAT was a nativist party and its unifying political platform came from its hostility to the "alien" Balubas, who had migrated in large numbers to traditional Lunda areas.[39] Tshombe's desire for secession was in part fed by the feeling that only secession could ensure that the Baluba threat be contained and Katanga's resources be enjoyed primarily by its "indigenous" inhabitants, whom he referred to "authentic Katangans."[40]

White settlers in Katanga came to see CONAKAT as an ally and the settler party merged into CONAKAT.[41] Playing a key role as advisors to CONAKAT leaders, white settlers bankrolled the party even prior to the secession.[42] However, as Miles Larmer and Erik Kennes explain, the

---

[36] All four regimes claimed to speak that chiefs and village headman were the true voice of Africans. For instance, in Transkei ex officio chiefs constituted half of the membership of the Transkei Parliament. See: N. Stultz, "Why Is Transkei Still Portrayed as a Stooge?" op-ed for *New York Times*, July 9, 1979. See also, J. R. T. Wood, *A Matter of Weeks Rather than Months: The Impasse between Harold Wilson and Ian Smith: Sanctions, Aborted Settlements and War 1965–1969* (Trafford, Victoria, 2008).

[37] Both Rhodesia and Transkei claimed support from their African populations through the votes from carefully selected chiefly representatives. Transkei's last election before declaring independence witnessed the widespread persecution and imprisonment of political opponents, and victory was assured for Kaiser Matanzima only because of the ex officio seats given to chiefs, many of whom received salaries from Pretoria. See: John Burns, "Transkei Bridles at Diplomatic Isolation," *New York Times*, October 24, 1976.

[38] See Hempstone, *Rebels, Mercenaries, and Dividends*, pp. 68–72.

[39] See J. Gerard-Libois, *Katanga Secession* (University of Wisconsin, Madison, 1966) pp. 11–30.

[40] Gerard-Libois, *Katanga Secession*, p. 12.

[41] J. Gerard-Libois, *Katanga Secession*, p. 26.

[42] Even so, Tshombe tried to distance himself from white settlers because they were a political liability and looked for funds elsewhere. Gerard-Libois, *Katanga Secession*, pp. 62–63. The Katangese whites' alliance with Tshombe was strengthened after many whites were embittered by the provocative speech made by Lumumba in front of the Belgian King, and even more so after the armed forces mutinied. See Gerard-Libois, *Katanga Secession*, p. 93.

concept of autochthony in Katanga was not as predictable or straightforward as it might first appear. For many Katangese, white settlers were
considered more of a legitimate presence in the new state than were
African migrants from Kasai and elsewhere who were seen as a direct threat
economically. It was only through this flexuous conception of Katangese
identity that white settlers and corporate interests could be indigenized in a
way that non-Katangese African migrants often could not be.[43]

Katanga and its supporters made arguments that the secession was a
local African problem and that it should be solved locally. Being invaded
by a United Nations force under the ultimate control of a Swedish then
later a Burmese Secretary-General, made up of soldiers from outside of
Africa, and funded primarily by American dollars, allowed pro-
Katangese propagandists to position Tshombe and Katanga as local
underdogs.[44] The Katangese government continued to exploit Western
sympathies for the underdog, making much of being a black country
attacked by international UN forces. Tapping into this sentiment,
Interior Minister Munungo said, "[we are] resolved to fight and die if
necessary. The United Nations may take our cities. There will remain
our villages and the bush. All the tribal chiefs are alerted. We are savages;
we are Negroes. So be it. We shall fight like savages with our arrows."[45]
Framing it this way was rhetorically useful in generating sympathy, but it
also appealed to Western rightists' fears of internationalism and the UN.
One pro-Katanga group, American Friends of Katanga, issued a fun-
draising appeal titled "Stop UN Colonialism! Hands off Katanga!"[46] The
American Committee for Aid to Katanga Freedom Fighters (ACAKFF)
also hammered home the idea that internationalist foreign meddlers were
violating Katanga's and, in a broader philosophical sense, Africa's sovereignty by intervening. An ACAKFF advertisement in the *Washington Post*
from August 1963 read: "Why not let the Congolese settle their own
affairs; It's time for the UN Army to get out of the Congo!"[47]

---

[43] Kennes and Larmer, *Katangese Gendarmes*, pp. 6–7. Larmer and Kennes make a
convincing case in their book that Katangese nationalism and the forces behind
separatism had autochthonous origins separate from the Western support that its
leaders no doubt used to their advantage.

[44] Group Research, Inc Archives, Box 6, ACAKFF, ACAKFF full-page advertisement in
Washington Post, "Why Not Let the Congolese Settle Their Own Affairs; It's Time for
the UN Army to Get Out of the Congo!" August 3, 1962.

[45] Hempstone, *Rebels, Mercenaries, and Dividends*, p. 188.

[46] Group Research, Inc Archives, Box 13, Folder: AFK, AFK charity appeal, March
27, 1962.

[47] Group Research, Inc Archives, Box 6, ACAKFF, ACAKFF full-page advertisement in
Washington Post, "Why Not Let the Congolese Settle Their Own Affairs; It's Time for
the UN Army to Get Out of the Congo!" August 3, 1962.

In a fascinating telegram exchange in the first weeks after the secession, Tshombe and Nkrumah debated the meaning of autochthony in the Katangese secession. Following the entry of UN troops, Tshombe wrote: "The entire population [of Katanga] is opposed to occupation by these [UN] troops ... And we also desire as soon as possible to see the establishment of African fraternity through an agreement between all African nations. Nevertheless, Katanga rejects the intrusion of any foreign ideology."[48] To this, Nkrumah replied: "The Government of Ghana in the interests of African solidarity cannot ... recognise the establishment of a so-called state of Katanga ... Regarding your idea of foreign ideology I do not understand what you mean. We know of one ideology only, African ideology."[49] On August 12, 1960, Nkrumah attempted one last time to persuade Tshombe to end the secession by linking it with foreign oppressors.

The whole world knows that your pretended State has been set up with the support of foreign interests. Your activities are applauded in South Africa and the Rhodesias and are condemned by every other Independent Africa State. This should give you food for thought. Your whole administration depends upon Belgian officials who are fundamentally opposed to African Independence and who are merely using you as their tool ... Your name is now linked openly with foreign exploiters and oppressors of your own country. In fact you have assembled in your support the foremost advocates of imperialism and colonialism in Africa and the most determined opponents of African freedom. How can you, as an African, do this?[50]

Tshombe was unimpressed by Nkrumah's appeals, and the battle for public support raged on. Nearly a year after Lumumba's removal from office, some stability in Leopoldville emerged in August 1961 when a new Congolese Prime Minister, Cyrille Adoula, was installed with the help of the CIA. His new Leopoldville government and the Elisabethville government often employed the same themes and tropes, but simply inverted their applications. Tshombe characterized Adoula's regime as being the puppet of the United States and the UN. On February 15, 1962, in an address to Katanga's provincial assembly Tshombe called for a summit between himself and Adoula: "The two of us, without any foreign interference – which was not the case, alas, at Kitona – will apply an African program, reserved to Africans and decided by Africans. The

---

[48] Tshombe's telegram to President Nkrumah, dated August 7, 1960, quoted in Nkrumah, *Challenge of the Congo*, p. 24.

[49] Nkrumah telegram to Tshombe, dated August 8, 1960, quoted in Nkrumah, *Challenge of the Congo*, p. 25.

[50] Nkrumah telegram to Tshombe, dated August 12, 1960, quoted in Nkrumah, *Challenge of the Congo*, pp. 25–26.

result will be peace for our people and peace for Africa."[51] In a public statement, the Katangese government followed on this theme of foreign exploitation of Katanga by asserting that the UN was interested only in securing Katanga's mineral wealth for the United States, a clever reversal of Leopoldville's claims regarding pro-Tshombe supporters.[52] Tshombe also pushed back on these accusations of the foreignness of his support, in particular the most damning of accusation of relying upon white mercenaries. In a message to UN local mission chief, Robert Gardiner, from September 1962, Tshombe huffed:

The matter of mercenaries is like the story of sea serpents or the abominable snowman. It is once more being used against Katanga. This happens whenever there is nothing new to be used against Katangese international public opinion or whenever the truth and justice of our cause and the moderation of our position have made progress in public opinion. We also know from experience that the mercenaries are the pretext constantly used as a prelude to new acts of force.[53]

The Rhodesian regime's claims of enjoying the support of authentic Africans were necessarily different than Katanga's since Rhodesia was forthrightly a white settler state, at least until the "internal settlement" and the creation of the short-lived Zimbabwe-Rhodesia. Nevertheless, its claims to authenticity were based upon the same supposed quiet support of the vast majority of traditional Africans in the villages.[54] As imagined by the Rhodesian regime, this largely silent mass was disinterested in formal politics, certainly formal national politics, but instead was solely concerned with local matters, and especially the conservative preservation of local cultures, traditions, and authority structures.[55] Indeed, once an African became interested in formal national politics they instantly ceased to be authentic. The opinions of the mass of authentic Africans, the Rhodesians argued, could only be truly discovered through tribal authorities via the local chiefs and headmen in what was called an Indaba. Rhodesians often repeated the accusation that outside forces were the primary causes behind all Rhodesia's political troubles, and often pointed out that their nationalist opponents and the guerrilla

---

[51] Hempstone, *Rebels, Mercenaries, and Dividends*, p. 228.

[52] Hempstone, *Rebels, Mercenaries, and Dividends*, p. 228.

[53] Kennedy Presidential Archives, Box 28A, NSF Series: Countries, Congo, Folder: Congo, General 9/1/62–10/16/62, Telegram from Elisabethville consulate to Sec State, relaying message from Tshombe to Gardiner, September 29, 1962.

[54] Relatedly, white Rhodesians took it as a given that they understood "their" Africans in a way that the international community did not, and could not. The author thanks David Kenrick for bringing this point to his attention.

[55] See: L. White, *Unpopular Sovereignty: Rhodesian Independence and African Decolonization* (University of Chicago Press, Chicago, 2015).

fighters they faced were fully supported by, trained by, and armed by the communist Chinese and the Russians.[56]

The question over what Rhodesia's African population actually felt about the regime came to a head with the 1972 Pearce Commission that aimed to gauge African public opinion about the 1971 Anglo-Rhodesian Settlement.[57] This test of acceptability was a condition insisted upon by the British, but initially resisted by the Rhodesians. Smith and his negotiators wanted any such test of acceptability to run only through an Indaba of chiefs and headmen, much like the Indaba Smith's government called in for the buildup to UDI.[58] The Smith government defended the Indaba's legitimacy at the time, saying "The Indaba system [w]as a more appropriate method of ascertaining the views of the mass of tribal Africans than alien practices which the British government and others desire to force the people to accept."[59] Smith cited the unanimous support of the chiefs in the Senate for the proposals and the vote in favor of the proposals by the National Council of Chiefs.[60] Unconvinced, the British insisted upon a method of gauging public opinion that went outside of chiefs and headman whose power and income were dependent upon the state. The result was a "No" vote, and the deal fell apart. The Smith regime countered that nationalist agitators and troublemakers had intimidated the rural population into that result.[61] As with Katanga, it was outsiders who were to blame for anti-government sentiment, and like the Katanga regime, Rhodesia too grumbled that the ultimate outsider, the United Nations in New York City, had no business meddling in the internal affairs of African states.

The Bantustans all rested their claims to the right of self-determination upon their peoples' supposedly distinct and deeply felt identities as

---

[56] Donal Lowry writes of how this externalization and internationalization of local African resistance to white rule in Rhodesia permeated white political culture and was fundamental to their conception of anti-communism. Donal Lowry, "The Impact of Anti-communism on White Rhodesian Political Culture, ca.1920s–1980," *Cold War History*, vol. 7, no. 2 (2007).

[57] The Anglo-Rhodesian Settlement was the result of a renewed British effort to end the six-year rebellion by the newly elected British Conservative leader, Edward Heath.

[58] For more on the relationship between the settler regime and African chiefs, see: Patrick O'Meara, *Rhodesia: Racial Conflict or Coexistence?* (Cornell University Press, Ithaca, 1975). See also: L. White, "'Normal Political Activities': Rhodesia, the Pearce Commission, and the African National Council," *The Journal of African History*, vol. 52, no. 3 (2011) p. 324.

[59] *The Domboshawa "Indaba": The Demand for Independence for Rhodesia (Consultation with African Tribesmen through Their Chiefs and Headmen)* (Government Printer, Salisbury, 1964), p. 15. Quoted in O'Meara, *Racial Conflict or Coexistence*," pp. 82–83.

[60] O'Meara, *Racial Conflict or Coexistence?*, p. 89.

[61] See: White, "'Normal Political Activities'."

ethnic nations. This was consistent with the bedrock apartheid principle that there was no single African population group in the republic, but instead a number of disjoined Bantu ethnicities. Just as Tshombe's regime made much of the fact that Katanga had preceded the Belgian Congo, Transkeians made similar claims about their ethnic basis in the Xhosa people and that it existed as an entity before the Union of South Africa was formed. An article on the United Press International (UPI) wire quoted Transkei's representative in Washington, Leslie Masimini, as saying, "We are not the creature of the apartheid homeland policy. Unlike the [other Bantustans], we existed before as a nation, and they know it. We have proof." As proof, Masimini would often unfurl an old nineteenth century map of Southern Africa which showed the existence of a "Transkei" north of the Kei River.[62] In a letter to the editor of the *New York Times*, Masimini explained:

Granted, uninformed members of the world community see my nation as a creation of the racial policies of the Republic of South Africa. The historical facts clearly refute this argument. The Transkeian Territories, as they were then known, were annexed to the Cape Province of South Africa by the British before the creation of the then Union of South Africa in 1910. Our historical identity is clear. We were older than the Republic of South Africa by many years. Our struggle for independence began almost immediately after the annexation, and was brought to fruition only a little more than a year ago. Apartheid may have been a part of the process, but our existence today as a nation is the product of many years work. South Africa may have agreed to our demands for her own motives.[63]

As Kaiser Matanzima once explained: "I am a disciple of the creed of nationalism ... Xhosa nationalism."[64] Like Tshombe's association with ancient tribal authority, Matanzima also made much of his status as a paramount chief. In his autobiography, Nelson Mandela recounts a discussion he had with his cousin and close friend from university, Kaiser Matanzima, where Mandela told the future leader of Transkei "... the [South African] government's policy was to try to put Africans into ethnic enclaves because they feared the power of African unity," to which, according to Mandela, Matanzima responded "... that he was trying to restore the status of the royal house that had been crushed by the British ... He too wanted a free South Africa, but thought the goal

[62] "Minister for Transkei: 'Loneliest Diplomat,'" UPI wire, June 4, 1978.
[63] "On Punishing South Africa – and Transkei," Letter to the Editor, Ngqondi Masimini, Minister at Large for North, Central, and South America, *New York Times*, November 1, 1977.
[64] Quoted in Gibbs, *Mandela's Kinsmen*, 24.

could be achieved faster and more peacefully through the government's policy of separate development."[65]

Like Mandela, other opponents of South Africa's Bantustan policy also presented Transkei and the later Bantustans as mere creations of South Africa's National Party. For instance, Liberia's permanent representative to the UN wrote to the secretary-general days before Transkei's purported independence calling the Bantustans a "diabolical and heinous scheme" designed to further the goals of apartheid South Africa.[66] UN Secretary-General at the time, Kurt Waldheim, agreed with the idea that Transkei was solely a creation of the apartheid system. In an official statement Waldheim wrote that Transkei was a part of the Bantustan project which was "designed to consolidate apartheid, to violate the unity and territorial integrity of the country, and to perpetuate minority rule."[67]

Lucas Mangope made great efforts to associate himself with Tswana's chieftancy and defend the proposition that Bophuthatswana was an organic homeland of the Tswana.[68] Wrapped up in the birth of Bophuthatswana were state-led efforts to establish the authenticity of the claim that it was in the territory of Bophuthatswana where the mystical ethnic origins of the Tswana people can be traced. Peris Sean Jones has written of how the placement, naming, architectural style, and the construction of the new capital city of Mmabatho were all infused with ideas of the legitimate ethnic origins of the nation and Mangope's right to lead it as a traditional leader.[69] Mangope, like Tshombe, Smith, and Matanzima, made efforts to distinguish between traditional tribally centered Africans (whom he claimed supported his regime) and the so-called detribalized Africans (whose rejection of his regime he dismissed).[70]

---

[65] Gibbs, *Mandela's Kinsmen*, p. 24.

[66] UN Archives, Country Files of the Sec-Gen Kurt Waldheim – Transkei, 25/10/1976–07/05/1978 S-0904-0039-07, Letter from Permanent Representative of Liberia to the Sec-Gen, "Policies of Apartheid of the Government of South Africa," October 22, 1976.

[67] "The Birth of Transkei Draws Fire at the UN," *New York Post*, October 26, 1976. Adding a degree of nuance to this construction of Transkei as a completely illegitimate product of apartheid is Timothy Gibbs' book, where he convincingly argues for "find[ing] a language that goes beyond the narrative of 'Bantustan stooges' and 'nationalist liberation movements' in order to incorporate the shades of grey ..." Gibbs, *Mandela's Kinsmen*, p. 6.

[68] Lawrence and Manson, "'Dog of the Boers'," p. 449.

[69] Jones, "Mmabatho 'Mother of the People'."

[70] Peris Sean Jones, "'To Come Together for Progress': Modernization and Nation-Building in South Africa's Bantustan Periphery – The Case of Bophuthatswana," *Journal of Southern African Studies*, vol. 25, no. 4 (1999) pp. 579–605.

As the 1980s wore on, Bophuthatswana began to move toward the idea of an ethnonational pan-Tswana connection with Botswana.[71] In this formulation, Bophuthatswana's independence was characterized as a return to precolonial freedom and a restoration of precolonial associations with their northern Tswana kin.[72] One problem with this pan-Tswana argument was that it leaned heavily on a mutuality of feeling from the northern Tswana, something that would have been most obviously expressed by recognition of Bophuthatswana by Botswana. Though there was also talk of a merger into Botswana – one government publication even equating the northern and southern Tswanas with the "two Germanies" – ultimately nothing came of it.[73] In 1977, Botswanan President Seretse Khama disputed Boputhatswana's British parentage, denouncing it as a "child of apartheid."[74]

In the rhetoric surrounding African authenticity there was a contest between friends and enemies of these aspirant states over what was truly African and what was not, and what non-African imports were legitimate, and which were not. However, arguments over authenticity and indigeneity were less about working out the true origins and autochthonous roots of these different lineages and more about ideology and politics. Beyond the appeal of the idea as a rhetorical flourish, no one on either side truly thought it possible or even desirable to recreate precolonial society whole cloth.[75] For both opponents and advocates, foreigners and foreign ideas were welcome if they pointed in the right direction, just as Africans were unwelcome if they pointed the wrong way.

[71] Lawrence and Manson, "'Dog of the Boers'."

[72] See Lawrence and Manson, "'Dog of the Boers'" and Jones, "Mmabatho 'Mother of the People'," p. 273. As Drummond writes, "According to this line of reasoning Bophuthatswana was not a child of apartheid but rather the bastard offspring of British colonial rule in Southern Africa." J. Drummond, "Reincorporating the Bantustans into South Africa: The Question of Bophuthatswana", *Geography*, vol. 76 (1991) pp. 373–396. Quoted in Jones, "Mmabatho 'Mother of the People'," p. 273.

[73] Jones, "Mmabatho 'Mother of the People'," p. 275.

[74] Quoted in J. Drummond and A. H. Manson, "The Evolution and Contemporary Significance of the Bophuthatswana–Botswana Border," in D. Rumley and J. V. Minghi (eds.), *The Geography of Border Landscapes* (Routledge, London, 1991) p. 234.

[75] Ryan Irwin points out: "The goal of nationalism was not to return Africa to precolonial conditions but to fuse African values with development planning and deliver a form of modernity in line with the continent's ideological proclivities." *Gordian Knot*, p. 34. "The end of formal [colonial] rule did not rend the relationship between Europe and Africa," Andrew W. M. Smith and Chris Jeppensen point out, "but simply unpicked some of the threads in a densely woven cloth." Andrew W. M. Smith and Chris Jeppensen (eds.), *Britain, France and the Decolonization of Africa: Future Imperfect?* (University College London Press, London, 2017) p. 12.

Katanga, Rhodesia, Transkei, and Bophuthatswana all made arguments that they were naturally oriented to the West, and much of their propaganda efforts went toward building an empathetic bridge with target audiences in Europe and North America. This pro-Western orientation took different forms, but most commonly included showing a strong commitment to anti-communism and free market philosophies, emphasizing their shared Christian values, and in some cases their close affection for different aspects of Western culture. For many anti-colonial nationalists and critics, though, the continued embrace of Western values by formerly colonized states delegitimated their independence. Frantz Fanon famously claimed that with true decolonization "the colonized masses thumb their noses at these very [Western] values, shower them with insults and vomit them up," as part of the wider struggle to "blow the colonial world to smithereens …"[76] Even for these four, their Western orientations were nuanced and partly contingent. But far from wishing the old order be blown to smithereens, these four pseudo-states pined for a West of the recent past, and their affinities were often expressed through temporal analogies wherein the alleged moral decadence and pusillanimity of the modern West was contrasted with the moral strength and confidence of the imperial era.[77] This temporal division allowed for a simultaneous longing for a past West and a disappointment with the modern, debased West. Adding another layer of distinction, these pseudo-states' criticisms of the West were typically aimed at current Western leaders, not those imagined Western masses that these regimes believed still held to the older values they admired.

From its very origins, Katanga was presented internationally as a stable, Christian, capitalistic, anti-communist bastion in a chaotic continent, a Western-oriented outpost of freedom standing alone against communist oppression. Its nationalist rivals were characterized as either communists themselves or were the dupes of foreign communist manipulators. Tshombe invoked the threat of a "communist dictatorship" in his independence declaration on July 11 as a primary justification for the "total independence" of Katanga.[78] His friends in the West adopted this theme. In announcing its arrival, the newly created pro-Katangese lobbying organization, ACAKFF, placed a full-page advertisement in the *New York Times*, titled "Katanga is the Hungary of 1961," situating Katanga within the familiar Cold War paradigm.[79] In a

[76] Fanon, *Wretched of the Earth*, pp. 8, 6.   [77] Brownell, "Out of Time."
[78] Gerard-Libois, *Katanga Secession*, pp. 328–329.
[79] *New York Times* advertisement, "Katanga Is the Hungary of 1961," December 14, 1961, ACAKFF.

1962 speech at a dinner for an American envoy sent to Katanga to try to negotiate peace, the American consul relayed Tshombe's remarks:

> on his relations with the US, Tshombe emphasized his American educational background and education by American missionaries. He said that the Belgians had been impressed by this to the extent that he had often been accused of being an American agent. Now the Americans opposed him ... the tragedy of Katanga and the Congo is that I who am the only Congo leader to have American influence and background and am a proven anticommunist. But I am marked for destruction by anticommunist America ... With something of a grin, Tshombe said he regretted hostile demonstrations and incidents at the [US] Consulate [in Elisabethville]; it wounded him to see broken windows and damage to US premises which were the result of the folly of the United States government.[80]

In pro-Katanga propaganda, there were creative efforts to make connections between American and Katangese cultures. The far-right John Birch Society created a documentary titled "Katanga: The Untold Story."[81] Among other themes, the film plays up the Christian culture of Katanga, placing emphasis on the fact that Tshombe was a Methodist. In addition to being a model of Christian piety and order, Katanga was made to be a modern exemplar of free-market capitalism, a "picture of flourishing business and property," where Air Katanga flew on "regular schedules." Katangese's family life and recreation was highlighted to show supposed similarities with Middle America. In one laughable section, the narrator describes how "in their off time, Katangese enjoy gymnastics and sports and for the enjoyment of old and young, games such as sack hopping and barrel-rolling." To exemplify their bourgeois domesticity one scene showed an African nuclear family, the Kutuwese, in their western ranch-style home. The father was in an armchair wearing a white shirt and a tie, filing through what appears to be family photos, the mother and the children lovingly gathered around behind. As the narrator explained: "In Katanga all social life centers around the family. The Kutuwese are representative of many thousands of married couples in this country. Their home is a modest one. It does not have many of the conveniences and luxuries of the West. But it is spotless and in striking contrast to the huts and shacks seen elsewhere in the Congo."[82] The *National Review* continued this rhetorical effort to pull the Katangese out of Africa in a maladroit attempt to render it more legible to the West. One article declared that they were "an orderly, industrious

---

[80] Fredericks Papers, Schomburg Center, Box 13, State Department Country and Region Files, Folder: SD, Country and Region Files (confidential), 1962, Airgram to Secretary Rusk from Amconsul Elisabethville, Jonathan Dean, "Tshombe Dinner for Undersecretary McGhee, Oct 4, 1962," October 13, 1962.

[81] "Katanga: The Untold Story," Produced and Directed by Stanford-Stuart.

[82] "Katanga: The Untold Story," Produced and Directed by Stanford-Stuart.

people – the most promising, in many respects in Africa."[83] More telling perhaps, was another *National Review* author's take on what made the Katangese unique in Africa: "All the natives I met were convinced that, for a long time to come, they needed European advice, European aid, European industrial and commercial relations. I have never met more level-headed people anywhere in Africa."[84]

Rhodesia made central to their propaganda, both overseas and at home, that they were a white, Christian nation in the middle of Africa surrounded by the forces of chaos and communism. In his radio broadcast announcing UDI, Smith famously proclaimed: "We have struck a blow for the preservation of justice, civilization and Christianity ..."[85] For Rhodesia, a major pillar of their appeals to American audiences was to emphasize the similarities of their (white) settler heritage with that of America's.[86] This theme did not only emerge from Rhodesia, but was reproduced by American allies of Rhodesia for American audiences. For example, a flyer from the American-based Friends of Rhodesian Independence (FRI) pleaded: "For the truth is that the Rhodesian experience exactly parallels our own history: pioneer settlers carving a civilized Nation out of hostile wilderness, then being abused and betrayed by their mother country, and asking only of the outside world that it not pass judgement before getting all the facts."[87] One FRI circular unblushingly declared that "if Washington and Jefferson and our Founding Fathers were alive today, they would be amazed at the exact parallel between the thirteen colonies and Rhodesia."[88] Another FRI newsletter ran a story about Rhodesia's similarities to the United States past and present under the title "Wild West in Mini-skirts." This was a forthrightly racialized and gendered affinity presumably targeting a readership of nostalgic white American males. It read:

Rhodesia today resembles nothing so much as the American West of a hundred years ago ... friendly natives aplenty. Fitting in perfectly with this vast potential of wealth is a highly intelligent and determined race of pioneers ready to fight to the death for their land. This is the greatest resource of all in Rhodesia: its people.

---

[83] Staniland, *American Intellectuals*, p. 239. Quoting from "Operation Smash, Phase III," *National Review*, January 15, 1963.

[84] Staniland, *American Intellectuals*, p. 239. Quoting from "What about Katanga?" *National Review*, October 21, 1961.

[85] Quoted in Alan Cowell, "Ian Smith, Defiant Symbol of White Rule in Africa, Is Dead at 88," *The New York Times*, November 21, 2007.

[86] See: Brownell, "Out of Time."

[87] Group Research Inc., Box 146, Folder FRI, Friends of Rhodesian Independence Flyer, "We Hold These Truths to be Self-Evident ... But ..." (undated).

[88] Group Research Inc., Box 146, Folder FRI, Friends of Rhodesian Independence Circular (undated, but April 1966).

Mostly of English stock, they have retained the best of their heritage and represent the best of their race. They are a handsome Nordic breed; a self-willed, good-living friendly people who would not tolerate a low standard of living for themselves any more than their stylish women would wear a low hemline ... Their kids are healthy, disciplined, well-scrubbed ... the decadent influences which are [destroying the West] are harder to find in Rhodesia.[89]

One theme that can be found in pro-Rhodesian propaganda in America was the idea that the doe-eyed Rhodesians were hurt and genuinely perplexed by American leaders' rejection. In 1969, the far-right American Southern Africa Council (ASAC) lobby reported:

We have asked Rhodesians about their feelings towards the US. While universally friendly, and recognizing the unique similarity between the Rhodesian and American experiences, they cannot understand why the American government is so deeply implicated in an international conspiracy to destroy the country.[90]

Transkei's promotional campaign ahead of its October 1976 independence emphasized the peaceful transfer of power and its inheritance of British-style systems of government. A Transkeian advertisement in the *Observer* published nine days before independence proclaimed: "On October 26 Westminster moves to Umtata" above a photograph of London's Houses of Parliament and Big Ben. The advertisement continued:

We have moved your Parliamentary system to our country. Statute by statute. It's been part of our peaceful evolution to total independence from South Africa. On October 26 we'll have full recognition for our language, our culture, and our own part of Southern Africa – Transkei, a country the size of Switzerland, in which we have lived and prospered over 300 years ... And so October 26 will see the birth of a beautiful new country, among those with the brightest economic prospects in Africa.

Beneath a map of Transkei, including a quartered map of the entire continent to show where it was, was the slogan: "Republic of Transkei: Africa's Quiet Independence."[91] In doing so Transkei drew a straight line from Westminster skipping past Pretoria and right to Umtata.

---

[89] Group Research Inc., Box 146, Folder FRI, Friends of Rhodesian Independence Newsletter, Fall 1970, vol. 3, no. 2, "Wild West in Mini-skirts."

[90] Group Research Archives, Columbia University, Box 22, Topical Files: ASAC File (American Southern Africa Council), *ASAC Review*, October–November 1969, photo caption from ASAC plaque to be presented to Ian Smith. The Group Research Report from 1967 claimed, "The ASAC is the newest Washington lobby, although it is a thinly disguised off-shoot of Liberty Lobby and is working the same side of the street as the JBS [John Birch Society]." Box 22, Group Research Report, February 15, 1967.

[91] Anti-Apartheid Movement archive, Weston Library, MSS AAM 980, Bantustans-General, H.S. Aspects of the Apartheid System, 1962–1994, Advertisement, "Republic of Transkei: Africa's Quiet Independence," *Observer*, October 17, 1976.

As with Katanga and Rhodesia, sometimes this Western orientation took on a Christian character in the Bantustans. In 1976, Matanzima reassured the clergy that he would never consider opening a casino in Transkei: "All the money in the world does not warrant the moral ruination of the peoples of the Transkei."[92] As will be detailed in the final chapter, this pledge did not last long. Lucas Mangope likewise positioned himself as a Christian leader, offering that "it was better to be streetcleaner in a Christian state than Prime Minister of a communist country."[93] In 1988, Mangope said, "We are living proof that the people of Southern Africa can live together in peace, harmony and prosperity irrespective of their race, ethnic roots or religious persuasion, under a democratic government that adheres to and respects the basic tenets of Christianity, the equality of all people and the free enterprise system."[94]

When Western leaders refused to openly support Katanga, Tshombe lashed out.[95] He made threats that even though he was inclined to be pro-Western, he was not bound to the West, and if the rejection continued he might look elsewhere for friends.[96] Whether this was a bluff or not, Katanga's biggest booster in the United States, Max Yergan, Chairman of the ACAKFF, lent credence to his threat.[97] Tshombe's faux-flirtations with the East did not have its intended effect of sparking a lover's jealousy from the West, but in fact provided some ammunition for maintaining their policy of a unified Congo. Releasing a statement "for

---

[92] "Transkei Won't Apply to Join UN-Kaiser," *Daily Dispatch*, June 24, 1976.

[93] Peris Sean Jones quoting Mangope from *Mafeking Mail* article from May 15, 1970. Peris Sean Jones "Etiquette of State-Building and Modernisation in Dependent States: Performing Stateness and the Normalisation of Separate Development in South Africa," *Geoforum*, vol. 33, no. 1 (February 2002) p. 30.

[94] Quoted in Jones, "Mmabatho 'Mother of the People'," p. 271. Mangope also made it a part of Bophuthatswana's propaganda push to present the state as a market economy ripe for Western investment, and a nonracial liberal democracy. Lawrence and Manson, "'Dog of the Boers'," p. 449.

[95] After signing his declaration ending the secession in January 1963, Tshombe, Munungo, and other cabinet members dined with UN officials in Kolwezi, and in a telegraph describing the meeting afterward, a UN participant wrote: "Atmosphere friendly, but throughout our conversation we felt Tshombe and Cabinet are extremely REPEAT extremely bitter about Europeans in general, Belgians in particular." Quoted in C. Othen, *Katanga 1960–1963: Mercenaries, Spies, and the African Nation that Waged War on the World* (The History Press, Gloucestershire, 2015) p. 216.

[96] SA National Archives, Pretoria, Box 1/112/3/1, vol. 11, 12 Congo, Secession of Katanga, Memorandum "Congo," from SA Ambassador to the US to Secretary DFA, August 17, 1962.

[97] See, for example: SA National Archives, Pretoria, Box 1/112/3/1, vol. 11, 12 Congo, Secession of Katanga, Memorandum "Congo," from SA Ambassador to the US to Secretary DFA, August 17, 1962.

background only" to the press in November 1961, the State Department proclaimed: "... Mr Tshombe's Government recently requested Soviet aid to protect secession in Katanga!"[98] The statement concluded that despite Tshombe's professed anti-communism his secession could actually invite communist intervention.[99]

Like Katanga, Transkei at times also faux-flirted with the Eastern Bloc. For example, Leslie Masimini, Transkei's pseudo-ambassador to the United States, said in an interview that the Soviet Union and China have shown some interest in the Transkei, but that Transkei would only look to them as a "last resort," emphasizing that "we are much more oriented to the West. All our foreign associations, our education, our political institutions are rooted in the West."[100] Transkei's boosters overseas likewise tried to make the argument that Transkei was similar to and was a natural ally of the West, but might be convinced to flip. Ralph De Toledano joked in a syndicated column that to gain recognition Transkei should denounce the CIA, ally with Cuba, arrest all the whites in the country, and ask the USSR for military aid.[101] On their end, Transkei seemed to take his advice and openly asked for communist aid and even offered to open a Cuban mission.[102] Like Katanga's threats, Transkei's were similarly ignored by both the West and the East. Smith's Rhodesia and Mangope's Bophuthatswana did not bother playing this coquettish game.[103]

This closeness with the West was at times a liability. One line of argument that would be used often in Katanga's bid for independence and which would later be repeated by the Bantustans was that these regimes were being punished for being too friendly with their former colonial rulers and had achieved sovereignty too peacefully. Fanon

[98] Kennedy Presidential Archives, Box 27A, National Security Files, Series: Countries: Congo, Folder: Congo, General 11/3/61–11/11/61, Department of State for the Press, "For Background Only," November 10, 1961.

[99] Kennedy Presidential Archives, Box 27A, National Security Files, Series: Countries: Congo, Folder: Congo, General 11/3/61–11/11/61, Department of State for the Press, "For Background Only," November 10, 1961.

[100] "Minister for Transkei: 'Loneliest Diplomat,'" *Sarasota Herald Tribune*, UPI wire, June 4, 1978.

[101] Syndicated column by Ralph de Toledano, "Carter, Young Anti-Africa Racists?" *Ludington Daily News*, April 4, 1977.

[102] Dan Geldenhuys, "International Attitudes on the Recognition of Transkei," Occasional paper given to the South African Institute of International Affairs, October 1979.

[103] These regimes were certainly not alone in this game. Kenneth Kaunda of Zambia made an explicit threat that if the United States and Britain did not help protect Zambia from Rhodesian military incursions he would be forced to turn to Havana and Moscow. David Ottaway, "Kaunda Coming to West with New Warnings on Rhodesia," *Washington Post*, May 14, 1978.

famously declared in the opening sentence of *The Wretched of the Earth* that "… decolonization is always a violent event."[104] But can decolonization be legitimate if it is not? In an interview from 1976, South African Prime Minister, Vorster, said,

> … it has occurred to me that if the Transkei fought us for independence, they would have been recognised, but because they get it peacefully they will refuse to recognise them. I sometimes wonder whether it would not be worthwhile for Kaiser Matanzima to just declare war on South Africa the day before independence, because then his chances of recognition would be much better.[105]

Matanzima himself argued that the UN only recognized new states if they were born through violence. "We are a peace-loving people in Transkei and we are not impressed by the noisy conglomeration of these blood-thirsty people."[106] Other homeland leaders used this same line of argument. Venda's President, Paramount Chief Patrick Mphephu, said in 1980 that "we [Venda] are being condemned and vilified for having achieved independence peacefully."[107]

Katanga, Rhodesia, Transkei, and Bophuthatswana all complained that they were blocked from making their cases directly to the people of the West. All four assigned blame for this to the West's leadership who fruitlessly pursued unreciprocated Third World friendships when their true and natural friends were these four. One aspect of this grievance was the difficulty their leaders faced traveling overseas which meant that their voices were either unheard or filtered through what they saw as a liberal media bias. For example, in March 1962, pro-Katanga groups in the United States invited Tshombe so that, as Katanga's pseudo-ambassador, Michel Streuelens, said, Tshombe could "tell his side of the story …"[108] He was denied entry, and critics saw this as the denial of

---

[104] Fanon, *Wretched of the Earth*, p. 1. "In its bare reality, decolonization reeks of red-hot cannonballs and bloody knives." p. 3.

[105] Interview with the South African Prime Minister, B. J. Vorster, by Clarence Rhodes of UPITN-TV on February 13, 1976. *The Times* of London agreed with Vorster's cynical assessment of Transkei's chances for recognition, as well as his tongue-in-cheek solution, offering this: "To prove its independence of South Africa the Transkei will necessarily have to be seen to do things inimical to South Africa." This article also identifies the self-fulfilling nature of Transkei's dependency on RSA as in part a result of its rejection by the world community. "Transkei Starts in Limbo," *The Times*, October 25, 1976.

[106] Quoted in, "Transkei-Matanzima," Reuter's News Wire, Umtata, Transkei, October 29, 1976.

[107] "Venda Chief's Unity Call," *Rand Daily Mail*, March 22, 1980.

[108] Group Research, Inc Archives, Box 13, Folder: American Friends of Katanga, AFK Charity Mailer, March 27, 1962.

free speech.[109] In February 1968, Ian Smith was invited by the University of Virginia's Law School to come speak in Charlottesville.[110] His visa request was also denied, sparking a similar hue and cry. But in addition to being physically blocked, these four alleged there was a Western media bias that blocked their viewpoints from a fair hearing. For example, the Friends of Rhodesian Independence wrote in their newsletter from 1970: "… liberals and other pro-communists are using economic blockades and twisted press coverage trying to snuff out this new outpost of freedom."[111] Another pro-Rhodesian lobbying group, ASAC, announced in 1969 a public relations effort in order to try to "break through the liberal news blanket."[112] This was indeed the larger goal of these domestic lobbies, to bypass what they saw as the unfair coverage of these regimes in the liberal press and the gatekeeping of their own government and present the true picture of these independence bids to the people of the West.

The largest family of shared arguments made favorable comparisons of these pseudo-states against the records of recognized African states, or their local nationalist rivals. Comparing themselves against independent Africa writ large provided these regimes with the rhetorical freedom to collect and generalize bad stories from around the continent into a wider narrative of African nationalist failure. This forced out into the light some of the disappointments of postcolonial African economic development and the widespread erosion of democratic governance, and it was used by these pseudo-states as both a defensive argument to respond to attacks on these four regimes, and also as a way to expose what they considered to be the double standards applied by the international community in denying their bids for self-determination. Other times, all four made more specific comparative arguments that their state structures were all that protected their vulnerable populations from the certain disaster that awaited them if either they were recaptured by the mother countries or if their internal African nationalist rivals were victorious. In these comparisons, the general and the specific were often purposely conflated such that nationalist failures anywhere portended nationalist failures everywhere.

[109] Dodd Papers, Box 193, Subseries E, Series III Press Release, "Statement by Senator Thomas J. Dodd on the State Department Suspension of the Visa of Mr. Michel Struelens, Director of the Katanga Information Service," October 11, 1961.

[110] Telegram from O'Neill, US Consulate Salisbury to Secretary of State, February 2, 1968, LBJ Archives, National Security File, Country File: Rhodesia, Box 97, vol. 2, 2/66–12/68.

[111] Group Research, Inc Archives, Box 146, Folder: Friends of Rhodesian Independence, "Help Keep the Spirit of 1776 Flaming in Rhodesia," *FRI Newsletter*, Spring 1970, vol. 3, no. 1.

[112] Group Research, Inc Archives, Box 22, Folder: American Southern African Council I, ASAC Circular by John Acord, October 1968.

Emerging as it did during the very first wave of decolonization, Katanga did not have the broad variety of comparisons to other African states that were available to those aspirant states that followed. It did, however, have the earliest failed African state to directly compare itself against, a state whose name would come to be almost metonymic with postcolonial state failure: its own mother state. The supposed "lesson" of the Congo was frequently employed by other critics of African nationalism, in particular the Rhodesians. In 1966, the Rhodesian Ministry of Information published a pamphlet distributed by the Rhodesia Information Office (RIO) in Washington, DC, titled "Rhodesia in the Context of Africa." Under a heading with a groan-inducing pun, "Freedom or Free-Doom," the pamphlet was intended to highlight the relative stability and affluence of Rhodesia as compared against the rest of Africa as a way to defend their new state and to convince readers that African nationalist rule meant only disaster. The destruction of Katanga at the hands of the UN was identified as an omen and a warning.

Rhodesians are fully aware of the problems of Africa, and were able to foresee the fate which has now overtaken these countries as the "African personality" asserted itself. The sorry sequence has been painted in blood across the face of Africa. The hopes and expectations of the masses who were stirred to fight for "uhuru" have been dashed in tragedy after tragedy ... As the pattern develops, the attacks against Rhodesia appear to become more virulent. Those countries whose records are the worst appear to be the most voluble in their threats ... [African independence] elsewhere brought only disastrous consequences ... One island of relative sanity remained in the richly endowed Katanga, under Moise Tshombe – the only African amongst Congo's millions who was capable of holding any part of the country together. But for academic reasons which sacrificed an entire country for expediency, Tshombe was to be destroyed. War was waged by the United Nations to destroy the secessionist or "rebel" government. This lack of human wisdom resulted in the elimination of the remaining civilization in the Congo and for six tragic years its 12,000,000 people have suffered the horrors of anarchy and privation ... But it is the fashion to turn a blind eye on the Congo tragedy, and even to suggest that it is an exceptional case from which Europeans in Rhodesia should not draw unwarranted conclusions. Embarrassing though it may be, its lessons are there to be learned – by the world no less than Rhodesia.[113]

Rhodesia's claim to sovereignty was based in large part on learning and applying that supposed Congolese lesson.[114]

---

[113] Group Research Inc, Archives, Columbia University, Box 287, Folder: Rhodesia Information Office, "Rhodesia in the Context of Africa," Ministry of Information, Immigration, and Tourism, June 1966 (RIO).

[114] As the Liberation War intensified, the Rhodesian Ministry of Information produced numerous pamphlets and booklets which they distributed widely overseas that luridly

Rhodesia hit the point hard and often that their government was better run than any other African country, and that as a result all Rhodesians, white and black, benefitted. Even before UDI, Marvin Liebman's American African Affairs Association (AAAA) warned of what it foresaw as the disastrous effect of imposing African majority rule on Rhodesia: "Today, as the wave of European control recedes, a score or more of infant nations have sprung into being – many of them with little or no political experience, and almost all of them without the economic strength to make their own way alone."[115] In the "Rhodesian Viewpoint" newsletter printed out of the RIO in Washington, the Rhodesian government again placed Rhodesia on a side-by-side with independent Africa.

It is Rhodesia's proud boast that, whatever her critics may say, her record in the fields of African health, education, wages, housing, and social welfare is superior to that in every one of the independent black African states. And it is submitted that, in a new nation with a civilized tradition of only 75 years, this is the only comparison which is valid.[116]

Ian Smith famously said that in Rhodesia one saw "the happiest Africans in the world."[117] Like Katanga and Rhodesia, Transkei compared itself against independent Africa, and made the case that their sovereign claims were unfairly dismissed. Prior to independence the South African government produced a great deal of propaganda favorably comparing Transkei against other African countries.[118] But it was primarily Lesotho, Swaziland, and Botswana against which Transkei and the other Bantustans compared their histories and self-determination claims. The reason the Bantustans wanted to be associated with the former High Commission Territories (HCTs) and not Zambia or Tanzania or any other former British colony in Africa was that these three all emerged out of the same complicated racial and ethnic milieu of British Southern Africa as did the Bantustans. They also were centered around a similar ethnic logic, which made them fundamentally different

---

documented the alleged atrocities of the African guerrilla armies with titles such as "Anatomy of Terror" and the "The Murder of Missionaries in Rhodesia." "Anatomy of Terror," Rhodesian Ministry of Information (January 1974); "The Murder of Missionaries in Rhodesia," Zimbabwe Rhodesia Ministry of Information (January 1978).

[115] Group Research Inc, Archives, Columbia University, Box 4, Folder: American African Affairs Association, AAAA Circular to Members, September 13, 1965.

[116] Group Research Inc, Archives, Columbia University, Box 287, Folder: Rhodesia Information Office, "Rhodesia Viewpoint," February 1967 (RIO).

[117] I. Smith, *Bitter Harvest: The Great Betrayal* (Blake, London, 2001), pp. 151–158.

[118] N. M. Stultz, *Transkei's Half Loaf: Race Separatism in South Africa* (Yale University Press, New Haven, 1981) p. 140.

kinds of nations than the pan-ethnic civic nationalisms to their north. Just as Botswana was the land of the Tswanas, Lesotho the land of the Sotho, and Swaziland the land of the Swazi, Transkei was to be the land of the Xhosa, and Bophuthatswana the land of the southern Tswana.

The HCTs were useful associations for the Bantustans in other ways. For one, all three were economically dependent upon South Africa, almost as islands of poverty in an affluent South African sea.[119] In his Independence Day speech, Kaiser Matanzima said that Transkei was at the moment economically dependent upon South Africa, but so too were Mozambique, Malawi, Lesotho, Swaziland, and Botswana, all of which enjoyed international recognition.[120] Newell Stultz, a political scientist who would later write a book titled *Transkei's Half-Loaf*, wrote an op-ed calling for recognition of Transkei. In it he argued that Transkei was as viable as many other African states, and in particular he noted that Transkei was materially better off than Lesotho, its legal neighbor to the north, and yet Lesotho's economic dependency on South Africa and its relative lack of resources "did not prevent Lesotho's getting international recognition when it became independent in 1966."[121] Since the Bantustans' legitimacy was questioned for these very same reasons of dependency, that the HCTs were in largely the same dependent position served as a powerful counter-argument.[122]

Historical chance played a major role. The Bantustans argued that they could have just as easily been designated as a protectorate as Bechuanaland, Swaziland, and Basutoland had been, and achieved independent recognition in the 1960s just as they had.[123] That these three HCTs were granted independence while the Bantustans were left inside South Africa was seen as a grave injustice.[124] In the months before and after Transkei's Independence Day, Transkei often made its case for sovereignty through historical accounts of their precolonial past which presented the case that they were a part of South Africa only by virtue of

---

[119] South African Prime Minister, Johannes Vorster, made the strengthening of economic ties between South Africa and the former HCTs a top priority. See: Irwin, *Gordian Knot*, pp. 159–160.

[120] "Transkei, a South African Black Area, Is Independent," *New York Times*, October 26, 1976.

[121] N. Stultz, "Why Is Transkei Still Being Portrayed as a Stooge?" op-ed, *The New York Times*, July 9, 1979.

[122] Stefan Talmon concludes that "Lesotho, Botswana, Malawi, or Swaziland were not much more independent from South Africa than the homeland states ..." Stefan Talmon "The Constitutive versus the Declaratory Theory of Recognition: Tertium Non Datur?" *British Yearbook of International Law*, vol. 75, no. 1 (2004) p. 112.

[123] "Are the Doubts about the Transkei Self-fulfilling?" *The Guardian*, October 21, 1976.

[124] This was what Peris Sean Jones called the Bantustans' tactic of "guilt-tripping" the British.

an "accident of history." For example, one government-issued propaganda document described Transkei's sovereign position this way:

[The HCTs], which are today members of the United Nations and the OAU, are no less South African countries than the Transkei is, bearing in mind that they each share long borders with South Africa, belong to the same customs union with South Africa, and are land-locked whereas the Transkei is a coastal state. The Transkei, however, was by an *accident of history* handed over to this Union of South Africa by the Cape Colony. The people of the Transkei were never consulted both about the formation of the Union and about their being handed over to it for administration. Its people accordingly became subject to segregation and discriminatory practices.[125]

Like Transkei, Bophuthatswana's claims for sovereign recognition often took the form of history lessons, recounting the decisions made by British colonists as they sliced and diced Southern Africa in the late nineteenth century trapping the southern Tswana in what would become the Union of South Africa, while setting in motion the eventual freedom of the northern Tswana.[126] This retelling of nineteenth century British decision-making was a narrative the regime returned to over and over again.[127]

The Bantustans made their claims for recognition not just through making favorable comparisons against independent Africa and drawing out their linkages with the HCTs, but sometimes by distinguishing themselves from each other. The South African minister at the US Embassy reported in a memorandum to Pretoria that he found the Transkeian diplomats-in-training were "sensitive" to any associations between Transkei and the other homelands, thinking Transkei to be a different case altogether.[128] As explained in a later chapter, Matanzima was later slow to recognize the other Bantustans as they became independent fearing that they would undermine his own state's claims. In the case of Bophuthatswana, its Finance Minister, Rowan Cronje, regularly placed Bophuthatswana's economy alongside other African nations.[129] Bophuthatswana's relative economic success as against independent

---

[125] SA National Archives, Box: Transkei 1/226/1/1, Independence Celebrations and Invitations. Long memorandum, "A New State: The Republic of Transkei" (undated).

[126] For more on the creation of this border, see: Drummond and Manson, "Bophuthatswana–Botswana Border."

[127] See for example: MSS AAM 981 Bophuthatswana 1981–1994, Letter from AIA Findlay to Gerard Omasta, January 28, 1991.

[128] SA National Archives, Box: Transkei: Independence Celebrations and Invitations, 1/226/1/1, "Transkei Diplomats" Letter from SA Ambassador the US, Shearer, to Secretary DFA, November 13, 1975.

[129] Jones, "Etiquette of State-Building," p. 34.

African countries as well as other Bantustans was put front and center in their appeals for recognition as to why it was different from the other Bantustans, including Transkei, which were all wholly dependent upon South Africa.[130] As if forcibly hugging together squabbling siblings into a family portrait, it was only due to South African pressure that the Bantustans ever recognized each other, and even afterward the relations were often less than familial.

Conclusion

As explained above, the three shared argument families that gave Katanga, Rhodesia, Transkei, and Bophuthatswana their unique ideological shape together formed a distinct discursive web. These four regimes and their friends abroad offered definitions of African authenticity and political legitimacy that ran in direct opposition to the core premises of postcolonial African nationalism. Emphasizing their tight ideological, political, economic, and cultural bonds with the West stood against the ideologies and deeply held beliefs of most postcolonial African nationalists about the true meaning of African self-determination. Finally, their criticisms of postcolonial African statehood were sustained, deep, and systemic, characterizing the entire process and results of decolonization under African nationalists as an abject failure that should be reexamined. This web implicated the foundational pillars of the postcolonial African state system, and as a result Katanga, Rhodesia, Transkei, and Bophuthatswana's shared ideological project was an existential threat to the entire African state system. These high ideological stakes were understood at the time, and the chapters that follow recount the battles and explore the diverse and bizarre battlefields of their struggles for sovereignty.

---

[130] These efforts to distinguish went all the way to the time of its incorporation. "Cronje and the other officials said Bophuthatswana should not be treated the same way as the other three nominally independent homelands – Ciskei, Transkei and Venda. They claim that while those three really are artificial creations of apartheid – and almost totally economically dependent on South Africa – Bop is the traditional home of the Tswana people, whom British colonialists arbitrarily divided between Botswana and South Africa." Keith Richburg, "Behold the Land of Bop: A Figment of Apartheid that Won't Go Away," *Washington Post*, September 16, 1993.

3   The Magical Hour of Midnight
Independence Days and National Commemorations

The mystical belief that beginnings augur fates is as old as humankind, and is something that continues on through the numerological and astrological fascinations with the timing and particulars of the moment of birth.[1] There is an almost inescapable tendency to anthropomorphize nation-states as individuals with human-like characteristics, and so the moments when new states are created and enter the international community are often compared to the moments of human birth, and commemorations of these sovereign moments have been analogized to celebrating birthdays.[2] And not only are state-persons "born" and become "international persons," but in secessionist conflicts the state from which the secessionist regime splits off is commonly referred to as the "mother country," further anthropomorphizing state-persons by gendering the actors in their reproduction. Like birthdays, dates of independence are thought to be definite and set, and like birthdays independence dates are memorized and are seen as a fundamental part of the state's biological reality.[3]

The moment when a new state is created is always granted a magical significance by national memory-makers, and the commemorations of these independence days are always invested with a great deal of symbolic

---

[1] Parts of this chapter on Rhodesia's and Transkei's commemorations are drawn substantially from a chapter by the author in an edited volume. J. Brownell, "'The Magical Hour of Midnight': The Annual Commemorations of Rhodesia's and Transkei's Independence Days," in Toyin Falola and Kenneth Kalu (eds.), *Exploitation and Misrule in Colonial and Postcolonial Africa* (Palgrave Macmillan, New York, 2018).

[2] This is what historian E. H. Carr famously coined the "fiction of the group-person." E. H. Carr, *The Twenty Years' Crisis* (Macmillan, London, 1946). But a few examples are: Joseph Heller, *The Birth of Israel: 1945–1949: Ben-Gurion and His Critics* (University Press of Florida, Gainesville, 2003); Joseph J. Ellis, *Revolutionary Summer: The Birth of American Independence* (Vintage Press, New York, 2014); Craig Nelson, *Thomas Paine: Enlightenment, Revolution, and the Birth of Modern Nations* (Penguin Books, New York, 2007); David Brewer, *The Greek War of Independence: The Struggle for Freedom and the Birth of Modern Greece* (Overlook Press, New York, 2011).

[3] For a superb exploration of this idea in fiction, see: Salman Rushdie's *Midnight's Children* (Random House, New York, 1981).

power.[4] Though the timing of independence days become saturated with meaning afterward, the decision taken regarding the timing beforehand is often the result of practical and prosaic considerations. Dating independence moments can be highly contested and indefinite and the moment of the creation of sovereignty ambiguous.[5] For instance, the dating of Katanga's independence moment was very fuzzy. As will be discussed below, earlier declarations of independence were advanced only to be withdrawn at the last minute, and the one Moise Tshombe publicly made on July 11, 1960 was later publicly retracted, then its retraction was retracted, and only later was it ratified by the Katangese provincial legislature, and throughout the secession important allies of the regime denied that Katanga had ever wanted full independence at all. Ian Smith's Rhodesian regime settled on November 11, 1965 to make his regime's declaration for a wide variety of seemingly unrelated factors, ranging from the economic (the timing of the tobacco crop harvest) to the administrative (the expiration of the preventative detention law) to the symbolic (having it overlap with Remembrance Day). Failing to achieve recognition after UDI and fearing that this was in part because its initial break with Britain was not thorough enough, the regime would then declare itself to be a republic on March 2, 1970, as a sort of second unilateral declaration of independence. Unlike the other regimes whose mother countries were hostile to their declarations, the dates of Transkei's Independence, October 26, 1976, and Bophuthatswana's, December 6, 1977, were matters of negotiation between the South African government and the nascent homeland governments of Transkei and Bophuthatswana. In deciding on the date for Transkei, the parties weighed, among other things, the short session of the Transkei National Assembly, the busy schedules of possible international attendees, and the timing of how the weekends fell in 1976, sounding more like the setting of a wedding date than that of a national independence day.

Unlike the growing literature on the important role of national day commemorations in the creation and reinforcement of national identity – in *nation-making* – little has been written on the role of national days in

---

[4] See M. E. Geisler, "The Calendar Conundrum: National Days as Unstable Signifiers," and M. Skey, "'We Wanna Show 'Em Who We Are' National Events in England," both in D. McCrone and G. MacPherson (eds.), *National Days: Constructing and Mobilising National Identity* (Palgrave Macmillan, London, 2009).

[5] Dating the ex-dominions' moment of full sovereignty is less than definite. See for instance: Stephen Marche, "Canada Doesn't Know How to Party," op-ed column, *New York Times*, June 23, 2017.

unrecognized states in performing sovereignty – in *state-making*.[6] Unlike sovereign states, commemorations of national days in contested states are necessarily provisional and aspirational, less about the remembrance of the moment of independence than a performance of sovereignty with an eye forward for what that day in the past might mean in the future, and how the commemoration itself could further that goal. With Katanga, Rhodesia, Transkei, and Bophuthatswana, here were cases in which the creation and formalization and repetition of the fledgling states' rituals were being performed by regimes that were denied legality and were under siege internationally. All four regimes understood the importance of their independence days and put a great deal of effort into making them appear to be authentically inspired, popularly supported, and internationally legitimated commemorations. Independence days were also performative – that is, attendance by an official delegation of a sovereign state has been interpreted by scholars of international law as being an act of implicit recognition.[7] It was this same understanding of the potentially performative role of independence day celebrations for these aspirant states that opponents of these pseudo-states tried to symbolically, politically, and even physically undermine these events. As will be shown below, all four contested states failed on all of these accounts, in part because of the active, as well as passive, resistance to these commemorations by opponents of these would-be states, inside and outside their territories. As a result, these regimes' ideological projects of nation-making and state-making were purposely disrupted by their opponents, with their performances heckled and national rites interrupted in part to stop the settling and hardening of their symbolic power through undisturbed repetition.[8] It was in part through denying the ability of the regimes to celebrate their birthdays that their enemies challenged the very notion that these pseudo-states had ever been born at all.

Despite the significance of these days, the aesthetic aspects of Katanga's, Rhodesia's, Transkei's, and Bophuthatswana's independence

---

[6] There is a rich literature on history and politics of commemorations and national memory making. See, for example: R. Charumbira, *Imagining a Nation: History and Memory in Making Zimbabwe* (University of Virginia Press, Charlottesville, 2015); L. Witz, *Apartheid's Festival: Contesting South Africa's National Pasts* (Indiana University Press, Bloomington, 2003). See also: D. McCrone and G. MacPherson (eds.), *National Days: Constructing and Mobilising National Identity* (Palgrave Macmillan, London, 2009); J. Gillis (ed.), *Commemorations: The Politics of National Identity* (Princeton University Press, Princeton, 1996).

[7] See Ker Lindsay, "Engagement without Recognition."

[8] B. Anderson, *Imagined Communities: Reflections of the Origin and Spread of Nationalism* (Verso, London, 1983); E. Hobsbawm and T. Ranger (eds.), *The Invention of Tradition* (Cambridge University Press, Cambridge, 1983).

bids have not been taken too seriously in the academic literature. But they should be. Katanga would have the opportunity to commemorate its so-called independence only twice, in 1961 and 1962. Rhodesia would commemorate UDI thirteen times, from 1966 to 1978, Transkei would have seventeen commemorations, from 1977 to 1993, and Bophuthatswana sixteen times from 1978 to 1993. Just as the elements of their original independence moments were refashioned as they first became commemorated, so too did the commemorations themselves change over time. These thoroughly edited and partly invented recreations of the past then become ritualized, and subsequent rituals reify earlier ones.[9] For national leaders these events provide platforms to tell their preferred national narratives. David Kertzer writes that political rituals, including commemorations, should not be seen as "mere embellishments," but as vital parts of modern politics, since it is only "through participation in the rites, [that citizens] of the modern state identif[y] with larger political forces that can only be seen in symbolic form."[10] As Kertzer further explains, "Symbolism is the stuff of which nations are made."[11] It will be argued below that it is the stuff of which states are made as well.

It will be contended below that the aesthetics of their independence days and their subsequent commemorations were not primarily the result of spontaneity or serendipity, and neither did they derive from ancient or traditional sources, but were new, purposeful, and self-consciously political choices. These aspirant states' aesthetic choices about how their independence days looked and sounded were used as opportunities to communicate to various audiences the natures of these aspirant states, what kinds of states they wanted to be associated with and from which they wanted to be dissociated, and how these regimes thought their states would fit into the world community, and they provided crucial elements of their shared discursive web.

Katanga

Katanga's purported independence was the shortest of the four, and its independent existence was politically, physically, and militarily challenged from the outset, with UN troops occupying Elisabethville and other strategic points for much of the secessionist period. The UN and the Congolese government were hostile to any expressions of Katangese

---

[9] See: Hobsbawm and Ranger, *The Invention of Tradition.*
[10] D. Kertzer, *Ritual, Politics, and Power* (Yale University Press, New Haven, 1988) pp. 1, 3.
[11] Kertzer, *Ritual*, p. 6.

independence and always looked to undermine the legitimacy of Tshombe's regime on a theoretical and political level, as well as to disrupt the creation of state institutions and traditions in very practical and physical ways. Like disrupting the drying action of wet paint by stirring it, the UN made deliberate efforts not to allow Katangese national traditions and rituals to develop and settle and acquire the legitimating patina of age and repetition.

Moise Tshombe's declaration of Katangese independence on July 11, 1960 was the most haphazard and ambiguous of the four regimes' independence declarations studied in this chapter. Supporters as well as opponents of the regime, and even seemingly Tshombe himself, were unsure as to what the Katangese regime was trying to achieve as its ultimate goal – whether it was complete sovereign independence, a federal Congolese state with significant Katangese autonomy, or a Katanga-dominated, unitary Congo. Tshombe had initially proposed the idea of declaring the independence of Katanga while it was still a part of the Belgian Congo, and both the Belgians and African politicians in Leopoldville took this threat of Katangese secession very seriously. On June 14, 1960, Tshombe's CONAKAT party had planned to issue a proclamation of independence from the Belgian Congo that would appeal for recognition directly from King Baudouin of Belgium, which was to be published in a newspaper the next day.[12] The plan could not be implemented as a Belgian officer physically stole the text from the offices of the local daily newspaper.[13] Tshombe's circle planned for another declaration of independence on June 28th, two days prior to Congolese independence, but Belgian authorities uncovered this second secessionist plan – the so-called Scheerlinck affair – and as described in the next chapter, promptly quashed it.[14]

The exiting colonial administration and incoming nationalist politicians were both hostile to these early Katangese secessionist attempts, resembling in some ways the conflict over Asanti separatism in the build-up to Ghana's independence. In that case, both the Gold Coast's British Governor as well as Kwame Nkrumah's nascent Convention People's Party (CPP) government opposed the Asanti movement.[15] Katanga's

---

[12] Gerard-Libois, *Katanga Secession*, p. 78.   [13] Gerard-Libois, *Katanga Secession*, p. 78.

[14] Gerard-Libois, *Katanga Secession*, p. 85. A third attempt was undertaken just a day before the Congo's independence in which reportedly on the initiative of Godefroid Munungo a European settler distributed copies of a proposed declaration to assembly members. Tshombe was not aware of this plan until he was informed of it by the Belgians. He did not support it, and it fizzled out quickly (pp. 88–89).

[15] See: Jean Marie Allman's, book, *Quills of the Porcupine: Asante Nationalism in an Emergent Ghana* (University of Wisconsin Press, Madison, 1993).

appeals over the heads of the nationalist politicians and colonial administrators on the spot and directly to the European monarch of the mother
state also mirrored the strategy of the Asanti separatist movement. It was
one that would be repeated again in the case of Rhodesia's attempted
independence, where the Rhodesians continued to claim the Queen as
their own – literally the Queen of Rhodesia – while rejecting the authority
of the British parliament.[16] In keeping with this idea, after Tshombe's
declaration of independence on July 11th, a Katangese delegation would
fly to Belgium to have an audience with King Baudouin in person in a
failed attempt to win Belgian recognition outside the normal channels of
the Belgian diplomacy.[17] This continued appeal to scale-jumping alliances straight to the imperial monarch reflects both an immediate strategy to win independence but also a deeper sentimentality for a return to
an older, imagined form of imperial rule that was based upon a shared
cross-cultural respect for chiefly and royal authority.[18]

The whole of the Congo became independent on June 30, 1960. In the
Leopoldville ceremony the new Congolese Prime Minister, Patrice
Lumumba, famously denounced the entire history of Belgian colonial
rule in front of an offended King Baudouin. Within days the Force
Publique mutinied across the Congo. Moise Tshombe, then the president of the Katanga Province, called for the intervention of Belgian,
Rhodesian, and British troops to restore order, a request that was beyond
his authority as a provincial president.[19] On July 10th, Belgian paratroop-
ers entered the Congo over the objections of Lumumba, as white settlers
began streaming over the Katangese border into the CAF. Rumors again
began to circulate in Brussels about the possibility of a Katangese declaration of independence.[20] The Belgians attempted to dissuade Tshombe
from declaring independence, communicating to him that they would
not recognize Katanga, and instead tried to reassure Tshombe about his
security concerns by promising that Belgian forces would stay to "as long

---

[16] D. Lowry, "The Queen of Rhodesia versus the Queen of the United Kingdom: Conflicts
of Allegiance in Rhodesians Unilateral Declaration of Independence," in
H. Kumarasingham (ed.), *Viceregalism: The Crown as Head of State in Political Crises in
the Postwar Commonwealth* (Palgrave MacMillan, London, 2020). See also: Kenrick,
Decolonization, Identity, and Nation in Rhodesia.

[17] *Keesing's Record of World Events* (formerly Keesing's Contemporary Archives), vol. 6,
November 1960 Congo Republic, Belgian, p. 17753.

[18] An insightful reexamination of the intra-imperial elite alliances that runs counter to most
scholarship on imperial power dynamics can be found in David Cannadine's book,
Ornamentalism: How the British Saw Their Empire (Oxford University Press,
Oxford, 2001).

[19] Gerard-Libois, *Katanga Secession*, pp. 96–97.

[20] Gerard-Libois, *Katanga Secession*, p. 97.

as necessary," regardless of the desires of the central government in
Leopoldville.[21] On July 11th, a state of exception was proclaimed in
Katanga as the Belgian troops arrived. Ostensibly there to ensure protection of European lives and possible evacuation of refugees, the Belgians
worked to solidify provincial control over the territory.[22]

At 8 p.m. Central Africa Time on the evening of July 11th, Moise
Tshombe went on the air at Radio Katanga and read out his
declaration:[23]

Belgium has granted independence to the Congo ... What do we behold at
present? Throughout the Congo and particularly in Katanga ... we see a tactic
of disorganization and terror at work, a tactic which we have seen applied in
numerous instances and in how many countries now under Communist
dictatorship ... The goal of these maneuvers and their premeditation were
amply proven by the repeated protests of the Prime Minister of the Congo
against the dispatch of Belgian troops from Belgium to protect property and
human lives. We declare that what the current central Congolese government
wants is nothing less than the disintegration of the whole military and
administrative apparatus, the installation of a regime of terror which ousts our
Belgian colleagues ... Under these circumstances ... the Katangan government
has decided to proclaim the independence of Katanga. This INDEPENDENCE
IS TOTAL. However, aware of the imperative necessity for economic
cooperation with Belgium, the Katangan government, to which Belgium has
just granted the assistance of its own troops to protect human life, calls upon
Belgium to join with Katanga in close economic community.[24]

Tshombe's address that night does not read like a text intended to be
saved or remembered as a national founding document. It was neither
philosophically high-minded nor a historically rooted call for Katangese
national self-determination; its grievances more political and immediate,
and its proclamations of sovereignty were slightly hedged. It is significant
that the details of the proclamation moment were subsequently thought
to be unimportant by the Katangese, and they were not incorporated into
the nation-building myths. This is in sharp contrast, for instance, with
the sanctification of the signing ceremony of the United States
Declaration of Independence or the Rhodesian Cabinet's signing of the
UDI document, as well as the elaborate "freedoms at midnight" rituals

---

[21] Gerard-Libois, *Katanga Secession*, pp. 97–98.
[22] Gerard-Libois, *Katanga Secession*, p. 99.
[23] There is some disagreement over whether or not the announcement was made at 8 p.m.
or 9:30 p.m. Christopher Othen claims 8 p.m. Othen, *Katanga 1960–1963*, p. 53. While
Michel Lupant, citing a press report, claimed 9:30 p.m. *Emblems of the State of Katanga,
1960–1963* (Belgian-European Flags Studies Centre (CEBED), Ottignies, Belgium, July
2004) p. 7, citing "La Libre Belgique" July 12, 1960, p. 1.
[24] Gerard-Libois, *Katanga Secession*, pp. 328–329.

performed around the globe during decolonization, including Transkei's and Bophuthatswana's faux independence ceremonies. Katanga's actual sovereign moment was so incidental as to be officially forgotten.

This indifference about the details of the proclamation was perhaps part of the more general ambivalence of the regime about whether or not the declaration of independence was really a declaration of independence at all. On his end, Tshombe walked back his proclamation almost as soon as he made it. In a communiqué on July 12, Tshombe said the Provincial Assembly and his government were reexamining the secession issue.[25] As reported in the *Rand Daily Mail*, Tshombe had a private meeting with foreign representatives and commerce and business interests in Katanga and gave the strong impression that he was "back-tracking."[26] A day later, Tshombe then told the Katangese people that he was "standing firm" on independence, and was not retracting it.[27] On their end, the South Africans believed that Tshombe wanted to secede all along but his vacillations "ha[d] been due to inability to obtain external support of recognition."[28] On July 17th, the Katanga Provincial Assembly finally ratified Tshombe's secession proclamation, an act which retroactively cast doubt on the meaning of the July 11th declaration, particularly in light of the subsequent retraction.

Adding to this uncertainty, from the date of the original declaration, July 11th, until the 18th, the new Congolese national flag still flew in Elisabethville parade ground of Camp Massart, and was still hoisted to the playing of "Vers L'Avenir," the new Congolese national anthem.[29] Only after the assembly ratified his declaration on July 17th did Tshombe introduce the new Katanga flag that would be hoisted the next day at a press conference.[30] The new red, green, white flag with the iconic three red crosses on the lower right section was designed only days before by a local German/Belgian architect.[31] These crosses were stylized copper ignots that would soon be found on Katangese postage stamps, on the tailfins of Air Katanga, and on the regime's new currency, the Katangese franc. Not only did this particular symbol have an undeniable precolonial pedigree, but it also provided a link between Katangese identity and copper mining which made the postcolonial corporate extraction of

[25] "Congo Urges US to Send Troops; Plea Is Rejected," *New York Times*, July 13, 1960.

[26] "Congo: America Asked to Send Troops," *Rand Daily Mail*, July 13, 1960.

[27] "Katanga Said Belgium Pledged Troops," *New York Times*, July 14, 1960.

[28] SA National Archives, Box 1/112/3/1 "Secession of Katanga," Telegram from SA High Commissioner in London to Secretary for External Affairs, Pretoria, July 14, 1960.

[29] Lupant, *Emblems*, p. 7.   [30] Lupant, *Emblems*, p. 7.   [31] Lupant, *Emblems*, pp. 8–9.

metals by UMHK more of a historical continuity with a precolonial past than a disjuncture brought on by colonialism.[32]

Even as the new flags flapped in Elisabethville, the Katangese regime's ambivalence toward seeking full independence can be seen in their odd responses to the Congo's first independence anniversary in June 1961. There are parallels to be made here with the American Confederacy's "pensive ambivalence" regarding American Independence Day on July 4th during the US Civil War.[33] At times the Tshombe regime wholly rejected any connection to Congolese independence. For example, the only postage stamp from the newly independent state of the Congo the Katangese regime chose to overprint carried enormous symbolic significance: the commemorative Congolese Independence stamp. The Katangese overprint simply printed "11 Juillet" over "30 Juin" and "De l'Etat Du Katanga" over "Congo."[34] That other Congo stamps were left alone besides this one served to reject the notion that the Congo had any authority over Katanga, and it disassociated Katanga from the Congolese sovereign through a supposedly straight line of continuity back through their former Belgian overlords as though those two weeks between Congolese independence and the secession never happened. However, speaking in Katanga on the first anniversary of the Congo's independence, Tshombe made the rather oblique statement that his policy was always to collaborate "with our brothers in the Congo," but at the same time to ensure that certain rights of Katanga be respected.[35]

On the first anniversary of the Congo's independence on June 30, 1961, Congolese soldiers in brand new uniforms paraded down Boulevard Albert in Leopoldville past President Kasavubu, Mobutu, and Prime Minister Joseph Ileo. This parade was led by Katangese soldiers wearing wide brimmed bush hats who were sent by Tshombe as a show of his willingness to keep to the agreement to bring the Katangese Army under central Congolese control.[36] Hardly the response one would expect of a fully sovereign state. This parade fell just a few weeks after talks with the central government broke down and after Tshombe himself had just been released from his imprisonment by the central authorities where he had been held for nearly two months. This show of unity would be short-lived, and Katanga would in effect be celebrating two independence anniversaries back-to-back.

---

[32] Kennes and Larmer, *Katangese Gendarmes*, p. 7.
[33] P. Quigley, "Independence Day Dilemmas in the American South, 1848–1865," *Journal of Southern History*, vol. 75, no. 2 (2009).
[34] Katanga's 1960 independence overprint (Scott # 40–49).
[35] "A Year of Self-rule in Congo," *Rand Daily Mail*, July 1, 1961.
[36] "Congolese Mark Year of Freedom," *New York Times*, July 1, 1961.

Amid these mixed signals, Katanga's establishment of the trappings and paraphernalia of statehood continued. In early 1961, Katanga established the so-called Presidential Guard for ceremonial purposes, consisting of a motorbike platoon and a horse platoon. The guard initially wore green uniforms with the Dragoon's helmet, a style that some described as looking out of the French Third Empire, or as others claimed, more like opera costuming.[37] The appearance of the outfits certainly added to what Susan Williams commented was a "Ruritanian atmosphere" to Katanga.[38] Adding to the sense of unreality, the Presidential Guards were present with all the requisite pomp for the pseudo-state visit of President Albert Kalonji of the semi-independent province of South Kasai when he visited Katanga in February 1961.[39] Tshombe also hosted President Fulbert Youlou of the Congo-Brazzaville when he came for a pseudo-state visit in early 1961, which offered another opportunity for Katanga to perform statehood.

On the day of its first anniversary, on July 11th, the Katangese Gendarmerie and Presidential Guards passed in review as Tshombe wore the sash of the Katangese Order of Merit.[40] From the moment of its secession and throughout its short existence, Katanga was engaged in several military conflicts, sometimes simultaneously, against the Congolese central government forces, the Baluba rebels in northern Katanga, and ONUC forces, so it is perhaps not surprising that the formal expressions of Katangese independence took on a distinctly martial character.[41] According to a chronicler of Katangese state symbols, as

---

[37] Lupant, *Emblems*, p. 27; B. Urquhart, *A Life in Peace and War* (W. W. Norton, New York, 1987), p. 184.

[38] Williams, *Who Killed Hammarskjold?* p. 34.

[39] South Kasai's desired sovereign status was even more ambiguous than Katanga's. Shortly after Tshombe declared Katanga's independence, Albert Kalonji declared that South Kasai was breaking away from the larger Kasai province and was thereafter to be known as the "Mining State of South Kasai." Crucially, South Kasai refused to send tax revenues to Leopoldville. The Congolese army conducted a brutal, but inconclusive invasion of the region in August 1960. During its brief existence South Kasai was informally allied with Katanga, and was even known as "the little Katanga." However, South Kasai never proclaimed itself to be a fully sovereign entity separate and apart from Leopoldville as did Katanga. David Halberstam, "Rich Diamond Mines at Stake in Congo-South Kasai Struggle," *New York Times*, February 19, 1962. See also: C. Young, *Politics in the Congo: Decolonization and Independence* (Oxford University Press, Oxford, 1965) pp. 537–539. For the pseudo-state visit, see: Lupant, *Emblems*, pp. 29–30.

[40] Lupant, *Emblems*, p. 26.

[41] Regarding the Baluba rebellion in northern Katanga, Tshombe's regime ironically employed the same slippery slope argument often employed against his regime. "Where would one end [asked the Katanga government White Book on the Baluba opposition] if each of the hundreds of tribes inhabiting the former Belgian Congo wanted to erect itself as [an] independent state?" Quoted in Staniland, *American Intellectuals*,

Figure 3.1 Moise Tshombe and Albert Kalonji, leader of the "Mining State of South Kasai," watch a formal military parade during the latter's pseudo-state visit to Katanga in early 1961.

part of the wider UN turn toward more direct confrontation with the secessionist regime, two months after Katanga's first anniversary UN forces "seized the stores and uniforms of the Presidential Guard," taking with them the green outfits with the Dragoon's helmets, some of which were reportedly later discovered in refugee camps and some even in Sweden.[42] According to UN representative Brian Urquhart, the seizures

p. 73 fn 53, citing Herbert Weiss, "The Tshombe Riddle," *New Leader*, no. 17 (September 1962).
[42] Lupant, *Emblems*, p. 30.

of these outfits greatly upset Tshombe, who was proud of the uniforms' operatic flair, and Tshombe tried unsuccessfully to have them returned.[43] Losing these uniforms in the UN fighting seems like a frivolous thing compared against the wider tragedies of the Congo Crisis, but it lends weight to the proposition that in instances of contested statehood symbolic repertoires were seen by all sides as important opportunities for the aspirant state to perform sovereignty.

Shortly after Katanga's first year anniversary, Cyrille Adoula became the Congo's new Prime Minister, and the Kennedy administration unequivocally threw its support behind the new central government against the secession.[44] Between the first- and second-year anniversaries, the Katangese Gendarmerie and UN forces engaged in two rounds of fighting. "Round One" in September 1961, officially called Operation Morthor, was militarily inconclusive but a political embarrassment for the UN. However, "Round Two" in December 1961 resulted in an almost complete UN victory that forced Tshombe to agree to end the secession and reincorporate Katanga into the Congo in the Kitona Agreement. From March 1962 until June 26, 1962, Tshombe and Congolese Prime Minister Cyrille Adoula took part in the Leopoldville talks to reintegrate Katanga into the Congo. Against the backdrop of this seemingly good faith attempt to find a workable formula for reintegration, commentators and political actors involved in the unfolding drama paid close attention to how the Katanga regime was going to mark the secession's second anniversary, as it was recognized as a demonstration of the regime's broader intentions and as a test for the regime's enemies.[45] Everyone waited to see what Tshombe was going to do.

Before the Leopoldville talks broke down, and as early as June 18th, the United Nations got wind of the Katanga regime's plans to have a large parade pass through Elisabethville on the second anniversary of Tshombe's equivocal declaration.[46] By the end of June, the UN reported to the British Consul, Derek Dodson, that the Katangese Gendarmerie planned on marching an additional thousand troops into Elisabethville

[43] Urquhart, *A Life in Peace and War*, p. 184.

[44] Thomas Noer, "New Frontiers and Old Priorities in Africa," in Thomas G. Paterson (ed.), *Kennedy's Quest for Victory, American Foreign Policy, 1961–1963* (Oxford University Press, Oxford, 1989) pp. 264–265

[45] David Halberstam, "Uneasy Katanga Marking Secession Anniversary," *New York Times*, July 10, 1962.

[46] Sir Roy Welensky Papers, Weston Library Oxford, African and Commonwealth Collection, Box 260, folder 1, Telegram from British Consulate Elisabethville to Foreign Office, June 12, 1962.

for the celebration.[47] UN Secretary-General, U Thant, spoke out strongly against Katanga's proposed military parade and the "so-called" independence celebrations more generally.[48] There then followed a great deal of diplomatic and political pressures from the UN and other quarters brought to bear on the Katangese regime in a vain attempt to convince the regime not to hold Independence Day celebrations, as they would be seen to be incompatible with the view to reintegrate Katanga back into the Congo.[49] The Adoula-Tshombe Leopoldville talks broke down four days before the Congo's second anniversary.

The United Nations aimed at least to blunt the political impact and the security risk of the parade by limiting its size. To hold a large-scale parade in the UN-occupied city of Elisabethville – in which ONUC forces controlled the airport, its troops ringed the city, and its soldiers patrolled the streets – the international organization held it would be necessary to have its permission.[50] The Secretary General's Office on July 1, 1962 reached out to the French, British, and American Consuls in Elisabethville to elicit their support in pleading with the Katangese to limit the size of their planned parade on July 11th.[51] The UN planned to first have their military commanders reach out to their opposite numbers in the Katangese Gendarmerie to ask them to reduce parade numbers out of security concerns.[52] There would be two very different interpretations coming out of the subsequent meeting of their military heads over the size of the Katangese military parade which would have large implications for the dustup that followed.

The immediate security concerns aside, the British Consul in Elisabethville, Dodson, was very worried about the inflammatory political effect of such a celebration, suggesting in a telegraph to London that he might suggest that Katangese officials move the celebrations to June 30th to correspond with the Congolese National Day.[53] Dodson was

[47] Welensky Papers, Box 260, folder 1, Telegram from British Consulate Elisabethville to Foreign Office, June 28, 1962, "Independence Celebrations."
[48] Welensky Papers, Box 260, "Congo," folder 2, Telegram from British Consulate New York to Foreign Office, London, June 30, 1962.
[49] Welensky Papers, Box 260, folder 2, Telegram from P. Davis, CAF Consulate in Elisabethville to L. Hawkins, Office of the Prime Minister, External Affairs, July 22, 1962.
[50] Welensky Papers, Box 260, folder 1, Telegram from British Consulate Elisabethville to Foreign Office, June 12, 1962.
[51] Welensky Papers, Box 260, folder 1, Telegram from British Consulate Elisabethville to Foreign Office, June 27, 1962, "Katanga Independence Celebrations."
[52] Welensky Papers, Box 260, folder 2, Telegram from British Consulate Elisabethville to Foreign Office, June 28, 1962, "Independence Celebrations."
[53] Welensky Papers, Box 260, folder 1, Telegram from British Consulate Elisabethville to Foreign Office, June 12, 1962.

instructed by the Foreign Office to take Britain's request to cancel Katanga's planned independence day celebrations to Evariste Kimba, Katanga's Foreign Minister, on June 26, 1962. After the meeting, Dodson relayed his conversation with Kimba in a telegram to London. He reported that he told Kimba that "such celebrations would make a very bad impression in almost all quarters abroad," especially coming as it would during sensitive negotiations with Leopoldville.[54] Nonetheless, he continued, "I said that I realised some sort of celebration was expected. But could these not be held on June 30th."[55] Having it overlap with the Congo's would be much less provocative, he argued. Kimba stood firm, saying that "the people would not stand for it" and according to the consul's recollection, he said, "pressure was always being put on Katanga," and that the British "paid too much attention to world opinion and especially Afro-Asian opinion."[56] He said Katanga was independent and that it was important to celebrate the anniversary of that independence, and that July 11th "would always remain an important date in their history." Kimba then reportedly thanked the British for their advice and said that the celebrations would go on as planned on July 11, ending, "They would run their country in their way."[57] As summed up separately by the CAF's consul in Elisabethville: "Despite British, American and UN protests, it became clear that the celebrations were to be given considerable priority."[58]

Prime Minister Roy Welensky's CAF government was sympathetic to Tshombe's cause, at least what they interpreted his cause to be, but like the British they were concerned about the potential political fallout were Tshombe to ostentatiously celebrate Katanga's independence. Furthermore, his government was concerned that the federation be not seen to encourage Tshombe in his intransigence. For instance, Katanga sent the federation an invitation to send a soccer team to Katanga to play in exhibition matches as part of their independence celebrations. Both the federation and the British saw this as a potentially embarrassing

---

[54] Welensky Papers, Box 260, folder 1, Telegram from British Consulate Elisabethville to Foreign Office, June 22, 1962, "Katangan Independence Celebrations."

[55] Welensky Papers, Box 260, folder 1, Telegram from British Consulate Elisabethville to Foreign Office, June 22, 1962, "Katangan Independence Celebrations."

[56] Welensky Papers, Box 260, folder 1, Telegram from British Consulate Elisabethville to Foreign Office, June 22, 1962, "Katangan Independence Celebrations."

[57] Welensky Papers, Box 260, folder 1, Telegram from British Consulate Elisabethville to Foreign Office, June 22, 1962, "Katangan Independence Celebrations."

[58] Welensky Papers, Box 260, folder 2, Telegram from P. Davis, CAF Consulate in Elisabethville to L. Hawkins, Office of the Prime Minister, External Affairs, July 22, 1962.

situation which should be avoided.[59] As a result, the federation deliberately delayed the processing of the invitation to Federal soccer teams to
play so as not to be a part of the independence celebrations, while also
not directly offending the Katangese.[60] In this same vein, the Federal and
British Consuls in Elisabethville both agreed not to attend or participate
in any festivities.[61]

A week out, on July 3, 1962, Tshombe, Welensky, and their respective
officials in charge of foreign affairs, including the future head of the
Rhodesia Information Office, Kenneth Towsey, met to discuss various
issues relating to the secession.[62] A time-pressed item on the meeting's
agenda was the upcoming Independence Day celebrations. In the meeting, Welensky directly asked Tshombe if he intended to go forward with
the independence celebrations on July 11th. According to the federation's record, "[Tshombe] said that it was necessary for local political
reasons that the celebrations should take place. To abandon them in
deference to United Nations pressure could lead to a dangerous situation. As it was, he had the situation well under control and he was
confident that he could guarantee that there would be no incidents on the
Katanga side."[63] It is unclear what exactly Tshombe meant by the
"dangerous situation," but it was likely a hint that he was politically
under pressure from more extreme elements in his own government.
This was similar, but slightly different, from Kimba's assertion to
Dodson that the calls for some sort of commemoration was something
that welled from the Katangese people, and was not directed solely from
the government. It appears from the record that Welensky did not push
the anniversary celebration issue further, even though the talking points
memoranda drawn up for Welensky before the meeting suggested he
emphasize that such celebrations would put Katanga in a bad light.[64]
According to the record, Tshombe did not ask Welensky about whether
or not the federation would take part in any official celebrations in

---

[59] Welensky Papers, Box 260, folder 1, Telegram from British Consulate Elisabethville to
Foreign Office, June 21, 1962.

[60] Welensky Papers, Box 260, folder 1, Telegram from Davis, CAF Consulate,
Elisabethville, to External Affairs, Salisbury, July 2, 1962.

[61] Welensky Papers, Box 260, folder 1, Telegram from Davis, CAF Consulate,
Elisabethville, to External Affairs, Salisbury, July 2, 1962.

[62] Welensky Papers, Box 260, folder 2, Record of Meeting at PM Welensky's Residence,
July 3, 1962. The others were Jean-Baptiste Kibwe, Evariste Kimba, H. N. Parry, and
Geoffrey Follows.

[63] Welensky Papers, Box 260, folder 2, Record of Meeting at PM Welensky's Residence,
July 3, 1962.

[64] Welensky Papers, Box 260, folder 2, Notes prepared for Welensky before Tshombe
meeting, "Katanga/Congo," July 3, 1962.

Katanga, which meant that Sir Roy did not have to express his government's opinion, as outlined in the pre-meeting notes, that "it would be imprudent for the Federation to be associated with any celebrations that may be held."[65]

All the while, Elisabethville crackled with tension, and rumors raced through the diplomatic community. Regime posters were placed around the city announcing "Independence 2," and both Elisabethville papers paid homage to the Katangese dead fighting the UN in the hostilities over the previous two years.[66] A secret CAF security assessment from early July 1962 described the increasing tensions in Elisabethville as a result of the upcoming Independence Day celebrations: "Independence celebrations for the 11th of July are, despite diplomatic and UN protests, still scheduled to take place and the atmosphere, duly tempered by heavy drinking and jollification, will probably be rife for incident." The assessment continued: "The celebrations period will also be marked by the effective 'bottling-up' of a considerable number of Katangese troops in Elisabethville, and if the Katangese were unwise enough to bring in large contingents from outside Elisabethville (Baya) a tempting situation favourable to UN military action would be presented."[67]

On July 9th, two days before the anniversary, the very active British Consul in Elisabethville, Dodson, relayed to the British mission in Leopoldville his meeting with UN military advisor Colonel Indar Jit Rikhye who was himself recounting his meeting with Tshombe from earlier that day.[68] Rikhye told Dodson how he and Tshombe had discussed the Independence Day celebrations and "after some initial argument Tshombe had agreed that numbers of troops participating should be decided by [their] Chiefs of Staff, and [Col] Kiembe [Gendarme Chief of Staff, who] had subsequently agreed with United Nations military on a ceiling of 300."[69]

---

[65] Were this hypothetical exchange to happen, the pre-meeting notes suggested the following points be made: "[Tshombe] will appreciate the reasons for our abstention, which we hope would not be interpreted in Katanga quarters as betokening any cooling of Federal friendship for the President's regime." Welensky Papers, Box 260, folder 2, Notes prepared for Welensky before Tshombe meeting, "Katanga/Congo," July 3, 1962.

[66] David Halberstam, "Uneasy Katanga Marking Secession Anniversary," *New York Times*, July 10, 1962.

[67] Welensky Papers, Box 260, folder 2, Federal Intelligence Report to External Affairs, July 17, 1962.

[68] Welensky Papers, Box 260, folder 2, Telegram from British Consulate in Elisabethville to British Embassy Leopoldville, July 7, 1962.

[69] Welensky Papers, Box 260, folder 2, Telegram from British Consulate in Elisabethville to British Embassy Leopoldville, July 7, 1962.

In the almost completely UN-occupied city of Elisabethville, the UN forces stationed in Katanga put Elisabethville as "out-of-bounds" to all its personnel until after the independence celebrations, explaining, "We do not recognise the cause of the celebrations."[70] No heads of state, consular officials, UN officials, or obviously Leopoldville representatives were present in the viewing stand, and only Katangese government ministers and officials from UMHK attended the day's events.[71] While the independence festivities were occurring in Africa, Katanga's second anniversary was also marked by some commemorations among sympathizers back in Belgium. In response, the Congolese central government sent an official protest to the Belgians for not shutting these celebrations down.[72]

To the assembled crowd in Elisabethville, Tshombe gave, as the *New York Times* reporter, David Halberstam, described it, a "somewhat mild and conciliatory speech," even while he was "sharply critical" of acting UN General Secretary U Thant, and defensive as to the influence of UMHK in Katangese politics.[73] Tshombe did, however, make a case for the historical continuity of an independent Katanga before the days of Belgian occupation, and asserted that the Belgians always recognized Katanga's "particularity," even as he did not emphasize the secession per se.[74] Tshombe used the speech to tell the story of the Katangese "nation" as a legitimate, authentic precolonial entity, in an unstated but obvious contrast to the artificial colonial creation of the Belgian Congo.[75] But while extrapolating upon the historical significance of July 11 for the Katangese nation, Tshombe was vague about what the July 11 declaration actually meant. He said, "July 11 did not represent Katanga's wish to secede but her wish to fight against chaos."[76] Taken in its entirety, Tshombe's speech cleverly left enough room for either side to draw from it what they wanted, and it crucially provided rhetorical space for

[70] "Elisabethville: Celebration Boycott," *Rand Daily Mail*, July 11, 1962.

[71] David Halberstam, "Katanga Troops Parade," *New York Times*, July 12, 1962.

[72] SA National Archives, Pretoria, Box 1/112/3/1, vol. 11, 12 Congo, Secession of Katanga, Letter from SA Accredited Diplomatic Representative in Salisbury to Secretary DFA, "Katanga," October 22, 1962.

[73] SA National Archives, Pretoria, Box 1/112/3/1, vol. 11, 12 Congo, Secession of Katanga, Letter from SA Accredited Diplomatic Representative in Salisbury to Secretary DFA, "Katanga," October 22, 1962.

[74] Welensky Papers, Box 260, folder 2, Telegram from British Consulate in Elisabethville to British Embassy Leopoldville, July 11, 1962.

[75] Quoted in Young, *Politics in the Congo*, pp. 500–501. Commenting on Tshombe's historical claims, Young writes, "Needless to say, much of this history requires some strained reinterpretation of what is generally accepted to be truth."

[76] Young, *Politics in the Congo*, pp. 500–501.

Katanga's friends overseas to argue in defense of Tshombe's reasonableness.

Watching from the privacy of a friend's balcony, Dodson described the parade: "It was headed by some one thousand, three hundred Gendarmerie followed by about three hundred and fifty para-commandos and six hundred police. All, including the police, were armed either with automatic rifles (Belgian Fal) or rifles. Detachments of school children, firemen, railwaymen, etc. followed."[77] He continued, "Turn-out and marching of troops and police was impressive and the whole parade went off without a hitch." But problems were again on the horizon. Dodson reported:

The number of armed men was far in excess of the three hundred supposedly agreed with the United Nations ... and my United States colleague, who has just seen [UN official Jean] Back tells me that he is furious, but that neither he nor UN military have yet decided what if anything they should do. My understanding had been that the United Nations were intending to prevent any additional troops entering the town.[78]

The New York Times quoted Jean Back as calling the large parade "a flagrant violation" of their agreement on parade size, adding, "Under these conditions, it will be difficult for the United Nations to accept [the Katangese regime's] word in the future."[79] It is significant that when the "thundering fireworks display" marking the independence celebrations began that evening a large number of Katangese thought that the third round of fighting had begun.[80]

In response to the Katangese parade, the UN sent a "stiff protest" to Katangese authorities, in which the UN claimed the parade far exceeded the agreed-upon size of 300 troops.[81] Whether it was out of what the federal consul speculated was "the feeling of pique and/or of being completely hoodwinked, or whether because of genuine fears for their own security in the light of what was interpreted as a Katangese show of strength," at 2 a.m. that morning the UN constructed a heavily fortified

---

[77] Welensky Papers, Box 260, folder 2, Telegram from British Consulate Elisabethville to British Embassy Leopoldville, July 12, 1962, "Independence Celebrations."

[78] Welensky Papers, Box 260, folder 2, Telegram from British Consulate Elisabethville to British Embassy Leopoldville, July 12, 1962, "Independence Celebrations."

[79] David Halberstam, "UN and Katanga Move up Troops," *New York Times*, July 15, 1962.

[80] David Halberstam, "Tshombe Is Still Keeping Katanga in Secession," *New York Times*, July 13, 1962.

[81] "UN Relax – Katanga Tension Eases," *Rand Daily Mail*, July 14, 1962.

roadblock on a popular Elisabethville street, the Avenue Tombeur.[82] This one route out of the capital city had up until then remained open. Two companies of Indian UN troops, a squadron of armored cars as well as UN field guns supported their position on the checkpoint.[83] In response, a company of heavily armed Katangese soldiers dug in on the other side of the barricade.[84]

For its part, the UN claimed that the controversial roadblock had been in place since December of 1961 and only been recently taken down as a "sweetener" for the recently failed Leopoldville talks on the understanding that the road could not be used to transport troops.[85] Permission was then allegedly granted for 300 Katangese to use the road for the purposes of the Independence Day parade, as there was no other way for them to get to Elisabethville.[86] When the Katangese "abused this permission, bringing in much larger numbers" the UN forces did not stop them out of fear of an armed clash.[87] "The natural result," the UN officials claimed, "was to make the Katangese cock-a-hoop" and the UN military contingent were afraid Katangese troops would begin to move their military freely around the capital in a dangerous and provocative manner.[88] The Katangese regime and the federation government both contested the UN's account that the roadblock existed before July 12th.[89]

All the while, Tshombe was furious about the roadblock, and he adamantly denied that his military commanders ever had any agreement with the UN regarding the size of the parade.[90] Reporting on a meeting with Tshombe and other Katangese Cabinet officials the day after the

[82] Welensky Papers, Box 260, folder 2, Telegram from P. Davis, CAF Consulate in Elisabethville to L. Hawkins, Office of the Prime Minister, External Affairs, July 22, 1962.

[83] Welensky Papers, Box 260, folder 2, Telegram from P. Davis, CAF Consulate in Elisabethville to L. Hawkins, Office of the Prime Minister, External Affairs, July 22, 1962.

[84] David Halberstam, "UN and Katanga Move up Troops," *New York Times*, July 13, 1962.

[85] Welensky Papers, Box 260, folder 2, Telegram from British Embassy in Leopoldville to Foreign Office, July 13, 1962.

[86] Welensky Papers, Box 260, folder 2, Telegram from British Embassy in Leopoldville to Foreign Office, July 13, 1962.

[87] Welensky Papers, Box 260, folder 2, Telegram from British Embassy in Leopoldville to Foreign Office, July 13, 1962.

[88] Welensky Papers, Box 260, folder 2, Telegram from British Embassy in Leopoldville to Foreign Office, July 13, 1962.

[89] Welensky Papers, Box 260, folder 2, Telegram from P. Davis, CAF Consulate in Elisabethville to L. Hawkins, Office of the Prime Minister, External Affairs, July 22, 1962.

[90] "UN Relax – Katanga Tension Eases," *Rand Daily Mail*, July 14, 1962.

celebrations, Dodson said that Tshombe argued that because of the UN's construction of the roadblock the night before "he was confronted with a highly dangerous situation."[91] After the meeting, and despite Tshombe's protestations to the contrary, Dodson concluded: "I have little doubt that Tshombe deceived the United Nations about the parade."[92] A violent incident occurred at the roadblock within the week. Historian Richard Mahoney contends that it was Katanga's Interior Minister, Godefroid Munungo, who was behind the "mob of 10,000 Katangese women and children armed with broomsticks" who stormed the UN checkpoint on July 17th.[93] During the course of the three-hour fight, three Katangese civilians died and fifteen others were injured, as well as the injury of about a dozen Indian UN soldiers.[94] The federation's consul in Elisabethville admitted that it is unclear who in fact shot and killed the Katangese civilians, and the consul accused both the Katangese and the UN of "cooking" the incident to make them appear in a more positive light.[95] This roadblock controversy marked the end of Katanga's second anniversary festivities.

There would be no third celebration since the regime was defeated in the battlefield by UN forces in January 1963. Tshombe fled the country, and after first being denied admission to France because he had no regular passport he was eventually allowed to enter. While in France, Tshombe applied for a new Congolese passport.[96] On June 30, 1963, UN troops marched past the Congolese National Army quarters in Elisabethville to celebrate Congolese independence, which was a symbolically powerful reaffirmation of the end to the secession.[97]

During its short existence as a pseudo-state, Katanga's commemorations were always contested and constantly disrupted. The seemingly petty interest taken in these ceremonies by the Congolese and UN exposed a deep concern that opponents had that Katanga was strengthening its symbolic claim to independence. The lack of official

---

[91] Welensky Papers, Box 260, folder 2, Telegram from British Consulate Elisabethville to Foreign Office, July 12, 1962.

[92] Welensky Papers, Box 260, folder 2, Telegram from British Consul in Elisabethville to British Embassy Leopoldville, July 12, 1962.

[93] Mahoney, *Ordeal in Africa*, p. 140.

[94] Welensky Papers, Box 260, folder 2, Telegram from P. Davis, CAF Consulate in Elisabethville to L. Hawkins, Office of the Prime Minister, External Affairs, July 22, 1962.

[95] Welensky Papers, Box 260, folder 2, Telegram from P. Davis, CAF Consulate in Elisabethville to L. Hawkins, Office of the Prime Minister, External Affairs, July 22, 1962.

[96] "Tshombe's Sickbed Is Guarded," *Rand Daily Mail*, July 1, 1963.

[97] "Tshombe's Sickbed Is Guarded," *Rand Daily Mail*, July 1, 1963.

representatives from sovereign states in attendance, even among Katanga's international friends, was a powerful message of its nonacceptance. In addition, the seizures of the uniforms in September 1961, the constraints imposed upon the size of the parade in July 1962, and the punitive roadblock imposed after the violation of the parade agreement, were all efforts to disrupt and undermine the establishment of Katangese national forms.

Rhodesia

Rhodesia's declaration of sovereign status did not occur in the same atmosphere of chaos and confusion as did Katanga's, and yet also it could not have the elaborate public displays of Transkei's or Bophuthatswana's first Independence Days. Even as understood by its strongest advocates, the Unilateral Declaration of Independence (UDI) was still an illegal act initially even if its supporters thought the resulting new state was legal. A month before he declared UDI, Ian Smith admitted that he thought such a break was morally justified, despite it being illegal "from a strictly constitutional point of view."[98] As such, even though nearly everyone expected a declaration at some point, it could not be advertised nor planned openly up to the very moment of the declaration.

When exactly UDI was going to be declared became a bit of a bettor's game. A rumor flew around British government circles in July 1965 that Ian Smith and his Rhodesian Front government were going to declare UDI on Rhodes Day on July 13th, piggybacking on the obvious symbolism of that day.[99] That day came and went. The Rhodesian High Commissioner in London, Andrew Skeen, argued that Rhodesia should break away before the British general election as this would ensure that Prime Minister, Harold Wilson, still only had a small majority in parliament, and could not afford to ignore pro-Rhodesia public opinion in Britain.[100] Historian Luise White notes that the Rhodesians were also weighing other considerations, having to do with the timing of the March tobacco harvest, in light of Britain's likely response of boycotting Rhodesia's biggest export, and the November expiration of the

---

[98] Ian Smith to Alexander Skeen (telegram), October 16, 1965. Quoted in J. R. T. Wood, *So Far and No Further: Rhodesia's Bid for Independence during the Retreat from Empire* (Trafford Publishing, Victoria, 2005) p. 395.

[99] Wood, *So Far and No Further*, p. 330.

[100] A. Skeen, *Prelude to Independence: Skeen's 115 Days* (Nasionale Boekhandel, Cape Town, 1966), pp. 59–61.

preventative detention law.[101] While J. R. T. Wood describes how the timing of UDI was possibly also influenced by the belief in Rhodesian circles that Britain was so preoccupied with the Kashmir crisis between India and Pakistan, that word of a UDI might actually relieve Britain of another unpleasant problem.[102] So the idea that a UDI was imminent was on everyone's minds, and there were arguments for when exactly it would come, but no one except a very small circle around Ian Smith knew exactly when.

Rhodesia's Declaration was eventually made at 11 a.m. on November 11, 1965, with the Rhodesian Front Cabinet members portentously gathering around a table in Government House to sign the scrolled document. The document itself was written in a frilly calligraphy with elaborate initials and decorations around the margins, as though it was an illuminated manuscript a participant would win at a local Renaissance Faire. The rebels signed the declaration under a portrait of the Queen, implying that she silently presided over the transfer of power. A famous photo was taken of the event, and later in the day Smith gave a speech over Rhodesian radio announcing the break with Britain. This entire tableau communicated an orderly and legal process belying that this was an illegal act of rebellion.

Which parts of their British heritage the regime clung to and which parts they discarded were vague and conditional. There was a great deal of loyalty to the Queen among whites in the early years after UDI, which ran alongside a deep hostility toward British politicians.[103] Secessionist movements always have to rationalize what aspects of the mother country's legacy they are seceding from and which they sought to still adhere to.[104] In this context the Rhodesian ambivalence toward their Britishness had a parallel almost exactly a century before and an ocean away with white southerners' ambivalence toward their Americanness during the confederacy's attempted secession from the United States. Paul Quigley notes that "Civil War-era white southerners' lingering affection for the Fourth of July [was a] part of their attempt to resolve tensions between southernness and Americanness."[105] Some white southerners saw their

---

[101] White, *Unpopular Sovereignty*, pp. 106–107.

[102] Wood, *So Far and No Further*, p. 363.

[103] For an interesting look at the loyalty issue around the time of UDI, see: C. Watts, "Killing Kith and Kin: The Viability of British Military Intervention in Rhodesia, 1964–5," *Twentieth Century British History*, vol. 16, no. 4 (January 2005).

[104] Many scholars have pointed out how even the American Declaration did not emerge out of whole cloth in 1776 but was itself written in a way to make it fit within a longer history of English liberties. See for example: D. Armitage, *The Declaration of Independence: A Global History* (Harvard University Press, Cambridge, 2007).

[105] Quigley, "Independence Day Dilemmas in the American South," pp. 236–237.

secession as a continuation of the process that began with the thirteen colonies breaking from Britain in 1776. By the mid-nineteenth century, the confederacy had begun to regularly make the case that their claims against what they portrayed as northern tyranny was directly akin to the colonies' claims against British tyranny.[106] This was consistent with the Rhodesian idea that Rhodesians were truer to core British ideals than were the modern British. Even though the UDI document was written in language shamelessly lifted from Jefferson's Declaration of a new republic, unlike the American Revolution, the goal of the Rhodesian's break from Britain was simply entry into the Commonwealth, as sovereign equals under the Queen.[107]

While there were a variety of reasons for the general timing of UDI, that it was on November 11, the same day as Remembrance Day, was not a coincidence. The armistice that officially ended World War I famously went into effect on the 11th hour of the 11th day of the 11th month, and UDI was declared not just on that same day, but at that same hour. Rhodesians always portrayed UDI as a patriotic rebellion; something not intended to be oxymoronic. For Rhodesians, Remembrance Day served as a stark reminder that Rhodesia had fought with Britain in two bloody world wars, but they were now denied their independence and shunned out of what the settlers considered to be political expediency.[108] The co-option of war remembrance was therefore a way to merge the concepts of rebellion and loyalty, reconciled by Rhodesian's insistence that they were loyal to an older, better Britain – the Imperial Britain of World War II and Winston Churchill.[109] Stacking UDI on top of Remembrance Day offered Rhodesians an annual propaganda truncheon as one symbolically rich site of contest during the rebellion was in the placing of wreaths on the Cenotaph in London and the planting of crosses in London's Field of Remembrance in St. Margaret's, Westminster.[110] It would become a recurring theme during the rebellion that on the anniversaries of UDI

---

[106] Quigley, "Independence Day Dilemmas in the American South," p. 253.

[107] Armitage, *Declaration of Independence*, p. 135. This mimicry was purposeful, as Ian Smith himself acknowledged. Smith, *Bitter Harvest*, p. 103.

[108] J. R. T. Wood, for one, claims that November 11 was chosen because of its symbolic attachment to the sacrifices made by Rhodesians during the two world wars. Wood, *A Matter of Weeks Rather than Months*, p. 463. See also: Camilla Schofield, *Enoch Powell and the Making of Postcolonial Britain* (Cambridge University Press, Cambridge, 2013).

[109] See: Brownell, "Out of Time."

[110] See for example: "War Dead Are Not Forgotten," *Rhodesia Herald*, November 8, 1969; British PRO, Letter from Neale to RAR Baltrop, November 15, 1966. Do 207/112; Letter from Watson to Neale, November 16, 1966; "Remembrance Day Ceremony (Rhodesia)," *Hansard*, HC Debate November 8, 1966. Mr. Biggs-Davison; Mr. Bowden.

Figure 3.2 Head of Rhodesia House, Sydney Brice, placing a
Rhodesian wreath on the Cenotaph in London during Remembrance
Day, November 1967.

and Remembrance Day there would be periodic clashes between anti-
Rhodesia protestors and supporters of the regime outside Rhodesia
House on the Strand.[111] This all contributed to the effective political
theater the Rhodesians created by overlapping these dates.[112]

The Bell of the Ball

Commemorating UDI in Rhodesia was always a white affair. But even
among whites it was only a small, elite group invited to the official
celebrations. Public Independence Day celebrations in the streets were
rare over the fifteen-year rebellion. Only the fifth-year anniversary in

---

[111] See: Brownell, "'A Sordid Tussle on the Strand'"; "Remembrance Sunday Is Mixed in
    London," *Rhodesia Herald*, November 10, 1975.
[112] "Honouring Rhodesians," *Rhodesia Herald*, November 10, 1977.

1970 featured a broader public celebration with a parade, but this was an anomaly that never happened before or after. In an unintentionally defensive editorial from 1969, the *Rhodesia Herald* describes how the Independence Day celebrations had, by their fourth year, established certain patterns of observance that evoked an image of a loveless marriage:

> Spontaneous celebration of any event is difficult to maintain year in year out. The anniversaries of UDI are marked by Independence Balls, statements by the Prime Minister and official receptions but not by street parades, flag waving or other such-like celebrations. Only ostentatious people carry their enthusiasm that far. Being largely of phlegmatic British stock, most Rhodesian Europeans were content to observe yesterday's Independence Day as just another holiday – very welcome as such but not calling especially for any obeisance or rejoicing. UDI is now firmly into its place in the Rhodesia calendar, to make of it what you will. The dedicated unilateralists seek out the formal celebrations, the others loaf or recreate – and presumably everybody is happy.[113]

On the first anniversary of UDI in 1966, there was, in a sense, a blank slate for the regime to perform this commemoration however it wanted. Rhodesia's UDI would come to be publicly celebrated primarily through the Independence Balls held on the night of November 10th. This started as a private charity ball the night before the public holiday hosted by the Lions Club of Salisbury in Harry Margolis Hall.[114] These were very much elite, white affairs, and narrower still, affairs for the governing Rhodesian Front party members, state functionaries, and their overseas visitors. It was only ever rendered public through the Rhodesian Broadcasting Corporation's (RBC) live broadcast over the radio that offered a glimpse inside the hall, but not actual access.

Within the hall that first night there was dinner and dancing building up to the climax at midnight. As midnight approached, Smith told the cheering crowd: "This is the beginning of a wonderful era." He then unveiled a 250-pound copper-bronze Bell that was modeled on the American Liberty Bell, with a native Mukwa wood frame.[115] The Independence Bell was inscribed: "I toll for justice, civilization, and Christianity," mirroring Smith's speech the year before in his announcement of UDI.[116] After the unveiling, Smith then rang the Bell twelve

---

[113] "Holiday Moods," *Rhodesia Herald*, editorial, November 12, 1969.

[114] The Margolis Hall event in 1972 was the first to be referred to as the "National Independence Ball." "UDI Celebrations This Weekend," *Rhodesia Herald*, November 7, 1972.

[115] "Smith Unveils 'Independence Bell' Gift," *Rhodesia Herald*, November 11, 1966; "PM Is a Dab Hand at Tolling that Bell," *Rhodesia Herald*, "Cabbages and Kings" section, November 10, 1971.

[116] "Rhodesian Calls Stand Unshaken," *New York Times*, November 12, 1966. Ian Smith Announcement of UDI, November 11, 1965.

times at midnight. He told the all-white partygoers: "Every time it rings it means a nail in the coffin of the people who want to interfere in the internal affairs of Rhodesia. Those days are gone forever."[117]

The symbolically freighted Bell became a cherished invented tradition. It sat in the Prime Minister's office for "363 or 364" days of the year, and only taken down to the site of the Independence Ball to be rung at the dance.[118] A column in the *Rhodesia Herald* from 1971 guessed that only three or four thousand Rhodesians, all those who had ever been to one of the Salisbury Balls, have ever seen the Bell, as very few have been inside Smith's office.[119] Many would hear it ring on the radio broadcast or see it in photographs in the press, but that was it: A tangible reflection of how small the circle of elites was that took part in official commemorations.

In inventing their national Independence Day traditions, Rhodesia's founding generation self-consciously wondered how future generations would view these events, and speculated how they would commemorate their actions. They were not alone in daydreaming of their young nation's future. On July 3, 1776, John Adams wrote to his wife Abigail about how he hoped American independence days might be celebrated in the future:

I am apt to believe that it will be celebrated, by succeeding Generations, as the great anniversary Festival. It ought to be commemorated, as the Day of Deliverance by solemn Acts of Devotion to God Almighty. It ought to be solemnized with Pomp and Parade, with Shews, Games, Sports, Guns, Bells, Bonfires and Illuminations from one End of this Continent to the other from this Time forward forever more.[120]

Directly mirroring Adams' thinking almost exactly 200 years later and a continent away, in the *Herald*'s light-hearted "Cabbages and Kings" column, the author dreamt of how Rhodesia's new public holiday might be commemorated in the future:

Someday [the Bell] has to be proudly positioned in some public place. No decision has been reached as to where, and perhaps it's a bit premature to go into deep argument on the matter. But being ever the optimist, I have decided that there is no better place than in some suitably imposing and floodlit tower or monument in Cecil Square, a spot already historically hallowed.[121]

---

[117] "'Wonderful Era' Predicted," *New York Times*, November 11, 1966.
[118] "PM Is a Dab Hand at Tolling that Bell," *Rhodesia Herald*, "Cabbages and Kings" section, November 10, 1971.
[119] "PM Is a Dab Hand at Tolling that Bell," *Rhodesia Herald*, "Cabbages and Kings" section, November 10, 1971.
[120] John Adams letter to Abigail Adams, July 3, 1776.
[121] "PM Is a Dab Hand at Tolling that Bell," *Rhodesia Herald*, "Cabbages and Kings" section, November 10, 1971.

Continuing on:

And each year at midnight on November 10 the populace will gather round to see and hear that 250lb copper bronze bell rung 12 times. "But why 12 times," young lads will ask, and old men will reply: "Because it always was 12 times right from 1966." The kids will look up at it and wonder about the bad old days, and the old men will go on to tell how Dorothy Goode saw a picture of the American Liberty Bell in an encyclopedia after UDI and thought Rhodesia should have one of its own. And how a new spare bell was found in Pretoria ... And how the Works Department carpenter made a mukwa frame for it to stand on pro tem, and how if you get close to it, you can read "I toll for Justice, Civilization, and Christianity – Independence, 11th November 1965."[122]

By imagining a future time when Rhodesia's national traditions would have acquired the legitimizing patina of age, as well as more popular participation, this fascinating column expressed without intending to a profound insecurity over the recentness of Rhodesia's invented traditions and how narrow a slice of the population who participated in them.

Striking the Bell at midnight was a retroactive placement of Rhodesia's UDI within the legal "managed" decolonizations to the north, the so-called freedoms at midnight, a legitimation attempted through a historical invention of the significance of midnight for the Rhodesians.[123] Quite obviously, Rhodesia did not receive its sovereignty at midnight. Even accepting their sovereign claims, they purportedly took it themselves when the cabinet signed the UDI document at 11 a.m. local Central Africa Time, or possibly when Ian Smith announced it on a twenty-minute radio broadcast on the RBC at 1:15 p.m.[124] Nothing in the declaration referenced the legal effect of midnight at all, but this was no barrier to the regime attaching itself to the symbolic significance of midnight as though Rhodesians did in fact receive legal independence at midnight like India, Ghana, and all other British ex-colonies that followed.

The Bell also linked Rhodesia to another aesthetico-ideological genre. In many ways Rhodesia's independence celebrations were pitched to appeal to American audiences, both those tourists inside the hall and those who would hear about it second-hand. Smith and his overseas

---

[122] "PM Is a Dab Hand at Tolling that Bell," *Rhodesia Herald*, "Cabbages and Kings" section, November 10, 1971. *The New York Times* reported that the Bell was "a former British warship's bell now the symbol of Rhodesia's rebellion against British rule." "Rhodesians celebrate 10 years of autonomy," *New York Times*, November 12, 1975.

[123] For more on the symbolism of midnight in these celebrations, see: R. Holland, S. Williams, and T. Barringer (eds.), *The Iconography of Independence: "Freedoms at Midnight,"* (Routledge, London, 2010).

[124] "Ten Years of UDI," *Rhodesia Herald*, November 11, 1975.

supporters were blatant in their attempts to marry 1776 and 1965 in American minds.[125] Conservative American groups were drawn to the idea of Rhodesia re-creating American history and many toured Rhodesia to see it happen live.[126] For American conservative groups, tours to Rhodesia were inextricably wrapped up in the politics of UDI, and having their tours overlap with the November 10/11th celebrations, which they often did, was not simply a happy coincidence.[127] For some American conservatives, Rhodesia's UDI was seen to be also *their* day, and celebrating that day in the United States, and especially in Rhodesia, was an act of ideological communion.[128]

After the countdown to midnight and the Bell striking, Smith and his wife and all assembled guests would then link arms as in the Hogmanay circle while everyone sang "Auld Lang Syne."[129] This song was another nod to the "freedoms at midnight" ceremonies.[130] But certain partygoers might have also had a disorienting deja vu as between UDI commemorations in November and Hogmanay in December since Margolis Hall was also the venue for the black tie Hogmanay Ball, where there was also a buffet dinner and dancing and, of course, as was Hogmanay tradition, "Auld Lange Syne" would be sung with linked arms after midnight.[131] This first ceremony as improvised and clubby as it was that first time

---

[125] This equation of 1776 and 1965 did not go uncontested. Prime Minister, Wilson, in particular challenged the linkage. See: James J. Kilpatrick, "Disservice to Jefferson's Postulate", op-ed, *Evening Star*, November 16, 1965; Arthur Krock, editorial, "In the Nation: Rhodesia and 1776," *New York Times*, November 16, 1965. The confederacy likewise tried to wed 1776 and 1861. This included their constitution and official symbols and iconography. As Quigley points out:

Even the official postsecession address of South Carolina to the other southern states drew the parallel explicitly. "The Southern States," it announced, "now stand exactly in the same position towards the Northern States that the Colonies did towards Great Britain .... [T]he Government of the United States has become a consolidated Government; and the people of the Southern States are compelled to meet the very despotism their fathers threw off in the Revolution of 1776." Quigley, "Independence Day Dilemmas in the American South," p. 253.

[126] See: Brownell, "Out of Time."

[127] For example, a 1970 advertisement for a "Special Independence Day Tour" organized by the far-right Liberty Lobby describes how their tour will arrive in Rhodesia "just in time for their biggest day – INDEPENDENCE DAY. You ride the crest of Rhodesian joy 'til the wee hours'." Group Research Inc. Box 146, FRI file, Friends of Rhodesia Newsletter, vol. 3, no. 2 (Fall 1970).

[128] See: Brownell, "Out of Time."

[129] "Should Auld Acquaintance Be Forgot?" *Rhodesia Herald*, November 12, 1969.

[130] See for example: Wm. Rogers Louis, *The Ends of British Imperialism: The Scramble for Empire, Suez, and Decolonization* (I. B. Tauris, London, 2007) p. 443.

[131] See for example the 1972 advertisement for the Hogmanay Ball at Margolis Hall. "8 pm–2 am. Dancing to the Tommy Campbell Band ... Book Early." *Rhodesia Herald*, November 13, 1972.

around proved to be the template for all future ceremonies, and efforts to replicate earlier Balls became a part of Rhodesia's nation-making project through the 1970s.

On the third-year anniversary of UDI in 1968 the regime introduced a new flag. The old colonial flag with the canton of the Union Jack was replaced with an entirely new flag displaying their new national colors of green and white.[132] A formal Retreat ceremony was then held with the lowering of the Union Jack flag from Cecil Square and the raising of the new flag, directly mimicking the ceremony from the managed decolonizations to their north, but with an oddly staggered timing, and significantly no representative from the mother country.[133] George Thompson, the British minister then in charge of negotiations to bring an end to the rebellion, was actually in Rhodesia at the time trying to salvage some accord after the failed HMS Fearless negotiations. In order to avoid any embarrassment of a high-ranking British official being present during the UDI anniversary celebrations, Thompson arranged for a few days visit to Central and East Africa, purposely missing the flag-swapping ceremony.[134] How symbolically different was this than the other freedoms at midnight celebrations with this representative of the mother country conspicuously retreating before the Beating the Retreat ceremony even began.

Rhodesia's UDI was an event celebrated abroad as well. In Pretoria, the Rhodesian diplomatic representatives hosted Independence Day parties at their official residence at Malvern House.[135] Kenneth Towsey, Rhodesia's pseudo-ambassador to the United States, hosted several UDI parties at his residence in Washington.[136] Rhodesia House in London likewise held UDI parties before the mission was shut down in 1969.[137] In Zambia, meanwhile, white residents were informed that they would be subject to arrest if they attempted to celebrate UDI, and this enforcement included checking on expatriate parties and clubs to ensure no celebrations occurred.[138] Zambia would eventually close all private clubs in the Copperbelt province, and bars would close early that day to

---

[132] For more on the creation of the new flag, see David Kenrick's book. *Decolonisation, Identity and Nation in Rhodesia*, p. 5. See also: B. Berry, "Flag of Defiance: The International Use of the Rhodesian Flag Following UDI," *South African Historical Journal*, vol. 71, no. 3 (2019).

[133] "Flag of Independence Is Raised," *Rhodesia Commentary*, vol. 2, no. 24, November 25, 1968.

[134] "Rift on Rhodesia Still Very Deep," *New York Times*, November 10, 1968.

[135] See for example: "Quiet Tone in Celebrations," *Rhodesia Herald*, November 12, 1969.

[136] Brownell, "Diplomatic Lepers."   [137] Brownell, "'A Sordid Tussle on the Strand'."

[138] "Zambia Bans Celebration of UDI," *Rhodesia Herald*, November 10, 1969.

preclude any sympathetic celebrations of UDI.[139] According to the *Herald*, Zambian authorities announced that some Zambian workers at these expatriate clubs reported that members shouted: "Long live UDI! Long Live Ian Smith!"[140]

The 1970 Independence Day celebrations marking the fifth year since UDI, and the first since their declaration of republic status, were something altogether different from earlier celebrations. At the main Independence Ball event at Margolis Hall that year, the theme was "New Nation – 1890–1970." Five hundred people attended the event, and the walls were decorated with blown-up images of Rhodesia's new dollar notes and postage stamps.[141] A giant map of the Rhodesian republic "dominated the scene," and there were large paintings of Cecil Rhodes, Clifford Dupont, the man who that year purportedly replaced the Queen as Head of State, and Prime Minister Ian Smith hanging in the hall as though they were the Soviet Trinity.[142]

The 1970 Independence Day parade would be the biggest ever held in Rhodesia.[143] Gone was the smug humility touted by the *Herald* editorial board the year before, and here were the "street parades" and "flag waving" enthusiasm formerly expressed only by "ostentatious people."[144] In preparation for the parade, the streets of central Salisbury were closed from 6 a.m. on the morning of the parade. All traffic would be stopped as the mile-long progression worked its way up Jameson Avenue.[145] The overflights before the parade included a squadron of helicopters, followed by fighter jets and bombers.[146] On the saluting dais was the new Rhodesia Head of State, Clifford Dupont, who was seated alongside Ian Smith and other cabinet officials and heads of the police and branches of the armed services.[147] Significantly, no foreign dignitaries were present for the festivities; even South Africa and

---

[139] "Zambia Acts to Stop UDI Revelry," *Rhodesia Herald*, November 11, 1969.

[140] "Zambia 'UDI Parties,'" *Rhodesia Herald*, November 13, 1973.

[141] For the significance of the new currency and postage stamps, see: J. Brownell, "The Visual Rhetoric of Settler Stamps: Rhodesia's Rebellion and the Projection of Sovereignty (1965–80)," in Yu-Ting Huang and Rebecca Weaver-Hightower (eds.), *Archiving Settler Colonialism: Culture, Space and Race (Empires and the Making of the Modern World, 1650–2000)* (Routledge, New York, 2018).

[142] Picture caption of Ian and Janet Smith, *Rhodesia Herald*, November 11, 1970.

[143] "Seven Flights of Planes for Big 'UDI Parade'" *Rhodesia Herald*, November 10, 1970.

[144] "Holiday Moods," *Rhodesia Herald*, editorial, November 12, 1969.

[145] "Closing of Streets on November 11," *Rhodesia Herald*, November 7, 1970.

[146] Leading the parade were 17 British South African Police (BSAP) motorcyclists in a V formation, then 16 mounted horsemen, the BSAP band, 31 units of troops, and a mechanized column including more than 200 vehicles. "Seven Flights of Planes for Big 'UDI Parade'" *Rhodesia Herald*, November 10, 1970.

[147] "Sunday Rehearsal for the Big Parade," *Rhodesia Herald*, November 2, 1970.

Portugal, which was the last colonial holdout in Africa, were notable in their absence. In this respect, the 1970 ceremony in Rhodesia was similar to Katanga's, Transkei's, and Bophuthatswana's independence ceremonials – tightly orchestrated, martial, and with an embarrassing absence of foreign delegations.

Ultimately it was estimated that more than 22,000 lined Jameson Avenue in Salisbury to watch the military parade in 1970, the majority of whom were white, which would actually make it a rather high percentage of Rhodesia's total white population. But the *Herald* noted that many Africans watched as well, including "21 chiefs, resplendent in their white topees, their mauve and scarlet robes and brass badges of office."[148] Several hundred other Africans also watched the parade, mainly from the Jameson Avenue parking structure. Interestingly, when those Africans who witnessed it from the structure were asked about the parade, they indicated that their attendance did not imply that they supported UDI, but only that they wanted to see the spectacle.[149] As reported by the *Herald*, Africans may have craned their necks and strained to catch the sights but they did not clap, because as one African interviewed said, "This is not our affair."[150] Continuing on, the unnamed African said, "If this day was to commemorate African independence, all the Africans from the townships would have assembled here. Most of the Africans are here simply to see what is going on."

The 1973 celebrations occurred under the shadow of a dramatic escalation of the guerrilla war. The theme was "early Rhodesian settlers" and the program featured Rhodesian pioneers on the cover.[151] In keeping with this theme, inside Harry Margolis Hall was a reconstructed settler-era camp with a replica wagon, and with sadza on the menu.[152] Despite the transient character of white Rhodesia, with most having only recently arrived into the territory, this display was part of a wider project connecting Rhodesia's rebellion more explicitly to an older Southern African settler tradition, and the African food alongside the wagon reinforced this attempted indigenization of the white settler in Africa.[153] As always, Smith rang the Bell twelve times, but the *Herald*

[148] "Parade Seen by 22,000," *Rhodesia Herald*, November 12, 1970.
[149] "Africans Came to See Pageantry," *Rhodesia Herald*, November 13, 1970.
[150] "Africans Came to See Pageantry," *Rhodesia Herald*, November 13, 1970.
[151] "Sadza to Be Independence Ball Treat," *Rhodesia Herald*, November 7, 1973.
[152] Phone interview with an American UDI commemoration participant, P. B. Gemma, notes with author, May 9, 2016.
[153] Kenrick identifies the appropriation of the Great Zimbabwe Bird on the Rhodesian crest as another manifestation of the attempt to indigenize white settlers. *Decolonization, Identity, and Nation in Rhodesia*, p. 98. For a great analysis of white settlers' senses of belonging in Rhodesia, see: D. McDermott Hughes, *Whiteness in Zimbabwe: Race,*

political reporter mistakenly thought he was supposed to ring it only eight times, one for each year of independence as opposed to twelve for midnight, and the reporter accused Smith of dropping a "clanger."[154] This was a common mistake. The next year's Ball, 1974, was bigger by some scale than earlier Balls. With 700 guests, Margolis Hall could no longer house the celebration and so it was moved to the auction floor of Tobacco Sales Limited in Salisbury, where it would remain for three years.[155]

At the tenth-year anniversary, new parts of Rhodesia's repertoire of state symbols were still being added. David Kenrick's study of the invention of their national symbols has shown how nationalism in Rhodesia was "neither static nor unchanging; it was amorphous and reactive, responding to internal and external developments."[156] As such new symbols were always being invented and older ones evolving. At the Independence Day reception in Gwelo, the minister of justice presented Mary Bloom with a check for R$500 for writing the winning entry for lyrics to Rhodesia's new national anthem, "Rise, O Voices of Rhodesia."[157] The ten-year anniversary was also a wartime commemoration. A *Herald* editorial captured this bleak mood explaining that enthusiasm for Independence Day was largely among those "eight out of ten white people who support the Rhodesian Front through thick and thin," but the other 20 percent of whites and the vast majority of the African population "cannot be expected to share the euphoria of today's anniversary."[158] In their reporting, the *New York Times*, like the *Rhodesia Herald*, were once again confused as to the number and significance of the Bell clangs and the origins of the Bell itself. They mistakenly reported that following the young nine-year-long tradition Smith rang the Bell ten times, one for each year of independence.[159]

In 1977 on Independence Day the Ball had been returned to its original home, the smaller venue, Harry Margolis Hall where it had been held from 1966 to 1973. Like the others, this was broadcast on the general service of the RBC during a regularly scheduled music program

---

Landscape and the Problem of Belonging (Palgrave Macmillan, New York, 2010). See also Brownell, "Out of Time."

[154] "They're Having a Ball," *Rhodesia Herald*, November 12, 1973.

[155] "PM Predicts 'Even Better' 10th Year of Independence," *Rhodesia Herald*, November 11, 1974.

[156] Kenrick, *Decolonization, Identity and Nation in Rhodesia*, p. 241.

[157] "Cheque Is Presented to Anthem Author," *Rhodesia Herald*, November 12, 1975.

[158] "After Ten Years," *Rhodesia Herald*, November 11, 1975.

[159] "Rhodesians Celebrate Ten Years of Autonomy," *New York Times*, November 12, 1975.

titled, "Making for Midnight."[160] In his broadcast, RBC host Tony Gaynor explained the significance of the Independence Bell, the twelve tolls of which, he said, "signify the departure of the old year and the dawning of a new one for Rhodesia."[161] The Master of Ceremonies announced before introducing Smith that "we are approaching *the magical hour of midnight*. Most of you here know the custom [of ringing the Bell] ..." As Gaynor explained, during the twelve occasions commemorating UDI, "This Bell has become as permanent a feature as Christmas trees are of Christmas." He added, "And I'm sure we all hope and pray that we shall continue to do so for years to come."[162]

In his speech, Ian Smith addressed the question over how many times the Bell will toll. "Now, just to get the record straight," Smith said,

In case you read a letter wondering how many times I was going to ring the Bell, and associating this with the years of independence. Those of you who come to these occasions know it that it has nothing to do with the years of independence. On the first such event, the Bell was wrung twelve times as it will be tonight, because this is the ringing in of midnight. I think it is the best plan, because if we were to ring once for every year of independence, you can imagine what the position would be when one of my successors in due time has to ring it one hundred ... one hundred times.

The crowd laughed. After the ringing of the Bell, the Master of Ceremonies raised his glass and announced: "Ladies and Gentlemen: Rhodesia!" To his radio audience Gaynor then added in a mellifluous voice: "May I suggest that wherever you may be that you too may raise your glass and toast 'Rhodesia.'"[163]

Because of the continuous state of emergency in Rhodesia and the state's wide security powers, including preventative detention, African resistance to the commemoration was more in the form of nonparticipation than counter-protests. For example, on the 13th anniversary in 1978, the national holiday led to the Salisbury city center being empty, but life went on as normal in the African townships of Harare and Highfield.[164] The ringing of the Bell in 1978 would be

---

[160] RBC "Making for Midnight," November 11, 1977. www.rhodesia.me.uk.

[161] Gaynor joined the RBC in 1974 and continued on for several years after Zimbabwean independence, but was immediately fired in 2000 after he opened the Zimbabwean Broadcasting Corporation's lunchtime news bulletin with the announcement: "This is the Rhodesia Broadcasting Corporation. The time is one o'clock." "Radio Man Axed for 'Rhodesia' Blunder," *Independent Online*, May 30, 2000, accessed August 2015, www.iol.co.za/news/africa/radio-man-axed-for-rhodesia-blunder-1.39093#.VcIa7hNVikp.

[162] Author's emphasis. RBC "Making for Midnight," November 11, 1977. www.rhodesia.me.uk.

[163] RBC "Making for Midnight," November 11, 1977. www.rhodesia.me.uk.

[164] Tom Wicker, "African Journey," *New York Times*, November 19, 1978.

the last.[165] Smith agreed to an "internal settlement" in 1978, a name change to Zimbabwe-Rhodesia, and elections that brought Bishop Muzorewa to power in June 1979. African politicians in the five-month-old new government thought it unfitting to celebrate the white supremacy enshrined in UDI and so the day was struck from the list of public holidays, but many whites reportedly still commemorated the day.[166] The UDI flag was lowered for the last time in Rhodesia on September 1, 1979, an event that reportedly went unnoticed.[167] Zimbabwe-Rhodesia produced another new flag and new symbols, but like the Smith regime that preceded it, it could never achieve recognition during its short lifespan. Zambian President Kenneth Kaunda captured what most observers thought of the "internal settlement": "What we have in Salisbury today is white power clad in black habiliments."[168]

Transkei

Unlike both Katanga's and Rhodesia's purported independence moments, Transkei's independence ceremonies were a choreographed series of public events that closely traced the forms of the "freedoms at midnight" celebrations. But while it mimicked their forms it lacked their legal and emotional substance. Transkei's featured big parades, military reviews, official delegations from the mother state, and at the climax, the lowering of the mother country's flag with the Beating the Retreat ceremony, the raising of the new state's flag at midnight, and a speech by the new leader. Transkei and South Africa took pains placing Transkeian independence within this recognizable aesthetico-ideological genre, and everything about the planning of the day went toward promoting the idea that this was an actual transfer of power and a legal transfer of sovereignty.

Unlike Katanga and Rhodesia, Transkei's mother state approved of the separation, not tacitly or grudgingly, but enthusiastically, and it was in part the degree of the republic's enthusiasm that rendered Transkei's independence so artificial for most observers. South Africa orchestrated it and pushed it forward, and the republic was the only state to ever recognize it. Apartheid planners hoped the creation of Bantustans could be sold to the world as a form of decolonization, and in furtherance of

[165] "Rhodesia, for the First Time, Fails to Mark Independence," *New York Times*, November 12, 1979.
[166] "Rhodesia, for the First Time, Fails to Mark Independence," *New York Times*, November 12, 1979.
[167] Berry, "Flag of Defiance," p. 29.
[168] Quoted in Jay Ross, "Britain Assails Nigerian Seizure of BP Interests," *Washington Post*, August 2, 1979.

this goal it was felt that they needed to *look* like decolonization. But noticeably absent from the festivities was the real joy of uhuru that was so much a part of the winning of independence elsewhere on the continent, what Alistair Cooke called the "ecstasy of Uhuru."[169] Where was the fun? While Transkei's independence moment was choreographed to mimic the decolonization ceremonies, its joyless and formulaic ceremony inadvertently served as the template for the other Bantustans which followed them, most immediately Bophuthatswana's.

The date for Transkei's Independence was a matter of negotiation between South Africa and the nascent Transkeian regime. Determining that foreign dignitaries were notoriously busy, it was believed that the date of Independence should be established at least twelve months in advance to give dignitaries time to put it on their schedules. Robert A. Du Plooy of the South African Department of Foreign Affairs, who would later serve as South Africa's Ambassador to Transkei, thought that the Transkeian Legislative Assembly term which was scheduled to meet on October 1, 1975 would be "an ideal opportunity" to announce the future date of independence a year hence.[170] Kaiser Matanzima, who was then the Transkeian Chief Minister, suggested that independence should take place during the month of October of the next year, perhaps on the 25th.[171] Noting that October 25th was also United Nations Day, Du Plooy wrote, perhaps ironically or mischievously, that he thought this to be "a good choice." But in 1976 the 25th was going to be a Monday, which meant organizing the arrangements for the celebration would be difficult with a weekend in front of it, he argued. It was therefore suggested that either Friday, October 22nd or Tuesday the 26th be chosen as the date, even though Austria and Iran also have the 26th as their national day – "[But] [t]here is no objection to this as many countries share national days."[172] It was finally decided that October 26th would be a public holiday with shops closed that day and the next.[173]

---

[169] Alistair Cooke, *Alistair Cooke's America* (Basic Books, New York, 2009) p. 100.

[170] National Archives of South Africa, Box: Transkei 1/226/1/1, "Independence Celebrations and Invitations," "The Date of Independence of the Republic of Transkei," Memorandum by R. A. Du Plooy.

[171] National Archives of South Africa, Box: Transkei 1/226/1/1, "Independence Celebrations and Invitations," "The Date of Independence of the Republic of Transkei," Memorandum by R. A. Du Plooy.

[172] National Archives of South Africa, Box: Transkei 1/226/1/1, "Independence Celebrations and Invitations," "The Date of Independence of the Republic of Transkei," Memorandum by R. A. Du Plooy.

[173] National Archives of South Africa, Box: Transkei 1/226/1/1, "Independence Celebrations and Invitations," "Minutes of Meeting of Committee on Transkei Independence Celebrations," February 24, 1976.

Figure 3.3 Kaiser Matanzima and South African Prime Minister John Vorster in Johannesburg in 1972.

With the date set, the South African government then focused on making the Transkei Independence celebrations a success. Initially hopes were high among the ceremony's planners that large numbers of foreigners would show up lending the event some legitimacy. To this end, the republic spent upward of $500,000 on an international campaign to promote the independence of Transkei in newspapers and magazines and other means, putting into motion the vast South African propaganda machinery toward this goal.[174] The South African Department of Information sent a circular to all of its offices abroad detailing their plans in regard to Transkeian independence celebrations.[175] These included special publications, audio-visual projects, and invitations to foreign television teams, to 160 foreign journalists, as well as foreign members of parliament.[176]

South Africa sent out circulars asking that local information department offices put forward names of foreign members of parliament who would likely agree to attend. One memorandum from an information official queried: "The question arises whether the invitations to foreign members of parliament should not be extended by the Transkei Legislative Assembly, or alternatively, by the South African Parliamentary Association, to disguise our hand somewhat and possibly make the invitations easier to accept."[177] Efforts to disguise South Africa's hand had instantly become that much more urgent, just two days after this memorandum was written. On June 16, thousands of black students in Soweto marched in protest of a new education mandate and the police forces fired into the unarmed crowd. This incident sparked what would become known as the Soweto uprising, which dragged the apartheid state back onto Western headlines. For

---

[174] "Transkei Bridles at Diplomatic Isolation," *New York Times*, October 24, 1976. See also: Rob Nixon, *Selling Apartheid: South Africa's Global Propaganda War* (Pluto Press, London, 2016).

[175] National Archives of South Africa, Box: Transkei 1/226/1/1, "Independence Celebrations and Invitations," "Invitation to Foreign Members of Parliament to Attend Transkei Independence Celebrations," Memorandum by N. Van Heerden, June 14, 1976.

[176] National Archives of South Africa, Box: Transkei 1/226/1/1, "Independence Celebrations and Invitations," "Invitation to Foreign Members of Parliament to Attend Transkei Independence Celebrations," Memorandum by N. Van Heerden, June 14, 1976.

[177] National Archives of South Africa, Box: Transkei 1/226/1/1, "Independence Celebrations and Invitations," "Invitation to Foreign Members of Parliament to Attend Transkei Independence Celebrations," Memorandum by N. Van Heerden, June 14, 1976.

apartheid planners and the nascent Transkei regime, who both were hoping for a successful rollout of the first Bantustan, the timing could have hardly been worse.

A month after Soweto, in July 1976, some early invitations had begun to go out.[178] Only three heads of state besides South Africa's were invited: these were the former High Commission Territories (HCTs) of Swaziland, Lesotho, and Botswana.[179] Earlier in the year, the chair of the Committee on Transkei Celebrations, H. J. R. Myburg, who also headed the Department of Bantu Administration and Development, stressed that the former HCTs needed to be invited and suggested that personal feelers by way of envoys were desirable before written invitations were actually extended, adding that "recognition of the Transkei by countries outside Africa would largely be conditioned by the stand taken by African countries."[180] In furtherance of this goal of gaining African support, Kaiser Matanzima said that he was sending his brother, George Matanzima, and a diplomatic trainee based out of Washington, Professor Mlahleni Njisane, "to certain countries outside South Africa to sound their feelings and to extend invitations. He revealed that any invitations that were accepted would be made known with a view to encouraging others to follow suit."[181] This idea of a cascading acceptance, of cautious countries waiting to follow the lead of bolder ones informed the regime's thinking as to how to break out from its diplomatic isolation, as it did for the other three regimes.

Invitations to delegations were also sent out to all foreign countries that were not overtly hostile to the apartheid regime.[182]

---

[178] National Archives of South Africa, Box: Transkei 1/226/1/1, "Independence Celebrations and Invitations," "Invitations as at 27 July, 1976."

[179] National Archives of South Africa, Box: Transkei 1/226/1/1, "Independence Celebrations and Invitations," "Minutes of Meeting with Chief Minister at His Office," February 24, 1976.

[180] National Archives of South Africa, Box: Transkei 1/226/1/1, "Independence Celebrations and Invitations," "Invitation to Foreign Members of Parliament to Attend Transkei Independence Celebrations," Memorandum by N. Van Heerden, June 14, 1976.

[181] National Archives of South Africa, Box: Transkei 1/226/1/1, "Independence Celebrations and Invitations," "Invitation to Foreign Members of Parliament to Attend Transkei Independence Celebrations," Memorandum by N. Van Heerden, June 14, 1976.

[182] Many of the South American invitations were to be handed to ministers of health. Sierra Leone's invitation was to be handed to the minister of justice, Ivory Coast's to the minister of justice, Taiwan's to the minister of agriculture. National Archives of South Africa, Box: Transkei 1/226/1/1, "Independence Celebrations and Invitations," "Invitations as at July 27, 1976."

South African officials already knew by July that many countries would not send an official delegation, but they still held out hope that some would, perhaps the fruits of Vorster's détente efforts.[183] On one South African Department of Foreign Affairs (DFA) memorandum from July 1976, it was revealed that Pretoria expected it could convince at least one of the former HCTs to attend the ceremony, and of the seventy-four invitations sent for foreign delegations they planned for ten to say "yes." They also planned to get sixty foreign members of parliament, and "seven or twelve" ministers of state.[184] This was the estimate used for approximating accommodations in Umtata.

Seven months out from their Independence Day, and facing preemptive boycotts from the UN and OAU, Transkei partially rested their hopes of recognition in Africa on the more friendly francophone African countries of the Ivory Coast and the Central African Republic (CAR).[185] The former French colonies in Sub-Saharan Africa won national independence through a very different process than the rest of Africa.[186] Observers have noted that the different systems of colonial administrations and different processes of decolonization, as well as the series of bilateral agreements between France and their former colonies left a postcolonial legacy such that in general francophone state leaders tended to maintain closer ties with the West than did anglophone state leaders.[187] It was for this reason that Vorster's foreign policy push of greater South African engagement with independent Africa proved most successful among the francophone states.[188] It is therefore not surprising that these francophone states were generally more friendly to four aspirant states than the rest of Africa. But as will be discovered, even they operated within certain prescribed parameters of state behavior toward these pariahs.

---

[183] Miller, *An African Volk.*

[184] National Archives of South Africa, Box: Transkei 1/226/1/1, "Independence Celebrations and Invitations," "Invitations as at July 27, 1976."

[185] "2 Countries Hold Transkei's Hopes," *Rand Daily Mail*, March 25, 1976.

[186] See: Frederick Cooper, *Citizenship between Empire and Nation: Remaking France and French Africa, 1945–1960* (Princeton University Press, Princeton, 2016).

[187] The ties between the francophone members of the so-called Brazzaville Group and their former colonizer, France, was a sticking point between them and the so-called Casablanca Group of African states, who characterized such relationships as "neocolonial." See: Andereggen, *France's Relationship*, chapter 6. Tensions between these ideological blocs, split over the meaning of pan-Africanism as well as the proper relations with the West, dissipated somewhat with the creation of the OAU in 1963. See: Irwin, "Sovereignty in the Congo Crisis," p. 212.

[188] See: Miller, *An African Volk*, pp. 67–70.

Even for pariahs, some friends could be embarrassing. The possible attendance at the Transkei ceremonies of the President of CAR, Jean Bedel Bokassa, who soon proclaimed himself to be the "Emperor of Central Africa," was reportedly a source of anxiety among the ceremonies planners.[189] A story leaked to the press indicated that were Bokassa to be the only leader to accept the invitation his acceptance would be rejected.[190] The article read: "The only foreign head of state who has expressed any interest in attending the Transkei Independence celebrations is Pres. Jean Bedel Bokassa of the Central African Republic – and the South African government has turned him down." Continuing on, the article read: "The South African government has decided against [allowing him to come] because of Pres. Bokassa's poor reputation internationally. Since coming to power by military coup in 1966. He has acquired a reputation as a 'Brutal Buffoon' and heavy drinker with bar-room habits."[191] Internally, the South African DFA discussed how to respond to the Bokassa press leak, concluding, "We will tell enquirers that it is for the Transkei Government to decide who it wishes to invite to Independence Celebrations and South African Government would not presume to influence choice of guests."[192] Bokassa's presence at the Transkei Independence Day events would likely have been acceptable had he been one of many, but it would have been a massive embarrassment had he been the only head of state to attend. This hypothetical came to nothing: The CAR, and its soon-to-be-crowned emperor, declined the invitation.

On September 15, 1976 Transkei received its first acceptance reply – from South Africa's minister of foreign affairs. The letter read like it was play-acting at a child's imaginary tea party:

I have the honour to thank you for your letter dated 16 August 1976, extending an invitation to the Republic of South Africa to be represented at the Independence Celebrations of Transkei during the period 25 to 27 October

---

[189] South Africa had been wooing Bokassa since 1974, offering and delivering large capital outlays for various prestige projects as part of what the DFA named "Operation Bokassa." Seven months before Transkei's independence, Bokassa welcomed the Matanzima brothers to Bangui and conveyed that he would recognize Transkei. He never did. Pfister, *Pariah to Middle Power*, pp. 79–83.

[190] "Thumbs Down for Transkei," *Rand Daily Mail*, August 16, 1976.

[191] National Archives of South Africa, Box: Transkei 1/226/1/1, "Independence Celebrations and Invitations," Telegram from Ntshongwana to Du Plooy, 1976.

[192] National Archives of South Africa, Box: Transkei 1/226/1/1, "Independence Celebrations and Invitations," Telegram from Secextern to Information Umtata, August 17, 1976.

1976. I take pleasure in informing you that the Republic of South Africa will be represented at the Independence Celebrations by the State President and Mrs. Diederichs, myself and Mrs. Muller and The Honourable M.C. Botha and Mrs. Botha. Particulars concerning the arrival and departure of the South African delegation will be communicated to your office separately. Please accept, Mr. Chief Minister, the assurance of my highest consideration.[193]

In late September, Transkei received a second acceptance, this time from the Rhodesian regime, which had been only belatedly invited. The Rhodesian Minister of Foreign Affairs, P. K. Van de Byl, wrote:

Your Excellency, am greatly honoured by invitation to Independence Celebrations. My formal reply indicating the very great pleasure I will have in being present at this history-making occasion has been despatched. May I offer Your Excellency sincerest congratulations as the day of destiny for your nation approaches, and may I extend profoundest good wishes. Assurances highest considerations.[194]

At this stage, with only South Africa and Rhodesia attending, it was likely the Rhodesian acceptance was a greater messaging burden than a benefit. Once again, the South Africans and Transkeians need not have worried, the day before independence *Rand Daily Mail* reported that "even Rhodesia, at one time the last hope for representation from an African country outside of South Africa, was given up [on]."[195] The Rhodesian regime, which was at the time preoccupied with the Geneva talks, ended up not sending anyone to Transkei's celebration.[196] A growing sense of panic began to overtake the planners as October approached and the RSVPs began to be returned.[197] African leaders formed a solid wall

[193] National Archives of South Africa, Box: BTS 1/226/1/1, vol. 3, "Transkei Independence Celebrations," Letter from H. Muller, Minister of Foreign Affairs, to Chief Minister of Transkei, Kaiser Matanzima, September 15, 1976.

[194] National Archives of South Africa, Box: BTS 1/226/1/1, vol. 3, "Transkei Independence Celebrations," Letter from SA Accredited Diplomatic Representative in Salisbury to Secretary DFA, quoting message from PK Van der Byl (undated, but September 1976).

[195] Patrick Laurence, Peter Kenny, "A Lonely Birth for Transkei," *Rand Daily Mail*, October 25, 1976.

[196] Interestingly, during Venda's Independence Day celebrations on September 15, 1979, the short-lived Zimbabwe-Rhodesia government sent a five-man delegation headed by the minister of manpower and social affairs. Press speculation as to whether this indicated that mutual recognition between the two was close at hand was shot down by a Zimbabwe-Rhodesian official who said their delegation represented "not approval, but a show of friendship to a neighboring country." State Department Telegram from US Embassy Pretoria to Secretary of State and Cape Town, "Venda Independence," September 15, 1979, accessed via Wikileaks: wikileaks.org/plusd/cables/1979PRETOR08406_e.html.

[197] National Archives of South Africa, Box: Transkei 1/226/1/1, "Independence Celebrations and Invitations," Telegram from Ntshongwana to Du Plooy, 1976.

against recognition of Transkei broadly, and more narrowly against attendance at the Independence ceremonies. The Zambian press, for instance, even called for any African heads of state who attended the ceremony to be deposed.[198]

To a Transkeian population which was indifferent to the proceedings, a black South African population who were largely opposed to it, and a wider world community who thought it was at best a farce and at worst a travesty, Umtata and Pretoria did their best to puff up interest and excitement in the independence celebrations by placing it within a larger narrative of black emancipation.[199] For Transkei to establish their external sovereignty through recognition, it was necessary to display to the world their "internal" support for independence among Transkeians inside and outside the aspiring state. On the buildup to the celebrations, Transkei authorities cracked down on possible disruptive elements within the territory.[200] Even with the heightened security, a boxing match between Nkosana "Happyboy" Mgxaji and Norman "Pangaman" Sekgapane at the Umtata Independence Stadium that was planned to coincide with independence celebrations had to be canceled because of threats made against one of the fighters and his family in South Africa by those opposing the birth of Transkei.[201] Likewise, two top professional soccer teams, the Orlando Pirates and Kaiser Chiefs backed out.[202] There was a strong police presence in the streets in the days and nights before the big day.

The millions of South African citizens who spoke the Nguni language of the Xhosa people were soon going lose their South African citizenship and be forced to take up Transkeian citizenship. This forced repatriation was a massively unpopular policy and was a sticking point prior to Transkei's independence just as it would be for Bophuthatswana. Even so, within South Africa the apartheid regime organized massive celebrations of Transkeian independence in several African townships across the republic. Despite the state's best efforts, these independence celebrations were often met with protests and violence in the townships.[203] Outside

---

[198] National Archives of South Africa, Box: BTS 1/226/1/1, vol. 3, "Transkei Independence Celebrations," "Zambian Press Comment on Transkei Independence," Letter from the SA Accredited Diplomatic Representative in Salisbury to Secretary for Foreign Affairs, September 30, 1976.

[199] See for example: "A Tough African Nationalist," *New York Times*, October 26, 1976.

[200] See chapter 1 in: Streek and Wicksteed, *Render unto Kaiser*.

[201] "Sport, Song and Celebration Will Herald the Birth of a New Transkei," *Rand Daily Mail*, October 14, 1976.

[202] "It Is All So Quiet as the Big Day Nears," *Rand Daily Mail*, October 25, 1976.

[203] "Youths Protest at Transkei Holiday," *New York Times*, October 17, 1976.

Cape Town, for instance, heavily armed South African riot police had to keep protestors away from the 1,000 attending a free feast of ox meat and beer in a stadium in the black township of Langa hosted by the Transkei government.[204] The Langa feast was part of several sponsored events around South Africa in anticipation of Transkei's independence. Matanzima addressed a crowd of 3,000 at one such celebration in Soweto's Dobsonville Stadium. In his speech, Matanzima said military confrontation with South Africa was suicidal and unnecessary since Transkei was getting what it wanted without firing a bullet.[205] Most Xhosa remained unimpressed, even those drinking the free beer.

In the days before the celebration, Umtata was decked out in the colors of green, ochre, and white, with the new Transkei flag unfurled across town.[206] As the preparations for the big day moved forward, they often provided irresistible comedic material for the foreign press. *The New York Times* correspondent John Burns used the quality of the Transkei Army Band and their tutelage under apartheid headmasters in the preparation for the independence celebrations as a metaphor for the entire Bantustan project:

A group of black men, none of whom played a musical instrument until a few months ago, sit in the center of a rugby field working their way laboriously through John Philip Sousa's "Manhattan Beach." In front of them, offering gentle exhortations, stands a South African Army bandmaster.[207]

Describing the new two million dollar presidential palace and the many new showcase buildings paid for by South Africa, Burns concluded that the army and the band, and Transkei itself, were all the products of apartheid South Africa.[208] The *Rand Daily Mail's* Tim Muil observed there was a "marked lack of enthusiasm" among Transkei Africans on the day of independence, and it was recognized to be "more the realization of a dream for Paramount Chief Kaiser Matanzima and the [ruling South African] National Party than cause for celebration for the masses."[209]

The day before independence the *Rand Daily Mail* ran a story titled, "A Lonely Birth for Transkei."[210] Revisiting this anthropomorphic

---

[204] "Youths Protest at Transkei Holiday," *New York Times*, October 17, 1976.

[205] "Youths Protest at Transkei Holiday," *New York Times*, October 16, 1976.

[206] "Youths Protest at Transkei Holiday," *New York Times*, October 17, 1976.

[207] John Burns, "Transkei Approaches Nationhood Helped, and Burdened, by Its Ties to South Africa," *New York Times*, October 22, 1976.

[208] John Burns, "Transkei Approaches Nationhood Helped, and Burdened, by Its Ties to South Africa," *New York Times*, October 22, 1976.

[209] "It Is All So Quiet as the Big Day Nears," *Rand Daily Mail*, October 25, 1976.

[210] Patrick Laurence, Peter Kenny, "A Lonely Birth for Transkei," *Rand Daily Mail*, October 25, 1976.

birth analogy, the article read: "The Transkei will celebrate its birth as an independent state at midnight tonight with South Africa as the midwife and sole official witness."[211] On the actual day, the only official representative was the South African State President. A couple dozen parliamentarians from Europe and South America were all there in their private capacities.[212] Andrew T. Hatcher, a black American public relations man hired by the South African government, brought fourteen Americans with him, all on South Africa's dime.[213] Other rumors made the rounds right up until the very day that official delegations from Malawi and Taiwan would be arriving, but they never did.[214] The lack of attendance was impossible to hide. The official guest list was released and as the *Rand Daily Mail* noted it was "conspicuous by its long list of blanks in place of the names of countries invited to attend the independence celebrations officially."[215] *The New York Times* reported:

The hastily erected independence Stadium showed wide open spaces in its stands prepared for 35,000 spectators. Only the smart marching of the newly formed Transvaal Battalion aroused any measure of enthusiasm. A steady flow of citizens headed for the exits during the speeches of the South African President and their Prime Minister. The streets of this capital of 30,000 were nearly deserted.[216]

Transkei's big show was a bust.

Internationally, Transkei's Independence Day was met with hostility. On the same day as the purported handover of power in Transkei, the acting President of the ANC, Oliver Tambo, and the Foreign Affairs Director of the PAC, David Sibeko, spoke to the UN General Assembly in New York City, and the international body voted 134 to zero to declare Transkei's independence "invalid" and prohibit members from any dealings with Transkei or any of the other homelands.[217] To mark the occasion the UN again passed a resolution rejecting Transkei's independence. The OAU held a "Festival of Rejection" during the week of

---

[211] Patrick Laurence, Peter Kenny, "A Lonely Birth for Transkei," *Rand Daily Mail*, October 25, 1976.

[212] Stultz, *Transkei's Half Loaf*, p. 118.

[213] "Transkei, a South African Black Area, Is Independent," *New York Times*, October 26, 1976.

[214] "Transkei, a South African Black Area, Is Independent," *New York Times*, October 26, 1976.

[215] "Transkei, a South African Black Area, Is Independent," *New York Times*, October 26, 1976.

[216] "Transkei, a South African Black Area, Is Independent," *New York Times*, October 26, 1976.

[217] Stultz, *Transkei's Half Loaf*, p. 118.

Transkei's ceremony.[218] Not that it mattered at all to world opinion, but even Rhodesia failed to formally recognize Transkei, and Transkei likewise never recognized Rhodesia.

The Transkei people by and large felt little ownership of the Day or the celebrations.[219] The glaring lack of enthusiasm was in stark contrast to the "freedoms at midnight" celebrations Transkei sought to mimic. *The Rhodesia Herald* correspondent sent to report on the ceremony wrote: "With the Transkei's independence less than a month away, visiting foreign journalists and diplomats are amazed by the absence of excitement and anticipation so characteristic of other African countries on the eve of 'Uhuru.'"[220] A Transkeian civil servant, who insisted on being unnamed due to security regulations, was quoted as saying, "It's like a great big puppet show with the whites pulling the strings and we blacks dancing about on the Matanzima stage." Another Transkeian citizen commented, "This is Kaiser's independence, not the peoples'. He wants to make every decision down to the last hymn to be sung on Independence Day. We might as well go on holiday and leave it all up to him and his white friends from Pretoria."[221]

After the formal handing over of the instruments of state at midnight in the Independence Stadium, and the 101-gun salute, Kaiser Matanzima made his first speech as the Prime Minister of the ostensibly independent state of Transkei. In his speech in front of the South African State President, Dr. Nicolaas Diedereichs, Matanzima expressed his "contempt" for the racial policies in South Africa that had typified life under white rule for centuries. "We utterly reject the racial discrimination which has been characteristic of much that is South African," Matanzima said.[222] This independence speech, with its public reckoning of the colonial legacy in front of the former colonial masters, was directly reminiscent of Patrice Lumumba's already famous humiliation of King Baudouin at the Congo's independence. Taking on the mantle of the martyr Lumumba was no coincidence. Nothing conveyed a sense of legitimacy more than a confrontation with the former colonizer, however stage-designed and manufactured it might have been. As much of a bust

---

[218] Southall, *South Africa's Transkei*, p. 3.

[219] Scholars have written of the spectrum of participation of the public in various national events. If plotted along this spectrum, the Transkeian event was on the very extreme end of a minimal public involvement, a completely top-down affair. J. Gillis (ed.), *Commemorations: The Politics of National Identity* (Princeton University Press, Princeton, 1996).

[220] "No 'Uhuru' Fervour in the Transkei," *Rhodesia Herald*, October 4, 1976.

[221] "No 'Uhuru' Fervour in the Transkei," *Rhodesia Herald*, October 4, 1976.

[222] "The Lonely Independence of Transkei," *The Guardian*, October 26, 1976.

as Transkei's independence celebrations proved to be, they would still become the template for the rest of the Bantustans.

A month before the first anniversary of independence in 1977, Matanzima said that Transkei would not have any official celebrations on its first anniversary due to a lack of money, and that independence celebrations would thereafter only be every five years.[223] If Matanzima's stated reason for not holding celebrations was in fact true, this would have been a budgetary decision without precedent even in the poorest of countries. Much more likely, Matanzima did not relish having another embarrassingly unenthusiastic celebration, especially after a year that had nothing to show for it in terms of international recognition. The hoped-for first break in their complete diplomatic quarantine that would result in a cascade of more recognition never happened, despite continued efforts on the part of the regime.

In Matanzima's speech during this low-key first anniversary he defined the threats facing the young state of Transkei as the same facing white settler Southern Africa, referencing the Rhodesian war against "terrorists" who target white and black civilians, as evidence of a communist march on South Africa and Transkei.[224] This anti-communist appeal was right in line with those made by the Katangese and Rhodesian regimes, and was similarly aimed at Cold Warriors in the West. Meanwhile in the United States, Leslie Masimini, the head of the Transkei Washington Bureau, attempted to organize a celebration of Transkei's first year of independence in Washington at the Museum of African Art on Capitol Hill. He quickly ran into problems trying to do so. After sending out some 500 invitations to US officials, members of the diplomatic corps, academics, and reporters to attend the celebration, Masimini was informed that the museum was pulling out of hosting the event due to political pressure.[225] The Transkei Embassy in South Africa marked the first-year anniversary by issuing a bellicose, if somewhat puzzling, statement on racial sovereignty in Africa: "Blacks are firm in their determination to keep Africa African, just as the tiger seeks to be more tigerish."[226]

In April 1978, Matanzima's government dramatically broke off diplomatic relations with South Africa, ostensibly over a land dispute, and would only restore formal diplomatic relations in 1980. As a result,

[223] Steve Kgame, "Matanzima Here to 'Bridge' Differences," *Rand Daily Mail*, September 15, 1977.

[224] "Matanzima Looks to Transkei's Future," *Rand Daily Mail*, October 27, 1977.

[225] Guy Bernard, "Birthday Party Problems," *Rand Daily Mail*, October 25, 1977.

[226] "Kaiser Aims to Liberate Africa," *Rand Daily Mail*, October 26, 1977.

Transkei's second and third-year anniversaries in 1978 and 1979, respectively, took place under much tighter finances, since South Africa supplied a large amount of Transkei's governmental budget. However, this break also meant that Transkei had an opportunity to claim its complete independence from South Africa which was seen as a possible opening for a diplomatic breakthrough, as detailed in the next chapter. Matanzima quickly took up the mantle of an anti-apartheid leader.[227] It always was a complex dance between the Bantustans and the ANC, as Timothy Gibbs has shown.[228] Recognizing the homelands as an essential part of the apartheid grand policy, the ANC knew they had to be outwardly rejected, yet the potentialities for new diffuse sources of power to serve as counterweights against Pretoria could not be ignored. Expressing this tension, an ANC statement from 1977 declared:

We have no alternative but to fight the Bantustan programme with ruthless determination, render it ineffective and unworkable. But also, and at the same time, since it is a weapon of destruction, while it lasts we must grab it from the enemy's grip and turn it against him and for the liberation of our country.[229]

In a reversal of Matanzima's earlier pledge not to hold celebrations as a money saving measure, Transkei's second-year anniversary in October 1978 was to be more ambitious in a desperate appeal to African leaders. Some weeks before, several African heads of state were invited to celebrate Transkei's independence in Umtata.[230] Of the celebrations, Matanzima said he wanted to make them "continental," since Transkei was a member of the world community. "We belong to the Organisation of African Unity," he said, "although we have not been officially admitted."[231] The full program of the second-year anniversary in 1978 was released to the press some days before Independence Day.[232] The afternoon was to have a "gymkhana and traditional festivities," and the day was to end with an official banquet at City Hall. Among other events, Matanzima was to address the nation at the Independence Stadium, and

---

[227] State Department Telegram from US Consulate Durban to Secretary of State and Others, "Matanzima Attacks SAG policies," Amrch 17, 1978, accessed via Wikileaks: wikileaks.org/plusd/cables/1978DURBAN00181_d.html.

[228] Gibbs, *Mandela's Kinsmen*.

[229] Quoted in Robert Fatton, Jr., "The African National Congress of South Africa: The Limitations of a Revolutionary Strategy," *Canadian Journal of African Studies / Revue Canadienne des Études Africaines*, vol. 18, no. 3 (1984).

[230] "Transkei Sends out Invitations," *Rand Daily Mail*, September 29, 1978.

[231] "Transkei Sends out Invitations," *Rand Daily Mail*, September 29, 1978.

[232] "Pomp at Kei Uhuru Party," *Rand Daily Mail*, October 23, 1978.

afterward "[p]igeons will be released into the air and traditional dances will add colour to the ceremony."[233] This was all very similar to the program at independence two years before, but with a new radical anti-apartheid message.

In his speech Matanzima called on the OAU to provide military training for Transkei so that his country could continue the fight against apartheid from a position of strength.[234] Completely reversing himself from the last year's speech, Matanzima argued the biggest security threat to Transkei was from apartheid South Africa, not the communist march he described a year before.[235] He said it was time for the world to reconsider its decision to ostracize Transkei.[236] While the program was released, the guest list was not. Just as at the actual independence ceremony, and the one-year anniversary, no African heads of state attended. The third Transkeian independence celebration was to be more subdued. There was to be none of the pomp and ceremony of the last anniversary. A government spokesmen said of the day's planned events: "I wouldn't exactly call them celebrations, the Ministers and MPs will address the meetings and then probably go home and watch television or something."[237]

With the restoration of diplomatic relations with South Africa in February 1980, Transkei's budget coffers were once again replenished with South African cash. Matanzima's October 26th message to the attendees in the Independence Stadium, which included the South African Ambassador to Transkei, Robert du Plooy, who stage-managed the original Independence Day events, was one of a country under siege.[238] Repositioning the greatest threat to Transkei as being once again from "revolutionary elements," and not from South Africa, this was a bitter and aggressive message of a duplicitous and naive West betraying Southern Africa to communism.[239] He said that Transkei's true friend was South Africa, and that this friendship had "aggravated the hatred" of the world community against Transkei.[240] He was correct.

[233] "We Won't Belly-Crawl – Matanzima," *Rand Daily Mail*, October 27, 1978.
[234] "Kei Calls on OAU," *Rand Daily Mail*, October 27, 1978.
[235] "Kei Calls on OAU," *Rand Daily Mail*, October 27, 1978.
[236] "We Won't Belly-Crawl – Matanzima," *Rand Daily Mail*, October 27, 1978.
[237] "We Won't Belly-Crawl – Matanzima," *Rand Daily Mail*, October 27, 1978.
[238] "Cash for Transkei Rebels Pours In, Says KD," *Rand Daily Mail*, October 27, 1980.
[239] "Cash for Transkei Rebels Pours In, Says KD," *Rand Daily Mail*, October 27, 1980.
[240] "Cash for Transkei Rebels Pours In, Says KD," *Rand Daily Mail*, October 27, 1980.

Bophuthatswana

Bophuthatswana's purported independence on December 6, 1977 followed more than a year after Transkei's. By that time, Bophuthatswana's and South Africa's leaders had already seen Transkei fail to win any international recognition, and Transkei would go on to have the muted commemoration of its one-year anniversary just before Bophuthatswana would declare its own independence in December. So, it was all laid out before them. Yet the ideological demands of the grand apartheid philosophy, the overwhelming inertia of such a massively ambitious set of policies with the powerful steam turbines of government bureaucracies churning, and the credibility of the National Party on the line, all meant that the process could not realistically be stopped. It had to churn straight forward toward another Bantustan independence.

Arguments were made, however, that Bophuthatswana was different than Transkei and that so too might its fate. The flip side of Transkei distancing itself from Bophuthatswana and the other Bantustans to better its own chances of recognition was Bophuthatswanan efforts to distinguish itself from the failed emergence of Transkei. But there were some inherent problems with this strategy. One was that there is no doubt that Bophuthatswana looked absurd on maps, some even quipped that it should be called "Jigsawland."[241] Commentators could never move past the two "anomalies" that at independence Bophuthatswana consisted of six separate pieces of territory, and that many more of its citizens still lived in South Africa than within its own, new borders – roughly two-thirds.[242] The latter was a weakness for Transkei as well, but not nearly as drastic.[243] In addition, Transkei had the geographic advantages of being roughly contiguous and having access to the sea, while Bophuthatswana was landlocked and with the exception of a strip abutting Botswana, it was completely surrounded by South Africa. Transkei also had an urban center in Umtata, which Bophuthatswana lacked. Because of its absurd geographical arrangement it was more reliant on

---

[241] AP newsreel, accessed April 9, 2019, www.youtube.com/watch?v=Qe3wYrB4kDo.

[242] "A New State Will Be Born at Midnight," *Rand Daily Mail*, December 5, 1977.

[243] Transkei and Ciskei combined had about 55 percent of its ethnic Xhosa citizens within the homelands, with only 1.6 percent in other homelands and 44 percent in designated white areas. Bophuthatswana had 35 percent of ethnic Tswanas inside, only .6 percent in other homelands, but 65 percent in white areas. Jeffrey Butler, Robert Rotberg, and John Adams, *The Black Homelands of South Africa: The Political and Economic Development of Bophuthatswana and KwaZulu* (University of California Press, Berkeley, 1977) p. 5, table 1.3.

South African goodwill for basic day-to-day business and travel between its various enclaves.

Yet despite these anomalies, Bophuthatswana was much better-off economically than Transkei. It attracted more industrial development than all other Bantustans combined, contained the second largest platinum company in the world, was generally rich in raw materials, and was seen to have had great potential for commercial agriculture.[244] Bophuthatswana also had the biggest budget of the Bantustans and the most developed security forces.[245] Even the argument that it was economically dependent upon South Africa did not distinguish it from many states of postcolonial Africa in terms of their economic dependence on international aid and foreign investment.[246] Bophuthatswana's weaknesses were therefore not unique to Africa. To the outside world, however, all these positive attributes and spirited defenses were bleached out against its inescapable association with Transkei and the apartheid-driven Bantustan system.

Lucas Mangope's regime recognized the objective problems these anomalies presented, and how these gravely damaged Bophuthatswana's legitimacy in the eyes of the world. He tried and failed to address both of these issues prior to independence, much as Matanzima had with both more land consolidation and the citizenship question.[247] He ultimately decided that it would be best to address these "anomalies" after independence rather than beforehand.[248] Within the territory all these sad notes were drown out by the trumpeting of the historic day of independence that was fast approaching. Like Transkei, the planning for the Independence Day events were a joint South African and Bantustan effort, with Pretoria footing the bill. As shown above, Transkei followed the Ghanaian independence script as closely as was possible, and Bophuthatswana in turn followed the Transkeian script closely. Because of this, the planning of Bophuthatswana's celebrations was much more straightforward since the Transkeian model from a year before had carved out a path already for other Bantustans to follow. As shown below, however, the Transkei model also provided some lessons that the later Bantustans would heed.

---

[244] "A New State Will Be Born at Midnight," *Rand Daily Mail*, December 5, 1977.

[245] "Chips Down for Mangope's New Army," *Rand Daily Mail*, December 18, 1977.

[246] And as James Ferguson points out, in terms of a specific dependency on South Africa, one needed to look no further than the independent and universally recognized state of Lesotho. Ferguson, *Global Shadows*.

[247] "A New State Will Be Born at Midnight," *Rand Daily Mail*, December 5, 1977.

[248] "A New State Will Be Born at Midnight," *Rand Daily Mail*, December 5, 1977.

As with Transkei, a crucial part of the preparations for Bophuthatswana's independence had to do with creating the infrastructures of sovereignty. These were primarily prestige projects located in the new capital cities, such as new government buildings, airports, and national stadiums, that could be shown off to outsiders – following the lead of most other new African states. This explosion of new construction that preceded every Bantustan independence transfer served a practical and a propagandic role, intended to convey that South Africa was taking these transfers of power seriously and that the resulting states were viable. It was also hoped that the newly spiffed-up capitals would serve as centripetal economic draws for the nonresident African populations to pull them away from white areas, as well as to serve as symbolic focal points for the new nations. But while Transkei had a natural capital in Umtata, Bophuthatswana had none. This was because Bophuthatswana's enclaves were scattered in and around larger white cities that remained in the republic after Bophuthatswana was to be excised out. So, that meant one had to be built, and fast. An article in the government-produced *Bophuthatswana Pioneer* magazine described the need for the new state to have a capital city: "We had to have a capital, since you cannot have a successful state and country without the heart from which to pump out life's blood. Our heart, the place that is ours and that is the mother of the people has always been ready and willing to spread its influence to the rest of the country and this has been done."[249]

South Africa injected massive sums of money into each Bantustan capital prior to independence. The site of Bophuthatswana's new capital was chosen in April 1976, and it was unsubtly named Mmabatho: mother of the people.[250] Design of the city was heavily influenced by Mangope himself, and it was explicitly to be a Tswana City, to be differentiated from the rectangular design of Mafeking. Mangope said, "I want a Tswana Town so my children won't lose their sense of identity ... I do not want a white town. I want a Tswana town. Tswanas build like this ... (and he held up his hands indicating a circular, embracing form)."[251] The (white) South African planners therefore embarked on an urban design which attempted to incorporate elements of Tswanan village life, a "rural vernacular architecture," as interpreted from

---

[249] *Bophuthatswana Pioneer*, no. 2, June 1985.

[250] Peris Sean Jones, PhD dissertation for Loughborough University, "Mmabatho, 'Mother of the People'.".

[251] Architectural consultant Professor Mallows, Quoted in Jones, "Mmabatho, 'Mother of the People'," p. 194.

Mangope's personal vision.[252] A tourist brochure from 1987 would eventually boast of Mmabatho: "Mushrooming from nothing but barren bush in only a few years, Bophuthatswana has given birth to Mmabatho, 'Mother of the People' – its new capital city and its spiritual home ... heart and soul of the Nation."[253]

The new capital would be yet another example of the visual rhetoric of independence. But timelines of independence and of the sovereign infrastructure did not match up. In June 1977, some five months out from independence, the Bophuthatswanan authorities sponsored a bus tour for forty journalists to show off their plans.[254] The journalists of the tour saw the R20 million "temporary" capital being built, because "in all of Bophuthatswana's six jigsaw pieces, there is no town big enough to act as a seat of government or as an arena for independence celebrations."[255] At the time of the June tour only the skeletons of administration buildings and trenches for sewers could be seen, and most of the planned work was not completed even as December came around.[256]

As the big day drew nearer, once again, like with Transkei, attendance was seen as a potential embarrassment. Planning for the Independence Day events, Mangope issued an open invitation for anyone to attend the celebrations.[257] This time around there could at least be no real surprise that no official state representatives attended. As a result, Bophuthatswana was slightly more reticent than was Transkei in touting its guest lists before the actual ceremony.[258] Once again, only one official representative of a recognized state attended – Dr. Nico Diederichs of South Africa. One unrecognized state representative did attend, along with several leaders of entities that would soon declare their own independence: Transkei's Matanzima attended Bophuthatswana's ceremony along with two cabinet officials.[259] Ciskei was represented by its Chief Minister, Lennox Sebe, and its interior minister. Despite his attendance at the celebration, Sebe refused to comment on whether or not his

---

[252] Architectural consultant Professor Mallows, Quoted in Jones, "Mmabatho, 'Mother of the People'," p. 194.

[253] Quoted in Jones, "Mmabatho, 'Mother of the People'," p. 204.

[254] Helen Zille, "A Crash Course in Freedom," *Rand Daily Mail*, June 20, 1977.

[255] Helen Zille, "A Crash Course in Freedom," *Rand Daily Mail*, June 20, 1977.

[256] Susan Parnell, "From Mafeking to Mafikeng: The Transformation of a South African Town," *GeoJournal*, vol. 12, no. 2, South Africa: Geography in a State of Emergency (March 1986) p. 205.

[257] "Vorster, Mangope Sign Pacts," *Rand Daily Mail*, November 16, 1977.

[258] Even so, the Bophuthatswana foreign secretary bizarrely boasted to the press that thirteen people from the Philippines would be attending, but it is unclear who these people actually were or if they indeed came. "Celebrations Begin," *Rand Daily Mail*, December 5, 1980.

[259] "Transkei and Ciskei Attend Celebrations," *Rand Daily Mail*, December 5, 1977.

attendance would indicate his support for Bophuthatswana's independence.[260] Bantustan leaders who rejected Bophuthatswana's independence outright were not invited.[261]

As the only heads of state to appear at the events, Matanzima and Diederichs allegedly drew more enthusiastic cheers than the arrival of Mangope himself, even though he was supposed to be the man of the hour.[262] Like Matanzima and Transkei, there was likewise not much enthusiasm for either Mangope or Bophuthatswanan independence among the majority of the Tswanas living outside the new state. For example, it was announced that among those arriving to celebrate were fifty-four Tswanas who were flown in from Cape Town by the South African Air Force, an embarrassing display of cost and effort when viewed against a population of over a million Tswanas living in the republic.[263] Seemingly having learned the lesson from Transkei's disastrous attempts to display homegrown support for independence through the free ox meat and beer rallies within the townships of South Africa, there did not seem to be any attempts to manufacture excitement for independence within the township Tswana populations.[264] Another lesson learned from Transkei was that Mmabatho was put under intensive security in the days before and during the celebration like Umtata was. Newspapers reported that there were police in uniforms everywhere during the events ensuring order.[265]

Following Transkei's template, the planned celebrations began with a sports program and other visual displays, starting on November 28th and running up to December 5th. However, unlike events in Umtata, the new Mmabatho Stadium that was the central stage for the visual displays during the independence ceremonies was not completed in time. Attendees had to file into a hastily constructed grandstands of scaffolding purpose-built for the occasion.[266] Nonetheless, according to the *Rand Daily Mail*, 40,000 people attended the independence ceremony in the

---

[260] "Transkei and Ciskei Attend Celebrations," *Rand Daily Mail*, December 5, 1977.

[261] "Slap in the Face for Me, Says Mopeli," *Rand Daily Mail*, December 6, 1977.

[262] "Independence Yawns ... to the Wrong Anthem," *Rand Daily Mail*, December 7, 1977.

[263] "Independence Yawns ... to the Wrong Anthem," *Rand Daily Mail*, December 7, 1977.

[264] In August 1976, students burned down Bophuthatswana's Legislative Assembly building. Or perhaps the lesson was even closer to home when Mangope's own car got stoned by black youths after a speech he gave in the Ikaheng Township outside Potchefstroom five months before independence. State Department Telegram from US Embassy Pretoria to Secretary of State and Cape Town, "An External Triumph and an Internal Rebuff," July 19, 1977, accessed via Wikileaks: wikileaks.org/plusd/cables/1977PRETOR03555_c.html.

[265] Doc Bikitsha's Finger on Your Pulse, "Freedom Ceremony Disjointed Affair," *Rand Daily Mail*, December 12, 1977.

[266] AP newsreel, accessed on April 8, 2019, www.youtube.com/watch?v=j8KHbLXi2JE.

stadium.[267] Yet attendance at these events should not be read entirely as support for the underlying purpose of the event. It was a spectacle, and much as many Rhodesian Africans filled the parking structure to watch the 1970 military parade out of curiosity but not support, possibly many Bophuthatswanans come to see the day's and evening's events out of this same curiosity. As an Associated Press newsreel narrator at the time put it: "For a while politics were forgotten as the people of Bophuthatswana submerged themselves in the pomp and pretentions of the celebrations."[268]

At midnight on December 6, 1977, South Africa purportedly bestowed independence on Bophuthatswana. As described in the *Rand Daily Mail*, at the climax of the celebration when Nico Diederichs handed over to Chief Lucas Mangope the "Status of Bophuthatswana Act, 1977" as well as the golden pen with which it was signed, the Master of Ceremonies reportedly had to "beg for applause and ululations from a crowd which [didn't] disguise its boredom."[269] The crowd did applaud for the gymnastics show in which dozens of young people performed a dance routine in orange and white athletic gear. There was also cheering for the drill of soldiers and police.[270] After the 101-gun salute, a group of twelve men in orange track suits ran through the stadium holding lit torches, and at the end a final man in all white jogged up a flight of stairs and set a large basin alight that Mangope dubbed the "the flame of independence."[271] This part of the spectacle looked almost identical to the iconic opening ceremonies of the Olympics.

There was, of course, the obligatory flag ceremony that had swept much of the rest of the world in the previous three decades. During what was supposed to be the solemn moment when South Africa lowered its flag, whistles and catcalls could be heard from the crowd, forcing the Master of Ceremonies to remind the crowd of the dignity of the occasion.[272] Perhaps most embarrassingly, when the Master of Ceremonies called on the crowd to sing the national anthem one section broke into the Xhosa anthem "Morena Bolacka Seehaba," a tune banned by Mangope. Only a few sang the anthem "Sefela SaSeehaba," which was relatively unknown, a scene reminiscent of Rhodesians not knowing the words to their own new anthem.[273] As independence was granted, the

---

[267] *Rand Daily Mail*, December 6, 1977.
[268] AP newsreel, accessed on April 9, 2019, www.youtube.com/watch?v=Qe3wYrB4kDo.
[269] "Independence Yawns ... to the Wrong anthem," *Rand Daily Mail*, December 7, 1977.
[270] "Independence Yawns ... to the Wrong Anthem," *Rand Daily Mail*, December 7, 1977.
[271] AP newsreel, accessed on April 8, 2019. www.youtube.com/watch?v=j8KHbLXi2JE.
[272] "Independence Yawns ... to the Wrong Anthem," *Rand Daily Mail*, December 7, 1977.
[273] "Independence Yawns ... to the Wrong Anthem," *Rand Daily Mail*, December 7, 1977.

Master of Ceremonies' triumphant shout of "Pula!" (rain), which should have prompted the response "A ene!" (let it rain), was met with silence.[274]

As was reported at the Umtata celebrations a year before, the crowd began to leave before the Mmabatho celebration was even over. The stadium was reportedly half empty by the time Mangope spoke.[275] In his speech, Mangope, like Matanzima a year before, directly confronted his former sovereign masters. He began by saying Bophuthatswana would be dedicated to racial justice, claiming that the "main reason for choosing independence is that we utterly abhor racial discrimination." But he said there would be no "retribution against our white fellow South Africans" despite the fact that their relations would at times be "naturally strained ... with our former colonial master, South Africa."[276]

Bophuthatswana's sovereign insecurities gurgled out from Mangope's independence speech. Directly attacking the South Africans for not consolidating its lands, Mangope declared that this geographical joke damaged the new state's chances for recognition. He went so far as to question the new state's new sovereignty – calling the supposed sovereign moment that had just occurred as merely granting Bophuthatswana "greater independence," rather than full independence.[277]

Just as it is born, our independence has already fallen to a fatal credibility gap which bears the stamp: made in Pretoria, by South Africa. It is not at all surprising, I'm afraid, that in overseas capitals they show me a map of the bits and pieces of Bophuthatswana and add the sarcastic remark: "Did you say independence. Please forgive our mouth we thought you were joking."[278]

This was a bizarre hedge, and it recalls in some ways Tshombe's calculated ambivalence over whether or not Katanga was truly declaring independence or was merely making a play at greater autonomy within the Congo. However, Mangope's calculation might have been the opposite of Tshombe's: That by threatening to undermine his new state's sovereign status he could extract more concessions from the mother country that wanted them out. The official South African representatives in attendance did not take offense as King Baudouin had during Lumumba's famous speech. This was all pro forma. At the state banquet afterward, Nico Diederichs addressed the attendees: "You are getting your republic without violence ... you are getting your republic after the

---

[274] "Independence Yawns ... to the Wrong Anthem," *Rand Daily Mail*, December 7, 1977.
[275] "Independence Yawns ... to the Wrong Anthem," *Rand Daily Mail*, December 7, 1977.
[276] "Independence Yawns ... to the Wrong Anthem," *Rand Daily Mail*, December 7, 1977.
[277] "Mangope Slates SA over Land," *Rand Daily Mail*, December 6, 1977.
[278] "Mangope Slates SA over Land," *Rand Daily Mail*, December 6, 1977.

Parliament of South Africa has voluntarily and with its very best wishes withdrawn its authority over you."[279] As with Transkei the Bophuthatswana people evidently were indifferent about the whole affair. As the *New York Times* editorial eloquently put it following Bophuthatswana's Independence Day: "[these homeland independence] ceremonies are part of an internal South African drama."[280]

Part of the festivities included a balloonist floating over Mmabatho three times to mark the event, with large printing on the side of the balloon in English: "Congratulations to the people of Bophuthatswana on your independence."[281] While the actual independence balloon floated up and away, the symbolic independence balloon never got off the ground. Like Transkei, the international community preemptively rejected Bophuthatswana even before the transfer ceremony. The OAU asked its member states to demonstrate on December 6th in protest against the Bantustan policy. The Mmabatho celebration was a "nonevent" in the rest of Africa, notably even in Botswana, the home of their Tswana brethren.[282] Gaborone was distinctly silent on the occasion even while their Tswana kith and kin ostensibly joined them in uhuru. The rejection by Botswana in particular stung the Mangope regime deeply since it undercut the would-be state's ethno-national legitimacy.

Western embassies in Pretoria emphasized to the *Rand Daily Mail* that they sent no official delegations to the ceremony and that those politicians and businesspeople from their countries who did attend were all in their private capacities, and none of the Western states recognized its independence.[283] In reporting on the Independence Day ceremonies, the South African press carried false stories that representatives of the United States and other countries were in attendance. As the US Ambassador to South Africa, William Bowdler, described in a telegram to Washington:

One [South African] newspaper said US "politicians" [were in attendance]. One television account showed the American flag flying with the South African and other flags as the newscaster spoke of the American representative. SABC radio in one broadcast referred to "the American Ambassador" and in another, "the American representative," as being in attendance along with the representatives of New Zealand and other countries.[284]

---

[279] "21-Gun Salute for Diederichs," *Rand Daily Mail*, December 6, 1977.
[280] "An Empty Ceremony in South Africa," *New York Times*, editorial, December 6, 1977.
[281] "Transkei and Ciskei Attend Celebrations," *Rand Daily Mail*, December 5, 1977.
[282] "It's a Non-event across the Border," *Rand Daily Mail*, December 6, 1977.
[283] "Whites in New Cabinet," *Rand Daily Mail*, December 7, 1977.
[284] State Department Telegram from US Embassy Pretoria to Secretary of State and Cape Town, "Bophuthatswana Reaches 'Greater Independence,'" December 7, 1977, accessed via Wikileaks: wikileaks.org/plusd/cables/1977PRETOR06671_c.html.

None of it was true, and the US Embassy forced them to retract the stories.[285]

The Western press generally either ignored the ceremony altogether, were outright hostile toward it, or brutally mocked it. *The New York Times* called Bophuthatswana's independence an "empty ceremony."[286] *The Times* of London wrote of Bophuthatswana as being "seven blocks of territory from the second independent homeland with that made-in-Pretoria look."[287] English language papers in South Africa likewise took potshots at the proceedings. The *Rand Daily Mail* featured the celebration in several articles and one large society piece, Doc Bikitsha's "Finger on Your Pulse."[288] Bikitsha described the day as having a "rather lacklustre atmosphere," a feeling of "indifferent expectancy," "… the faces of people I passed to the stadium where the takeover was to take place, were not radiant or happy. There was a dull sort of 'let's go and see what's going to take place' look about them … No spunk."[289] Another newspaper described the ceremony as being typical of a Mangope-staged production, combining "raw tribalism with twentieth century pizzazz – bare boobs, bands and some Barnum and Bailey."[290]

The annual commemorations of Bophuthatswana's independence displayed the very same push-pull tension regarding South Africa as did Transkei's, although Bophuthatswana never took the dramatic step of breaking off relations.[291] Unpopular as they were, Mangope's regime made attendance at the annual celebrations mandatory and their coercive efforts only became harsher as time went on.[292] For instance, civil servants and politicians were forced to contribute money to the ceremonies or else forgo their salaries. In addition, the chiefs in the rural areas were pressured to encourage participation among their villagers.[293] These were authoritarian celebrations, where everyone was forced to be happy, but few truly were.

---

[285] State Department Telegram from US Embassy Pretoria to Secretary of State and Cape Town, "Bophuthatswana Reaches 'Greater Independence,'" December 7, 1977, accessed via Wikileaks: wikileaks.org/plusd/cables/1977PRETOR06671_c.html.

[286] "An Empty Ceremony in South Africa," *New York Times*, December 6, 1977.

[287] "'Hollow Monument to an Idea of the Past," *Rand Daily Mail*, December 7, 1977.

[288] Doc Bikitsha's Finger on Your Pulse, "Freedom Ceremony Disjointed Affair," *Rand Daily Mail*, December 12, 1977.

[289] Doc Bikitsha's Finger on Your Pulse, "Freedom Ceremony Disjointed Affair," *Rand Daily Mail*, December 12, 1977.

[290] *Star*, December 10, 1977. Quoted in Jones, "Mmabatho, 'Mother of the People'," p. 125.

[291] See for instance: "SA Risks 'Sinister' Big Brother Image," *Rand Daily Mail*, December 9, 1980.

[292] Jones, "Mmabatho, 'Mother of the People'," p. 135.

[293] Jones, "Mmabatho, 'Mother of the People'," p. 135.

Conclusion

Katanga, Rhodesia, Transkei, and Bophuthatswana performed their Independence Days and subsequent commemorations for multiple audiences, inside and outside their borders. None of the four aspirant states were able to gather any official international support for the celebrations. Katanga was unable to convince even its closest allies to lend official support, or to even send a soccer team. Rhodesia likewise was never able to have official delegations present at its celebrations, even for its large fifth-year celebration in 1970. With the exception of its mother country, South Africa, Transkei and Bophuthatswana were also never able to attract official foreign delegations to either the Independence Day ceremonies, or to subsequent commemorations, even during Transkei's diplomatic break with South Africa.

In staging their Independence Days, all four consciously linked their regimes to different aesthetico-ideological genres. While each of the four was ideologically and politically opposed to African nationalism as it formed across most of the continent, all four were nonetheless drawn to the aesthetic themes of managed decolonization as a legitimizing factor in their own struggles to achieve sovereignty. As such the forms of the independence at midnight ceremonies were exactly mimicked in Transkei, Bophuthatswana, and Rhodesia and were alluded to in Katanga's commemorations. All four also tried to indicate their ideologically friendly positions vis-à-vis the West, especially in terms of continued economic ties, anti-communism, and shared Christian roots, and these can be seen in the commemorations and Independence Day speeches. As each of their commemorations evolved, these national days were also seen as opportunities to craft their national narratives in the images of their respective ruling parties which increasingly became indistinguishable from their states.

The independence narratives of all four aspirant states were contested and disrupted by their opponents. In Katanga's celebrations the physical performances were interrupted, the costuming confiscated, and the day's events regulated by outside forces. In the buildup to Transkei's day, those who participated in organized independence rallies were physically attacked in the republic, its celebrants heckled, and the exhibition boxing match canceled because of the threat of violence to the boxers' families. Bophuthatswana avoided any rallies which could demonstrate the would-be state's lack of popularity, but even so its actual flag swapping was marred by catcalling from the crowd. Katanga's, Rhodesia's, Transkei's, and Bophuthatswana's narratives were upended by the affirmative boycotts placed upon official attendance or participation in their

Independence Day celebrations. Overseas these regimes' days proved to be rallying calls for friends and foes alike. As much as these regimes invested in making their Independence Days and subsequent celebrations a success, opponents of these regimes saw the failure of these events as equally important. As a result, even as their clocks struck twelve during their annual celebrations, for these four, no magic ever came at the midnight hour.

4   The Quest for Recognition

The Historical Importance of Diplomatic Recognition and the Pursuit of International Acceptance

International recognition mattered a great deal to these four pseudo-states, as it continues to matter for all contested states today.[1] Recognition held out potentially dramatic domestic benefits for these regimes and dangled out the opportunity for international aid, access to international markets, and military alliances that could protect their states from threats both internal and external. Widespread recognition would bring these contested states under the same international protections as legal states, guaranteeing their territorial integrity and protecting them from the unlawful use of force. It is not without reason that it has been said that state recognition "is the holy grail of legitimacy."[2] And its denial, as one author wrote, was often "lethal" to aspirant states.[3] This chapter will describe the legal, political, and practical importance of recognition generally, as well as compare and contrast the individual quests for recognition by Katanga, Rhodesia, Transkei, and Bophuthatswana.

While each of their quests was unique in some ways, several through lines can be pulled out that ran through all of them. For one, all four regimes made public statements and gestures that swung back and forth from an extreme optimism bordering on the delusional as to their prospects for recognition, to an equally extreme defeatism and bitterness at the betrayals at the hands of their supposed friends on the other. All four regimes shared the same notion that international recognition could act like a cascade such that if one or two states would break with the collective ban on recognition there would then follow a critical mass of support coming from other states that were too afraid to act independently. Because of this cascade notion, these four states all searched for

---

[1] See: D. Geldenhuys, *Contested States in World Politics* (Palgrave Macmillan, New York, 2009); Bahcheli, *De Facto States*; Caspersen, *Unrecognized States*; Fabry, *Recognizing States*.

[2] Quoted in C. P. Watts, *Rhodesia's Unilateral Declaration of Independence: An International History* (New York: Palgrave Macmillan, 2012) p. 144.

[3] Fabry, *Recognizing States*, p. 7.

that elusive first state to break with the world community anywhere they could find them, through any channels they could discover, and were willing to use any means at their disposal to secure. Each also believed, or purported to believe, that recognition could be achieved in bits and pieces over time, through small concessions of sovereignty. After no state ever came forward to recognize them after their declarations of independence, these aspirant states sometimes made a dramatic gesture that was intended to display to the world their full independence from their former mother states. Finally, after being constantly rejected by the international community, all four retreated to a position that emphasized that recognition per se was not so important after all, and that while the international community would eventually come to see that they were functioning and stable states, in the interim they were content with the status quo. This was, of course, compensatory and untrue.

Diplomatic recognition sits at the intersection of domestic politics and international law.[4] At its core, diplomatic recognition is an existing state acknowledging that an aspiring state has become a fully independent entity separate and apart from any other state, with its own international personality, and is a full and equal member of international society. There are several methods by which recognition may be granted – bilateral or collective, and implicit or explicit – and it can take the direct form of a treaty or a public statement, or an action such as the establishment of embassies or the exchange of resident ambassadors, but can also be inferred from more subtle acts of legal states.[5] There have been several instances of coordinated recognition and nonrecognition, including League of Nations and UN decisions that could be ostensibly binding on member states, nonetheless, diplomatic recognition remains the prerogative of individual states.[6] Writing about the first example of coordinated nonrecognition, the Japanese puppet state of Manchukuo, Joseph O'Mahoney concludes that collective nonrecognition is perhaps best seen as a "symbolic sanction" and not merely a failed attempt at coercion or domestic political posturing, but a "means of creating common knowledge" and "shared understandings" as it concerns international norms of behavior.[7] In addition to expressing these "shared understandings"

---

[4] See: Fabry, *Recognizing States*, p. 7.
[5] For an analysis of these various methods, see: Ker Lindsay, "Engagement without Recognition."
[6] Fabry, *Recognizing States*, p. 8.
[7] See: J. O'Mahoney, "Proclaiming Principles: The Logic of the Nonrecognition of the Spoils of War," *Journal of Global Security Studies*, vol. 2, no. 3 (July 2017) pp. 204–219. Legal scholar Stefan Talmon argues that collective nonrecognition of would-be states that run afoul of international norms should merely "withhold the rights inherent in statehood

about the undesirability of a contested state for recognition, the UN Security Council could also obviously deny a nascent state membership to the body.[8] All four aspirant states in this book were denied membership in the UN, and in the cases of Rhodesia and the Bantustans, the UN General Assembly called on member states not to recognize the new aspirant states even before they declared independence which precluded the possibility that they would apply for membership.[9] With its evolution toward universality and the presumption of state membership, the distinctions between the denial of admission to the UN and collective nonrecognition have become somewhat blurred.[10]

The question of what recognition, or its denial, means in a legal sense has been called the "great debate" among international lawyers; with a broad division in this regard being between the so-called declaratory and constitutive theories.[11] Legal scholars subscribing to the declaratory theory contend that recognition by other states is merely a precondition for the establishment of diplomatic relations and it has no bearing on whether the aspiring state is legal or not.[12] For them, an entity is a state if it meets certain empirical conditions of statehood – sometimes referred to as the Montevideo criteria – regardless of whether or not any other state chooses to recognize it.[13] This is the "prevalent contemporary

from a new state," but that collective nonrecognition alone cannot determine whether an entity is a state or not. "Constitutive versus the Declarative Theory," p. 180.

[8] Talmon makes the point that collective nonrecognition has never been about shared understandings of an aspirant state failing to meet the objective criteria of statehood. "Constitutive versus the Declarative Theory," p. 120.

[9] Admission to the United Nations has often been seen as the functional equivalent of attaining statehood, but UN membership and the achievement of legal statehood are not the same thing. Thomas Grant has traced the evolution of the United Nation's membership criteria from its founding to date and describes a marked change in how the United Nations dealt with membership applications from the early years of the organization when the substantive criteria were taken very seriously, to a "permissive admission practice" which laid the groundwork for near-universal state membership. Thomas Grant, *Admission to the United Nations: Charter Article 4 and the Rise of Universal Organization* (Martinus Nijhoff Publishers, Leiden, 2009).

[10] Quoting Grant: "… recognition remains a part of State practice, and admission to the UN remains at most a 'near analogue' to collective recognition." Grant, *Admission to the United Nations*, p. 256.

[11] For an excellent article analyzing the legal meaning of recognition and nonrecognition, see: Talmon, "The Constitutive versus the Declaratory Theory," p. 101. See also: Fabry, *Recognizing States*.

[12] This accords with Stefan Talmon's argument about the effects of recognition and nonrecognition. "Constitutive versus the Declarative Theory."

[13] Talmon writes, "The now predominant view in the literature is that recognition merely establishes, confirms, or provides evidence of the objective legal situation, that is the existence of the state" ("Constitutive versus the Declarative Theory," p. 105). The Montevideo Convention's empirical criteria for statehood are that the entity must have: (1) a defined territory, (2) a permanent population, (3) a government, and (4) a

view," among legal scholars, one that "... discounts the [legal] significance of recognition," believing it to be only "status-confirming."[14] In contrast, supporters of the constitutive theory argue that a political entity only becomes a legal state through the mechanism of diplomatic recognition, and that "without international recognition, without external sovereignty, any talk of sovereignty is nonsensical, and without sovereignty it makes no sense to talk of statehood ... a state is either recognized or it is not a state."[15] The fulfillment of objective criteria, they argue, does not matter if the entity is not accepted as a part of the international community, and they therefore hold that recognition is not merely "status-confirming," but "status-creating."[16] Put another way, for declaratory theorists if a tree falls in the forest it makes a sound even if no one is there to hear it, but for constitutive theorists, in an empty forest falling trees crash in silence.[17]

In his book *Recognizing States*, Mikulas Fabry focuses on the practice of state recognition rather than the competing legal theories as to its effect, and in it he describes a change over time in how aspirant states have been recognized or denied recognition.[18] From at least the mid-nineteenth century, the international community had generally conceived of self-determination as a negative right – that third parties should not interfere in a people's struggle for sovereignty against their mother state – and only if that new entity were to be successful in establishing sovereign control "as an observable fact" would third parties recognize the new state.[19] But this practice of recognizing sovereign "facts" on the ground would come to be displaced by the 1950s. It was President Woodrow Wilson who would most famously be associated with the refashioning of the notion of self-determination into a positive right that resided with a people that had nothing to do with an aspirant state's actual attainment of the empirical

capacity to enter into relations with other states. Montevideo Convention on the Rights and Duties of States, enacted 1933, accessed via https://treaties.un.org/pages/showdetails.aspx?objid=0800000280166aef, January 24, 2021.

[14] Fabry, *Recognizing States*, p. 2; Talmon, "Constitutive versus the Declarative Theory," p. 101.

[15] Caspersen describes this as the "traditional" or "classical" view of sovereignty, in which a state either possesses sovereignty or does not possess it. She ascribes to the idea that sovereignty should be viewed less as a binary and more as a fluid and nuanced concept. Caspersen, *Unrecognized States*, pp. 13–15.

[16] "Constitutive versus the Declarative Theory," p. 101.

[17] Caspersen argues that recognition matters more than any empirical criteria. Caspersen, *Unrecognized States*.

[18] See: Fabry, *Recognizing States*.   [19] See: Fabry, *Recognizing States*.

criteria of statehood.[20] Only after the Second World War, however, did this principle began to truly become dominant. Afterward, it would be juridical rights that would trump empirical criteria when it came to recognition.[21] No longer would recognition simply be an acknowledgment of facts on the ground that a state already existed, but instead recognition created a protected space for a state to be created.[22] As Mikulas Fabry succinctly summarizes it, state recognition had evolved from "assessing fact to evaluating right."[23]

In this new international environment, the empirical conditions of statehood for a colonial territory were seen as inapplicable, or in any case irrelevant to the peoples' claim for sovereign independence, since only in rare cases had colonial peoples fully liberated their territory from the colonizers. In December 1960, the UN General Assembly passed Resolution 1514, the "Declaration on the Granting of Independence to Colonial Countries and Peoples," which stated that self-determination was a right for "all peoples" and that the colonial powers should "transfer all powers to the peoples of those territories, without any conditions or reservations ..." In doing so, "inadequacy of political, economic, social or educational preparedness should never serve as a pretext for delaying independence."[24] It was hoped, almost as a matter of faith, that the conditions of statehood would be met following independence and international recognition. As Nkrumah famously advised, "Seek ye first the political kingdom and all things shall be added unto you." This was the exact opposite order of the old paradigm.[25] Recognition of ex-colonies by existing states would become, by and large, "automatic."[26] So despite

---

[20] While Wilson intended this concept to apply exclusively to European nationalist claims against the losers of the First World War, his idea nonetheless would serve as an inspiration for non-European peoples around the world under the European empires of the victors of the Second World War. E. Manela, *The Wilsonian Moment: Self-Determination and the International Origins of Anticolonial Nationalism* (Oxford University Press, Oxford, 2007).

[21] Caspersen writes that "the origins of the state may have been added as an additional criterion for international recognition following the end of World War I but it now became the *only* criterion." Caspersen, *Unrecognized States*, p. 18.

[22] Pointing to the example of the UN's policy toward Kosovo in the early 2000s of "standards before status," Caspersen claims that empirical criteria could possibly be reemerging as a trend. This has been termed "earned sovereignty." *Unrecognized States*, p. 20.

[23] Fabry, *Recognizing States*, p. 148.   [24] UNGA Res. 1514.

[25] One result of this, notes Barry Bartmann, is that "we are faced with an absurd combination of states and would-be states existing in a legal fog: some widely recognized states can claim only rudimentary conditions for statehood ... In other cases, fully-functioning and self-contained states are quarantined as pariahs ..." "Political Realities and Legal Anomalies," p. 12.

[26] Fabry, *Recognizing States*, p. 157.

the declaratory theory being in the ascendency as to the legal effect of recognition, with decolonization a whole host of new states achieved widespread recognition "[which] have plainly not met the criteria postulated by the theory or to have been considered as states prior to their recognition," yet at the same time other entities "have met these criteria but are not deemed states."[27]

Once the European empires had broken up into state units mostly corresponding to their former colonial borders, the right to self-determination became once again subordinated to the new states' rights to territorial integrity.[28] "[W]ith its right hand," Rupert Emerson writes, "[the UN] endowed all peoples with the right of self-determination, but with its left hand it denied that people embraced within the newly independent states might appeal to the right on their own behalf ... secession from what purported to be national states was outlawed."[29] Often it was these sovereign rights under international law, including that of territorial integrity, which allowed the new states to survive at all, especially as against domestic challenges to their authority through fragmentation or irredentism.[30] State sovereignty, as Robert Jackson aptly describes it, is "rationed and regulated by those who currently enjoy it."[31] This international turn against secession found its most clear expression in the role the United Nations played in crushing the Katangese secession.[32] In 1970, a decade after Katanga seceded, U Thant outlined how the UN was hostile to any and all secessions, explaining that the United Nations "spent over $500 million in the Congo primarily to prevent the secession of Katanga ... The United Nations' attitude is unequivocal. As an international organization, the UN has never accepted and does not

---

[27] Fabry, *Recognizing States*, p. 4.   [28] Fabry, *Recognizing States*, p. 149.

[29] Emerson, "The New Higher Law of Anti-Colonialism," p. 173.

[30] This argument has been most closely associated with Robert Jackson. See: *Quasi-states*.

[31] Fabry, *Recognizing States*, p. 4, quoting Robert Jackson, *The Global Covenant: Human Conduct in the World of States* (Oxford University Press, Oxford, 2000). As Hillgruber eloquently describes it: "existing states continue to be the 'masters' of the [state admission] procedure." C. Hillgruber, "The Admission of New States to the International Community," *European Journal of International Law* 9 (1998) p. 503. M. Rafiqul Islam argues, that among others, one of the major reasons the Katanga and Biafra secessions failed while Bangladesh succeeded was the fear that these precedents would lead to fragmentation of their own states. Rafiqul Islam, "Secessionist Self-Determination," p. 214.

[32] The generalized prohibition against secession was that it violated the territorial integrity of the mother state, but that was only one rationale for collective nonrecognition. Others included that the contested state violated one of the several peremptory norms of international law. J. Crawford, *The Creation of States in International Law* (Oxford University Press, Oxford, 2006).

accept the principle of secession of a part of its member state."[33] It was on top of this dry, barren international ground that these four would-be states dropped their seeds.

A peculiar aspect of the struggles for recognition of these contested states was that there were certain shared understandings between opponents and proponents. Some of these shared understandings were rooted more in myth and conjecture than evidence, but regardless of their underlying validity, these understandings helped shape the contours of these struggles. One shared understanding was that there was such a thing as "creeping recognition," wherein a sovereign state could unintentionally recognize a contested state through an accumulation of certain behaviors and actions that taken together acknowledged the legitimacy of the aspiring state.[34] In several instances concerning these aspirant states, the US State Department, the British Foreign Office, and South African DFA debated the possible inadvertent legal effects of certain actions and interactions and agonized over the possibility that recognition could be accidentally conferred. Parallel to this, all four aspirant states forthrightly pursued the strategy of creeping recognition as a path toward international acceptance – a strategy that Rhodesia's last High Commissioner in London, Alexander Skeen, sneeringly termed the "softly, softly catchee monkey" approach.[35]

It is in retrospect surprising that both opponents and supporters of these aspirant states believed in this possibility of inadvertent recognition when the bulk of international practice and legal opinion concludes that

[33] Secretary-General Press Conference in Dakar, Senegal, January 4, 1970. *UN Monthly Chronicle*, no. 7 (February 1970), quoted in Fabry, *Recognizing States*, p. 167. Some apparent exceptions to this general rule did emerge, in particular in cases of extreme human rights violations, known as "remedial secession," such as in Bangladesh's secession from Pakistan, as well as Kosovo's secession from Serbia. The latter's recognition has split the international community. Whether or not this exception exists as a matter of international law, and when it applies, is not without controversy. Biafra, for instance, made legitimate claims for statehood based in part upon the central government's pogroms against the Igbo people. Nevertheless, Biafra was not recognized by the majority of states and was rejected by the OAU and UN.

[34] Creeping recognition of a government, as opposed to a state, had occurred in the past, as with Britain's implicit recognition of Franco's Spain in the 1930s. In the case of Franco's Spain, the British Opposition feared that Franco's government would gain recognition in stages, and that Britain's *de facto* recognition would ripen to *de jure* status, a prediction that proved true as Britain granted de jure recognition to Franco in 1939. H. W. Briggs, "Relations Officieuses and Intent to Recognize: British Recognition of Franco," *The American Journal of International Law*, vol. 34, no. 1 (January 1940) pp. 50–52. British recognition of Franco's government would be an example of what Talmon would describe as recognition *of a State*, as opposed to recognition *as a State*. There was no question as to whether or not Spain existed as a state, only what government represented Spain. Talmon, "Constitutive versus the Declarative Theory," p. 108.

[35] Skeen, *Prelude*, p. 50.

creeping recognition was largely a myth.[36] An explicit policy of nonre-cognition cannot be negated by any subsequent actions that may imply recognition. For instance, the United States maintained commercial and economic connections with Manchukuo despite being the political force behind Manchukuo's collective nonrecognition.[37] More recently, the Turkish Republic of Northern Cyprus (TRNC) has been recognized by no other country besides Turkey, yet the United States, Britain, and Germany maintain "information offices" in Northern Nicosia, and the TRNC maintains unaccredited liaison offices in several foreign cap-itals.[38] Somaliland, which has not been formally recognized by any other state or international organization, has established informal ties with Ethiopia and other neighboring states, and it is home to several offices from European Union and UN aid agencies.[39] But despite these diplo-matic interactions that might seem to imply a form of recognition, political scientist James Ker Lindsay argues persuasively that "intent is crucial," and that if a state avoids only those acts which are indisputably acts of recognition, then their stated intentions on the matter are dis-positive.[40] Similarly, Thomas De Waal summarized the bulk of inter-national legal opinion and claimed that fears of creeping recognition are unfounded. He writes, "Concerns in the recognized states that greater engagement will lead to 'creeping recognition' of the territories is not borne out by legal opinion, which concludes that recognition is a con-scious act and cannot be conferred by accident."[41]

If the creeping approach could not actually result in inadvertent rec-ognition then why did all sides choose to behave as though this was a real possibility? It was likely because this was a useful fiction. For Western opponents of these regimes, the notion of creeping sovereignty raised the stakes of seemingly small actions or omissions and served as a useful rhetorical weapon to hammer their own governments for being too soft on these regimes. These would-be states and their friends abroad had more straightforward reasons to contend that creeping sovereignty was a backdoor to diplomatic recognition: This was the only argument they

---

[36] In correspondence with the author James Ker-Lindsay has indicated that in all of its instances, the strategy of creeping sovereignty has never been able to push an aspirant state over that final threshold of recognition.

[37] Caspersen, *Unrecognized States*, p. 43.

[38] In 2014, then-Vice President Joe Biden even met with the Turkish Cypriot leader in the contested state. Ker Lindsay, "Engagement without Recognition."

[39] See Caspersen, *Unrecognized States*.

[40] Ker Lindsay, "Engagement without Recognition."

[41] Thomas De Waal, *Uncertain Ground: Engaging with Europe's De Facto States and Breakaway Territories* (Carnegie Endowment for International Peace, Washington, DC, 2018) p. 1.

had. There were both foreign and domestic reasons for these regimes to argue that recognition was not simply a binary switch that was permanently shut off for them but instead to emphasize that they were incrementally making progress toward securing acceptance. Creeping sovereignty was a way to fit small victories into a larger narrative of struggle and these crumbs provided vital political nutrients.

From the perspective of Western governments, fine-tuning status-raising contacts with these unrecognized states held out political advantages domestically and internationally. Within Britain and the United States (and in the case of Katanga, Belgium) there were powerful political forces pushing for the recognition of these states, and contrary forces pushing the other way, including significant diplomatic pressures applied by African states.[42] What is notable is that Western political swings between the right and the left did result in alternating softer and harder policies toward these aspirant states, but they all operated within certain parameters. In Belgium the replacement of Prime Minister Gaston Eyskens' government with that of Theo Lefevre's in April 1961 brought with it a decidedly less friendly attitude toward Katanga.[43] In the United States, the Eisenhower administration was much less concerned with the Katanga secession than Leopoldville's possible communist drift, and even though Kennedy's administration would move toward a more aggressive stance against Tshombe his administration tempered its policies in response to the powerful Katanga lobby. In Britain, Harold Macmillan's Conservative government was sympathetic to Katanga even while formally correct in its dealings with the illegal regime.[44] Always implacably hostile toward Rhodesia's UDI, Harold Wilson's Labour government nonetheless moved cautiously against it, allowing, for instance, the continued operation of Rhodesia House until 1969. With the election of Edward Heath in 1970 there was a reengagement with Rhodesia that ultimately led to the doomed Anglo-Rhodesian agreement, and the rebellion continued. Richard Nixon was much more lenient toward Rhodesia, and Southern Africa generally, than was Lyndon Johnson's administration, but this leniency never rose to the level of formal relations. And though the Carter administration was morally

---

[42] For more on African diplomatic efforts to bring an end to apartheid, in particular the "Africa Group," see: Irwin, *Gordian Knot*.

[43] Gerard-Libois, *Katanga Secession*.

[44] Alan James describes how part of Britain's relatively sympathetic attitude toward the Katangese secession can be traced to the close ties between elites in the CAF, who were predominantly white Rhodesians, and members of the Tory Party in Britain. See A. James, *Britain and the Congo Crisis, 1960–63* (MacMillan Press, London, 1996) chapter 13.

opposed to the white settler government in Rhodesia, he still was hesitant to shut down the RIO for fear of butting up against the strong pro-Rhodesian lobby.[45] The election of Margaret Thatcher in 1979 seemed to indicate a change in British policy toward recognition of the newly constituted Zimbabwe Rhodesia, but her government did not change Britain's long-standing policy on nonrecognition, a decision that was influenced by Carter's decision to also withhold recognition.[46] Neither did Thatcher's government recognize the Bantustans. Finally, Ronald Reagan's defeat of Jimmy Carter raised hopes among some that he would recognize the Bantustans, but while his administration's policy of "constructive engagement" did mark a shift toward a more conciliatory approach to South Africa, recognition was still off the table. As will be seen, Western governments on the right instituted more friendly relations toward these aspirant states short of full recognition, and those on the left put into place more unfriendly policies but were themselves keenly aware of the domestic backlash of moving too aggressively. Accordingly, the binary of recognition or nonrecognition was politically too crude of an instrument to be useful, so the dialing-up or dialing-down pressure on these contested states were used as finely calibrated gifts or punishments that could be granted to domestic lobbies on both sides of these struggles.

The idea of cascading recognition was another understanding shared by both sides of these struggles. Despite international recognition being within the prerogative of individual states, the order and pacing of recognition certainly mattered, and legal states factored in the likely actions of other states in their recognition decisions. Even if a sovereign state were sympathetic to a secessionist project, being out-front and alone on the question of recognition could put that state in a risky political position. Not only did it often mean angering the mother state – indeed, it could be seen as an act of war – but it could also mean attracting the ire of the broader international community and possibly significant sections of domestic popular opinion. These risks were possibly abated if the recognizing state were part of a cascade of support for the secessionist project and not isolated. Related to this, in the international politics of African decolonization, the West generally deferred to African states on the issue of the recognition. Against the international

---

[45] See: A. Lake, *The "Tar Baby" Option: American Policy toward Southern Rhodesia* (Columbia University Press, New York, 1976); Eddie Michel, "'This Outcome Gives Me No Pleasure. It Is Extremely Painful for Me to Be the Instrument of Their Fate': White House Policy on Rhodesia during the UDI Era (1965–1979)," *South African Historical Journal*, vol. 71, no. 3 (2018).

[46] Michel, "This Outcome," p. 21.

context of the assumption of a cascade effect, it made sense that these aspirant states probed the walls of their collective nonrecognition looking for loose bricks.[47] In response, the international community's fear of a cascade of recognition spurred a parallel effort to maintain the integrity of the international wall and ensure that every legal state continued to refuse recognition.[48]

Once again, the example of Biafra looms large. In that conflict, as in the ones discussed here, a major effort was made to sell the Biafran cause abroad to win support and ultimately recognition.[49] Eventually, Tanzania, Zambia, Gabon, the Ivory Coast, and Haiti each recognized Biafran independence. But these states' decisions did not lead to a flood of recognition from the West as Ojukwu had hoped. Ojukwu claimed that South Africa very nearly recognized Biafra, and France as well.[50] As was the case with Transkei, where the United States and Western Europe were supposedly waiting on the decisions of African countries, Ojukwu had suspected that other African countries were waiting on France to move first, or was using them for political cover to mask their own inaction.[51] Completing the circle, in a September 1968 meeting between French and Biafran representatives in Paris, the French expressed their support for the secessionist state, but stated that official recognition would not be forthcoming until more African states recognized Biafra first.[52] They never did, so France never did, and no cascade occurred.

Because of these two shared beliefs on both sides of these conflicts over the recognition of these four contested states – of the possibility of creeping recognition and of the nature of cascading recognition – these four conflicts played out in very similar ways. Katanga, Rhodesia, Transkei, and Bophuthatswana all tried to make incremental gains internationally, pushing their diplomatic statuses overseas in one direction until no more progress could be made, then turning and trying from a different angle. Each small instance of progress celebrated, and each small setback decried as an injustice. And all the while, they entertained dreams that once a single brave country recognized them, especially were it an African country, then diplomatic recognition would fall onto them like confetti from a ticker-tape parade.

---

[47] The small island state of Naura, in the Pacific Ocean, which besides its sovereign status has little economic prospects, has even made it a practice of selling recognition in return for international aid. Ellen Barry, "Abkhazia Is Recognized – By Nauru," *New York Times*, December 15, 2009.

[48] J. Nkala, *The United Nations, International Law, and the Rhodesian Independence Crisis* (Clarendon Press, Oxford, 1985) pp. 67–68, chapter 4.

[49] Gould, *The Biafran War*, p. 75.   [50] Gould, *The Biafran War*, p. 109.

[51] Gould, *The Biafran War*, p. 109.   [52] Gould, *The Biafran War*, p. 116.

Katanga

Even before Katanga's final declaration of independence on July 11, 1960, Katangese officials already knew that formal recognition would be a formidable task. Tshombe's and his CONAKAT party's intention to break away from the rest of the Congo was widely known even before Congolese independence, and Belgium and the world community already signaled that the new state would not exactly be welcomed with open arms. On June 25, Belgian authorities became aware of a secessionist plot that was in the works, one that seemed to be further along than the one they had thwarted only ten days before. It was discovered that Tshombe had reached out to a former Belgian police officer in Katanga, Francois Scheerlink. The plot was to have Scheerlink act as a "special ambassador" for the state of Katanga, and an airplane itinerary had him flying to Elisabethville, Brussels, New York, and Washington.[53] His accreditation letter presaged Tshombe's letter to Michel Struelens, the future head of the Katanga Information Service (KIS) in New York. Both Scheerlink and Struelens would be charged with the same small task of winning overseas support and recognition for the breakaway region. Under Belgian interrogation, Scheerlink outlined Tshombe's plan:

Separation [of Katanga] would be effected by a proclamation of the provincial government asking recognition for the independence of Katanga from Belgium and the United States. Recognition was also to be sought in the countries bordering the Congo, and in England and Portugal. Simultaneously, an appeal would be made to the UN. For the Katangan provincial government, it would be a race against the clock.[54]

The plot failed, and Scheerlinck was arrested by the Belgians five days before Congolese independence.[55] But the idea never disappeared.[56]

The Congo became independent on June 30, 1960. Prior to Tshombe's declaration a week and a half later, Belgium's Foreign Minister Pierre Wigny had sent out telegrams to several Western powers explaining why Belgium would not recognize Katangese

---

[53] Othen, *Katanga 1960–1963*, pp. 49–51.
[54] Quoted in Gerard-Libois, *Katanga Secession*, pp. 86–87.
[55] Othen, *Katanga 1960–1963*, p. 49.
[56] The South African consul in Elisabethville reported on the day of Congo's independence that Tshombe had approached South Africa with his intention to secede and what this might mean for South Africa. National Archives of South Africa, Box 1/112/3/1, Secession of Katanga, Telegram from SA Consul Elisabethville to Secretary External Affairs, Pretoria, June 30, 1960. #467.

independence.[57] Many of the reasons offered for this rejection were familiar: That Katanga leaving would render the rest of the Congo economically unviable and therefore easy prey for communists, but interestingly also that if Belgium recognized Tshombe it would actually undermine Tshombe's legitimacy and render him a neocolonial stooge.[58] This is very similar to the uncomfortable dance South Africa would play with its Bantustans, in which the former mother state worried about how their breakaway states could be seen as their puppets. Tshombe had hoped that Belgium would be the first state to recognize his regime after which others would soon follow its lead. Undeterred, Tshombe made his declaration.

From Katanga's perspective, Belgium was sending mixed signals, simultaneously providing significant technical and military assistance to Katanga, especially in the early months of the secession, but avoiding formal relations. A delegation from Katanga was sent out to Brussels several weeks after the proclamation and was received by King Baudouin I himself, but no recognition followed. Katanga's Minister of the Interior, Godfroid Munungo, expressed his "surprise, disappointment, and sadness" at Belgium's failure to recognize Katanga.[59] Munungo rhetorically asked whether Katanga should have fostered disorder and violence like Lumumba's government in order to be recognized: "Must we have murders first?"[60] Munongo's response would be repeated in slightly different variations by the leaders of the two Bantustans in this study. Kaiser Matanzima and Lucas Mangope often made a similar self-pitying claim that Transkei and Bophuthatswana, respectively, were unfairly targeted by the world community because they achieved independence from their former master peacefully and without bloodshed.[61] Four days after Transkei's independence, Matanzima boomed in an angry speech to the National Assembly that the UN was "a noisy conglomeration of ... bloodthirsty people," and argued that only states born of violence were to be recognized by the UN.[62] This argument was often accompanied by a tongue-in-cheek joke that such bloodshed could still be delivered if that would help.

While all four aspirant states assumed that recognition, if it came at all, would be in a cascade, no sovereign state wanted to be the first and only

---

[57] Alexis Heraclides, *The Self-Determination of Minorities in International Politics* (Taylor & Francis, New York, 1991).
[58] Heraclides, *Self-Determination of Minorities*, p. 72.
[59] "Katanga's Self-Gov Hopes Fade," *Rand Daily Mail*, July 25, 1960.
[60] "Katanga's Self-Gov Hopes Fade," *Rand Daily Mail*, July 25, 1960.
[61] "Transkei Won't Apply to Join UN-Kaiser," *Daily Dispatch*, June 24, 1976.
[62] Quoted in Stultz, *Transkei's Half Loaf*, p. 121.

state to expose itself by recognizing one of these states if no other state followed. As reported by the South African government in a secret telegram, in early August 1960 the Belgians were on the cusp of recognizing Katanga, but their concern was that they did not want to hang out there for long as the sole recognizing state. The message was relayed by a senior official at Sabena to the South African minister of transport.

[H]e was bringing a message from Belgian Government that they would decide this afternoon whether or not to recognize Katanga and they hoped that if they did Union would follow suit immediately. He explained that channel used was because of secrecy.[63]

As it turned out, the Belgian Cabinet met on August 2 and announced that its position on recognition had not changed.[64]

When recognition never came in the months after the secession, it was Tshombe this time who aimed his fire at his former colonial leaders. In a statement made on October 9, 1960, Tshombe said, "There will be a diplomatic rupture if things go on like this. We have had enough. If Belgium was a sincere and honest country she would recognise Katanga's independence. We want to collaborate with everyone, but we do not want them interfering in our affairs ... [the Belgians must] consider themselves as foreigners in Katanga."[65] This line of argument was a clever pivot from accusations that these regimes were in fact still controlled by their former masters. Katanga's threats against Belgium, much like Transkei's later threats against South Africa, were intended for an audience other than their former colonial masters. Just as Katanga had many continued links and lines of communication with Belgium, the Bantustans had numerous ongoing formal and informal ways they could convey messages directly to South Africa had that truly been the intent. Instead, these were public fights for the international community to witness as evidence of the breakaway states' freedom of movement.

Hours before he was to declare Katanga's independence, Tshombe told the American consul in Elisabethville of his intentions and demanded recognition.[66] At first, the United States was noncommittal, acting on the State Department's vague instruction beforehand: "In general we wish Tshombe discouraged [sic], but we do not wish to close

---

[63] SA National Archives, Box 1/112/3/1, "Secession of Katanga," Telegram from Secretary of External Affairs, Pretoria, to SA Embassy in Brussels, August 2, 1960.

[64] SA National Archives, Box 1/112/3/1, "Secession of Katanga," Telegram from SA Embassy in Brussels to Secretary of External Affairs, Pretoria, August 3, 1960.

[65] "Tshombe's Threat to Belgium," Rand Daily Mail, October 10, 1960.

[66] SA National Archives, Box 1/112/3/1, "Secession of Katanga," Telegram from SA High Commissioner in London to Secretary for External Affairs, Pretoria, July 14, 1960.

door completely since detachment Katanga could conceivably be in interest West if rest of Congo continues in present status."[67] On July 14, 1960, Tshombe sent out a priority telegram to several foreign ministries, including the United States, making a direct plea for recognition. In its style it was very different from his initial declaration three days before, though the substance was largely the same.[68] The view of the United States toward Tshombe's telegram was summarized in a diplomatic cable by the South Africans:

United States Government replied to Tshombe that they were not prepared at this stage to consider extending recognition. United States view is that dust must be allowed to settle first. However, their basis thinking is that Africa should not be broken up into large number of economically non-viable States. United States certainly would be unable to meet all demands for economic aid without which these States would be easy prey for communism. By itself Katanga would be economically viable, but not so Congo without it.[69]

While not immediately dismissing the idea of recognizing Katanga, the United States decided it could not go first. If other states came around on recognition, some in the State Department thought that "the US might reconsider its position."[70] But that was as close as the United States ever came.

The British Foreign Office adopted a similar line of argument as the United States in denying formal recognition to Katanga. This was how the South African High Commission in London summarized the position of the British Foreign Office in the days after the declaration:

Present thinking is that Western Countries cannot afford to give Tshombe encouragement to secede as secession of Katanga would make Congo dangerously weak economically and any country which supports such a step would incur heavy censure for aiding break-up of Congo, it is felt that in these circumstances even Belgians unlikely to risk recognition at this stage.[71]

---

[67] Quoting State Department Telegram. Othen, *Katanga 1960–1963*, p. 53.

[68] SA National Archives, Box 1/112/3/1, "Secession of Katanga," En Clair Telegram from Moise Tshombe to Secretary for External Affairs, Pretoria, July 14, 1960.

[69] SA National Archives, Box 1/112/3/1, "Secession of Katanga," Telegram from SA Embassy in Washington to Secretary for External Affairs, July 15, 1960.

[70] Mahoney quoting from a State Department Telegram cited in Analytical Chronology. R. D. Mahoney, *JFK: Ordeal in Africa* (Oxford University Press, Oxford, 1983), p. 54, fn. 108.

[71] SA National Archives, Box 1/112/3/1, "Secession of Katanga," Telegram from SA High Commission to Secretary External Affairs, July 16, 1960.

The Foreign Office received Tshombe's telegram from July 14th calling for recognition, but decided not to reply back.[72] For one, the Foreign Office was not convinced that Tshombe had achieved de facto independence, citing the presence of Belgian troops and their imminent replacement with UN troops, reverting to the Montevideo criteria of effective statehood.[73] Throughout the secession, Britain walked a very thin line, and while it never openly supported Katanga, it was unenthusiastic, to say the least, about the UN mission in the Congo and President Kennedy's efforts to bring the secession to a swift end.

Britain and the quasi-dominion of CAF were always publicly cautious and correct with regard to Katanga, but behind the scenes Salisbury and London clashed over the Congo Crisis. Because of its geographic location surrounding Katanga like a holster to a gun, the CAF was probably Katanga's most important regional ally. Prime Minister Sir Roy Welensky's government supported the breakaway state in numerous ways, and tried in vain to have Britain officially recognize Katanga – Welensky argued that doing so would be for "the good of the Free World."[74] But the federation was an especially odd case because it was itself not a fully sovereign state, even though the British government treated it as a quasi-dominion. Though it did not have the legal capacity to recognize new states, Welensky was careful not to overtly support Katanga's secession, as evidenced by the hesitation to be seen participating in the independence celebrations discussed in the previous chapter.[75] Reporting on a meeting with federation officials, the South Africans relayed that the federation government thought if it was seen that they were openly on the side of Tshombe it "would probably do his cause more harm than good. It was obvious that the opposition of the Afro-Asian group to Tshombe's regime was provoked by the feeling that he was nothing more than a stooge for the Belgians. If the Federation

---

[72] SA National Archives, Box 1/112/3/1, "Secession of Katanga," Memorandum from Harold Taswell, SA High Commission in London, to Secretary External Affairs, July 19, 1960.

[73] SA National Archives, Box 1/112/3/1, "Secession of Katanga," Memorandum from Harold Taswell, SA High Commission in London, to Secretary External Affairs, July 19, 1960.

[74] Quoted in Heraclides, *Self-Determination of Minorities*, p. 73.

[75] Heraclides claims Welensky's support for Katanga was "total and uninhibited," but while his government was constantly pressuring Britain to makes its support for Katanga more overt, Welensky too was cautious at times not to get too out-front on the Katanga issue. For example, he always made pains to emphasize that Tshombe was not really a secessionist, but a frustrated federalist. Heraclides, *Self-Determination of Minorities* p. 72.

supported him it would only strengthen the group's feeling."[76] Like the South Africans, the federation sent a private message of sympathy to Tshombe.

South Africa proved to be a friend of Katanga that demanded to operate behind-the-scenes and unofficially, like Belgium and the federation. The republic did not comply with United Nations policies regarding Katanga, both out of an innate sympathy for Tshombe's cause but more so out of principle that such interventions could become a precedent that would later be turned against the republic. The republic was an open recruiting ground for Katangese mercenaries, something that was at least tacitly approved of by the government, it traded openly with Katanga in defiance of UN resolutions, and publicly opposed all UN initiatives putting any kind of pressure on Tshombe.[77] In the days after the declaration, South Africa received Tshombe's formal plea for recognition. Like the British, South Africa did not reply to the telegram directly. The advice expressed by the South African high commissioner in London to Pretoria following a report on British nonrecognition, suggested "... you may wish to defer reply to Tshombe until de facto situation develops to degree where recognition becomes unexceptional."[78] Those conditions were never seen to be met, and so recognition from South Africa never followed. South Africa expressed their support of Tshombe privately, and never granted Katanga formal recognition.[79]

Harold Taswell, who would later become the South African Ambassador to the United States, was in 1960 the South African High Commissioner in Salisbury in the federation. He wrote a memorandum on the issue of formal recognition which he sent to the DFA in Pretoria. Taswell's memorandum concluded:

My own feeling for what it is worth is that it probably would not do the Union or Tshombe any good for us to be the first to recognize him. While there are a considerable number of arguments against it, there might be some merit in [P.R.] Killen's crossing the border to have an informal talk with Tshombe and say that

---

[76] SA National Archives, Box 1/112/3/1, "Secession of Katanga," Memorandum from Harold Taswell, SA High Commission in Salisbury, to Secretary External Affairs, "Katanga and the Federation," August 9, 1960.

[77] Pfister, *Pariah to Middle Power*, pp. 33–36.

[78] SA National Archives, Box 1/112/3/1, "Secession of Katanga," Telegram from SA High Commission to Secretary External Affairs, July 16, 1960.

[79] For an excellent study of South Africa's policy regarding Katanga, see: Passemiers, "Safeguarding White Minority Power."

whereas we have great sympathy with his cause recognition of his Government at this stage might cause more embarrassment than good.[80]

Taswell's last observation would be a consistent line through the pursuit of recognition for all four pseudo-states, namely that their relationships with South Africa were mixed blessings which might better at times be hidden from view rather than celebrated, a view that accorded well with South Africa's own interests. Taswell would elaborate on this point in another memorandum three days later after speaking with two Belgians who formerly held senior positions in Katanga: "On the question of recognition both [Belgian] officials feel that if we [South Africa] were the first to recognize the Katanga we would be doing Tshombe's cause a disservice rather than a favour because of our unpopularity with black states generally."[81]

There were other states that were also privately sympathetic to Katanga, but fell short of formal recognition. These included several states in francophone Africa, including the Central African Republic, Madagascar, Cameroon, the Ivory Coast, and Niger.[82] It is no surprise that it was again these same francophone countries where South Africa believed it could achieve the recognition breakthrough with the Bantustans a decade and a half later.[83] France itself was sympathetic to Katanga: supporting Belgium internationally and opposing UN involvement, looking the other way at mercenary recruitment, and selling weaponry into the territory. French Equatorial Africa also denied airspace to ONUC and US military planes in support of ONUC, while allowing Katangese flyover rights.[84] According to Gerard-Libois, French recognition seemed close to happening in April 1961 when France made certain overtures to Katanga that it would support the pro-western Brazzaville Group countries recognition of Katanga and would itself open a

---

[80] SA National Archives, Box 1/112/3/1, "Secession of Katanga," Memorandum from Harold Taswell, SA High Commission in Salisbury, to Secretary External Affairs, "Recognition of Tshombe's Government," July 16, 1960.

[81] SA National Archives, Box 1/112/3/1, "Secession of Katanga," Memorandum from Harold Taswell, SA High Commission in Salisbury, to Secretary External Affairs, "Recognition of Katanga's Independence," July 19, 1960.

[82] Heraclides, *Self-Determination of Minorities*, p. 76.

[83] The Brazzaville Group, with Ivory Coast's Felix Houphouet-Boigny at the forefront, was seen by many to be a moderate counterweight to the more radical Casablanca Group headed by Ghana and Guinea. Generally, France and its former sub-Saharan colonies maintained very close ties, cemented in part through various bilateral cooperation and aid agreements created in the early 1960s. As a result, they tended to be far less interested in accusations of neocolonialism since many among them had been labeled the same. See: Andereggen, *France's Relationship*, chapter 6.

[84] Heraclides, *Self-Determination of Minorities*, p. 72.

consulate in Elisabethville.[85] Presaging what would be its position toward Biafra, France would provide hope and material support but never grant official recognition to Katanga.

Portugal was also friendly to Katanga. Lisbon did everything it could to thwart ONUC, denying UN overflights and not allowing the stationing of a UN observer in Portuguese Angola to monitor the mercenary paths into Katanga.[86] Angola remained a vital link to and from South Africa to Katanga, providing a friendly route for mercenaries and military equipment.[87] It was also through Angola and the Benguela Railroad that Katanga was able to export most of its vitally important minerals. The Katangese sent a delegation headed by Evariste Kimba, the soon-to-be foreign minister of Katanga, to Lisbon in the first several weeks after Tshombe's declaration.[88] Predictably, the question of recognition was brought up in the meeting. The Portuguese relayed their conversation with the delegation to the South African Embassy who sent it on to Pretoria:

The question of recognition was also raised and Dr. Nogueira [Director-General of Political Affairs in the Portuguese Foreign Office] explained to them that under the present political constellation, recognition by Portugal or by the Rhodesian Federation or the Union, would play into the hands of their enemies and suggested that they might sound out countries like Nigeria or Senegal to take the initial step.[89]

The closest Katanga came to achieving formal recognition was from President Fulbert Youlou's Congo-Brazzaville. Youlou was reportedly considering recognizing Katanga just prior to Lumumba's assassination in January, and even afterward he treated Katanga as a de facto state. Youlou interacted with Tshombe as though he were a Head of State, inviting him to the 1960 Brazzaville Conference as the President of Katanga, and even paying a pseudo-state visit to Katanga in 1961.[90] Yet even these actions were not enough to imply full recognition.

---

[85] Gerard-Libois, *Katanga Secession*, p. 184.

[86] Heraclides, *Self-Determination of Minorities*, p. 75.

[87] Heraclides, *Self-Determination of Minorities*, p. 75. Katanga also had an unofficial representative in Lisbon, "a somewhat shadowy figure" named H. A. Lester through whom Katangese requests to Portugal for arms and assistance were routed. See: de Meneses and McNamara, *The White Redoubt*, p. 90.

[88] SA National Archives, Box 1/112/3/1, "Secession of Katanga," Memorandum from AHH Mertsch, SA Ambassador to Portugal to Acting Secretary for External Affairs, Pretoria, "Visit to Lisbon of Katanga Delegation," September 2, 1960.

[89] SA National Archives, Box 1/112/3/1, "Secession of Katanga," Memorandum from AHH Mertsch, SA Ambassador to Portugal to Acting Secretary for External Affairs, Pretoria, "Visit to Lisbon of Katanga Delegation," September 2, 1960.

[90] Heraclides, *Self-Determination of Minorities*, p. 74.

Katanga's rejection by the international community took various forms. Sometimes these were formal diplomatic statements of nonrecognition by individual states, and there were also collective responses, such as that of UN Resolution 169 rejecting Katanga's claim to be a sovereign nation. But far more often they took the form of small denials of direct contacts and forced re-routings of state-to-state communications. For instance, on July 18, 1960 the Katanga government under Tshombe sent an ultimatum to the UN headquarters demanding a decision on the recognition of Katanga's independence within 48 hours.[91] There was no reply, there could not be: The UN did not think Katanga existed as an entity to which it could respond. An illustration of how the UN Secretariat shunned Katanga can be seen in February 1961, when Michel Struelens, Katanga's pseudo-ambassador to the United States whose activities are analyzed in detail in another chapter, delivered a message from Tshombe directly to Secretary-General Dag Hammarskjold's offices in the UN headquarters, which was only a few blocks away from Streulens' Katanga Information Service (KIS) office. In response to the message, Hammarskjold sent a telegram directly from New York to the UN office in Elisabethville advising them to pass the following message on to Tshombe:

The Secretary General of the United Nations is not in a position to accept any message from Mr. Tshombe sent to him by an agency which is not recognised instrumentality of the Republic of the Congo. For messages to the Secretary General the channels established by the United Nations in the Republic of the Congo are available.[92]

The UN was careful throughout every interaction with Katanga to ensure that nothing it did could imply recognition. Yet sometimes it drifted very close. To bring an end to the fighting during Operation Morthor on September 20, 1961, Tshombe and Mahmoud Khiary, the UN Civilian Operations Chief, signed a ceasefire agreement in Ndola, Northern Rhodesia. The text of the ceasefire read that it was a "protocol agreement between the Katanga authorities and ONUC" and it was signed by "President Tshombe on behalf of the Katanga Government" and Khiary for the UN, and the document was approved by the UN

---

[91] "Uprising Is Feared in Congo," *Rand Daily Mail*, July 19, 1960.

[92] UN Archives, S-0793-0019-10, "Subject Files: Special Assistant to Chief UN Representative – Mercenaries and Political Advisors: Case Files – Struelens, Michel – Political Advisors Part III," February 11–17, 1961. "Telegram from ONUC Leopoldville to ONUC Elisabethville," February 1961.

Secretariat in New York.[93] This document opened up a slew of problems for the UN, because it seemingly acknowledged Tshombe's title and authority. In approving the ceasefire document, the UN Secretariat clarified that this was of a strictly military nature and did not imply recognition.[94] The Soviet Union, for one, was not satisfied, charging that by engaging with the "mercenary and separatist bands [the UN was] thereby appearing to recognize the legality of their existence and their official status."[95] Leopoldville was upset as well, arguing that "no agreement may be concluded between the United Nations and a provincial government ... except where the legally invested Central Government has been consulted and its prior agreement obtained."[96] But as R. Simmonds rightly points out, the UN had little choice but to deal with Tshombe as though he was the authority in Katanga, because he was the only authority in Katanga.[97]

On their end, the Katangese were emboldened by the ceasefire, which was read by the regime as a victory on multiple fronts. Increasing tensions between the Katangese Gendarmerie and UN forces, combined with the questions swirling around Dag Hammarskjold's plane crash in Northern Rhodesia, led the UN Security Council to pass Resolution 169, which among other things was the most explicit expression of the UN's policy of the nonrecognition of Katanga.[98] The resolution also seems to read as a response to the criticisms lobbed at the UN after the ceasefire and the apparent slide toward recognition.

As trivial as they seemed, and belying their small size, postage stamps can be evidence of statehood, and one of the stranger examples of the UN's efforts to preempt Katangese expressions of sovereignty was in U Thant's response to Katanga's issuing of postage stamps. Katangese stamps were accepted as valid postage by some state members of the Universal Postal Union (UPU), the specialized agency of the UN that is the regulating body for international postage. Seeing this potential slide into de facto recognition through the acceptance of their rebel province's stamps, the Congolese central government protested and in 1962 the United Nations General Secretary U Thant wrote to all UN member

---

[93] R. Simmonds, *Legal Problems Arising from the United Nations Military Operations in the Congo* (Martinus Nijhoff, Leiden, 1968) p. 211.

[94] Simmonds, *Legal Problems*, p. 212.   [95] Quoted in Simmonds, *Legal Problems*, p. 212.

[96] Quoted in Simmonds, *Legal Problems*, p. 212.

[97] Simmonds, *Legal Problems*, p. 213. Negotiations regarding ceasefire and ending of hostilities was also one of the exceptions cited by James Ker-Lindsay to the normal implications that engaging with contested states on a state-to-state level could imply recognition. Ker Lindsay, "Engagement without Recognition."

[98] J. Koops, N. MacQueen, T. Tardy, and P. D. Williams (eds.), *Oxford Handbook of UN Peacekeeping Operations* (Oxford University Press, Oxford, 2015) p. 165.

states, the UPU, and a separate letter to the South African Permanent Representative to the UN, urging them all not to treat Katangese stamps as valid postage, reminding all concerned that only the central Congolese authorities out of Leopoldville had the legal authority to issue stamps.[99] The denial of the stamps by all states, and in particular Katanga's ally of South Africa, was seen by Thant as being crucial to solving, "the problem of Katanga."[100]

In what would turn out to be the dying days of state of Katanga, Tshombe made a last appeal for recognition through an international alliance. In November 1962, Tshombe visited Roy Welensky in Salisbury. He proposed to Welensky that a pact be formed between Katanga, the federation, Mozambique and Angola, and South Africa.[101] Welensky reportedly agreed to pass the information on but reiterated to Tshombe the same policy line taken by South Africa and Portugal from the beginning of the secession: "... Sir Roy said he doubted the wisdom of an actual pact which could do the Katanga more harm than good. All countries were friendly and could be relied upon to help one another in certain circumstances." Tshombe also mentioned to Welensky that he thought the time was right for Katanga and South Africa to have formal trade talks, and that among the many items on a possible agenda would be the fact that Katanga wanted to move away from buying so much French wine and buy more South African wine.[102] Katanga later approached the South Africans in December 1962 about the possibility of establishing a Katanga trade office in South Africa to facilitate Katanga placing orders in the republic, which Katangese officials complained was complicated by layers of intermediaries.[103] The South Africans rebuffed the offer and repeated the line that such an office would do more harm than good for both South Africa and Katanga and open them to further attacks. Instead, the South Africans suggested that

---

[99] South African National Archives, Pretoria, Box 1/112/3/1, vol. 11, 12, Congo: Secession of Katanga, Letter from Secretary General of the UN, U Thant, to SA Permanent Representative to the UN, December 4, 1962.

[100] South African National Archives, Pretoria, Box 1/112/3/1, vol. 11, 12, Congo: Secession of Katanga, Letter from Secretary General of the UN, U Thant, to SA Permanent Representative to the UN, December 4, 1962.

[101] SA National Archives, Pretoria, Box 1/112/3/1, vol. 11, 12 Congo: Secession of Katanga, Telegram from SA Accredited Diplomatic Representative in Salisbury to Secretary for Foreign Affairs, Pretoria, November 14, 1962.

[102] SA National Archives, Pretoria, Box 1/112/3/1, vol. 11, 12 Congo: Secession of Katanga, Telegram from SA Accredited Diplomatic Representative in Salisbury to Secretary for Foreign Affairs, Pretoria, November 14, 1962.

[103] SA National Archives, Pretoria, Box 1/112/3/1, vol. 11, 12 Congo: Secession of Katanga, Record of discussion between JR Taels, President Tshombe's Commercial Advisor, and Mr. Sole, "Katanga Purchases in South Africa," December 3, 1962.

the Katangese appoint a South African purchasing agent to ease transactions. As will be detailed in later chapters, Katanga pursued other more comically inept means to win recognition, including outright bribery, but all failed.

Because of the birth order of these four states, Katanga's search for recognition in some ways put it in the best position of the four. There were very few precedents for collectively rejecting a new state from entry into the international order, no real template to follow except possibly that of Manchuoko. The arguments against Katanga's chances at recognition still had to be formed in real time in response to events on the ground. Once this cut became grooved in, the particular arguments of the aspirant states that followed did not matter as much, and their specific merits or demerits were washed down the grooved path toward nonrecognition.

Rhodesia[104]

As with all other declarations of independence, Rhodesia's UDI in 1965 was an invitation to the world community to recognize it as a full member of the family of nations.[105] Rhodesia's public case for recognition was stronger in some respects than Katanga's and weaker in others. Because it was a settler state whose independence was in part premised upon the preservation of white supremacy, it was certainly more offensive to large sections of the world community than the more amorphous concept of Katanga's neocolonial ties to Belgium and Western mining interests. However, unlike Katanga's secession from the newly independent state of the Congo, Rhodesia's was truly an anti-colonial rebellion against a European empire. Alone among the four, Rhodesia's claims to self-determination did not entail a redrawing of internationals borders. It should be remembered that it was Zambian and Malawian nationalists, not the white settlers in Rhodesia, who had successfully pushed for the dissolution of the CAF and who subsequently won independence, transforming what were formerly internal federal boundaries into new international borders.[106] In addition, no argument could be made that Rhodesia was a puppet of any regime, even as Rhodesia in the 1970s

---

[104] This section of the chapter draws heavily upon a chapter published in an edited volume: Brownell, "The Visual Rhetoric of Settler Stamps."

[105] For an excellent study of the international politics of UDI, see Watts, *Rhodesia's Unilateral Declaration of Independence*; See also: Nkala, "International Recognition," pp. 53–76.

[106] The CAF's constitutional structure merging two protectorates and a colony was bafflingly complicated. Robert Blake wrote of the CAF: "The Federation of Rhodesia

became increasingly dependent for its economic survival upon South Africa. Britain could never make a colorable claim that it was able to exercise any control whatsoever within the territory, and the UN never set foot in the territory. Its real strength, though, would only appear later on, paradoxically after any real chance for international recognition had dried up. This was its ability to survive on its own for fifteen years, easily meeting the Montevideo standards of de facto state capacity. Under the old paradigm of state recognition prior to the early 1950s, Rhodesia would have been accepted as a new state. But this was a new age.

Ian Smith's government in Rhodesia signaled that a unilateral break with Britain had been in the cards for some time, and this allowed opponents of his regime to prepare for UDI when it eventually did come on November 11, 1965. For the first time in its history, the United Nations preemptively rejected recognition to a state before it had even declared its independence.[107] Additionally, the day after UDI, the UN passed Resolution 216, which once again called upon member states not to recognize Rhodesia. On that same day, the State Department issued a statement saying that "no request for recognition had been received from Salisbury, none was expected and it would not be granted if it were sent."[108] Western supporters of the regime were furious at what they saw as their government's unfair treatment meted out to Rhodesia compared against other young states. The treasurer of the pro-Rhodesia lobbying organization, AAAA, bitterly wrote:

Since the end of World War II, 34 former African colonies and territories have gained independence. Each time this happened, most of the world applauded. Economic aid, technical advice, a seat in the UN and diplomatic relations were instantly made available. On November 11, 1965 Rhodesia declared its independence. But how different world reaction was this time! Instead of economic and technical help, the new state was quarantined ... [109]

The quest for recognition was a high priority for the Smith government. From his experiences living and researching in post-UDI Rhodesia, Harry Strack observed, "[one] cannot fail to notice the longing for recognition – the reaching out for any 'scrap' of recognition."[110] Among its Southern African friends, Rhodesia ran up against an

and Nyasaland was one of the most elaborately governed countries in the world." *A History of Rhodesia* (Knopf, New York, 1978) p. 284.

[107] UNGA Res. 2012 (October 12, 1965).

[108] Nkala, "International Recognition," p. 67, citing *The Times*, November 12, 1965.

[109] Liebman Papers, Box 2, Circular from Robert Richardson, AAAA Treasurer, to members and friends (undated, but spring 1966).

[110] H. Strack, "The International Relations of Rhodesia under Sanctions" (PhD dissertation, University of Iowa, 1974) p. 152.

argument that would have been all too familiar to the Katangese when they sought recognition a few years before: that someone else had better go first. Only two days after UDI, the Portuguese ambassador in Pretoria informed the Rhodesian accredited diplomatic representative, John Gaunt: "In the face of the international reaction, both Portugal and South Africa would be better placed to help Rhodesia in this difficult emergency if they did not recognize its independence immediately, but rather waited for another power, more disinterested, with fewer direct links, to do so first."[111]

Rhodesia had to struggle to find direct access to people to whom it could even make its case for independence. Whether it was out of a psychological need for self-affirmation or an actual belief, Rhodesian officials often proffered the idea that their rebellion was popular among the people of the West, and that it was only the top rung of Western national leaders and civil servant mandarins in their foreign ministries who rejected them, people who in modern right-wing political parlance would be slandered as being a part of the "deep state." In 1967, Smith tried to send a personal message directly to President Lyndon Johnson through an intermediary, the former head of the Chrysler Corporation, L. L. "Tex" Colbert, asking for recognition, bypassing the layers of senior staff which Rhodesians felt were hostile to their cause.[112] The ploy did not work.

As another attempt to bypass these filters, in March of 1966, the Rhodesian Minister of Foreign Affairs, Lord Graham, issued an appeal to several foreign ministers from countries Rhodesia believed were potentially sympathetic to its cause.[113] These included: Italy, Holland, Belgium, West Germany, Spain, Australia, New Zealand, Austria, Greece, Sweden, Norway, Finland, Denmark, Switzerland, Brazil, Argentina, Japan, United States, and Turkey. As explained in a note by the South African representative in Salisbury, France was earlier sent a substantially similar letter, which was why it was not included, and Canada was seen by the Rhodesians as being implacably hostile to Rhodesia and was therefore excluded.[114] Graham's message to these

---

[111] Quoted in de Meneses and McNamara, *White Redoubt*, p. 56.

[112] T. Noer, *Cold War and Black Liberation: The United States and White Rule in Africa, 1948–1968* (University of Missouri Press, Columbia, 1985) p. 231.

[113] DFA Archives, Pretoria, Box 1/156/1/7, UDI: Recognition of Rhodesian Government and Formulae for Contacts with Rhodesia, Letter with attachment from South African Accredited Diplomatic Representative in Salisbury to Secretary of Department of Foreign Affairs, "Lord Graham's Appeal on behalf of Rhodesia," March 23, 1966.

[114] DFA Archives, Pretoria, Box 1/156/1/7, UDI: Recognition of Rhodesian Government and Formulae for Contacts with Rhodesia, Letter with attachment from South African

ministers had an urgent and sincere tone, which forthrightly laid out Rhodesia's problems in getting its message out in the face of a hostile world press, British interference, and the so-called Afro-Asian Bloc which he claimed polluted the image of Rhodesia internationally. It began as an almost apologetic entreaty:

While I fully appreciate the obstacles at present existing to any formal or official communication between us, I believe the time may well be appropriate for me, as a private individual, to put before you a true and factual account of the present position in Rhodesia. I think we all know of the propensity of the World Press to slant reporting, and to interpret events in their own way, and I dare hope, therefore, that you will, in the interests of hearing both sides, for a moment forget my position as Minister of External Affairs, and accept this brief account of me personally.[115]

After three pages of Graham touting Rhodesia's political peace and social calm, its booming economy, the state of race relations, and the reasons for declaring independence, Graham made a final direct appeal to the ministers for recognition:

To sense the spirit of unity among our people (black and white) and their determination not to be diverted from a policy that they know to be right is a stimulating experience. We all believe this must be continued and that, in due course, other nations will give us that "recognition" that is our right. The truth about the Rhodesian situation is so far removed from what is to be read in the Press that I would end by asking you, however informally it may be done, to send someone here who may then give you a first-hand report about my country. I would be pleased to give my personal attention to assisting such an observer in every way I can.[116]

Graham's appeal would be the last direct state-to-state appeal of the Rhodesians to win recognition. But their quest continued through other means.

In the longer term, Rhodesian government officials believed that the best way to eventually win acceptance by other states was to continue to strengthen Rhodesia's trade contacts and economic relations. This was a slow, backdoor method of achieving *de facto* then *de jure* recognition. As

Accredited Diplomatic Representative in Salisbury to Secretary of Department of Foreign Affairs, "Lord Graham's Appeal on behalf of Rhodesia," March 23, 1966.

[115] DFA Archives, Pretoria, Box 1/156/1/7, UDI: Recognition of Rhodesian Government and Formulae for Contacts with Rhodesia, Letter with attachment from South African Accredited Diplomatic Representative in Salisbury to Secretary of Department of Foreign Affairs, "Lord Graham's Appeal on behalf of Rhodesia," March 23, 1966.

[116] DFA Archives, Pretoria, Box 1/156/1/7, UDI: Recognition of Rhodesian Government and Formulae for Contacts with Rhodesia, Letter with attachment from South African Accredited Diplomatic Representative in Salisbury to Secretary of Department of Foreign Affairs, "Lord Graham's Appeal on behalf of Rhodesia," March 23, 1966.

the minister of external affairs described in 1966, "just as in the past it used to be said that the flag followed trade, so today I am quite certain that recognition will not be long in following trade also.[117]" Betraying a less brave face, Smith conceded in another interview: "... being an optimist, I hope it won't be too long before some government recognition does come our way."[118]

Regardless of what the rest of the international community believed after UDI, Rhodesian leaders sometimes boasted that their state was already fully independent. The Rhodesian Minister of Internal Affairs, Desmond Lardner-Burke, claimed as early as 1967 that in his view Rhodesia had already gained implicit, or practical, recognition from the international community.[119] Ian Smith was even bolder, claiming in 1967 that "practical recognition has been adopted by many countries who are continuing to trade with us and whose sympathies lie entirely with us."[120] Rhodesia's Foreign Minister, Jack Howman, said to the Rhodesian Parliament in 1970: "In terms of internationally accepted standards, Rhodesia possesses all the requirements of statehood, namely: a permanent population, a defined territory, a stable and effective government and the capacity to enter into relations with other states. In international parlance, it is accepted too, that the political existence of a state is independent of recognition by other states."[121] Whether Howman and the others were truly passionate partisans of the declaratory school of statehood all along or found themselves there out of necessity, this was an argument Rhodesians were always forced to make.

Despite the invaluable support it provided the regime, South Africa never recognized Rhodesia, and in fact their relationship was not always friendly behind closed doors.[122] "South Africa's support for Rhodesia," Miller explains in his book, "was ... consistently less strident or automatic than was often perceived."[123] On the day of UDI, Prime Minister Hendrik Verwoerd issued a press statement to respond to questions about whether or not the republic would recognize Rhodesia. Verwoerd's statement relayed that the republic had a policy of "non-interference" in the affairs of Rhodesia, and that it intended to "maintain

---

[117] Rhodesian Parliamentary Debates, vol. 64, July 6, 1966, col. 608.
[118] Strack, "International Relations," p. 152.
[119] Strack, "International Relations," p. 150.
[120] Strack, "International Relations," p. 151.
[121] Rhodesian Parliamentary Debates, vol. 77, June 16, 1970, col. 589. In view of their notorious transience, it is arguable whether in fact Rhodesia's white population was "permanent." See, J. Brownell, "The Hole in Rhodesia's Bucket: White Emigration and the End of Settler Rule," *The Journal of Southern African Studies*, vol. 34, no. 3 (September 2008) pp. 591–610.
[122] See: Miller, *An African Volk*.   [123] Miller, *An African Volk*, p. 100.

normal, friendly relations with both Rhodesia and the United Kingdom," and that South Africa and Rhodesia would continue to have relations and that "the measure and character of this intercourse is such that its continuation is unavoidable, irrespective of who exercises effective authority in Rhodesia."[124] This was not a statement of recognition, though it did express that South Africa considered the Smith regime to be the de facto authority in the territory.[125] This was less than what Rhodesia hoped for, but was as good as they could get, and even this stance displeased the British.

Perhaps he was truly happy with South Africa's policy or maybe he was just being a good sport, either way, Ian Smith thanked the South Africans for their stance of "correctness" since it maintained friendly relations and continued engagement while avoiding the question of recognition. In a meeting just days after UDI with the South African accredited representative in Salisbury, Smith gushed: "[P]lease say to your Prime Minister how much my Cabinet and I appreciated his statement and the fact that it came so soon after our declaration of independence. It gave us strength and moral support at a difficult time, please thank him for it."[126] The telegram communicated that Smith "accepts the need for a policy of 'correctness' to safeguard South Africa's position and realizes that it could assist the Republic's attitude of helpfulness to Rhodesia."[127]

This supposedly "neutral" stance of South Africa regarding the Rhodesian/British conflict did not provide a clear road map for future state-to-state interaction. For instance, it did not answer such practical problems such as the procedure for allowing Rhodesians to enter the republic with Rhodesian papers, especially since South African domestic law at the time mandated that people entering the country must produce travel documents of a recognized state. For its part, Britain formally

[124] DFA Archives, Pretoria, Box 1/156/1/7, UDI: Recognition of Rhodesian Government and Formulae for Contacts with Rhodesia, "Admission of Rhodesian Citizens: Recognition of Rhodesian Passports," Memorandum by AL Badenhorst, Secretary for Justice to Secretary of the Interior and Secretary for Foreign Affairs, December 22, 1965.

[125] DFA Archives, Pretoria, Box 1/156/1/7, UDI: Recognition of Rhodesian Government and Formulae for Contacts with Rhodesia, "Admission of Rhodesian Citizens: Recognition of Rhodesian Passports," Memorandum by AL Badenhorst, Secretary for Justice to Secretary of the Interior and Secretary for Foreign Affairs, December 22, 1965.

[126] DFA Archives, Pretoria, Box 1/156/1/1, vols. 1, 2, 3 UDI, Telegram from SA Accredited Diplomatic Representative in Salisbury to Secretary for Foreign Affairs, Pretoria, November 19, 1965.

[127] DFA Archives, Pretoria, Box 1/156/1/1, vols. 1, 2, 3 UDI, Telegram from SA Accredited Diplomatic Representative in Salisbury to Secretary for Foreign Affairs, Pretoria, November 19, 1965.

appealed to South Africa to reject Rhodesian passports.[128] Since Rhodesia was not recognized, the work-around rule that was settled upon was that the South African consul in Rhodesia would issue a document allowing for entry: The precedent for this that was cited by the Justice Secretary was a 1933 League of Nations opinion on Manchukuo.[129] South Africa's cautious and legalistic attitude toward Rhodesia's passports clearly suggests a fear of inadvertently conferring recognition, but the country's ultimate legal conclusion was that their government's intention was the crucial factor, and that engaging with Rhodesia would not trigger recognition: "Just as non-intercourse does not necessarily signify non-recognition, so non-recognition does not compel non-intercourse."[130] Traveling for Rhodesians under Rhodesian documents remained difficult, but this travel problem was eased by the transient nature of the white settler society since a high percentage of whites never took up citizenship and always traveled under non-Rhodesian passports. Even the Rhodesian Foreign Minister, P. K. Van der Byl, formally approached the South Africans himself while trying to obtain South African passport since he found it difficult to travel in Europe under his diplomatic Rhodesian passport.[131] Van der Byl later withdrew the request, citing "practical difficulties and inadvisability considering his position [as Foreign Minister]."[132]

[128] DFA Archives, Pretoria, Box 1/156/1/7, UDI: Recognition of Rhodesian Government and Formulae for Contacts with Rhodesia, "Admission of Rhodesian Citizens: Recognition of Rhodesian Passports," Memorandum by A. L. Badenhorst, Secretary for Justice to Secretary of the Interior and Secretary for Foreign Affairs, December 22, 1965. Lesotho and Swaziland were not parties to this arrangement and forthrightly denied Rhodesian passport-holders. DFA Archives, Pretoria, Box 1/156/1/7, UDI: Recognition of Rhodesian Government and Formulae for Contacts with Rhodesia, "Rhodesian Passports Considered Invalid: Lesotho" (unsigned report) August 14, 1968.

[129] DFA Archives, Pretoria, Box 1/156/1/7, UDI: Recognition of Rhodesian Government and Formulae for Contacts with Rhodesia, "Admission of Rhodesian Citizens: Recognition of Rhodesian Passports," Memorandum by AL Badenhorst, Secretary for Justice to Secretary of the Interior and Secretary for Foreign Affairs, December 22, 1965.

[130] DFA Archives, Pretoria, Box 1/156/1/7, UDI: Recognition of Rhodesian Government and Formulae for Contacts with Rhodesia, "Admission of Rhodesian Citizens: Recognition of Rhodesian Passports," Memorandum by A. L. Badenhorst, Secretary for Justice to Secretary of the Interior and Secretary for Foreign Affairs, December 22, 1965. Citing J. G. Starke, *Introduction to International Law*, 5th ed. (Butterworth, London, 1963) p. 133.

[131] DFA Archives, Pretoria, Box 1/156/1/7, UDI: Recognition of Rhodesian Government and Formulae for Contacts with Rhodesia, Code telegram from South African Accredited Diplomatic Representative in Salisbury to Secretary for Foreign Affairs, Pretoria, December 30, 1966.

[132] DFA Archives, Pretoria, Box 1/156/1/7, UDI: Recognition of Rhodesian Government and Formulae for Contacts with Rhodesia, Code telegram from South African

Prime Minister Vorster, who became the prime minister following Verwoerd's assassination in 1966, pursued a Rhodesian policy that was a balancing act between maintaining some public distance from the rebel state to help win moderate African states over to the idea of détente, while still being seen to be doing enough to support the white settler regime that was so domestically popular within the republic, especially among English speakers.[133] South Africa's application of the "correctness" formula did seem to change over time. For instance, on the advice of the South African DFA the head of the South African mission in Salisbury turned down an invitation from the speaker of the Rhodesian parliament to attend the opening session in 1966, some five months after UDI.[134] It was feared at the time that a South African representative attending an official Rhodesian ceremony such as the "Opening of Parliament" might imply recognition.[135] As a result, the only official foreign guest at that first year's opening ceremony was the Portuguese consul-general. South Africa's DFA reply to the accredited diplomatic representative on the question of attendance in the 1967 opening session was categorical and exactly opposite to that of the 1966 answer: "There is no (repeat no) objection to acceptance of invitation to attend the formal opening of Rhodesian Parliament on 19th April."[136] Over time, South Africa grew less concerned about how its relations with Rhodesia played out on the world stage, or what sorts of intercourse could be implied to mean South African recognition of Rhodesia. For instance, in 1970 the presence of South African Police units in Rhodesia prompted the British ambassador to ask the South African DFA if this presence implied recognition. The South Africans again responded with the formula that their relations with Rhodesia were merely the continuation of their pre-UDI relations, and this did not affect their stance on recognition.[137]

Accredited Diplomatic Representative in Salisbury to Secretary for Foreign Affairs, Pretoria, January 4, 1967.

[133] Miller, *An African Volk*.

[134] DFA Archives, Pretoria, Box 1/156/1/7, UDI: Recognition of Rhodesian Government and Formulae for Contacts with Rhodesia, Letter from the Accredited Diplomatic Representative in Salisbury to the Secretary of Foreign Affairs, Cape Town, "Opening of Rhodesian Parliament," March 9, 1967.

[135] DFA Archives, Pretoria, Box Note by Pik Botha, May 25, 1966.

[136] 1/156/1/7, UDI: Recognition of Rhodesian Government and Formulae for Contacts with Rhodesia, Telegram from Department of Foreign Affairs, Cape Town, to the Accredited Diplomatic Representative in Salisbury to the "Opening of Rhodesian Parliament," March 23, 1967.

[137] DFA Archives, Pretoria, Box 1/156/1/7, UDI: Recognition of Rhodesian Government and Formulae for Contacts with Rhodesia, Letter from the South African DFA to Arthur Snelling, British Ambassador to South Africa, October 21, 1970.

State funerals were notable occasions where the conflicts over Rhodesia's international status were very publicly contested. These began even before UDI amid growing tensions with Britain during Rhodesian independence negotiations. Smith flew out to London in January 1965 for Winston Churchill's funeral. After the ceremony at St. Paul's Cathedral, the Metropolitan Police sought out the vehicles of those invited to the lunch afterward at Buckingham Palace. Ian Smith's driver had been told to join the convoy, but Smith indicated that he had actually never been invited to the lunch and Smith instead ordered his driver to return to his Hyde Park Hotel. An emissary from Buckingham Palace then called at Smith's hotel room and told him that he was in fact invited, but Smith still insisted that he was not. According to press reports, it was only when the emissary said, "The Queen commands ..." that Smith agreed to then head to Buckingham Palace for the lunch.[138] An accumulation of little slights such as this before UDI added to the Smith government's anger that it was treated as something less than an equal.

After Hendrik Verwoerd, the architect of apartheid, was assassinated, Ian Smith was asked to attend Verwoerd's state funeral in September 1966, nearly a year after UDI. In response to this request, the South African diplomatic representative in Salisbury believed that rejecting Smith's request could have had negative consequences for the republic. "In view of the overwhelming and deeply emotional expression of sympathy throughout Rhodesia, a refusal at this stage could be construed as a rebuff to the people of Rhodesia who we firmly believe would expect no lesser a person to represent them."[139] At the same time, South Africa could not afford Smith the same status as the head of a sovereign state. The compromise arrived at was that Smith would be allowed to attend but only in his personal capacity.[140]

Status and titular questions for Rhodesian representatives came up again for the funeral of another titan in Southern African politics. António de Oliveira Salazar, the longtime ruler of Portugal died on July 27, 1970. The South Africans were shocked that the Rhodesian

---

[138] DFA Archives, Pretoria, Box 1/156/1/1, vols. 1, 2, 3 UDI, Telegram from SA Charge D'affaires, J. Van Dalsen, to Secretary of Foreign Affairs, Pretoria, "Southern Rhodesia," February 5, 1965.

[139] DFA Archives, Pretoria, Box 1/156/1/14, UDI visits of Rhodesian PM, other ministers to RSA and vice versa, Telegram from SA Accredited Diplomatic Representative, Salisbury to Secretary for Foreign Affairs, Cape Town, September 7, 1966.

[140] DFA Archives, Pretoria, Box 1/156/1/14, UDI visits of Rhodesian PM, other ministers to RSA and vice versa, Telegram from Secretary for Foreign Affairs, Cape Town, to SA Accredited Diplomatic Representative, Salisbury to September 7, 1966.

accredited representative in Portugal who succeeded Harry Reedman, Colonel W. M. Knox, was given a special status equal to that of other mission heads and seated in the cathedral during an official event honoring the life of Salazar.[141] Knox's status apparently raised a flutter among diplomatic circles, who are particularly attuned to such things. Predictably upset by this, the British approached the Portuguese about this challenge to their sovereignty over Rhodesia. Apparently, the Portuguese responded by saying that the granting of a special status to Knox was a blunder by the Portuguese protocol department and was not approved by higher officials. They assured the British that this would not happen again.[142]

As it was with all major international bodies, Rhodesia was rejected for membership in the Universal Postal Union. Rhodesia's philatelic rejection had a precedent in Katanga. Rejection of UPU membership is not the same thing, however, as the rejection of Rhodesian postage overseas, which required constant enforcement on the ground by each individual member's postal authorities. These states' cumulative decisions, to ban the stamps or not to ban them, were known to carry some legal effect on the issuing regime's status as a de facto state. The British did not call on the UPU to ban all Rhodesian postage stamps, however, but only specific issues.[143] These stamp issues included the UDI commemorative stamp created just weeks after the declaration; the Rhodesian overprints in which the new regime simply had "Independence" stamped on top of Rhodesian colonial-era stamps; and the entire decimal definitive series that Rhodesia had timed to correspond with its republic status in 1970, a series the British thought was purposely provocative, in particular one featuring the new Rhodesian flag. The thrust behind Britain's push to ban these stamps was encapsulated in the following internal memorandum from the Foreign Office calling for a ban on the 1970 definitive stamps: "If we ignore the stamps we will give the impression that pressures against the regime are being allowed to slide at a time when we will be taking every possible step to ensure that other countries do not move towards recognition." The fear was that in innumerable small ways the

---

[141] DFA Archives, Box 1/156/6, UDI External representation, Letter from SA Ambassador to Portugal, B. J. van der Walt, to Secretary of Department of Foreign Affairs, "Spesiale status vir rhodesiese verteenwoordiger by die begrafnis van Dr Salazar," August 21, 1970.

[142] DFA Archives, Box 1/156/6, UDI External representation, Letter from SA Ambassador to Portugal, B. J. van der Walt, to Secretary of Department of Foreign Affairs, "Spesiale status vir rhodesiese verteenwoordiger by die begrafnis van Dr Salazar," August 21, 1970.

[143] For an examination of the battle over Rhodesian stamps, see: Brownell, "The Visual Rhetoric of Settler Stamps."

regime's illegal status internationally had to be actively enforced and reinforced, and stamps, as small as they were, were one such field of contest.[144]

In June 1969, the Rhodesian electorate overwhelmingly voted in favor of a republican constitution, ostensibly cutting its ties to Britain and the Commonwealth. The Smith regime had hoped that becoming a republic would clarify its international status by fully severing any residual British ties and thereby help in gaining international recognition.[145] But the new constitution had the opposite effect and shunted Rhodesia further into isolation. In 1970, the UN Security Council passed a resolution making nonrecognition mandatory for member states.[146] This redoubled effort to tighten the fence internationally around Rhodesia was part of Britain's self-described "post-republic posture."[147] Manifestations of this new posture included urging those countries that still had them to close their Salisbury consulates, which most did only in March 1970, after the British threatened to withdraw the exequaturs from their consulates.[148] This also included the closing down of both the British Residual Mission in Rhodesia and the withdrawal of the governor, and the shutting down of Rhodesia House in London that will be explored in a later chapter.[149]

Rhodesia made one last dramatic drive for recognition before it fully collapsed. In March 1978, Smith's regime signed an agreement with several moderate African nationalist leaders to form a new constitution. This was known as the "internal settlement." The Patriotic Front, whose nationalist armies remained actively engaged against the Rhodesian defense forces, was excluded from the agreement. In spite of the name change to Zimbabwe Rhodesia and the opening up of the franchise to black Africans, the constitution retained significant powers for the white minority to the extent that many saw white settlers as still being in control. This led critics to assert that this was the same old Rhodesia. After an election a new government headed by Bishop Abel Muzorewa

---

[144] PREM 13/3444, "Rhodesian Postage Stamps," Memorandum from FCO to PM Wilson, February 16, 1970, undated penned note at the top, signed "H.W."

[145] A. Quentin-Baxter, *Rhodesia and the Law: A Commentary on the Constitutional and International Law Aspects of the Rhodesian Situation* (New Zealand Institute of International Affairs, Wellington, 1970) p. 18.

[146] UNSC Resolution 277 (March 18, 1970).

[147] PREM 13/3444, Memorandum for the Prime Minister, "Rhodesian Postage Stamps," March 3, 1970.

[148] "Consular Representation in Rhodesia," Telegram from Ellsworth, US Mission to NATO to State Department, 17 October, 1969. US National Archives at College Park, MD: NACP. Central Files 1967–1969, RG 59, Box 2445; Lake, *"Tar Baby" Option*, pp. 142–143.

[149] See: Brownell, "'A Sordid Tussle on the Strand'."

Figure 4.1 Ian Smith watching the officer administering the government, Clifford Dupont, sign the new constitution bill in 1969 that would make Rhodesia a republic the following year.

took power in June 1979, the beginning of what would end up being the six-month lifespan of Zimbabwe Rhodesia. Predictably, international organizations maintained their opposition. The UN continued to withhold support, and the OAU rejected the government out of hand, calling Muzorewa's government a "gigantic fraud."[150] Speaking for the so-called front-line states, Tanzania warned that any Anglo-American support for the Muzorewa government would be seen as "tantamount to declaring war" on black Africa.[151]

Despite vocal international opposition, the possibility of recognition for the illegal regime appeared to be as close as it ever was since the first

---

[150] "Modest Aid to Zimbabwe," *Washington Post*, March 7, 1981.
[151] "Modest Aid to Zimbabwe," *Washington Post*, March 7, 1981.

days after UDI. A public relations blitz was unleashed in the West to convince Western states that Rhodesia had essentially "done enough." Some powerful politicians in both Britain and the United States pushed hard for an end to the sanctions and to recognize the new regime. North Carolina Senator, Jesse Helms, was behind an aggressive push in Congress in 1979 to lift sanctions on Zimbabwe Rhodesia and recognize the new state. On his initiative, the Senate overwhelmingly passed a nonbinding resolution in May calling for an end to sanctions, and in a White House news conference President Jimmy Carter was forced to admit that majorities in both chambers supported the lifting of sanctions on Muzorewa's government. But Carter held strong.[152] Margaret Thatcher reversed her campaign pledge regarding recognition of the "internal settlement" government, and withheld recognition as well. As a result, despite inching closer to a break, Zimbabwe Rhodesia could never break free.[153]

Transkei

It was Transkei's relationship with South Africa that always presented the greatest political, practical, and messaging barriers to its claims for independence. There were some precedents for denying recognition to a nascent state because it retained too many ties to the mother country. This rationale was initially employed by the United States regarding Syria, Lebanon, and Transjordan's independence.[154] Transkei's responses to criticisms of their dependency on South Africa cleverly turned the arguments back on their opponents. Transkei and their friends argued they would not be overly dependent upon South Africa if they were to be recognized by the international community. This was the irony identified by Newell Stultz and others, that the international quarantine of Transkei forced it to be dependent on South Africa, which reinforced the international charge of them being South Africa's puppet. Stultz writes, "The Transkei state is thus in the grip of a peculiar vicious circle. Its financial dependence on South Africa is seen by other countries in part as grounds for not recognizing Transkei, but nonrecognition prevents the development of alternative sources of assistance that could

---

[152] See: Graham Hovey, "President Refuses to Lift Trade Ban against Rhodesians," *New York Times*, June 8, 1979.

[153] N. Waddy, "The Strange Death of 'Zimbabwe-Rhodesia': The Question of British Recognition of the Muzorewa Regime in Rhodesian Public Opinion, 1979," *South African Historical Journal*, vol. 66, no. 2 (2013) pp. 227–248.

[154] Crawford, *The Creation of States in International Law*, p. 84; Fabry, *Recognizing States*, p. 156.

lessen the dependence."[155] Cutting their relationship off immediately without an alternative revenue stream would have been disastrous, and with no other states recognizing Transkei these budget shortfalls would have gone on indefinitely. This self-fulfilling effect of isolation was picked up by others.[156] A little more than a month before independence, Professor Mlahleni Njisane, the former diplomat-in-training in Washington, who was by then slotted to become Transkei's ambassador to South Africa, said, "We're in a real bind, aren't we? ... For us, independence is a chance to break the shackles of apartheid. If we reject it [independence offered by South Africa] to show that we reject apartheid, the shackles could last forever."[157]

Transkei's first year of independence was dominated by the question of recognition – it was, as Newell Stultz points out, the "central issue" for the regime.[158] Some six months before its independence, the *Rand Daily Mail* reported that some of the factors weighing on African leaders' decisions regarding Transkei recognition would be the progression of other homelands toward independence, something that always worried Transkei with Bophuthatswana following so closely behind it in independence.[159] This affected Transkei's recognition strategy. A year out from independence, Transkei's Washington diplomats-in-training, T. T. Letlaka and Njisane, made their rounds to the embassies in Washington of African countries. The South African minister assigned to the diplomats-in-training, Jeremy Shearer, noted that there was an "obvious need [for Letlaka and Njisane] to dissociate the Transkei from the homelands, linking its past with that of the ex-High Commission Territories, partially for competitive reasons but principally at this stage not to jeopardise any faint chances of recognition."[160] According to Letlaka's written report to Umtata, the initial soundings from the ambassadors of the former HCTs were positive.[161] When George Matanzima, Kaiser's brother, visited the United States in May 1976 the South African Ambassador to the United States, Pik Botha, personally took him around to Lesotho's, Swaziland's,

[155] Stultz, *Transkei's Half Loaf*, p. 129.
[156] "Are the Doubts about the Transkei Self-fulfilling?" *The Guardian*, October 21, 1976.
[157] John Burns, "Transkei, as It Prepares for Independence, Finds Itself to Be Outcast among Nations," *New York Times*, September 8, 1976.
[158] Stultz, *Transkei's Half Loaf*, p. 116.
[159] "Security Laws May Knock Hopes," *Rand Daily Mail*, April 24, 1976.
[160] SA National Archives, Box: Transkei: Independence Celebrations and Invitations, 1/226/1/1, "Transkei Diplomats" Letter from SA Ambassador the US, Shearer, to Secretary DFA, November 13, 1975.
[161] SA National Archives, Pretoria, Box: Transkei 1/226/1/1, "Independence Celebrations and Invitations," Letter from Letlaka to Chief Minister Matanzima, Umtata, December 15, 1975.

and Botswana's embassies and leaned on each of them to recognize Transkei.[162]

Beyond the HCTs, Transkei thought its best hopes for recognition lay with the francophone countries. As explained in Chapter 3, Bokassa's CAR looked to be the most sympathetic, but Letlaka and Njisane also called on the Ivorian Embassy and the Mauritanian director of the African department of the IMF.[163] Outside of the francophone countries, there was likewise a positive report after meeting the Malawian ambassador. Even African states that were overtly hostile to the Bantustan policy were approached, and according to Letlaka, the results were none too bad. The Ghanaian counselor they met gave Letlaka the impression that Ghana might even be possibly open to recognition. All these meetings were summarized in the optimistic consolidated report Letlaka sent back to Umtata.[164]

This early optimistic attitude about recognition was expressed by several Transkeian officials. In February 1976, Transkei's Interior Minister, Stella Sigcau, bragged publicly that "there are countries in Africa that have indicated they will be open-minded about the question of recognizing the Transkei."[165] Sigcau added, "There are things in the air." In London, Digby Koyana was doing much the same thing as Letlaka and Njisane were doing in Washington. For his part, Koyana told reporters that on the recognition issue Transkei had "taken the matter very far, both here and in America."[166] In January 1976, Koyana sounded out several London-based African diplomats on Transkeian independence. Among other impressions Koyana came away with was that there was marked difference in attitudes between the loud public rejections of the Bantustan system generally and the more welcoming attitude they found in private discussions.[167] At every embassy he visited Koyana gave his pitch for independence and he delivered his supplemental papers in support of Transkeian independence. He even

---

[162] P. Koyana-Letlaka, *This Is My Life: A South African Journey* (Xlibris, Bloomington, 2014) p. 242.

[163] SA National Archives, Pretoria, Box: Transkei 1/226/1/1, "Independence Celebrations and Invitations," Letter from Letlaka to Chief Minister Matanzima, Umtata, January 20, 1976.

[164] SA National Archives, Pretoria, Box: Transkei 1/226/1/1, "Independence Celebrations and Invitations," Letter from Letlaka to Chief Minister Matanzima, Umtata, December 15, 1975.

[165] "Umtata Backing from Africa?" *Daily Dispatch*, February 14, 1976.

[166] "Umtata Backing from Africa?" *Daily Dispatch*, February 14, 1976.

[167] SA National Archives, Pretoria, Box: Transkei 1/226/1/1, "Independence Celebrations and Invitations," Memorandum by S. S. Koyana, "Transkeian Trainee Diplomat: Progress Report," January 2, 1976.

came away with the impression that Ghana and Zambia were open to recognition.[168] Like Letlaka's report, Koyana's too was a summary of all diplomatic initiatives he had undertaken sent on to Umtata and presented a similarly sunny picture.[169]

In July 1976, these hopes were raised even more when a former Lesotho cabinet minister was quoted as saying that Lesotho would be forced to recognize Transkei soon after the October 26 independence handover.[170] If South Africans, Transkeian officials, and their supporters were searching for positive signs that at least one of the HCTs would recognize them, those signs were out there. But most signs pointed the other way. The most damaging news to arrive regarding Transkei's recognition was received about four months after Koyana's rosy report out of London. It came from a BBC interview of Chief Leabua Jonathan of Lesotho. When asked about Transkeian recognition, Jonathan said, "Well we shall declare our position when that time comes. We shall cross that bridge when we come to it ..."[171] The interviewer then asked Jonathan what he thought about the South Africans argument that not recognizing Transkei would be hypocritical because Transkei was just as viable as many other fully sovereign African states: "[D]oes this argument impress you at all or will it affect your decision which way to jump, to recognize or not recognize?" Jonathan replied, "Well that might be their view. It doesn't impress me in the least. They seem to compare an independent viable Lesotho with Transkei – I'm not at all impressed by their views." The interviewer followed up: "Am I detecting an approach that you probably will not recognize the Transkei?" To which Jonathan answered, "Let us wait until we come to the bridge and see if we can cross it."[172] Lesotho never crossed the bridge.

In April 1976, rumors began to circulate that South Africa was to free Nelson Mandela from Robben Island as a signal of its willingness to open dialogues with the rest of Africa and the world.[173] This was viewed by sources for the *Rand Daily Mail* as a "trump card" for Matanzima to

---

[168] SA National Archives, Pretoria, Box: Transkei 1/226/1/1, "Independence Celebrations and Invitations," Memorandum by S. S. Koyana, "Transkeian Trainee Diplomat: Progress Report," January 2, 1976.

[169] SA National Archives, Pretoria, Box: Transkei 1/226/1/1, "Independence Celebrations and Invitations," Memorandum by S. S. Koyana, "Transkeian Trainee Diplomat: Progress Report," January 2, 1976.

[170] "Transkei Will Be Recognised – Ex-minister," *Rand Daily Mail*, July 26, 1976.

[171] SA National Archives, Pretoria, Box: Transkei 1/226/1/1, "Independence Celebrations and Invitations," Excerpt from May 11, 1976 BBC interview with Chief Jonathan.

[172] SA National Archives, Pretoria, Box: Transkei 1/226/1/1, "Independence Celebrations and Invitations," Excerpt from May 11, 1976 BBC interview with Chief Jonathan.

[173] "Mandela May Be Free in August – UN View," *Rand Daily Mail*, April 7, 1976.

achieve recognition for Transkei.[174] Mandela was a Xhosa from the Transkei region and a cousin of Matanzima.[175] Observers speculated that such a move might be enough to allow countries such as Ivory Coast, the CAR, and perhaps Swaziland to break the UN and OAU boycott and recognize Transkei. This in turn, it was hoped by Transkeian officials, would encourage the United States and Britain, who were both waiting for Africa to take the lead on this issue, to follow suit.[176] South African officials, however, were firm in their dismissals of any such idea, and Mandela was firmly opposed to the Bantustan project, so it never happened.

Outside of Africa, Transkei received mixed signals regarding possible recognition. In the middle of March 1976, more than six months before independence, a press report from London's *Daily Dispatch* cited "informed sources" that France was going to go against the rest of the European Union and recognize Transkei upon its independence.[177] The article pointed to the state-level treatment afforded to recent Bantustan visitors to France and alleged promises made to them that they could expect French economic and cultural assistance.[178] The South African Embassy in Paris shot down this enthusiasm the very next day.

Our own impression is further that it is too early for France to have taken a firm decision on this matter. Our feeling is that the French attitude will to a large extent be influenced by the decision of the Western European group – where matter has apparently already been discussed. Western European group in turn will be guided by reaction of the African countries. [179]

The United States had been one of the abstentions in a UN General Assembly vote in November 1975 which preemptively called on members not to recognize Transkei, and there was some speculation that Transkeian recognition could be a possible bargaining chip in US efforts to draw South Africa into Henry Kissinger's efforts to end the Rhodesian

[174] "Mandela May Be Free in August – UN View," *Rand Daily Mail,* April 7, 1976.
[175] Gibbs, *Mandela's Kinsmen.*
[176] "Mandela May Be Free in August – UN View," *Rand Daily Mail,* April 7, 1976.
[177] SA National Archives, Pretoria, Box: Transkei 1/226/1/1, "Independence Celebrations and Invitations," Telegram from Secretary DFA to SA Embassy in Paris, March 17, 1976.
[178] SA National Archives, Pretoria, Box: Transkei 1/226/1/1, "Independence Celebrations and Invitations," Telegram from Secretary DFA to SA Embassy in Paris, March 17, 1976.
[179] SA National Archives, Pretoria, Box: Transkei 1/226/1/1, "Independence Celebrations and Invitations," Telegram from SA Embassy in Paris to Secretary DFA, March 18, 1976.

rebellion, or possibly in exchange for South African concessions in the tug of war over Namibia.[180] Pretoria certainly hoped that their work on the Rhodesian negotiations would translate to US help in regard to Transkei.[181] But two days after the telegram from France, South African and Transkeian authorities received very similar news from the United States. In his testimony before a Senate subcommittee, US Assistant Secretary of State for African Affairs, William Everett Schaufele, outlined US policy toward Transkei, which the South African Embassy in turn relayed to the DFA: "United States will not make decision on recognition at present time. Attitude of African countries will be important factor in United States decision-making. Presume most African countries opposed to Transkei independence."[182] While the State Department hesitated in coming out and declaring its intentions clearly, the Democratic presidential nominee, Jimmy Carter, urged the US government not to recognize the "sham" independence of Transkei.[183]

In June came an unequivocal no from Canada.[184] Canada was the only major Western country in which the Transkeians did not even bother to send an invitation to their Independence Day celebrations. Still the United States waited to announce their decision not to recognize Transkei. Only days before independence did a State Department spokesman respond to a direct *New York Times* query that the United States would not recognize the regime, but that answer was expected by all but the most starry-eyed supporters of Transkei.[185] At that time, State Department officials told the *New York Times* that the Ford administration had never seriously considered recognizing Transkei, but Secretary of State Henry Kissinger did not want to publicly embarrass Vorster, especially as the Rhodesian peace talks were underway.[186] Britain likewise denied recognition. Furious at Britain's denial of recognition, Matanzima queried whether Transkei should recognize Britain:

---

[180] Stultz, *Transkei's Half Loaf*, p. 117.   [181] Southall, *South Africa's Transkei*, p. 55.

[182] SA National Archives, Pretoria, Box: Transkei 1/226/1/1, "Independence Celebrations and Invitations," Telegram from SA Embassy in Washington to Secretary DFA, Cape Town, March 20, 1976.

[183] "Carter Urges US to Reject Kei 'Sham,'" *Rand Daily Mail*, October 18, 1976.

[184] SA National Archives, Pretoria, Box: Transkei 1/226/1/1, "Independence Celebrations and Invitations," Telegram from SA Embassy in Ottawa to Secretary DFA, June 30, 1976.

[185] B. Gwertzman, "U.S. Will Not Recognize Transkei after Its Independence Next Week," *New York Times*, October 22, 1976.

[186] B. Gwertzman, "U.S. Will Not Recognize Transkei after Its Independence Next Week," *New York Times*, October 22, 1976.

"After all, they are going down the drain, a country ruled by trade unions."[187]

In the year leading up to its independence date one after another international organizations preemptively rejected Transkei's independence. Transkei applied for membership to the OAU, but in a July 1976 resolution the organization denounced the would-be state, declaring that South Africa's Bantustan system of which Transkei was the flagship was "the cornerstone of Apartheid."[188] In August 1976, the Conference of Heads of State of Governments of Non-Aligned Countries voted not to recognize any of South Africa's Bantustans.[189] Following suit, in September, the nine members of the European Economic Community declared that they would not recognize the independence of Transkei.[190] As early as November 1975 the UN General Assembly passed a resolution calling upon all members not to recognize Transkei or any other Bantustan.[191] In June 1976, Matanzima publicly said that Transkei would not bother applying to join the United Nations. He said this was due to the "unhealthy spirit which prevailed at the United Nations."[192] This statement on applying for membership was a reversal of his pledge a year out from independence that Transkei would apply regardless of its likely rejection.[193] On its end, the United Nations did not wait for Transkei's declaration to foreclose the possibility of recognition, as on October 24, two days before independence, the General Assembly once again condemned the creation of South Africa's Bantustans.[194] On the actual day of independence, the UN General Assembly passed another resolution calling on "all Governments to deny any form of recognition to the so-called independent Transkei and to refrain from having any dealings with the so-called independent Transkei or other Bantustans."[195]

---

[187] "Transkei-Matanzima," Reuters News Wire, Umtata, October 29, 1976.
[188] Donald A. Heydt, "Nonrecognition of the Independence of Transkei,"*Case Western Reserve Journal of International Law*, vol. 10 (1978) p. 167, quoting June 28, 1976. O.A.U. Doc. CM/Res. 493 (XXVII).
[189] Heydt, "Nonrecognition."
[190] EE statement quoted in Heydt, "Nonrecognition," 167.
[191] UNGA Res. 3411 D [XXX].
[192] "Transkei Won't Apply to Join UN-Kaiser," *Daily Dispatch*, June 24, 1976.
[193] SA National Archives, Pretoria, Box: Transkei 1/226/1/1, "Independence Celebrations and Invitations," "Press Statement by Chief Minister of Transkei, Paramount Chief the Honourable K. D. Matanzima," October 31, 1975.
[194] UNGA Agenda Item 53 (October 24, 1976).
[195] UNGA. Res. 31/6 A, 31 U.N. GAOR, Supp. (No. 39) 10, U.N. Doc. A/31/39 (1976). The United States abstained.

Immediately after independence, Transkei's push to have Lesotho recognize them became more coercive.[196] In November 1976, Transkei began demanding that Lesotho citizens present Transkeian visas if they wished to cross the border, something which many Basotho had to do often to work or trade in South Africa. Refusing to communicate directly with Umtata, Lesotho complained to Pretoria and eventually appealed to the UN Secretary-General claiming that South Africa's border closure caused Lesotho significant financial distress. The UN Security Council passed a resolution commending Lesotho for not recognizing Transkei and condemned South Africa for pressuring them to do so.[197] In March 1978, a more bizarre occurrence happened when 139 head of cattle wandered over the border from Lesotho into Transkei. After Transkei impounded the cattle, Lesotho appealed directly to Pretoria to have them returned, but South Africa directed them back to Umtata, claiming that it no longer had sovereign control over Transkei. Once again Lesotho refused to contact Umtata and appealed to the UN. Transkei would not budge. Ultimately Lesotho issued passports to the cattle owners "under duress" who were then allowed to come over and retrieve their cattle, under the stipulation that this one-off issuance did not imply recognition.[198]

Being outside normal, legal channels available to other states, unable or unwilling to vet various people coming to offer aid, Transkei was particularly vulnerable to exploitation by some individuals looking to take advantage of their desperate position. Numerous individuals drew from the Transkeian treasury under these auspices ostensibly for the purposes of winning recognition and attracting investment. In the United States Transkei first hired a black American public relations man named Andrew Hatcher.[199] As late as October 1976, Hatcher announced that at least six countries would recognize Transkei immediately following independence, though he refused to name them besides indicating that four were from Africa and the other two from the Far East.[200] Nothing came of his prediction. A *Rand Daily Mail* exposé from

---

[196] For more on the Lesotho/Transkeian border conflicts, see the draft article in preparation for publication by John Aerni-Flessner and Chitja Twala, tentatively titled "Bargaining with Land: Borders, Bantustans, and Sovereignty in 1970s Southern Africa" (in author's possession).

[197] UNSC Res 402 (1976). Heydt, "Nonrecognition," p. 190. This also resulted in an outpouring of international aid to Lesotho.

[198] United Nations Archives, Country Files of the Secretary General – Kurt Waldheim-Transkei, 25/10/1976–07/05/1978, S-0904-0039-07, "Lesotho/Transkei Situation," Note for the File, March 1978.

[199] Streek and Wicksteed, *Render unto Kaiser*, p. 200.

[200] Streek and Wicksteed, *Render unto Kaiser*, p. 200.

May 1978 detailed the Transkeian public funds spent on overseas agents.[201] The process, or lack of process, of how Transkei time and again fell for the expensive promises of outsiders promising diplomatic connections was described by the secretary for foreign affairs to the National Assembly in 1978:

> [there were people in other countries] who try in various ways to project the image of Transkei, and these people are paid. Some of the people who are included amongst these lobbyists are not appointed by the department. They merely come from the Prime Minister's department. The Prime Minister brings people from his department and we have to pay them. The moment he has agreed or has made it possible that they represent Transkei in some way we have to pay them. We have therefore had to pay some gentlemen, for instance, with whom we had not entered into any contract as a department.[202]

This same idea of the prime minister's end-around the normal appointment procedure was later expressed by the deputy secretary of foreign affairs: "Sometimes the department gets a directive and it comes from the Prime Minister that he should be given so much and it is not easy for the department to say 'no' if the Prime Minister says he must be given so much."[203]

Perhaps the most embarrassing episode of Transkei's search for recognition was the so-called Ecuador breakthrough. The South African *Sunday Tribune* reported that Transkei's hopes of breaking through its international "Blanket of Hostility" was greater in South America than elsewhere.[204] In August 1976, a delegation from Transkei visited Argentina, Brazil, Chile, Paraguay, and Uruguay.[205] The trip was planned by the South African DFA, and included high-level Transkeian officials, including soon-to-be appointed Foreign Minister Digby Koyana. Leslie Masimini, the so-called Minister at Large representing Transkei in the North, Central, and South America, told the *Rand Daily Mail* three months before independence that he thought there

---

[201] "R30,000 Bill to Promote Transkei," *Rand Daily Mail*, May 29, 1978. See also: Streek and Wicksteed, *Render unto Kaiser*, pp. 204–205.

[202] Minutes of Select Committee on Public Accounts, Debates of the National Assembly, 1978, quoted in: Streek and Wicksteed, *Render unto Kaiser*, p. 203.

[203] Minutes of Select Committee on Public Accounts, Debates of the National Assembly, 1978, quoted in: Streek and Wicksteed, *Render unto Kaiser*, p. 204.

[204] See: US State Department Telegram from Durban to Secretary of State, Washington, "Transkei Delegation to Visit South America," July 26, 1976, accessed via Wikileaks on June 9, 2017: wikileaks.org/plusd/cables/1976DURBAN00353_b.html.

[205] See: US State Department Telegram from Durban to Secretary of State, Washington, "Transkei Delegation to Visit South America," July 26, 1976, accessed via Wikileaks on June 9, 2017: wikileaks.org/plusd/cables/1976DURBAN00353_b.html.

were several South American countries looking to break Transkei's isolation, and he believed that South America would definitely be "the key to world recognition of Transkei."[206]

Almost five months after Transkei's putative independence, the Ecuador affair became news on April 4, 1977, when the Transkei National Assembly welcomed a delegation from Ecuador led by Vice Admiral Maldonado Mino. When Mino addressed the National Assembly he sent greetings from the president of Ecuador, and invited Kaiser Matanzima to visit Ecuador.[207] Afterward, Matanzima spoke in the assembly: "On this day, in the full glare of all humanity, the free and sovereign people of Ecuador and Transkei have found each other."[208] The *Die Burger* newspaper called the Ecuador visit a "great breakthrough" and it appeared that Ecuador had recognized Transkei.[209] To the Transkeian regime, this seemed to be the rip in the blanket they had waited for. A week later, Digby Koyana announced to the assembly that this upcoming state visit to Ecuador "could escalate visits and returns of visits to other countries, particularly Third World countries," and he added that more good news was likely on the way.[210] Mino's visit seemed to lead to a concrete trade deal between the two countries that was signed in Transkei. But things soon started to fall apart. On May 11, 1977, Ecuador's Foreign Ministry denied that Mino's delegation had any official status: "[Ecuador] has not accredited any official mission encharged with political responsibility to that region of Africa."[211] Ecuador then reaffirmed their support of the UN's position on the nonrecognition of Transkei. A clearly embarrassed Koyana asserted that this reversal must have been the result of outside pressure. As time wore on it became clear that the Transkeian regime had been the victims of a scam.[212]

This scam was very close in substance to the Guatemalan recognition scam that duped the Katangese. A "mysterious lobbyist/diplomat" named Dr. Richard Blom was at the center of this particular Ecuadorian scam.[213] A wealthy Australian businessman, Blom, resided in East London in the Cape Province. Transkei had appointed Blom as a roving ambassador on the basis of Blom's promises of foreign connections. In his speech to the National Assembly, Mino praised Blom for

[206] "Off to Washington," *Rand Daily Mail,* July 9, 1977.
[207] Streek and Wicksteed, *Render unto Kaiser,* p. 205.
[208] Quoted in Streek and Wicksteed, *Render unto Kaiser,* p. 205.
[209] Streek and Wicksteed, *Render unto Kaiser,* p. 205.
[210] Quoted in Streek and Wicksteed, *Render unto Kaiser,* p. 205.
[211] Streek and Wicksteed, *Render unto Kaiser,* p. 206.
[212] Streek and Wicksteed, *Render unto Kaiser,* p. 206.
[213] Streek and Wicksteed, *Render unto Kaiser,* p. 206.

arranging the Ecuadorian visit, something which boosted Blom's credibility in Matanzima's circle.[214] What later became public was that on September 14, 1977 Blom and Transkei's Chief of Protocol, Liston Ntshongwana, left on a mission for South America for which they were paid R10,000 each.[215] Blom never came back. The Transkei regime tried without luck to reach him in Ecuador. The reasons for him never returning to South Africa became more obvious when the East London authorities issued a writ against Blom for back taxes. Soon the Transkeian authorities issued their own writ against him, and it became known that Australia had a long-standing warrant out for him for currency violations.[216]

Like the other pseudo-states in this book, Transkei's illegal status meant that they could not as easily avail themselves of the more thorough background checks and vetting processes for individuals doing business with the regime that would have been possible through normal state-to-state communications, and it obviously could not enter into extradition agreements with other states. In 1966, L. Ron Hubbard, the founder of Scientology, was initially welcomed into Rhodesia as a mysterious American millionaire with big development plans and ambitious political ideas, and he briefly set up his headquarters in the break-away state. But at the end of six months the Rhodesians had had enough and refused to extend his visa forcing him to leave.[217] James Earl Ray was believed to be making his way to Rhodesia when he was nabbed in Heathrow Airport and extradited to the United States for killing Dr. Martin Luther King.[218] Other unsavory types drifted in and out of these aspirant states.[219] In 1979, George Matanzima, the Minister of Foreign Affairs, admitted this was a problem for Transkei:

There are wolves hovering around, promising Transkei the moon and the stars, but when once a person promises the moon and the stars you know what generally happens. We never get to the stars, and the stars never come to us, nor the moon for that matter. It is time that we become very careful of whom we bring into Transkei, and we are determined to do so.[220]

---

[214] Streek and Wicksteed, *Render unto Kaiser*, p. 206.

[215] Streek and Wicksteed, *Render unto Kaiser*, p. 206.

[216] Streek and Wicksteed, *Render unto Kaiser*, p. 207.

[217] Erin Conway-Smith, "Inside L. Ron Hubbard's Johannesburg Mansion, Where Scientology's Toughest Test Was Born," *The Week*, June 29, 2015.

[218] "Rhodesia-US Link in Manhunt: Immigration Query by Luther King Suspect: Government Assurance of Watch Is Reported," *Rhodesia Herald*, June 14, 1968.

[219] See: Brownell, *Collapse of Rhodesia*.

[220] Quoted in Streek and Wicksteed, *Render unto Kaiser*, pp. 212–213.

It was not uncommon for drifters and grifters, uhuru hoppers, and other ne'er-do-wells to end up in these territories from all over Africa and further afield, giving these illegal states the look of the Mos Eisley Cantina in the movie *Star Wars*.[221]

Another instance of Transkei's vulnerability to scams was the Berkeley affair. Aptly summarizing the whole affair, authors Streek and Wicksteed wrote: "It was odd: there is simply no other way to describe the situation, which became odder as it went on."[222] A former Conservative MP, who later joined the Labour Party only to switch to the Social Democratic Party before ultimately returning to Labour, Humphry Berkeley, would improbably become an important political and diplomatic advisor for Matanzima for a year.[223] Berkeley was a gay rights advocate as well as a prominent anti-apartheid activist. He was an honorary Vice President of the British-based Anti-Apartheid Movement, and was therefore a prohibited immigrant in the republic.

A London-based West Indian public relations man named Scobie Loblack first introduced Berkeley to Transkeian affairs.[224] As far back as July 1976, Loblack was on Digby Koyana's list to attend Transkei's independence celebration.[225] Berkeley visited Umtata in April 1978 along with Loblack and a man named Paul Dwyer, where he met Kaiser Matanzima in person. He was soon given a R100,000 a year job. Transkei's public relations presence in London at the time was swelling with staff and showered with Transkei tax money. Those receiving this Transkeian tax money included Berkeley and Loblack, but also the Business Expansion firm headed by Paul Dwyer, who was described as "Transkei's information and publicity representative."[226] Describing his role in London at the time, Loblack said, "My job is to explain to Britain and Europe that Transkei is not a homeland. Neither is it some place ridden with mud huts and shacks."[227] This was all done by Matanzima against the wishes of the Foreign Minister, Koyana.[228]

In July 1978, Matanzima shuffled his cabinet around, and significantly absorbed the foreign affairs and information portfolios into the prime minister's own office, stripping it from Koyana, who was then given the

[221] *Star Wars: A New Hope* directed by George Lucas, Lucasfilm Ltd. (1977).
[222] Streek and Wicksteed, *Render unto Kaiser*, pp. 207–208.
[223] Streek and Wicksteed, *Render unto Kaiser*, p. 207.
[224] Streek and Wicksteed, *Render unto Kaiser*, p. 208.
[225] SA National Archives, Pretoria, Box: Transkei 1/226/1/1, "Independence Celebrations and Invitations," "Invitations as of 27 July 1976."
[226] Streek and Wicksteed, *Render unto Kaiser*, p. 208.
[227] Quoted in Stultz, *Transkei's Half Loaf*, p. 120.
[228] Streek and Wicksteed, *Render unto Kaiser*, p. 208.

Ministry of Justice and Prisons.[229] As reported by the US State Department, a source in Umtata said that the move was driven by Matanzima's dissatisfaction with the "inability of Koyana to obtain recognition for Transkei."[230] Other related reports claim that the move was also in part the result of a "personal feud" between Koyana and Humphry Berkeley.[231] Berkeley admitted to a *Washington Post* reporter his dislike for Koyana and his desire to run Transkei's foreign affairs.[232] A few days after the cabinet reshuffling, Matanzima announced Humphry Berkeley, a former Conservative MP, to the new post of "Diplomatic Representative for Transkei" on July 21, 1978.[233]

This new team had lofty goals for Transkei's outreach.[234] In April 1978, while Berkeley, Loblack, and Dwyer were all in Umtata, Transkei broke relations with Pretoria, which was widely read in South Africa as something prompted by Berkeley.[235] Not hiding his intentions at all, Matanzima combined his call to end diplomatic ties with South Africa with a simultaneous renewed drive to win diplomatic recognition in the West.[236] Among other things, Berkeley advised Matanzima not to recognize Bophuthatswana, "a step he argued would only cheapen Transkei's claim to unique status."[237] He pitched to Western audiences the

---

[229] See: US State Department Telegram from Durban to Secretary of State, Washington, "Cabinet Reshuffled; Prime Minister Assumes Foreign Affairs," July 21, 1978, accessed via Wikileaks on June 9, 2017: https://wikileaks.org/plusd/cables/1978DURBAN00437_d .html.

[230] See: US State Department Telegram from Durban to Secretary of State, Washington, "Cabinet Reshuffled; Prime Minister Assumes Foreign Affairs," July 21, 1978, accessed via Wikileaks on June 9, 2017: https://wikileaks.org/plusd/cables/1978DURBAN00437_d .html.

[231] See: US State Department Telegram from Durban to Secretary of State, Washington, "Cabinet Reshuffled; Prime Minister Assumes Foreign Affairs," July 21, 1978, accessed via Wikileaks on June 9, 2017: https://wikileaks.org/plusd/cables/1978DURBAN00437_d .html.

[232] See: US State Department Telegram from Durban to Secretary of State, Washington, "Former British MP Appointed Diplomatic Representative for Transkei," July 26, 1978, accessed via Wikileaks on June 9, 2017: wikileaks.org/plusd/cables/1978DURBAN00445_ d.html.

[233] See: US State Department Telegram from Durban to Secretary of State, Washington, "Former British MP Appointed Diplomatic Representative for Transkei," July 26, 1978, accessed via Wikileaks on June 9, 2017: wikileaks.org/plusd/cables/1978DURBAN00445_ d.html.

[234] See: Streek and Wicksteed, *Render unto Kaiser*, p. 215.

[235] Streek and Wicksteed argue that Berkeley likely "confirmed and strengthened" the idea of the diplomatic break that had already been around for some time as a play for international recognition. Streek and Wicksteed, *Render unto Kaiser*, p. 209.

[236] John Burns, "Transkei Breaks Diplomatic Tie, Its Only One, with South Africans," *New York Times*, April 11, 1978.

[237] See: US State Department Telegram from Durban to Secretary of State, Washington, "Former British MP Appointed Diplomatic Representative for Transkei," July 26,

possibility of a naval station on the Transkei coast, free from the apartheid baggage that came with the Simonstown base. To do this, he argued for the construction of a new seaport. And, "his schemes got more grandiose as they went along."[238]

In the announcement of the break, Matanzima said that Transkei was withdrawing all diplomatic staff from South Africa and he expected Pretoria to do the same. In a fiery speech to the National Assembly he called on the West to recognize Transkeian independence, but said he would accept military and economic assistance from any country, Western or Communist.[239] Chief Matanzima told the assembly that the South African government had "callously slaughtered millions of blacks in the enforcement of their obnoxious laws."[240] He said he expected South Africa to punish Transkei for the break and asked for aid from the West to protect them. He then made explicit Transkei's new policy of supporting liberation movements: "We have been compelled to join in the liberatory movements and claim the whole of South Africa as belonging to whites and blacks, with blacks controlling the majority. Henceforth this will be the fundamental policy of our struggle for liberation."[241]

If Matanzima expected an immediate and positive reaction overseas to Transkei's break with South Africa, he was sorely disappointed. As John Burns reported, the South African popular press responded to Matanzima's diplomatic break and threat of war with "a collective shrug."[242] And the *Rand Daily Mail* reported that black South African exiles in London and Western diplomats were all "suspending judgment" on the issue.[243] The newspaper's sources relayed that those interviewed were waiting to see how far Matanzima would go in breaking with Pretoria to see if he was indeed serious.[244] Britain's reaction to his announcement was "decidedly cool."[245] The US State Department issued a statement about the diplomatic break:

We do not believe that the announcement of a break in diplomatic relations between Transkei and South Africa changes the fundamental character of the

1978, accessed via Wikileaks on June 9, 2017: wikileaks.org/plusd/cables/1978DURBAN00445_d.html.

[238] Streek and Wicksteed, *Render unto Kaiser*, p. 209.

[239] "Transkei Cuts Ties," *Rand Daily Mail*, April 11, 1978.

[240] "Transkei Cuts Ties," *Rand Daily Mail*, April 11, 1978.

[241] "Transkei Cuts Ties," *Rand Daily Mail*, April 11, 1978.

[242] John Burns, "Transkei Breaks Diplomatic Tie, Its Only One, with South Africans," *New York Times*, April 11, 1978.

[243] "West Plays Waiting Game," *Rand Daily Mail*, April 11, 1978.

[244] "West Plays Waiting Game," *Rand Daily Mail*, April 11, 1978.

[245] "Transkei Cuts Ties," *Rand Daily Mail*, April 11, 1978.

relationship between them. We have never recognized Transkei as an independent entity, and there is not question of our doing so now ... We do not recognize the Transkei as an independent nation.[246]

According to initial reports, Vorster and Pik Botha "were apparently astounded at the development" and it was seen as a blow to their homeland policy, which had Transkei as its "showpiece."[247] But it is quite possible that South Africa's purported shock was a charade.

Five months after the diplomatic break, in September 1978, an official delegation from the Ivory Coast did arrive in Umtata, and unlike the Ecuadorian debacle a year before, their credentials checked out.[248] The delegation again seemed to augur the beginning of a cascade of recognition. Leslie Masimini said in September 1978, nearly two years after Transkei's independence with no other country besides South Africa recognizing them, that he still expected twenty African countries were ready to recognize Transkei.[249] Berkeley had built up expectations for the second-year anniversary in October as a grand opportunity for Transkei to display its newfound freedom of movement and its new international position.[250] But as explained in Chapter 3, the second-year independence celebration came and went without any foreign dignitaries attending.

To make the break with South Africa viable, Transkei needed new sources of money. It was thought by some that the way out was to unilaterally break with Pretoria and hope that another state or states would step in. Maybe Nigeria would be the answer. Berkeley would later claim in a *Spectator* article he wrote that he had successfully arranged for a Nigerian delegation to visit Umtata and that they agreed to train the military and police, and give Transkei a loan to finance the harbor, the sort of too-good-to-be-true windfall that is reminiscent of the internet era's "Nigerian Prince" hoaxes.[251] Later, he alleged that Matanzima inexplicably left the Nigerian delegation waiting in Umtata while he went away to East London, which scuttled the potential deal. Berkeley publicly claimed that South Africa was behind the death of the Nigerian deal, and with it the only chances for Transkeian recognition.[252] No other new patrons appeared.

---

[246] State Department press briefing, DPC, 67, April 11, 1978.
[247] "Transkei Cuts Ties," *Rand Daily Mail*, April 11, 1978.
[248] Streek and Wicksteed, *Render unto Kaiser*, p. 211.
[249] Streek and Wicksteed, *Render unto Kaiser*, p. 201.
[250] Streek and Wicksteed, *Render unto Kaiser*, p. 211.
[251] H. Berkeley, "The Mission that Failed," *The Spectator*, August 4, 1979.
[252] H. Berkeley, "The Mission that Failed," *The Spectator*, August 4, 1979.

On February 19, 1979, Berkeley was eating at the Umtata Holiday Inn when two men approached his table, one claiming he was a police-man.[253] The men escorted him out of the restaurant and into a car, and then drove him to a remote location outside Umtata. He was taken out and allegedly beaten and whipped with belts.[254] He was then thrown into the trunk and driven to another spot where they took him out and pointed a gun at him threatening to kill him. Berkeley was left by the side of the road just over the border in South Africa. He made his way back to Transkei afterward, but not surprisingly, Berkeley soon discovered he was fired from his role as diplomatic representative.[255] The story behind Berkeley's Nigerian plan began to unravel over the course of year when Transkeian foreign affairs officials began chasing down their mysterious Nigerian contacts, and they soon found that much of Berkeley's story was false.[256] George Matanzima piled on: "Mr Berkeley is making colossal efforts to bluff the world, just as he attempted to bluff the government of Transkei by faking what he knew he was incapable of performing."[257] Berkeley would always contend that his swift (and violent) firing and removal from Transkei was the work of South Africa.

To the extent that the break with Pretoria was an effort to win recog-nition, it failed. Interestingly South Africa did not retaliate against Transkei for the diplomatic affront.[258] South African patience and mag-nanimity in the wake of Transkei's actions certainly seemed less merciful than fishy. All the same, with South Africa's military withdrawal, Transkei turned to the battle-hardened Rhodesian military for help in training its soldiers.[259] This farcical, pantomime diplomatic fight ended in April 1980 with South Africa ceding a portion of East Griqualand to Transkei and relations were restored. But the exercise highlighted the dependent relationship between the two, especially since the inter-national community continued to shun Transkei.

The election of Ronald Reagan was seen by hopeful observers in South Africa, Transkei, and elsewhere as a last chance of a diplomatic

[253] Streek and Wicksteed, *Render unto Kaiser*, p. 217.
[254] Streek and Wicksteed, *Render unto Kaiser*, p. 219.
[255] Streek and Wicksteed, *Render unto Kaiser*, p. 222–223.
[256] Streek and Wicksteed, *Render unto Kaiser*, p. 216.
[257] Quoted in Streek and Wicksteed, *Render unto Kaiser*, p. 215.
[258] South Africa still bailed Transkei out, granting an emergency grant to pay Transkei civil servants. Patrick Lawrence, "Transkei Is Fighting on Two Fronts," *Rand Daily Mail*, October 16, 1979. In April 1978, just a few weeks after the flamboyant break, Transkei suffered horrible flooding along its coastline and had to come to South Africa asking for aid relief. Southall, *South Africa's Transkei*, p. 271.
[259] Southall, *South Africa's Transkei*, p. 272.

breakthrough for Transkei recognition.[260] With Reagan's victory came the advancement of J. A. Parker, who had worked on Transkeian public relations in Washington, to Reagan's transition team. Parker would later be appointed to the Reagan administration. In an interview in Umtata in 1981, Masimini announced that he had been invited to attend Ronald Reagan's inauguration in 1981 as the Transkeian representative.[261] But by January 10, 1981, it became clear that Masimini had not been invited by the official inaugural committee to the inauguration ceremony.[262] The invitation Masimini received was only to one of the many unofficial private functions associated with the inauguration and the invitation was for him to attend in his personal capacity.[263]

Bophuthatswana

Much as the nonrecognition of Katanga served as a general model for rejecting later secessionist movements in Africa, the nonrecognition of Bophuthatswana by the international community followed the more specific template created for Transkei a year before. This allowed the international community to effectively ignore the specific arguments made by Bophuthatswana by collapsing it into the broader anti-Bantustan policy. Since Transkei was a tailor-made template for Bophuthatswana and all the later Bantustans, the suit was already cut and fitted and only needed to be draped over each one as they declared independence. This did not mean that Bophuthatswana did not try to shake off this tailored precedent.

In its search for international recognition, Bophuthatswana shared many of the same propaganda themes as Transkei, even as it tried to distinguish itself from its predecessor. The primary theme shared by both was that they were not South Africa's puppets and were not the artificial creations of apartheid.[264] Like Matanzima, Lucas Mangope pleaded that

---

[260] "Reagan Win May Be Good News for Transkei," *Rand Daily Mail*, July 28, 1980.

[261] John Matisonn, "No Official Invitation for Kei's Man in US," *Rand Daily Mail*, January 10, 1981.

[262] The US State Department issued what must have been a devastatingly clear statement on the matter. "Foreign agents, including the agent of the so-called Republic of Transkei, have no diplomatic status in the US. No invitation was or will be issued to Transkei. The US does not recognize the Transkei but considers it to be an integral part of the Republic of South Africa. We do not believe that the homelands offer a viable solution to South Africa's racial problems, and we are not willing to recognize any solution which is imposed on the black majority without their consent." Quoted in Streek and Wicksteed, *Render unto Kaiser*, p. 357.

[263] John Matisonn, "No Official Invitation for Kei's Man in US," *Rand Daily Mail*, January 10, 1981.

[264] See for example: "Mangope Speaks Out on Key Issues," *Rand Daily Mail*, July 3, 1981.

he hoped that Bophuthatswana would be judged on its own merits and not judged by the unpopularity of apartheid more generally. Related to their arguments that they were not simply the by-products of apartheid, each Bantustan presented the case that they had an existence that preceded that of the Union of South Africa and contained a logic outside that of apartheid – even if their independence also benefited South Africa.

What weakened this argument was that all the Bantustans were released one by one by South Africa under conditions set by the South Africans as part of South Africa's grand policy. The introduction of new Bantustans hurt each existing Bantustan's claim for individuality. Mangope addressed the relationship between Bophuthatswana's claims for independence and those of the other Bantustans when asked about it in 1981:

When it comes to the question of recognition, any country – Great Britain for example – should define its criteria for recognition and apply such criteria to us. If they are also interested in considering recognition for Transkei they should do the same. But then they should decide on merit on recognition for us, on merit for Transkei and on merit for Venda. I believe we are definitely not the same. Not even twins are the same you know.[265]

Mangope was always much more generous to the other Bantustans' claims than was Matanzima, who positioned Transkei as a unique case, a result likely less due to Mangope's more magnanimous personality than to the fact that Bophuthatswana was the second and not the first Bantustan released for independence.

Kaiser Matanzima attended Bophuthatswana's independence celebrations on December 6, 1977, in its new capital of Mmabatho. Despite attending its independence ceremony, Mangope failed to win immediate official diplomatic recognition from Transkei.[266] A month after Transkei's break with South Africa, Mangope visited Transkei on a state visit in May 1978, an occasion which Transkei took as an opportunity to display all the requisite protocols and pomp of a state visit – including a 21-gun salute from a muzzle loading cannon – in welcoming the head of the new Bophuthatswanan state.[267] This visit was reminiscent of the pseudo-state visit of the leader of the breakaway region of South Kasai

---

[265] "Mangope Speaks Out on Key Issues," *Rand Daily Mail*, July 3, 1981.

[266] State Department Telegram from US Consulate Durban to Secretary of State and Other Posts, "Transkei and Bophuthatswana Fail to Establish Diplomatic Links," June 7, 1978, accessed via Wikileaks: wikileaks.org/plusd/cables/1978DURBAN00342_d.html.

[267] State Department Telegram from US Consulate Durban to Secretary of State and Other Posts, "Transkei and Bophuthatswana Fail to Establish Diplomatic Links," June 7, 1978, accessed via Wikileaks: wikileaks.org/plusd/cables/1978DURBAN00342_d.html.

to Tshombe's Katanga. The Transkei visit was the first time since Bophuthatswana's independence that the two leaders had met and Mangope had hoped to use the occasion to exchange ambassadors with Transkei, but was unable to convince Matanzima to do so.[268] Umtata's official line was that of all the other homelands only Transkei could justifiably call itself a sovereign nation. Employing an argument closely associated with Berkeley, who was at that time still in favor in Umtata, Matanzima reportedly held out that unlike Transkei, Bophuthatswana was a true creature of apartheid and that were Transkei to be too closely associated with the other "artificial" Bantustans it would harm claims to Transkei's historical uniqueness and destroy its chances at international recognition.[269] Eventually, Matanzima relented under South African pressure and finally recognized Bophuthatswana.

Matanzima's capitulation regarding Bophuthatswana's recognition did not automatically apply to the other Bantustans as they were released. Prior to the independence of the third Bantustan, Venda, in 1979, Matanzima dismissed the new Bantustan as a fraudulent country that had no historical claim to independence like Transkei and (presumably, now) Bophuthatswana. Once again, under pressure from Pretoria Matanzima would back away from this view of Venda as well.[270] In 1981, Umtata eventually hosted the President of Venda, Chief Patrick Mphephu, in an official pseudo-state visit.[271] Mphephu flattered Matanzima by telling him he aimed to model Venda on Transkei and wanted his delegation to note everything they saw and learn during their visit.[272] It was a different case with the creation of Ciskei in 1981. Ciskei was also ethnically Xhosa, which undermined Transkei's ethno-national claim for self-determination, as well as exposing the National Party's self-serving application of the tribalized nature of the Bantustans. George Matanzima made a public statement that Transkei had the "rightful claim" to be the sole representative of the Xhosa and that Transkei would not sit with Ciskei in any constellation of states.[273] "I wish to urge South Africa," Matanzima pleaded, "not to create problems for itself by granting independence to Ciskei separately from Transkei."[274] Furious,

---

[268] "Mangope's Kei Visit 'Fruitless," *Rand Daily Mail*, May 23, 1978.
[269] State Department Telegram from US Consulate Durban to Secretary of State and Other Posts, "Transkei and Bophuthatswana Fail to Establish Diplomatic Links," June 7, 1978, accessed via Wikileaks: wikileaks.org/plusd/cables/1978DURBAN00342_d.html.
[270] Streek and Wicksteed, *Render unto Kaiser*, p. 361.
[271] Streek and Wicksteed, *Render unto Kaiser*, p. 361.
[272] Streek and Wicksteed, *Render unto Kaiser*, p. 361.
[273] Streek and Wicksteed, *Render unto Kaiser*, p. 360.
[274] Quoted in Streek and Wicksteed, *Render unto Kaiser*, p. 360.

Chief Lennox Sebe, the Chief Minister of Ciskei stated that Ciskei would indeed get independence just like Transkei: "Our people voiced their feelings about independence in a referendum. We believe their wishes are sacred. The nation says it wants independence. Where does Chief Matanzima come into it? Who is he?"[275] South Africa was embarrassed that two of its three Bantustans would not recognize each other, but once again, Transkei did come around to recognize Ciskei and all the Bantustans would come to exchange embassies in each other's capitals. However, the tensions between Transkei and Ciskei never abated.[276]

On the cusp of its independence, Bophuthatswana sent diplomatic trainees to Pretoria and later to foreign postings under South African tutelage just like Transkei.[277] Also like Transkei, Bophuthatswana focused its recognition appeal on the former HCTs. Among other themes, the regime elaborated upon their supposedly authentic ethnic basis among the Tswana peoples. This argument was harmed by the negative responses of their purported ethnic Tswana brethren across the border. On the day of Bophuthatswana's independence celebrations, the Botswana minister of external affairs announced:

We reject the Bantustan policy because we believe it unjust. Therefore, it cannot be the answer to the racial problems of South Africa. The Botswana Government, therefore, decided that it would not recognize the independence of any Bantustan. Bophuthatswana will not be an exception to this policy.[278]

Months after their disappointing independence ceremony, Bophuthatswana's prospects for recognition were still dreary. At the official opening of the National Assembly, Mangope complained that informal high-level contacts with countries in Africa were "extremely heartening" but Bophuthatswana had yet to win any formal recognition.[279] He said that although all the international legal requirements for recognition had been met, only two unnamed countries had "the

---

[275] Quoted in Streek and Wicksteed, *Render unto Kaiser*, p. 360.

[276] Former Rhodesian Selous Scout commandos under Reid Daly, then the head of the Transkei Defense Forces, conducted several operations intended to disrupt and overthrow the Ciskeian government, but they were unsuccessful. It would be the feuding Matanzima brothers themselves who were ousted in a military coup in October 1987. Maj. Gen. Bantu Holomisa would take control of Transkei in December. See: Alan Cowel, "Pretoria Puzzle: 'Homelands' at Odds," *New York Times*, October 20, 1986; John F. Burns, "Army Coup in South African Homeland," *New York Times*, December 31, 1987.

[277] See: US State Department Telegram from Pretoria to Secretary of State, Washington, "Tswana Diplomatic Trainees," June 22, 1977, accessed via Wikileaks on June 9, 2017: wikileaks.org/plusd/cables/1977PRETOR03057_c.html.

[278] "It's a Non-event across the Border," *Rand Daily Mail*, December 6, 1977.

[279] "Mangope Hits at 'Africa's Unrealism'," *Rand Daily Mail*, March 8, 1978.

courage to speak up." He must have been referring to South Africa and Transkei.[280] In his fury at the alleged hypocrisy of the international community in singling his pseudo-state out for international opprobrium, Mangope's speech mirrored those of Tshombe, Smith, and Matanzima:

The remainder of our brother countries still regrettably adhere to outdated slogans and guidelines in policy which are rapidly being overtaken by realities and events as shown by the conflicts elsewhere on this continent. The sooner our brothers in Africa show a sense of realism in the face of our human plight, the easier it will be to undo the untold damage which is being inflicted on the cause of African unity as long as they withhold their recognition from us.[281]

Just as Transkei's wooing of its neighbor Lesotho turned from courtship to outright animosity, so too did Bophuthatswana's attempted association with Botswana turn bitter. An example of Bophuthatswana's efforts to coerce Botswana into recognition concerned international water rights. The Ngotwane and Molopo rivers begin in Bophuthatswana and flow into Botswana, where the water is relied upon for domestic and agricultural purposes.[282] In 1979, Bophuthatswana began the construction of the Ngotwane Dam to provide water for irrigation. Bophuthatswana also dammed the Molopo River for agriculture and recreational purposes. Together these dams cut the water flow into Botswana.[283] Earlier, South Africa had agreed to consult Botswana before any potential damming of the headwaters of the Limpopo River, and because of this supposedly inherited agreement, Bophuthatswana offered to bring in Botswanan officials to take part in the decision-making process, but Botswana refused to engage with the illegal state. Instead, they issued a complaint directly to South Africa. Bophuthatswana denied that South Africa had anything to do with the dam building projects since sovereignty had been transferred in December of 1977.[284]

A second border dispute between Bophuthatswana and Botswana began on the last day of 1986 when Bophuthatswana informed Botswana that Botswanan citizens would from then on require a visa to enter Bophuthatswana that they must apply for, thirty days before departure.[285] This adversely affected transport in and out of Botswana into South Africa, upon which it was dependent.[286] Lucas Mangope used the

---

[280] "Mangope Hits at 'Africa's Unrealism'," *Rand Daily Mail*, March 8, 1978.
[281] "Mangope Hits at 'Africa's Unrealism'," *Rand Daily Mail*, March 8, 1978.
[282] Drummond and Manson, "Bophuthatswana–Botswana Border," p. 234.
[283] Drummond and Manson, "Bophuthatswana–Botswana Border," p. 235.
[284] Drummond and Manson, "Bophuthatswana–Botswana Border," p. 235.
[285] Drummond and Manson, "Bophuthatswana–Botswana Border," p. 235.
[286] Drummond and Manson, "Bophuthatswana–Botswana Border," p. 236.

occasion of Bophuthatswana's ninth independence commemoration on December 6, 1986 to discuss the unilateral move: "If Botswana cannot change its foreign policy on Bophuthatswana and continues with its mudslinging, then Bophuthatswana will be left with no option but to retaliate ... and ... in quite a few areas of our coexistence we could be difficult to the extreme discomfort of Botswana."[287] As with the conflict over water rights, Botswana refused to interact with Bophuthatswana directly and communicated only with South Africa in order to persuade them to pressure Mangope. The South Africans agreed to intervene, and this led to Bophuthatswana quietly dropping the visa requirement in August 1987.[288] As with Transkei, Bophuthatswana's strong-arm tactics failed.

Just as Transkei and South Africa held out hope for the break in the wall of nonrecognition coming from francophone Africa, so too did Bophuthatswana. Five months before independence, Leopold Senghor of Senegal welcomed an official delegation from Bophuthatswana. *The Rand Daily Mail* characterized the meeting as a "triumph," and it raised hopes that Senegal would attend the ceremony and recognize the new state.[289] Within days, however, the Senegalese denied the meeting was of an official nature and their policy was still in line with that of the OAU – no recognition.[290] Like Senegal, other francophone countries similarly made slight nods toward recognition, but none ever went all the way. As described in an earlier chapter, no official delegation from francophone Africa, or anywhere else attended Bophuthatswana's independence ceremony.

American policy toward the Bantustans was set with Transkei and was repeated verbatim with regard to Bophuthatswana, and later Venda and Ciskei.[291] The Carter administration made its position on recognizing Bophuthatswana clear months before their Independence Day.[292] In keeping with international consensus, American foreign policy held that

---

[287] Drummond and Manson, "Bophuthatswana–Botswana Border," p. 236.

[288] Drummond and Manson, "Bophuthatswana–Botswana Border," pp. 236–237.

[289] State Department Telegram from US Embassy Pretoria to Secretary of State and Cape Town, "An External Triumph and an Internal Rebuff," July 19, 1977, accessed via Wikileaks: wikileaks.org/plusd/cables/1977PRETOR03555_c.html.

[290] State Department Telegram from US Embassy Dakar to Secretary of State and Cape Town, "Senegal Asserts Continued Opposition to Bantustans," September 22, 1977, accessed via Wikileaks: wikileaks.org/plusd/cables/1977DAKAR04974_c.html.

[291] State Department Telegram from US Embassy Pretoria to Secretary of State and Cape Town, "Official Contacts with the 'Independent' Homelands," September 29, 1979, accessed via Wikileaks: wikileaks.org/plusd/cables/1979PRETOR08945_e.html.

[292] In a speech in July 1977, Secretary of State Cyrus Vance said, "The South African Government's policy of establishing separate homelands for black South Africans was devised without reference to the wishes of the blacks themselves. For this reason, and

all the Bantustans remained an integral part of South Africa. But the State Department had a very complicated view as to how to treat Bophuthatswana, and their citizenry – most of whom the US government knew did not accept that they were citizens of the new pseudo-state. The excerpt below addresses some of these complications:

... in our view, the homeland areas of South Africa are nothing more than administrative units, of the same nature as any of the four South African provinces: Natal, the Cape, Transvaal, or the Orange Free State. There is no question we should continue to refuse to recognize the so-called independent homelands and to eschew any form of contact with officials of those "governments" (except possibly in the case of an emergency). While there are obvious limits to the argument that setting up an international barrier against travel to or dealings with the unrecognized "independent states" confers a form of negative recognition, we believe the embassy should simply ignore these unrecognized boundaries and officials to the extent permitted by the "state" in question. This policy leaves us free to maintain contact with the unwilling "citizens" of those areas as South African citizens, which we assert they are, or should be.[293]

It was therefore rather oddly in the freedom of US officials to travel to and from the Bantustans, not in avoiding going to them altogether, where nonrecognition tangibly expressed itself.

The high-water mark for Bophuthatswana's recognition campaign came in 1987 in Britain. It also was, as Peris Sean Jones put it, "[the] greatest reflection of Bophuthatswana's influence within the Conservative Party."[294] The occasion was when the British Parliament's Foreign Affairs Committee allowed the Bophuthatswanan government to present evidence and give direct testimony in support of its claims to statehood .[295] Ultimately, despite this full airing of arguments in front of an official body, the committee nonetheless decided that Bophuthatswana was still an integral part of South Africa.[296] Britain did not recognize it as a state,

---

because we do not believe it constitutes a fair or viable solution to South Africa's problems, we oppose this policy. We did not recognize the Transkei, and we will not recognize Bophuthatswana if its independence is proclaimed in December, as scheduled." FRUS, 1977–1980, vol. 1, p. 214, Address by Secretary of State Vance, St. Louis, Missouri, July 1, 1977.

[293] State Department Telegram from US Embassy Pretoria to Secretary of State and Cape Town, "Official Contacts with the 'Independent' Homelands," September 29, 1979, accessed via Wikileaks: wikileaks.org/plusd/cables/1979PRETOR08945_e.html.

[294] Peris Sean Jones, "Etiquette of State-Building," p. 36.

[295] Peris Sean Jones, "Etiquette of State-Building," p. 36. See also: British Foreign Affairs Committee, Session 1986–1987, 11.5, 1987, Minutes of Evidence from the Government of the Republic of Bophuthatswana.

[296] Peris Sean Jones, "Etiquette of State-Building," p. 36.

and South Africa remained the only country to ever recognize Bophuthatswana.

Conclusion

Why did these aspirant states expend so much political energy and government resources pursuing the fool's errand of recognition? Nina Caspersen's answer about unrecognized regimes' futile searches for recognition generally, is applicable to these four: that the search itself was vital. She writes, "However much we talk about globalization, erosion of the state, and the increasing irrelevance of territory, statehood remains the top prize; it legitimizes the struggle, guarantees protection for the inhabitants and prestige and power for the leaders."[297] The dream of fully realized statehood is a powerful legitimizing force for unrecognized regimes, and giving up on seeking recognition, even when the choice of giving up is an objectively rational one, risks sacrificing their internal legitimacy. As a result, and again quoting Caspersen: "Unrecognized states are continuously trying to find their place in an international system that has no place for them, and they consequently seem almost doomed to a transient existence, always chasing the elusive goal of recognition."[298] What this meant in the four cases studied here was an almost continuous process of raising hopes of recognition, the exaggeration of small successes, the promise of near breakthroughs, and the idea that legality and international acceptance was right around the corner. In this sense these regimes' internal propaganda sounded much like the state equivalent of Willy Loman from the play *Death of a Salesman*, relentlessly, tragically optimistic.

---

[297] Caspersen, *Unrecognized States*, p. 68.   [298] Caspersen, *Unrecognized States*, p. 111.

5   Establishing Foreign Missions in America
The Katanga Information Service, Rhodesia
Information Office, and Transkei's Washington Bureau

Diplomatic missions always carry great symbolic importance.[1] As physical manifestations of foreign states, mission buildings and their grounds have often been viewed as sites of disloyalty and hostility, and especially so when the sending state's actions or ideologies offend significant portions of popular opinion within the host country.[2] As a consequence, throughout the development of modern international relations mission sites have attracted protests and occasionally violence.[3] In the case of the Rhodesia Information Office (RIO), which was situated in a quiet residential neighborhood in leafy Northwest Washington, DC, a group opposing the regimes of white Southern Africa actually exploded a bomb in front of the mission shattering its windows and damaging the facade. Rhodesia House in London was firebombed twice, and more than once the American Consulate in Elisabethville was attacked by Katangese demonstrators, on one occasion the windows were smashed, the American flag ripped down, and an out-building on the grounds set aflame.[4] While this degree of violence directed toward missions and their inhabitants was unusual, these missions did serve as powerfully emotive

---

[1] Parts of this section are derived from an article written by the author and published in the *International Journal of African Historical Studies*. "Diplomatic Lepers."

[2] See for example: I. Gournay and J. C. Loeffler, "Washington and Ottawa: A Tale of Two Embassies," *The Journal of the Society of Architectural Historians*, vol. 61, no. 4 (December 2002) pp. 480–507.

[3] Contemporaneously with post-UDI Rhodesia, the United States embassy off of Grosvenor Square in London was a regular site of protests against various American policies, beginning with anti-Vietnam War demonstrations in the 1960s and 1970s. A decade later, the US Embassy in London was the site of numerous demonstrations against the United States nuclear policies, and more recently, Grosvenor Square has again been the site of frequent anti-Iraq War demonstrations. Outside of Britain, US embassies have been the target of numerous violent attacks, as in Tehran, Beirut, Nairobi, and Dar es Salaam. See for example: "Thousands in London Protest US A-Arms Policy," *The New York Times*, June 10, 1984; Gournay and Loeffler, "Washington and Ottawa," pp. 481–482.

[4] "Katangese Stone US Consulate; Student Mob Assails Kennedy," *New York Times*, December 20, 1962.

points of convergence for broader ideological and political battles over the future of Africa, as well as serving as important sites of conflict in the racial politics of the host countries. As such these battles being waged over small pieces of real estate in Washington and New York were understood to be important parts of a multifaceted geopolitical conflict.

After their declarations of independence, all four would-be states and their representatives were immediately confronted with an international and domestic policy of nonrecognition. This was a diplomatic quarantine that imposed a set of conditions that would define how these missions would operate and function in the host countries.[5] Moise Tshombe's Katangese regime opened a foreign mission in New York City, three months after the province of Katanga declared its independence from the Congo. Five years later, almost immediately after Rhodesia declared its independence from Britain on November 11, Ian Smith's regime established its foreign mission in Washington, DC. Transkei set up its mission in Washington in July of 1977, nine months after Transkei's declared independence. Bophuthatswana's efforts to establish a diplomatic presence in the United States were more tentative, but Lucas Mangope's regime did operate from an information office out of a suburban home in Washington, DC and later out of an office off of Dupont Circle from 1980 to 1983. This chapter will look at how these aspirant states and their representatives in these missions tried to negotiate their precarious statuses in the United States against the backdrop of the wider conflicts over their sovereign existences.

While it is true that they were forced to operate without the privileges and immunities of legally recognized diplomatic missions and that their representatives were in some ways treated as "lepers" in the diplomatic community, this did not mean that these representatives had no influence.[6] Michel Struelens of the Katanga Information Services (KIS) and Kenneth Towsey of the RIO both had a remarkable degree of access and influence, especially considering their statuses as unrecognized diplomats from illegal regimes. In contrast, Masimini of the Transkei Washington Bureau was under the information and lobbying umbrella of South Africa, and unlike Struelens and Towsey who both had direct access to powerful congressmen and senior government officials, Masimini found it difficult to bend many ears on Capitol Hill. But

---

[5] Stultz refers to Transkei's international position as "a country under involuntary quarantine." *Transkei's Half Loaf*, p. 120.

[6] In a newspaper interview Towsey claimed he was treated like a leper by the diplomatic community in Washington. "Rhodesians Treated as Diplomatic 'Lepers,'" *Washington Post, Times Herald*, December 26, 1967.

whether through South Africa as a conduit, or directly as was the case with Katanga and Rhodesia, all four regimes still had access to conservative opinion-makers throughout the country, which facilitated their ability to spread their messages widely. In the case of Struelens, President Kennedy more than once discussed his political impact and his legal status in the country, not a small indication of his outsized importance. Similarly, Towsey and the RIO were the frequent topic of high-level discussions in four successive administrations, as well as the direct subject of UN Security Council resolutions. Similarly, Masimini's presence in the United States and the operation of his Washington Bureau drew the attention of the OAU, and the State Department agonized over how best to address his status publicly.

Many friends and enemies of these regimes, as well as a number of neutral political observers at the time, recognized the similarities among the stories of these four regimes. This was because the struggles in the United States and Britain over the legal statuses of these missions and their occupants mirrored one another. In the United States the contests were fought among largely the same people, with their same institutional strengths and weaknesses, and with the same sites of conflict. Domestic political battles in the United States over the recognition of Katanga, Rhodesia, Transkei, and Bophuthatswana pitted those who operated the gate-keeping functions of the international state system against those with domestic legislative and oversight power who attempted to pull planks away from the fences of this same system. In the United States, right-wing friends of all four breakaway regimes had a powerful base in the US Congress, especially, but not exclusively, among southern conservatives, while opponents of the regimes were typically grouped in certain sections of the State Department. Because of their institutional strengths and weaknesses, friends of these regimes had the negative power to criticize, frustrate, and gum up foreign policy, but lacked the positive ability to shape and direct it. American presidents, regardless of their natural sympathies for or against these regimes, were typically careful not to disturb either of these roughly balanced institutional forces. And as will be described, when viewed against the wider sweep of American foreign policy, Africa as a continent was rarely seen as a top priority by most senior policymakers. Nonetheless, there were certain vocal sections of the American public on both the right and the left for whom the fate of Africa was of utmost importance, and the magnetic poles for their efforts in the United States to either defend or destroy these aspirant states often drew both sides to the small physical buildings and grounds of these mission sites in New York and Washington.

Katanga

Katanga's international presence was expressed through several unofficial foreign missions.[7] As part of this effort to establish an international personality, Tshombe directed that Michel Struelens, an "urbane and soft-spoken" Belgian national who had been working on tourism promotion in the Congo, serve as the Katangese representative in the United States.[8] Citing a well-placed source, an internal State Department memorandum reported that Struelens had intended to continue to work on tourist promotion in the United States for the Congo after independence, but that Lumumba insisted he be replaced, only at which point did Tshombe hire him on as a pseudo-diplomatic representative for the breakaway Katangese state. The memorandum noted: "It was ironic that Struelens had never been to Katanga, and might have devoted his talents to the cause of the Central Government if Lumumba had not fired him in the wild period of July 1960."[9] On September 29, 1960, the American consul in Brussels attached a foreign media, or "I" visa, to his Belgian passport, allowing him to enter the United States, even though his declared purpose in coming to the United States meant he should have been issued another category of visa.[10] This seemingly small instance of bureaucratic negligence would later loom large. At that time, Struelens was in possession of several documents that together give a picture of what the secessionist Katangese regime thought he was and what role they intended that he perform in the United States. These included a letter from Tshombe designating Struelens as the diplomatic representative of Katanga in the United States.[11] Struelens also carried with him letters of credentials signed by Tshombe addressed to the State Department and the United

---

[7] For a discussion of Katanga's other international missions, see Gerard-Libois, *Katanga Secession*, pp. 182–183.

[8] "Envoy for Tshombe," *New York Times*, August 3, 1964.

[9] Fredericks Papers, Schomberg Center, Memorandum of conversation, Leopoldville Embassy: McGhee; Fredericks; Daniel F. Margolies, Counselor for Economic Affairs, American Embassy Leopoldville; Fernand de Pooter, President Federation des Entreprises Congolais, October 6, 1962.

[10] "Visa Procedures of Department of State: The Struelens Case," *Report of the Subcommittee to Investigate the Administration of the Internal Security Act and other Internal Security Laws to the Senate Committee on the Judiciary* (Washington, DC: US Government Printing Office, August 6, 1962) p. 2.

[11] "Struelens Case," p. 2.

Nations. Together, these documents made a claim as to Katanga's sovereign status.[12]

Struelens arrived in the United States under his new visa on October 3, 1960 and registered with the Department of Justice as an agent of the Katanga government as required under the Foreign Agents Registration Act (FARA). Setting up in a four-room suite in midtown New York for himself, his assistant, and his secretary, this office operated as "a miniature embassy."[13] The mission of the KIS, as described by Struelens, was "to tell the Katanga story in the Western Hemisphere, based on the belief that Katanga is the only barrier against communist influence in the Congo."[14] His work included traveling around the United States making speeches and meeting conservative opinion-makers. His efforts included producing and distributing a newsletter titled "Katanga Calling ..." This short publication often published Tshombe's speeches or statements, and was supplemented by cherry-picked news reports favorable to Katanga's secession, all under a colored banner which included Katanga's new flag. By the end of 1961, Streulens boasted having 3,000 names on the KIS mailing list.[15] Importantly, he was adept at handling the American press.[16] As described in the *New York Times*, Struelens managed his press conferences "with the aplomb of a diplomat and the sincerity of a parson."[17]

For the first several months of his work at the KIS, the Eisenhower administration did not see Katanga as the biggest threat to US interests in the Congo, as they were much more concerned with Patrice Lumumba and possible communist infiltration in Leopoldville. Richard Mahoney concluded that it was Eisenhower's sympathetic attitude toward the secession and the decision to allow Struelens to enter the country and set up shop during these early months of the secession, which made the secession so difficult to uproot during the Kennedy administration.[18] Nevertheless, while Struelens benefited from this tolerant attitude toward Tshombe in these first months, Katanga was consistently denied any of the manifestations of statehood, and he was

---

[12] For a discussion of the forms of claims to sovereignty, see Hillgruber, "The Admission of New States to the International Community," p. 492.

[13] "Aide Here Denies Drive by Katanga," *New York Times*, December 29, 1961; Weissman, *American Foreign Policy*, p. 103.

[14] "Envoy for Tshombe," *New York Times*, August 3, 1964.

[15] This was an estimate his assistant lowered to 2,000. "Aide Here Denies Drive by Katanga," *New York Times*, December 29, 1961.

[16] C. Hoskyns, *The Congo since Independence* (Oxford: Oxford University Press, 1965) p. 411.

[17] "Envoy for Tshombe," *New York Times*, August 3, 1964.

[18] Mahoney, *Ordeal in Africa*, p. 54.

Figure 5.1 Michael Struelens giving a speech to an audience in Los Angeles, California, February 1962.

accordingly denied the privileges and immunities that representatives of fully recognized states enjoyed.[19]

---

[19] See, for example: United Nations Archives, New York City, S-0793-0019-10, "Subject Files: Special Assistant to Chief UN Representative – Mercenaries and Political Advisors: Case Files – Struelens, Michel – Political Advisors Part III," February

Support for Katanga in the United States did not rely as much on any special affection for Katanga per se as it did a strong, uniting dislike of Katanga's enemies. The American right-wing was suspicious of African nationalists' intentions, and for some a clear parallel was drawn between domestic racial politics and events in Africa.[20] Alongside the undeniable racial backdrop of the domestic civil rights movement and the rise of nationalism in Africa, the Katangese, Rhodesian, Transkeian, and Bophuthatswanan causes were also framed in nonracial language so as to appeal to a wider range of potential allies in the United States. Some powerful members of Congress were eventually drawn to the cause of Katanga, led by Senator Thomas Dodd from Connecticut, who had earned a liberal reputation on domestic civil rights. To Dodd, Tshombe was the only reliably noncommunist leader in the whole of the Congo. Dodd and others would argue that all of the Congo was doomed to a bleak communist future if Katanga were not allowed to remain strong and autonomous.

It is unclear the extent to which Dodd found Struelens or Struelens found Dodd, but like the only two lepidopterists at a party, they soon found each other.[21] So much of a champion was Dodd to Tshombe that White House officials joked that Tshombe's memoirs should be titled, "Dodd is my Co-Pilot."[22] Struelens had a particularly close relationship with Dodd's office, as well as with other congressmen, but conservatives always dismissed as liberal propaganda the claim that there was such a thing as a single, monolithic "Katanga Lobby" under Struelens' direction.[23] Mocking tales of Struelens' superhuman influence, one editorial

11–17, 1961, "Telegram from ONUC Leopoldville to ONUC Elisabethville," February 1961; John F. Kennedy Presidential Library, Box 27A, Congo, National Security Files, General, May–September 1961, Series: Countries, Congo, Memorandum for McGeorge Bundy from Melvin Manful, State Department, "Letter to President from Interior Minister of Katanga," June 2, 1961, and Telegram from Rostow to Sheppard for President and Salinger, September 23, 1961.

[20] The racial parallels were drawn by both sides of the debate. See T. Borstelmann, *The Cold War and the Color Line: American Race Relations in the Global Arena* (Harvard University Press, Cambridge, MA, 2001). See also Noer, *Cold War and Black Liberation*.

[21] Mahoney writes, "Thanks to Belgian propagandist Michel Struelens, Katanga had meanwhile found her apostle in Washington – Connecticut Senator Thomas Dodd . ..." Mahoney, *Ordeal in Africa*, p. 110. Urquhart wrote that Dodd "had hitched onto, or been recruited by, Tshombe's public relations campaign." Urquhart, *A Life in Peace and War*, p. 179. Weissman writes that "Struelens' mailings to Congress had lit a fire under Senator Thomas Dodd ...." Weissman, *American Foreign Policy*, p. 159. See: Brownell, "Diplomatic Lepers," p. 215.

[22] Mahoney, *Ordeal in Africa*, p. 110.

[23] See Weissman, *American Foreign Policy*, p. 175, fn 78. Thomas J. Dodd Papers, University of Connecticut, Box 256, Subseries IV, Letter from Dodd to Rusk, February 8, 1962.

read: "[I]f one Belgian press man can outwit the combined brains of the whole press corps of State Department publicists – including [Carl T.] Rowan – Uncle Sam had better hire the Belgian and fire the Washington crew."[24] On their end, a frustrated State Department official was quoted in the *New York Times* as saying, "Streulens is a clever man. I wished he worked for us."[25]

At first, the State Department not only tolerated Struelens existence, but in July and August of 1961 – overlapping with Katanga's first-year anniversary – it even tried to use him as an intermediary in its dealing with Tshombe when the threat of a Leftist challenge to the central government appeared most threatening.[26] However, once the Kennedy administration successfully orchestrated the installation of Cyrille Adoula in the Congolese premiership in Leopoldville in August 1961, this ended the tentative search for a deal with Tshombe.[27] It soon became apparent to the administration that Adoula's survival depended on the successful reintegration of Katanga into the Congo, and Adoula's draining support became a sort of hourglass that served as the timekeeper for the administration's Katanga policy.[28] Because of this, the United States then took a harder line against Tshombe's year-old regime, and by extension Streulens' KIS. With affected outrage, Dodd would often repeat that the State Department used Struelens to further its ends and then discarded him when he was no longer needed.[29]

In mid-September 1961, serious fighting broke out with UN and Katanese forces clashing in what the UN called Operation Morthor. As the fighting dragged on with Katanga getting the better of it, Struelens and the Katanga government began pumping out a steady flow of pro-Katanga propaganda. Describing his work during this period, Struelens said: "When the UN says it has committed no atrocities in Katanga, I distribute pictures of atrocities and so give proof of the bloody mess of the UN in Katanga."[30] Newspaper headlines around the world carried

---

[24] *Chicago Daily News*, reprinted from *New York Herald Tribune*, January 9, 1962. Quoted in Mahoney, *Ordeal in Africa*, p. 137.

[25] Quoted in Howe and Trott, *Power Peddlers*, p. 180.

[26] See "Telegram from the Department of State to the Embassy in the Congo," July 28, 1961, Doc. 89, FRUS, vol. XX. See also Hoskyns, *The Congo since Independence*, p. 377.

[27] Mahoney, *Ordeal in Africa*, p. 87.

[28] See Noer, "New Frontiers and Old Priorities in Africa," pp. 253–283. Mahoney convincingly makes the argument that the Adoula installation was the turning point in Kennedy policy towards Katanga. Mahoney, *Ordeal in Africa*, p. 131.

[29] "Struelens Case," p. 8.

[30] "Aide Here Denies Drive by Katanga," *New York Times*, December 29, 1961.

stories of UN atrocities.[31] At home, a small group of congressmen led by
Dodd attacked Kennedy's Congo policy. The volume of domestic hostility against the UN fighting in Katanga shocked the Kennedy administration.[32] After Morthor and the backlash that followed, Kennedy
wanted to avoid any further fighting in the Congo, unless it was explicitly
clear that Katanga was the aggressor.[33]

After the hullabaloo he raised over Morthor, the days of the State
Department tolerating Struelens were over. In early October 1961,
Newsweek reported that the State Department was canceling Struelens'
visa.[34] Like almost everyone else, Struelens read this off the news-
stands.[35] Several days later, his visa was officially canceled with the
explanation that he had been acting outside the terms of his "I" visa.[36]
Just two months before this, the State Department had renewed his visa
to allow him to go to Katanga (and to be allowed to return) for the
purposes of furthering State Department policy. But much had changed
from July. As George McGhee would later say in congressional testimony
about the August to October 1961 turn: "Now, Mr. Struelens appeared
to be, as a good representative, carrying out this policy [in July and
August], and suddenly [in October] we in the State Department found
that rather than a man who had been cooperative, that he appeared to be
working against our policy in a variety of ways."[37] Before the cancellation, the State Department had asked the FBI to investigate the possibility of Struelens violating his status or the law more broadly.[38] The FBI
broke into his office looking for anything that could get him deported,
and Attorney General Robert F. Kennedy authorized the FBI to tap the
KIS phones.[39] Thereafter, the State Department received daily reports of
his communications with Tshombe.[40]

---

[31] Mahoney, *Ordeal in Africa*, p. 100.

[32] Stephen Weissman describes Kennedy's caution in response to the Katanga lobby as
unwarranted and "panicky." Weissman, *American Foreign Policy*, p. 193. JFK Archives,
Box 27A, National Security Files, Series: Countries, Congo, Congo: General,
November 3–11, 1961, Memorandum for the President from Rusk, "Next Steps in the
Congo," November 11, 1961.

[33] JFK Archives, Box 27A, National Security Files, Congo: General, October 1–November
2, 1961, Series: Countries, Congo, Memorandum for McGeorge Bundy from L. D.
Battle, State Department, "Status Report on the Congo," November 2, 1961.

[34] "Ahead with the Headlines," *Newsweek*, October 9, 1961. M. Struelens, *ONUC (United
Nations in the Congo) and International Politics* (American University Press, Washington,
DC, 1968) p. 152.

[35] Quoted in "Struelens Case," p. 17.   [36] "Struelens Case," p. 17.

[37] "Struelens Case," p. 142.   [38] "Struelens Case," p. 31.

[39] Mahoney, *Ordeal in Africa*, p. 137. Struelens apparently knew his phones were tapped
and his telex monitored, and when he confronted McGhee with this McGhee did not
deny it. "Struelens Case," pp. 59–60.

[40] Mahoney, *Ordeal in Africa*, p. 137.

Using the technical violation of his visa status was a pretext, as department officials admitted the Brussels consul had made a mistake in giving him the "I" visa when his intended activities in the United States were clear.[41] In an exchange before a congressional hearing on the Struelens affair, Republican Senator Roman Hruska asked if the "I" visa had been issued by mistake if it would not be "more decent and more civilized" to have reissued him the appropriate visa: "Would that not have been much nicer?" To which a State Department official responded: "I think, at that time, the Department was not interested in being too nice to Mr. Struelens."[42]

Quickly springing to Struelens' defense, Dodd wrote directly to Secretary of State, Dean Rusk, expressing his outrage at the cancellation of Struelens' visa.[43] As a result of Dodd's letter, and the fear of greater blowback, all action to deport Struelens was halted.[44] Thereafter, Struelens was allowed to stay in the United States, but he could not leave and have any hope of returning. The visa cancellation also led to Senator Dodd's decision to open a congressional investigation to be co-chaired by segregationist Senator James Eastland from Mississippi, who would later become an outspoken defender of Rhodesia, to determine whether the department had abused its visa power in their treatment of Struelens.[45]

In December 1961, "Round two" of the UN/Katangese fighting began. As with Morthor, the Katanga lobby and the Struelens propaganda mill went into action. It was in the midst of the December 1961 fighting when the ACAKFF announced its formation with a full-page advertisement in the *New York Times* carrying the title "Katanga is the Hungary of 1961."[46] Once again, this combined propaganda had an effect on US public opinion inside and outside Congress. Senator Hubert Humphrey suggested that the administration needed to make its case better to the American public, arguing that Kennedy and the UN were losing the propaganda war against the Katanga lobby. He said unless they made their case better, the UN would be "crucified on this cross of the Congo with Mr. Tshombe emerging as a patron saint, which he ain't, to put it in the vernacular."[47] In the race between a UN military victory in Katanga and the political pressure on Kennedy to stop the fighting, the latter won out, and Kennedy decided to break the

---

[41] Quoted in "Struelens Case," p. 26.   [42] "Struelens Case," p. 70.

[43] Quoted in "Struelens Case."   [44] "Struelens Case," p. 30.

[45] Dodd Papers, Box 193, Press Release by Dodd's Office, October 11, 1961.

[46] Group Research Inc. Archives, Box 6, Folder ACAKFF, ACAKFF Advertisement, *New York Times*, December 14, 1961.

[47] Mahoney, *Ordeal in Africa*, p. 119.

government's past and future practice by responding directly to a communication from Tshombe to negotiate a truce.[48] After Katanga had almost been completely crushed, Tshombe was escorted by American officials to negotiate his surrender at Kitona, which he signed on December 21, 1961. Upon his safe return to Elisabethville, however, slippery Tshombe began to wiggle away from the agreement.

Over the holiday season of 1961/1962, the department took the offensive in the propaganda war against the Katanga lobby. Its origins began in early November when the State Department issued background information to the press on the Katanga crisis.[49] This State Department document outlined the legal and moral arguments against Tshombe's claim for Katangese self-determination, arguing, among other things, that Tshombe did not speak for a majority of Katangese, and the secession movement was an artificial creation of white settlers and European industrial interests.[50] Kennedy then asked George Ball to make the case for the administration's Congo policy, which he did in a sober and articulate speech that the State Department would later publish as a pamphlet.[51]

This was, however, too little, too late, and too polite for some in the Africa Bureau. Assistant Secretary of State for African Affairs, G. Mennen "Soapy" Williams, was growing increasingly unhappy with Kennedy's cautious approach and decided to go public with his feelings despite warnings from Washington.[52] On December 27, Williams made a speech charging that public sympathy for Katanga during the conflict was the result of "a well-financed propaganda machine speaking for Mr. Tshombe and against the UN."[53] On the same day, another State Department official, Carl T. Rowan, stated that "there has been a clever

---

[48] All previous communications had been ignored or answered informally by the consul in Elisabethville. See, for example, JFK Archives, Box 27A, National Security Files, Series: Countries, Congo, Congo: General, May–September 1961, Memorandum for McGeorge Bundy from Melvin Manful, State Department, "Letter to President from Interior Minister of Katanga," June 2, 1961, and Telegram from Rostow to Sheppard for President and Salinger, September 23, 1961; see also Mahoney, *Ordeal in Africa*, p. 122.

[49] JFK Archives, Box 27A, National Security Files, Congo: General, Series: Countries, Congo, November 3–11, 1961, Department of State press document, "For Background Only," November 10, 1961.

[50] JFK Archives, Box 27A, National Security Files, Congo: General, Series: Countries, Congo, November 3–11, 1961, Department of State press document, "For Background Only," November 10, 1961.

[51] JFK Archives, Oral History, JFK OH-GWB-03, George Ball Oral History Interview – JFK #3, February 16, 1968.

[52] Noer, *Soapy*, p. 253.   [53] Quoted in "Struelens Case," p. 40.

big money campaign to convince Americans that they ought to support Katangan secession." This speech identified whom he thought was behind this mysterious Lobby: "Heading up this campaign is a former Belgian civil servant, Michel Struelens, who operates out of some rather plush quarters in New York ... [and through 'spreading around' cash] Struelens has gotten some extremely vocal help in dispensing a string of myths and a stream of misinformation about Katanga and the Congo."[54] In the midst of their printed propaganda exchange, Williams and Streulens actually debated each other on the same stage at a Boston University Law School forum, a battle in which the student newspaper claimed that Streulens won.[55]

The day after Christmas in 1961, two FBI agents contacted Struelens and asked if he had ever engaged in any illegal efforts to try to obtain recognition of Katanga.[56] Struelens denied the charge. Several days later, a State Department spokesman publicly accused Struelens of trying to bribe Costa Rican officials to grant recognition to Katanga in exchange for one million dollars cash, repeating an accusation first made in the *New York Times*.[57] This attempted bribe, which seemed to result in Struelens and Katanga being conned, was not Struelens and Katanga's last, as they would also try to negotiate a deal with Guatemala.[58]

When asked about the bribe accusation regarding Costa Rica, Struelens told the *New York Times*: "Even if the story were true, which it is not, I cannot understand why the United States would be so concerned about diplomatic efforts made by another government."[59] Some aspects of the story were confirmed, however, by Dr. Gonzalo Ortiz-Martin, Costa Rica's chief representative at the UN.[60] When questioned about the matter in the Dodd hearings, Struelens pleaded "diplomatic" secrecy, and was let off the hook.[61] The official investigation into these

---

[54] Quoted in "Struelens Case," p. 40. Mahoney indicates that during one meeting in the Oval Office with Kennedy, Dodd reacted with some sensitivity to the implied accusation from Kennedy that perhaps he was on the receiving end of some of Struelens' cash. Mahoney, *Ordeal in Africa*, 146. In his memoir, Brian Urquhart offers a hearsay quote from Tshombe in which he claimed that Dodd was on the take from Katanga, but Urquhart added that he was not sure whether or not this was true. Urquhart, *A Life in Peace and War*, p. 179.

[55] Howe and Trot, *Power Peddlers*, p. 177.   [56] "Struelens Case," p. 40.

[57] See: "Bribe Plan Linked to Katanga Aide," *New York Times*, January 4, 1962.

[58] "Struelens Case," p. 57.

[59] Russell Baker, "Aide of Katanga Is Said to Offer Recognition Bribe," *New York Times*, January 3, 1962.

[60] Russell Baker, "Aide of Katanga Is Said to Offer Recognition Bribe," *New York Times*, January 3, 1962.

[61] Howe and Trott describe how Struelens was treated with "infinite gentleness" during the Dodd hearings. Howe and Trott, *Power Peddlers*, p. 182.

deals went nowhere as the information the government had acquired on the bribe had been illegally obtained.[62] It is also unclear what law this exchange would have violated.[63] Undersecretary George Ball realized the embarrassment that these charges caused the department, and he commented to a colleague that in going after Struelens unsuccessfully the department had been "very stupid ... we will look sick because we have nothing on this fellow."[64] Or more correctly, nothing they could use in court.

According to sworn testimony, Struelens also twice paid for an alleged friend of the Guatemalan president to go to Guatemala and try to obtain diplomatic recognition, but to no avail.[65] This account can be buttressed by an unusual meeting in Salisbury, Rhodesia in early 1962. Days after the bribery story broke in *New York Times*, Miguel Ydigoras-Laparra, the son of the Guatemalan president and a self-described Guatemalan diplomat, arrived in Salisbury, along with his brother-in-law, Hugh Ian McGarvie-Munn, the British-born Commander of the Guatemalan Navy and husband of President Fuentes' daughter, in order to have a meeting with Prime Minister Welensky and the secretary of external relations.[66] In the meeting, Munn told Welensky that in December 1961 the Katangese government, most likely through Struelens, had reached out to the Costa Rican government via a New York dentist to try to negotiate a deal by which the Katangese would pay $1,250,000 to the Costa Ricans in exchange for recognition, with the intermediary taking a sizable cut off the top, but the State Department got wind of it and the deal exploded into the press.[67] According to the Guatemalan delegation, Tshombe then offered $1,000,000 in exchange for Guatemalan recognition, a proposal Munn claimed remained undiscovered by the State Department. The delegation members said that their main interest in Katanga was not the money, but that Tshombe shared their government's anti-communist priorities. They had been instructed

---

[62] See G. Mennen William's testimony in "Struelens Case."

[63] *The Times* reported that legal experts did not see any illegality in this potential exchange. Russell Baker, "Aide of Katanga Is Said to Offer Recognition Bribe," *New York Times*, January 3, 1962.

[64] Quoted in Mahoney, *Ordeal in Africa*, p. 137.

[65] It is worth noting that Dodd had a long-standing, and ethically questionable, relationship with the Guatemalan government. Howe and Trott, *Power Peddlers*, p. 176. See D. Koskoff, *The Senator from Central Casting* (New American Political Press, New Haven, CT, 2011).

[66] Welensky papers, Bodeleian Library, Federal Immigration Declarations, January 18, 1962. Record of a Meeting in the Prime Minister's Office, January 19, 1962.

[67] Welensky papers, Bodeleian Library, Record of a Meeting in the Prime Minister's Office, January 19, 1962.

to speak first with Welensky before moving forward. Munn and Ydigoras-Laparra boasted that they had "considerable experience over a number of years of dirty politics ... [and] had helped governments to power and got them out of power." Further, they claimed that their government had positioned a Guatemalan diplomat, Jose Rolz-Bennett, into the position he held at the United Nations as the ONUC representative in Katanga, but because he "had property and relations in Guatemala [he] could therefore be controlled."[68] Their scheme, according to the CAF readout of the meeting, was the following:

With Mr. Rolz-Bennett in the position he now was, [Munn and Ydigoras-Laparra] believed that it would be possible to get United Nations out of Katanga without fighting, and thereafter to proceed, in secrecy, to tackle the State Department. There were several things the State Department wanted of Guatemala and much could be gained in return. By a series of intrigues [the delegation] believed it would be possible to have Katanga recognised as an independent state, but it would take time, possibly six months.[69]

The federation officials were dumbfounded. In replying to this outrageous presentation, Welensky reiterated his belief that despite Tshombe's declaration of independence he thought the Katangese leader was always committed to work within the framework of the Congo, and that it was the federation's policy to advise Tshombe to work toward a federal solution for the Congo.[70] While Welensky was convinced of his visitors' "bona fides," he advised the delegation to talk to Tshombe directly, and the meeting ended. To the extent that the Welensky government took the meeting seriously beforehand, it appeared that afterward they regarded the meeting and the delegation's "series of intrigues" as a farce.[71] It is not known whether the delegation was ever received by Tshombe, or whether money was ever exchanged, but certainly no recognition was given.

In January 1962, Kennedy proposed that the United States purchase $100 million of the UN's $200 million bond issue to cover expenses for the Congo Operation, which at that point was millions in debt.[72] The

---

[68] Welensky papers, Bodeleian Library, Record of a Meeting in the Prime Minister's Office, January 19, 1962.

[69] Welensky papers, Bodeleian Library, Record of a Meeting in the Prime Minister's Office, January 19, 1962.

[70] Welensky papers, Bodeleian Library, Record of a Meeting in the Prime Minister's Office, January 19, 1962.

[71] In a handwritten note on the top, a federal official present at the meeting wrote on the forwarded minutes to another official: "For your information and possible amusement ..." Note by W. B. Parker to "Bob," Welensky papers, Bodeleian Library, Record of a Meeting in the Prime Minister's Office, January 19, 1962.

[72] Weissman, *American Foreign Policy*, p. 177.

bond bill forced Kennedy's Congo policy directly into the maw of Dodd and the congressional Katanga lobby.[73] Suddenly the government's pressure on Struelens eased up. This was attributable to Kennedy wanting to avoid antagonizing Struelens' friends inside and outside of Congress. Reaching out to Struelens, the State Department allegedly told the pseudo-diplomat: "Mr. Struelens we want to give you your visa back."[74] After this brief courtship ended, the department would later assert that no prior commitment on his visa could have been made before it received an actual application. Furthermore, in keeping with typical practice any application would have to be received by a consulate overseas.[75] Struelens therefore remained an "alien out of status" within the United States.

Another part of Kennedy's UN bond bill campaign was to have Prime Minister Adoula visit the UN and Washington as the new face of the Congolese central government. Concurrent with Adoula's first visit to the United States as the Congolese premier, Struelens decided that Tshombe should also visit the United States as a way to scuttle Adoula's tidy public relations tour and to kill the UN bond bill.[76] Struelens saw a fight over Tshombe's visa as a public relations win even if his visa was ultimately rejected.[77] The conservative group Young Americans for Freedom had proclaimed Tshombe to be that year's top "defender of freedom," and former President Herbert Hoover was to present Tshombe with a plaque at a rally in Madison Square Garden.[78] The effect of Tshombe visiting around the time of the Adoula visit was taken very seriously by the administration. Struelens met with State Department officials to discuss Tshombe's visa on February 1, 1962.[79] Despite being the professed head of a sovereign state, department officials insisted that Tshombe could not enter the United States on a Katangese passport nor with his old passport from the Belgian Congo.[80] Dodd attempted to assert pressure on the administration regarding the visa situation by writing a threatening letter to Rusk.[81] In his letter, the Connecticut senator expressed his shock and dismay that, despite what was indicated to him recently, the State Department was

---

[73] The Katanga lobby groups focused much of their attention on the UN bond issue. See for example: Group Research Inc. Archive, Box 6, Folder ACAKFF, "The War in Katanga: The United Nations in the Congo, Report of a Mission."

[74] "Struelens Case," p. 59.   [75] "Struelens Case," p. 64.

[76] Howe and Trott, *Power Peddlers*, p. 180.   [77] Howe and Trott, *Power Peddlers*, p. 180.

[78] Howe and Trott, *Power Peddlers*, p. 180. In the event, neither Hoover nor Tshombe were present.

[79] "Struelens Case," p. 65.   [80] "Struelens Case," p. 65.

[81] Dodd Papers, Box 256, Series IV, Subseries D: Congo: Correspondence 1961–1962, folder 6749, Letter from Dodd to Rusk, February 8, 1962.

"still carrying on their war against Mr. Tshombe and against Mr. Struelens and that completely fanciful monster, the Katanga Lobby."[82]

Characteristically, the administration was split over Tshombe's visa request. The State Department Legal Advisor, Abram Chayes, was against using the visa power for political reasons since he felt it violated free speech protections.[83] The Africanists in the administration argued for the visa to be denied. Williams wrote a forceful note to Kennedy arguing that allowing Tshombe to visit at this time would gravely damage US relations with the rest of Africa.[84] Reportedly, Kennedy asked Chayes point blank if he was legally required to grant him a visa, and when Chayes said he was not, Kennedy answered: "Why should I permit Tshombe a visa? I don't want to."[85]

Not surprisingly, the Katanga lobby was outraged. The right saw attempts to shut down these regimes' US foreign missions and the denial of visitor visas to the regimes' leaders as "indirect censorship of the worst order," and examples of a blatant ideological double standard.[86] William F. Buckley Jr. emphasized this theme of uneven treatment in an article about the denial of Tshombe's visitor visa to the United States, writing, "Tshombe, at a time when he represented the forces of law and anti-communism in the Congo, was shot at by a United Nations expeditionary force ... and was denied a visa to come to the United States. Meanwhile, we relaxed the controls governing the visits to this country by our former enemies."[87] Max Yergan, Chairman of ACAKFF wrote to Secretary of State Dean Rusk expressing his outrage at the denial of Tshombe's visa, while the United States "ceremoniously welcomed ... Nikita Khrushchev, Fidel Castro, the late Patrice Lumumba, and Holden Roberto."[88] This sensitivity was in part because they knew how incredibly important these visits to the United States were in terms of

---

[82] Papers, Box 256, Subseries IV, letter from Dodd to Rusk, February 8, 1962.

[83] Mahoney, *Ordeal in Africa*, p. 136.   [84] Noer, *Soapy*, p. 254.

[85] Quoted by J. Wayne Fredericks in J. Wayne Fredericks Papers, Schomburg Center for Research in Black Culture, New York Public Library, Manuscripts and Archives Section, Box 13, "Chronology of the Congo" memorandum (undated), Folder: State Department, ACF Memos Re: Kennedy Policy in Congo. Ambassador Guillon remembered Kennedy as responding to Chayes' answer that he was not legally obligated to grant Tshombe a visa as being: "Then I won't." Quoted in Mahoney, *Ordeal in Africa*, p. 136.

[86] Dodd Papers Box 193, Subseries E, Series III, Press Release, "Statement by Senator Thomas J. Dodd on the State Department Suspension of the Visa of Mr. Michel Struelens, Director of the Katanga Information Service," October 11, 1961.

[87] W. F. Buckley, "On the Right," syndicated column, December 18 or 19, 1965.

[88] Liebman Papers, Box 56, Telegram from Yergan to Sec. of State, Dean Rusk, February 15, 1962.

influencing US public opinion on the Katanga question.[89] In the case of Tshombe's visa denial, it did not dampen the opposition's anger over Congo policy. Nor did it stop the pro-Katanga Madison Square Garden rally held in Tshombe's honor where Senators John Tower and Barry Goldwater were among those who made speeches praising the righteousness of Katangese cause.[90] In response to the uproar over Tshombe's visa, the administration decided to postpone the UN bond bill.[91] A watered-down bond purchase was only passed by Congress in September of that year.

In March 1962, the US ambassador to Belgium met with the Belgian Foreign Minister, Paul-Henri Spaak. Spaak said he had trouble understanding how the US government allowed Struelens to operate out of New York City when he was doing "great damage" to US policy objectives in the Congo.[92] The ambassador replied that the administration was finding it difficult to establish legal grounds for expelling him. Like the Belgians, the Adoula government called on the State Department to ask why Struelens had not yet been kicked out of the country.[93] Repeating the ambassador's excuse to Spaak, the response was that there were no legal grounds to kick him out.[94]

In response to these criticisms over the KIS, Samuel Belk, a staffer from the National Security Council, asked to reopen the possibility of deporting Struelens, a different legal issue than merely invalidating his visa. In forwarding on cables from Brussels and London in which the Struelens affair was a point of embarrassment, he expressed his frustration that calls to deport Struelens had always "been met with a rebuff from the State legal people who, of course, adopt a very legalistic attitude toward the problem." "I cannot believe," Belk continued, "that faced as we are with Struelens' repeated efforts to justify an independent Katanga in complete contradiction to U.S. policies, we can't find some means to

---

[89] See, for example: Liebman Papers, Box 56, "Federation of Rhodesia and Nyasaland," Attached prospectus to letter from Liebman to Yergan, February 2, 1962.

[90] Howe and Trott, *Power Peddlers*, pp. 180–181. See also: L. Kaplan, "The United States, Belgium, and the Congo Crisis of 1960," *The Review of Politics*, vol. 29, no. 2 (April 1967) p. 248.

[91] Mahoney, *Ordeal in Africa*, p. 136.

[92] FRUS, vol. XX, Congo, Doc. 212, "Telegram from the Embassy in Belgium to the Department of State," March 4, 1962.

[93] FRUS, vol. XX, Congo, Doc. 256, "Telegram from the Department of State to the Embassy of the Congo," July 7, 1962; FRUS, vol. XX, Congo, Doc. 273, "Telegram from Embassy in the Congo to the Department of State," August 11, 1962.

[94] FRUS, vol. XX, Congo, Doc. 256, "Telegram from the Department of State to the Embassy of the Congo," July 7, 1962; FRUS, vol. XX, Congo, Doc. 271, "Telegram from the Department of State to the Embassy of the Congo," August 10, 1962.

export this darling of the Katanga Lobby for good."[95] Replying to the NSC's inquiry, the State Department indicated that there were two grounds to deport him: that he violated his visa status, or that his activities were prejudicial to the US public interest, endangered the welfare safety, or security of the United States. It recommended against basing deportation on either one.[96] But as the administration hemmed and hawed over the legal issues involved, concern over Struelens' bad influence on Tshombe continued.[97]

In the late fall of 1962, the Kennedy administration saw that time was running out for the Adoula regime unless something could be done about Katanga. Over the course of several high-level meetings in November, the administration finally decided to move against Struelens.[98] In one White House meeting Kennedy reportedly asked: "Can we throw him [Struelens] out?"[99] Deputy National Security Advisor, Carl Kaysen, replied that there would inevitably be a court case and Struelens would get a hearing. Kennedy then directed Kaysen to reexamine the issue of expelling Struelens.[100] Nearly two weeks later, Kaysen reported that Struelens had forced a decision by applying for a change from non-immigrant status to permanent resident status from inside the country. The INS had asked the State Department for a recommendation, and the department had yet to give one. Tellingly, Kaysen wrote, "The problem still remains Dodd.... The argument in favor of moving now [against Struelens] is that Tshombe is beginning to show signs of worry and this action would act as a further warning to him.

---

[95] JFK Archives, Series: Countries, Congo, National Security Files, Box 28, Congo: General, February 20–March 9, 1962, Memorandum for Ralph Dungan from Samuel Belk, National Security Council, "Activities of Michael Struelens in the United States," March 6, 1962.

[96] JFK Archives, Series: Countries, Congo, National Security Files, Box 28, Congo: General, February 20–March 9, 1962, Memorandum for McGeorge Bundy from Manfull, State Department, "Michel Struelens," March 9, 1962.

[97] FRUS, vol. XX, Congo, Doc. 230, "Telegram from the Department of State to the Embassy in the United Kingdom," May 11, 1962.

[98] FRUS, vol. XX, Congo, Doc. 323, "Memorandum of Conversation," November 5, 1962; FRUS, vol. XX, Congo, Doc. 325, "Memorandum for the Record," November 8, 1962.

[99] Fredericks Papers, Box 13, Folder: State Department, Country and Region Files, Congo Handwritten Notes, J. Wayne Fredericks handwritten notes on the November 5, 1962 White House meeting on the Congo, dated November 11, 1962.

[100] JFK Archives, National Security Files, Congo: General November 6–10, 1962, Box 28A, Memorandum for Brubeck, State Department from Carl Kaysen, "Congo Review," November 7, 1962. Fredericks remembers Kennedy directing Kaysen not merely to investigate the expulsion of Struelens, but to "produce means of expulsion." J. Wayne Fredericks Papers, Box 13, Folder: State Department, Country and Region Files, Congo Handwritten Notes, J. Wayne Fredericks handwritten notes on the November 5, 1962 White House meeting on the Congo, dated November 11, 1962.

The argument against, of course, is the question of how Dodd might react." In early December 1962, his application for permanent residence status was denied by the INS on the request of the State Department.[101] He was asked to leave within fifteen days or face deportation proceedings.[102]

In reaction to the move to expel Struelens, Dodd carried out an earlier threat he had made and released the findings of his congressional hearings on the Struelens case.[103] Predictably, the findings concluded that the department's treatment of Struelens had been a "glaring abuse" of its visa power.[104] But it was too late to influence the course of events. In the third round of fighting the newly fortified UN military force brought the Katangese secession to an end through conquest in early 1963. Struelens did not finally leave the country until that summer, which ended the lengthy deportation process.[105] Struelens would portentously characterize his visa fight this way: "It is not my battle, it is the battle of Katanga."[106]

Rhodesia

Katanga's and Rhodesia's independence bids never overlapped, and so the KIS and the RIO never coexisted. Shortly after Rhodesia's UDI in 1965, the staff of the Southern Rhodesia Affairs Office in the British Embassy in Washington were made to sign a pledge of loyalty to the Crown or lose their diplomatic status.[107] This loyalty pledge was concurrent with the loyalty pledge distributed to members of the staff at Rhodesia House in London, discussed in the next chapter.[108] Of the five staff members, only the lone black staffer, Lot Senda, signed the pledge.

---

[101] "Tshombe Aide Here Ordered Out by US," *New York Times*, December 7, 1962.

[102] "Tshombe Aide Here Ordered Out by US," *New York Times*, December 7, 1962.

[103] Dodd Papers, Subseries D: Congo, Series IV, Box 256, folder 6749: Correspondence 1961–1962, Letter from Dodd to McGhee, November 5, 1962.

[104] See generally: "Struelens Case."

[105] "Ex-Aide of Katanga Leaves for Canada," *New York Times*, August 9, 1963.

[106] "Envoy for Tshombe," *New York Times*, August 3, 1964. Streulens eventually became a professor at American University in Washington, DC. When asked in the 1970s by Howe and Trott about his relationship with Dodd and Katanga's right-wing supporters in America, Streulens reportedly said that Dodd and others had "no interest" in Katanga but merely used it as a stick to beat Kennedy. Howe and Trott cast some doubt over this retrospective remembrance by Streulens. *Power Peddlers*, p. 182.

[107] "They're Still Doing a Job for Rhodesia," *Washington Post*, February 13, 1966.

[108] The Rhodesia House loyalty pledge turned into a political embarrassment for the Wilson government, forcing a public retreat on the issue. See Brownell, "'A Sordid Tussle on the Strand'."

Senda's decision was neither preordained, nor without some "considerable heart-searching."[109] One of the first African lawyers in Rhodesia, Senda had formerly been attached to the United Nations delegation from Southern Rhodesia.[110] According to an internal South African cable, in that role he had been subject to a great deal of abuse from the representatives of the independent African states who "accused him of treason to their side."[111] After UDI, when first asked by the British Charge d'Affaires whether or not he supported the "rebel illegal government" or remained loyal to the Crown, Senda reportedly replied that his allegiance was to Ian Smith's government, but upon further reflection and considering his relatives back in Rhodesia he opted in favor of the Crown.[112] The other members of the Rhodesian mission staff did not try to influence his decision. According to the South Africans, his former colleagues "appear[ed] sympathetic to his particular circumstances," and he was subsequently reassigned to the British Embassy.

Officially, the State Department refused to see the Head of the Rhodesian mission, Air Vice-Marshal Alfred "Raff" Bentley, but State's Desk Officer informed Bentley that the Rhodesia mission no longer enjoyed any official status or immunity, that members of the staff had to regularize their status with US immigration authorities, and that no Rhodesian passports issued or amended after UDI would be recognized.[113] Refusing to pledge loyalty to the Crown, Bentley returned to Salisbury on November 18, but only after asking the South Africans to store certain files in the South African Embassy so as not to have them

[109] South African Department of Foreign Affairs, Box 1/156/6, "UDI External Representation," Telegram from South African Ambassador to the US, Taswell, to Secretary of DFA, Pretoria, "Rhodesian Representation, Washington; Termination of Appointments," November 17, 1965.
[110] Senda went on to be a prominent lawyer in Zimbabwe and was a PF-ZAPU MP in Parliament."Veteran Lawyer, Lot Senda's, Burial Today," *The Chronicle*, December 30, 2016.
[111] South African DFA, Box 1/156/6, "UDI External Representation," Telegram from South African Ambassador to the United States, Taswell, to Secretary of DFA, Pretoria, "Rhodesian Representation, Washington; Termination of Appointments," November 17, 1965.
[112] South African DFA, Box 1/156/6, "UDI External Representation," Telegram from South African Ambassador to the United States, Taswell, to Secretary of DFA, Pretoria, "Rhodesian Representation, Washington; Termination of Appointments," November 17, 1965.
[113] South African DFA Archives, Box 1/156/1/19/1, "UDI Rhodesia's Position re: International Organizations and Agencies," Telegram from South African Embassy Washington to Secretary DFA, Pretoria, November 14, 1965.

fall into hostile hands, with the idea that they could eventually be returned to Rhodesia.[114]

The remaining three staffers, Kenneth Towsey, Henry J. C. Hooper, and Arnold Saich, refused to sign the pledge and lost their diplomatic status.[115] The three were removed from Britain's diplomatic list and were "out of status," but the State Department decided not to move for deportation as long as they remained "quiescent."[116] Instead of leaving the country though, the three continued to work out of their former office, except now for the Smith regime.[117] Outside this pseudo-embassy at 2852 McGill Terrace NW the name plaque was changed to read: "Rhodesia Information Office."[118] It would become, as an article in the *Rand Daily Mail* described: "The loneliest 'embassy' in Washington." [119]

The US government only learned about the RIO's existence through press reports.[120] In February 1966, RIO staffer John Hooper officially registered with the Justice Department under the FARA as an agent of the "Department of External Affairs, Ministry of Information, Government of Rhodesia," a move that, from the Lyndon Johnson administration's perspective, generated much unwanted attention.[121] The department issued a statement following the RIO's filing emphasizing that the registration under the FARA in no way implied recognition, and it concluded with a reiteration of the policy of nonrecognition of the "rebel regime."[122] Although the RIO, just like the KIS a few years earlier,

---

114 South African DFA Archives, Box 1/156/1/19/1, "UDI Rhodesia's Position re: International Organizations and Agencies," Telegram from South African Embassy Washington to Secretary DFA, Pretoria, November 14, 1965.

115 Towsey and Hooper stayed on, but Arnold Saich left the United States in 1967.

116 Lyndon B. Johnson Presidential Library, National Security File, Country File: Rhodesia, Box 97, vol. 2, 2/66-12/68 "Rhodesia/Zambia Situation Report," no. 18, January 18–February 11, 1966.

117 "They're Still Doing a Job for Rhodesia," *Washington Post*, February 13, 1966.

118 "Rhodesia Retains Information Office Here as Lobbying Center," *Washington Post*, March 19, 1970.

119 "Untitled 'Diplomats' in Loneliest Embassy," *Rand Daily Mail*, February 24, 1966.

120 For the Johnson administration's initial reaction to the RIO, see: Eddie Michel, "Those Bothersome Rho-dents: Lyndon B. Johnson and the Rhodesian Information Office," *Safundi* vol. 19, no. 2 (2018) pp. 227–245.

121 Lyndon B. Johnson Presidential Library, National Security File, Country File: Rhodesia, Box 97, vol. 2, 2/66-12/68 "Rhodesia/Zambia Situation Report," no. 18, January 18–February 11, 1966.

122 Lyndon B. Johnson Presidential Library, National Security File, Country File: Rhodesia, Box 97, vol. 2, 2/66-12/68 "Rhodesia/Zambia Situation Report," no. 19, February 12–14, 1966. In 1987, the Reagan administration "capitulated to political pressure," including most notably a Senate bill with forty-nine co-sponsors, calling for the shutting down of the Palestine Information Office. Like the KIS, RIO, and Washington Bureau, the PIO was registered as an office of a foreign agent, this one

clearly fell within the intended scope of the FARA, and despite the department's clarifying statements that the foreign principal did not necessarily have to be a recognized state, the registration seemed to imply some degree of official acceptance of the regime to African diplomats and domestic liberals.[123] With the news of the FARA registration, a group of demonstrators calling itself the "Afro-American Citizens of Washington" along with some African diplomats began mobilizing to protest the RIO.[124]

Shortly after news of the FARA registration, Zambian President Kenneth Kaunda visited the US ambassador in Lusaka to inquire about the mission.[125] The ambassador informed Kaunda that there were no legal grounds to close it, pointing out that "we had a similar case with Struelens' Katanga office."[126] On February 17, 1966, nearly all the African ambassadors in Washington met at the home of the Zambian ambassador to discuss the RIO during which a group of them agreed to call on "Soapy" Williams to clarify the Johnson administration's position.[127] As summarized in a memorandum to Johnson from this same day: "The Rhodesian situation is heating up again and attracting a lot more press coverage – some of it with adverse ramifications on us."[128] Williams met the delegation, but on February 23, 1966, Zambia nonetheless issued an official protest note about the establishment of the

being the Palestine Liberation Organization. The administration's strategy was unique, categorizing the PIO as a "foreign mission," even though it never held itself out as one, in order for it not to be protected by the First Amendment, and fully under State Department control, so that it could be shut down. This was due to strong lobbying on the part of Israel. Anthony Lewis, "Abroad at Home; Shot in the Foot," *New York Times*, December 3, 1987.

[123] Lyndon B. Johnson Presidential Library, National Security File, Country File: Rhodesia, Box 97, vol. 2, 2/66-12/68 "Rhodesia/Zambia Situation Report," no. 18, January 18–February 11, 1966.

[124] Fredericks Papers, Box: Rhodesia, Folder: Department of State-Rhodesia Telegrams, UPI Wire (Rhodesia) February 17, 1966.

[125] Lyndon B. Johnson Presidential Library, National Security File, Country File: Rhodesia, Box 97, vol. 2, 2/66-12/68 "Rhodesia/Zambia Situation Report," no. 22, February 17, 1966.

[126] Lyndon B. Johnson Presidential Library, National Security File, Country File: Rhodesia, Box 97, vol. 2, 2/66-12/68 "Rhodesia/Zambia Situation Report," no. 22, February 17, 1966.

[127] Lyndon B. Johnson Presidential Library, National Security File, Country File: Rhodesia, Box 97, vol. 2, 2/66-12/68 "Rhodesia/Zambia Situation Report," no. 23, February 18, 1966.

[128] Lyndon B. Johnson Presidential Library, National Security File, Country File: Rhodesia, Box 97, vol. 2, 2/66-12/68 "Memorandum for the President," from the President's Deputy Special Assistant for National Security Affairs R. W. Komer, February 17, 1966.

RIO.[129] The governments of Ghana and Nigeria also issued formal protests.[130]

Carl T. Rowan, formerly of the State Department, who along with Soapy Williams were the bêtes noires of the Katanga lobby, also played that role for the Rhodesia lobby. As a columnist Rowan wrote an invective in 1966 where he noted the existence of the RIO and declared that the Rhodesia lobby was merely a racist and "reactionary reincarnation" of the right-wing Katanga lobby with many of the same leading figures inside and outside Congress.[131] A National Security Council staffer in charge of African affairs felt compelled to respond to Rowan and other critics by asserting that the existence of the RIO did not signify recognition, and that China and Cuba (both unrecognized by the United States) ran similar offices.[132] Because of the pressure to do something, on February 26, Thomas Mann, the Undersecretary of State for Economic Affairs, wrote a letter to John Hooper.[133] Mann's letter suggested that Hooper apply for an adjustment of his visa status to reflect his new role, and demanded that the RIO not represent itself as an instrument of the "Government of Rhodesia," but instead as an organ of a foreign principle.[134] In a "relaxed" and "amiable" personal meeting with Hooper at his home, a State Department official further explained to Hooper that while he had been allowed to remain out of status since UDI, African pressure since the publication of the FARA filing had forced the government's hand and Hooper must now "regularize" his status in the country.[135] Hooper was informed that Mann's letter was to be circulated in the United Nations in response to protests from certain African governments. Initially Hooper attempted to distance himself from Towsey and Saich, holding himself out as the lone foreign agent,

[129] Lyndon B. Johnson Presidential Library, National Security File, Country File: Rhodesia, Box 97, vol. 2, 2/66-12/68 "Rhodesia/Zambia Situation Report," no. 26, February 25, 1966.

[130] Lyndon B. Johnson Presidential Library, National Security File, Country File: Rhodesia, Box 97, vol. 2, 2/66-12/68 "Memorandum for the President," from R. W. Komer, February 17, 1966.

[131] Carl T. Rowan, "Another Racist Club," *The Evening Star*, February 26, 1966.

[132] A. DeRoche, *Black, White and Chrome: The United States and Zimbabwe, 1953–1998* (Africa World Press, Trenton, 2001) p. 146.

[133] Lyndon B. Johnson Presidential Library, National Security File, Country File: Rhodesia, Box 97, vol. 2, 2/66-12/68 "Rhodesia/Zambia Situation Report," no. 27, February 26–March 1, 1966 Memo from Thomas McElhiney to Thomas Mann.

[134] Lyndon B. Johnson Presidential Library, National Security File, Country File: Rhodesia, Box 97, vol. 2, 2/66-12/68 Memorandum from Rick Haynes for Hayes Redmon, re: RIO, April 8, 1966.

[135] Lyndon B. Johnson Presidential Library, National Security File, Country File: Rhodesia, Box 97, vol. 2, 2/66-12/68 "Rhodesia/Zambia Situation Report," no. 27, February 26–March 1, 1966, Memo from Thomas McElhiney to Thomas Mann.

and that they as private individuals were not involved, but this paper-thin separation did not last long.[136]

These interactions with Hooper and Towsey revealed the bind in which the State Department found itself. The Rhodesians and their American friends knew Hooper and the RIO were not breaking the law, yet the government felt compelled by international and domestic pressure to move against them. An internal State Department memorandum admitted that "Mr. Hooper is on firmer ground than we are," as it concerned the legality of the operation of the RIO.[137] In response to the publication of Mann's letter to Hooper, letters poured into the White House pleading with President Johnson to leave Hooper alone – letters clearly prompted by direct mailings from the Rhodesia lobby.[138] Almost as soon as the RIO opened, the Johnson administration had noted the connections between the RIO and "extreme right-wing US groups" and was not at all interested in stirring them up unnecessarily.[139] But the Hooper episode certainly stirred them up. In Hooper's eventual reply to the State Department, he wrote that "it has not been my intention to lay claim to any official capacity in the United States ..." and with that the controversy temporarily abated.[140]

The diplomatic pressure on the United States over the RIO continued, and in response State Department official Rick Haynes wrote a memorandum advocating that the government initiate deportation proceedings against the three Rhodesians and close the RIO. The memorandum was written in language very close to Samuel Belk's memorandum about Struelens four years before.[141] To support his argument, Haynes pointed

---

[136] Raymond Heard, "Untitled 'Diplomats' in Loneliest Embassy," *Rand Daily Mail*, February 24, 1966.

[137] Lyndon B. Johnson Presidential Library, National Security File, Country File: Rhodesia, Box 97, vol. 2, 2/66-12/68 "Rhodesia/Zambia Situation Report," no. 27, February 26–March 1, 1966, Memo from Thomas McElhiney to Thomas Mann.

[138] These letters all referenced certain details about the FARA and emphasized the same talking points, which strongly indicates that they were written in response to a plea from the Rhodesia lobby. See, for example, Lyndon B. Johnson Presidential Library, White House Central File, Name File: J. Hooper, Letter from S. D. Gardner, Jr., to President Johnson, April 18, 1966.

[139] Lyndon B. Johnson Presidential Library, National Security File, Country File: Rhodesia, Box 97, vol. 2, 2/66-12/68 "Memorandum for the President," from the President's Deputy Special Assistant for National Security Affairs R. W. Komer, February 17, 1966.

[140] Lyndon B. Johnson Presidential Library, National Security File, Country File: Rhodesia, Box 97, vol. 2, 2/66-12/68 "Rhodesia/Zambia Situation Report," no. 27, February 26–March 1, 1966 for Thomas Mann from McElhiney.

[141] Lyndon B. Johnson Presidential Library, National Security File, Country File: Rhodesia, Box 97, vol. 2, 2/66-12/68 "Memorandum from Rick Haynes for Hayes Redmon," re: RIO, April 8, 1966.

to the criticism they were getting from the African ambassadors and the wider United Nations, but also to the pressure from domestic civil rights groups, noting how the Student Non-Violent Coordinating Committee (SNCC) had recently picketed the RIO.[142] Haynes pointed out that since the RIO is registered under the FARA "the Office has been going ahead full steam turning out propaganda critical of both the US and the UK. It has lined up support from a most vocal and unsavory bunch of right-wing reactionary types."[143] Haynes argued, that not following up on Mann's letter to Hooper would be read by critics at home and abroad as the government "condoning" the RIO's activities.[144] Hayne's proposal went nowhere and the RIO remained open.

One of the factors weighing against the immediate deportation of the RIO representatives was one that was shared by the British government in regard to Rhodesia House in London. This was that Salisbury would respond by deporting the US representatives and shutting down the American mission in Rhodesia, a potential act both the United States and Britain saw as embarrassing and contrary to their broader policy goals with respect to Rhodesia.[145] It was also posited that if faced with a fait accompli of Rhodesia closing their Salisbury missions this could legally constitute de facto recognition of the Smith regime, under the rationale that this sort of expulsion was a power only sovereign states possessed.[146] So, in a dizzying turn of logic similar to the rationale allowing Americans to travel to the Bantustans, the mission of the unrecognized regime was allowed to stay open because closing it could possibly afford the regime more status.

Kenneth Towsey came to be the acknowledged "Ambassador-out-of-the-Ordinary" for Rhodesia, with John Hooper as the office's information officer.[147] Towsey was described by one reporter as being "well-groomed ... and spoke in a quiet voice with an accent straight from the playing fields of England."[148] During the Katanga secession Towsey had

---

[142] Lyndon B. Johnson Presidential Library, National Security File, Country File: Rhodesia, Box 97, vol. 2, 2/66-12/68 "Memorandum from Rick Haynes for Hayes Redmon," re: RIO, April 8, 1966.

[143] Haynes noted the full-page advertisement placed in the *Washington Post* on April 5 by "their American supporters." Lyndon B. Johnson Presidential Library, National Security File, Country File: Rhodesia, Box 97, vol. 2, 2/66-12/68 "Memorandum from Rick Haynes for Hayes Redmon," re: RIO, April 8, 1966.

[144] Lyndon B. Johnson Presidential Library, National Security File, Country File: Rhodesia, Box 97, vol. 2, 2/66-12/68 "Memorandum from Rick Haynes for Hayes Redmon," re: RIO, April 8, 1966.

[145] Michel, "Those Bothersome Rho-dents," p. 12.

[146] Michel, "Those Bothersome Rho-dents."

[147] "The Twilight Diplomats," *Washington Post*, July 27, 1977.

[148] "Rhodesia: Two Men, Two Cases," *Washington Post*, July 8, 1973.

been at the Ministry of External Affairs in Salisbury, and was intimately involved with creating the federation's policy throughout that crisis. Only two years later, propaganda flowed from his office in Washington about the nature of independent Rhodesia and the nature of its enemies. These materials included a newsletter titled "Rhodesian Commentary" printed in Salisbury and sent to Washington, and "Rhodesian Viewpoint," which was a collection of favorable newspaper clippings drawn from around the United States and reprinted out of the RIO.[149] As a regular part of his operations, Towsey directly wrote letters to the editor, issued press releases under RIO stationery, and maintained correspondence with conservative American politicians and opinion makers. The RIO also regularly gave prepared materials to sympathetic congressmen who inserted them directly into the *Congressional Record*.[150] In many ways the RIO staff held themselves out as diplomats – they were still driven around in a chauffeured black car around Washington, albeit one that was stripped of its diplomatic plates.[151] Sensitive to what they perceived as a series of petty slights from the official Washington diplomatic crowd, the RIO staff publicly described themselves as diplomatic "lepers."[152] Belying their self-pitying portrayal of their social ostracization, the RIO hosted regular cocktail parties, much as Rhodesia House did in London.[153] And in 1973, First Lady Pat Nixon actually invited Mrs. Towsey to a fall party for diplomatic wives at the White House – one could only hope to be so ostracized in Washington circles.[154]

Shortly after the opening of the RIO, a British Embassy spokesman explained: "As far as we're concerned, [the RIO] has no status at all.... We take no cognizance of it; it is without significance."[155] But it was, of course, quite significant. Anthony Lake describes the RIO as "easily the most effective of the pro-Smith groups operating in the US,"[156] and Andrew DeRoche describes how the establishment of the RIO "sparked

[149] See generally, Group Research Inc. files on Rhodesia. See also "Rhodesia Cites US Poll Seeking Policy Change," *Washington Post*, March 16, 1969.
[150] R. Arsenault, "White on Chrome: Southern Congressmen and Rhodesia, 1962–1971," *Issue: A Journal of Opinion*, vol. 2, no. 4 (Winter, 1972) p. 49.
[151] "Rhodesians Treated as Diplomatic 'Lepers'," *Washington Post, Times Herald*, December 26, 1967.
[152] "Rhodesians Treated as Diplomatic 'Lepers'," *Washington Post, Times Herald*, December 26, 1967.
[153] Howe and Trott, *Power Peddlers*, p. 210.
[154] Howe and Trott, *Power Peddlers*, p. 210.
[155] "Rhodesia Retains Information Office Here as Lobbying Center," *Washington Post*, March 19, 1970.
[156] Lake, *"Tar Baby" Option*, p. 104.

a gradual increase in American public criticism" of Johnson's sanctions policy.[157]

Though it was tucked in a residential neighborhood, the mission building did not go unnoticed.[158] On the night of August 29, 1970, two bombs exploded within minutes of each other, the first in front of the residence of the Portuguese ambassador at 11:30 p.m., and the second bomb blew up just across the narrow Rock Creek Park in front of the RIO on McGill Terrace at 11:40 p.m. Dozens of windows in both buildings and surrounding homes and buildings were smashed, which "shattered the night's tranquility in two of Washington's most elegant and sedate sections," but the blasts resulted in no injuries.[159] The Portuguese ambassador was out of town on vacation leaving his personal staff in the building, and no one was in the RIO at the time. *The Washington Post* quoted a spooked neighbor as saying, "We're not safe anywhere, are we? I think it's dangerous to be near these embassies now."[160] As a result of these bombs, the Executive Protective Service of the Secret Service added additional patrols and "fixed post" patrols at both sites.[161] Towsey was quoted as saying that while Rhodesia "is sometimes supposed to be in an explosive situation. It's not as explosive as this."[162]

Following the blasts, Towsey offered the following bland and patently obvious observation: "One could only suppose from the fact that our office and the Portuguese Embassy received attention at approximately the same time that there was some kind of political motivation from people with ideological positions in regard to southern Africa."[163] In fact, the so-called Revolutionary Action Party had already claimed responsibility for the bombs, and said in a note mailed to the Associated Press that the two explosions were in retaliation for the oppression of blacks in Africa.[164] *The Washington Post* article reporting

---

[157] DeRoche, *Black, White and Chrome*, p. 145.
[158] "Blasts Spur Tight Guard on 2 Missions," *Washington Post*, August 31, 1970.
[159] "Bombings Shock Residents in Area," *Washington Post*, August 31, 1970
[160] "Bombings Shock Residents in Area," *Washington Post*, August 31, 1970
[161] "Blasts Spur Tight Guard on 2 Missions," *Washington Post*, August 31, 1970.
[162] "Bombings Shock Residents in Area," *Washington Post*, August 31, 1970.
[163] "Blasts Spur Tight Guard on 2 Missions," *Washington Post*, August 31, 1970.
[164] In full their manifesto read:

> We are an African people and we are at war with all nationalistic institutions, organizations and governments, etc. that conduct and lend support to exploitation and oppression of African people around the world. Angola, Mozambique, Zimbabwe shall and will be freed. Revolutionary Action Party. ("Blasts Spur Tight Guard on 2 Missions," Washington Post, August 31, 1970)

the blast showed a large photograph of Washington Mayor, Walter E. Washington, standing alongside Hooper and Towsey in front of the RIO inspecting the bomb damage. A better publicity article and photo could hardly have been developed by the Rhodesian public relations men themselves, displaying as it did the sober and thoughtful pseudo-diplomats alongside Washington's black mayor in front of the site of the Leftist terror attack. The article explains that the State Department was preparing a statement of apology for the Portuguese government, but because the United States did not recognize the Rhodesian government no similar statement was being prepared for the Rhodesians.[165] To what entity could they apologize except the British Embassy?

If in some ways Towsey and the RIO took the form of Struelens and the KIS, then another Connecticuter, former Secretary of State Dean Acheson, played the role of Senator Dodd, as the face of the opposition to US policy toward Rhodesia. During the Congo Crisis and after, Acheson was outside the State Department lobbying the Kennedy and Johnson administrations against taking Africanist positions.[166] But behind these northeasterners, the Katanga and Rhodesia lobbies were driven largely by the broad support of southern conservatives and the anti-communists of the New Right.[167]

The major organizations of the Rhodesia lobby grew out of the old organizations of the Katanga lobby. The founder of the most influential pro-Katanga organization, ACAKFF, was also the founder of the most influential pro-Rhodesia organization, the AAAA: conservative public relations guru, Marvin Liebman. Describing his professional niche, Liebman explained: "If I were to define my expertise, I would say that I am an expert at agitation and propaganda – the 'agit-prop' that Marxism has used so effectively over the years."[168] The chairman of the ACAKFF and the co-chairman of the AAAA was a black man named Max Yergan.[169] William A. Rusher, the publisher of the *National Review*, was instrumental in founding both the ACAKFF and the AAAA, the

---

[165] "Blasts Spur Tight Guard on 2 Missions," *Washington Post*, August 31, 1970.

[166] Brinkley, *Dean Acheson*, p. 305.

[167] This was not merely clever Cold War marketing on behalf of the Rhodesians. Anti-communism formed a crucial part of their political ideology. Lowry, "The Impact of Anti-communism." Raymond Arsenault convincingly makes the case that support for Rhodesia in the US Congress was deeply rooted in the South. Arsenault, "White on Chrome." See also V. McKay, "The Domino Theory of the Rhodesian Lobby," *Africa Report* (June 1967).

[168] William A. Rusher Papers, Library of Congress, Box 52, General Correspondence, Memorandum by Liebman, "Professional Resume and Notes," November 24, 1980.

[169] For an interesting and nuanced and ultimately sympathetic portrait of Yergan's life, see Anthony III, *Max Yergan*.

latter of which he was the co-chairman alongside Yergan. Matching the names involved in both the ACAKFF and the AAAA quickly reveals that atop their letterheads had quite nearly the same list of supporters.[170] The address for Liebman's public relations firm was 79 Madison Avenue, the same mailing address as the ACAKFF, and the AAAA's original mailing address was also 79 Madison Avenue.[171] In 1966, it was revealed that the AAAA's new headquarters on Fifth Avenue shared the same postage meter as the Rhodesian government.[172] Rusher explained in a letter to the editor that the AAAA and the Rhodesian government both employed the same public relations firm: Marvin Liebman Associates.[173]

There was a tension, though, between these groups associated with the *National Review* magazine, and the more radical groups linked with the John Birch Society and the Liberty Lobby such as the American Friends of Katanga (AFK), the Friends of Rhodesian Independence (FRI), and the American Southern African Council (ASAC).[174] But among these more radical groups there was a great deal of overlap as well. The FRI was run out of an office on 132 3rd Street in Washington, DC, the same address as the far-right Liberty Lobby, which publicly proclaimed the independence of its lobbying organization.[175] The ASAC and the FRI were linked as well, with the former providing all the public relations work for the latter.[176]

These lobbying organizations, especially the Liebman groups, worked closely with the foreign missions. There was, for instance, quite close coordination in messaging between Struelen's KIS, the Tshombe regime, and the ACAKFF.[177] Rusher and Towsey also corresponded regularly over the course of several years, and Rusher facilitated Towsey's introductions to various individuals in the media.[178] One area

---

[170] Contemporaries identified these organizational overlaps as well. See for example D. Pearson and Jack Anderson, "The Washington Merry-Go-Round," syndicated column, June 9, 1967.

[171] Group Research Inc., Box 4, folder AAAA, "Certificate of incorporation of AAAA," February 16, 1965. The AAAA later moved to 5th Avenue. Noer correctly identifies AAAA as being "an outgrowth of the old 'Katanga Lobby,'" and the organization's connection with the *National Review*. Noer, *Cold War and Black Liberation*, p. 223.

[172] "Moon Shines on Apartheid," *Washington Notes on Africa*, Summer 1982.

[173] Group Research Inc., Box 4, folder AAAA, Rusher Letter to the Editor to *The Nation*, January 16, 1967.

[174] *Washington Post* columnists identified this split in the lobby as early as 1966. R. Evans and R. Novak, "Inside Report," *Washington Post*, May 3, 1966.

[175] See Group Research Inc., Box 146, Folder FRI.

[176] See generally, Group Research Inc., Box 22, Folder ASAC.

[177] See, for example, Liebman Papers, Box 56, Letter from Liebman to Sidney O. Hershman and Struelens, July 23, 1962.

[178] William A. Rusher Papers, Library of Congress, Washington, DC, Box 76, Letter from Rusher to Towsey, October 26, 1971.

of close coordination between Towsey and all the domestic groups, was in the organization of Potemkin-style tours of Rhodesia for American conservatives.[179]

The more radical Bircherite groups were seen to be rather embarrassing friends by the Katangese and Rhodesians, but their grassroots base and energy made them useful to these would-be states. In a letter to his former boss, Roy Welensky, Kenneth Towsey wrote that while he was forced to work alongside some extremists in America, "We have considered it prudent to sup with them with a long spoon."[180] Expressing this same idea, Hooper wrote a letter to Under Secretary of State, Thomas Mann, that Salisbury would lose the propaganda war if the wider American public saw them in the same way as they saw domestic racist groups.[181]

In early 1967, the administration decided to push back against the pro-Rhodesian forces, a reprise of the State Department's counteroffensive against the Katanga lobby during the winter of 1961/1962. UN Ambassador, Arthur Goldberg, gave a series of lectures taking on the arguments of Acheson and others, and State officials began to meet with congressional leaders to make their case. The State Department issued a "background paper" on UDI, which in form and intention mirrored the background paper the department issued during the Kennedy administration's counteroffensive against Katanga in November 1961.[182]

All the while, Towsey and his information officer, John Hooper, remained "out of status" since refusing to sign the loyalty pledge. On May 4, 1967, Towsey applied for an adjustment of his visa status. As with other aspects of Johnson's Rhodesian policy, with this visa matter the specter of Katanga loomed large. The Africa Bureau feared that moving against Towsey might create another "Struelens case" in which the current administration would draw unwanted fire from the Rhodesia lobby just as Kennedy had from the Katanga lobby.[183] Towsey's application was approved by the INS after the State Department indicated they had no objection to the status change.[184] Towsey then became a permanent resident alien in early January 1968, a status that Struelens had been unable to obtain when in the service of the KIS.

---

[179] See for example: Liebman Papers, Box 40, Letter from Liebman to Ralph de Toledano, January 11, 1966; Box 41, Letter from Liebman to Rene Wormser, February 13, 1967; Box 40, Letter from Liebman to Ralph de Toledano, January 11, 1966.

[180] Quoted in Gerald Horne, *From the Barrel of a Gun: The United States and the War Against Zimbabwe, 1965–1980* (University of North Carolina Press, Chapel Hill, 2015) p. 104.

[181] Michel, "Those Bothersome Rho-dents," p. 10.

[182] Noer, *Cold War and Black Liberation*, p. 232.   [183] Lake, *"Tar Baby" Option*, p. 106.

[184] Lake, *"Tar Baby" Option*, p. 105.

This did not indicate any broader trends regarding the RIO as Salisbury had hoped. Following an Executive Order implementing UNSC Resolution 253, the US Treasury Department froze the bank accounts of the RIO in the United States. Towsey's and Hooper's personal accounts in the United States were also frozen. This treasury action sparked outrage from the Rhodesia lobby. Towsey worked his congressional connections who then leaned on the administration, and almost as soon as the personal accounts were frozen, they were unfrozen again.[185] As for the RIO's accounts, those were restored with a new funding system whereby the RIO had access to money in accounts in New York that were funded by various religious and charitable groups, which were in turn reimbursed by the Rhodesian government.[186] Once again, this characteristic attack and counterattack left the mission in a state of legal limbo.

John Hooper's application for a change in his visa status was a different issue from Towsey's. He applied for the same change of status as Towsey, but crucially he did so two months later. While Hooper's change of status was being processed, the Security Council passed Resolution 253.[187] Among other things, this resolution required that all member states deny entry to Rhodesian supporters of the Smith regime. British Prime Minister, Harold Wilson, considered Hooper's status to be so symbolically important as to send a letter to Secretary of State, Dean Rusk, asking him to deny the visa request.[188] The State Department concluded that Hooper's application fell within the meaning of the new resolution, but that Towsey's came in just under the wire.[189] As a result of these considerations, the department recommended to the INS that they deny Hooper's request.

Pushing back against this, of course, was the Rhodesia lobby. In a replay of the Struelens affair, interested congressmen pressed hard on the State Department not to take action against Hooper, with Senator James Eastland, the former co-chairman of the committee investigating the State Department's handling of the Struelens affair, at the fore. A member of Eastland's Judiciary Committee staff urged the INS to sit on Hooper's application and take no action.[190] Eastland eventually took up the issue directly with Nixon's Secretary of State, William Rogers, and

---

[185] See the syndicated column by William F. Buckley: "US Attempts to Put Gag on Rhodesia Info Agency," syndicated column, *Beaver County Times*, October 15, 1968.
[186] See: Lake, *"Tar Baby" Option*, p. 108.   [187] Lake, *"Tar Baby" Option*, p. 106.
[188] Lake, *"Tar Baby" Option*, p. 107.   [189] Lake, *"Tar Baby" Option*, p. 106.
[190] "Implications for US International Legal Obligations of the Presence of the RIO in the US," subcommittee on Africa, Foreign Affairs Committee House of Representatives, May 15, 17, 1973.

in March 1973, the department finally acquiesced in permanently freezing the application.[191] As a result, Hooper could stay indefinitely, but he could not leave the United States and expect to be allowed back in – the same state of passport limbo as Struelens found himself in the early 1960s.

The 1971 Byrd Amendment (Section 503 of the Armed Services Authorization), which carved out a limited exception to UN sanctions on Rhodesian imports pertaining to chrome and other metals, was the major triumph of the Rhodesia lobby in the United States.[192] Couched in Cold War language, Section 503 was pushed through by a coalition of anti-communists, corporate interests, and pro-Rhodesian segregationists.[193] The RIO hosted a Christmas party to celebrate the Byrd Amendment and a satirical song for the occasion was written to the tune of "O Tannenbaum." Verse VII of the song read:

> Oh, Kenneth, T.; oh, Kenneth T.
> Ambassador one day you'll be.
> And may John Hooper follow thee
> To posts of great authority.
> Next winter may it be your lot
> To spend your Christmas where it's hot.
> Please raise a toast in Salisbury
> In memory of 503.[194]

The party did not last. In late 1972, the Rhodesian guerrilla war began in earnest. As Towsey bitterly noted in an op-ed piece in the *Washington Post*, "[now] the Armageddon boys are whooping it up over Rhodesia. 'Race war' and 'blood bath' spring readily to their lips."[195] The Byrd Amendment was repealed in 1977, and in that same year the Carter administration moved against the RIO. The Justice Department began scrutinizing the activities of the RIO to ensure conformity with the provisions of the FARA, and sent FBI agents to the RIO to examine its records.[196] In May, the UN Security Council passed Resolution 409, which was intended to stop the transfer of funds to Rhodesian agents or

---

[191] "Implications for US International Legal Obligations of the Presence of the RIO in the US," subcommittee on Africa, Foreign Affairs Committee House of Representatives, May 15, 17, 1973.

[192] Lake, *"Tar Baby" Option.*

[193] Lake, *"Tar Baby" Option.* See also: Horne, *From the Barrel of a Gun.*

[194] "The Absolutely Tentatively Provisional Official Marching Song of 'The 503 Club,'" in Howe and Trott, *Power Peddlers*, p. 212.

[195] "Rhodesia's Situation: 'An Ideological Tussle,'" *Washington Post*, April 13, 1976.

[196] "Rhodesia Lobby under Scrutiny by Justice Department," *Washington Post*, March 29, 1977.

information offices overseas.[197] The resolution targeted the RIO and the Rhodesia Information Centre in Australia. This outraged those in conservative circles in both countries. For instance, William F. Buckley Jr.'s *Firing Line*, an American public affairs television series, dedicated an episode to what it called "Rhodesia Blackout."[198] Were it put into effect the resolution would have cut off the RIO from direct funding from Salisbury and would have to rely solely upon what private donations it received from US sources, which would have made it impossible for the RIO to remain open.[199] In July, the Treasury Department informed Towsey that he needed to wind up the RIO's accounts and close the office if he wished to remain in the United States.[200]

The State Department wrongly assumed that this notification by itself would be enough to close it down.[201] But to implement the treasury warning, it was necessary that President Carter issue an Executive Order giving the treasury the legal authority to do so. As explained in a State Department cable from August 1977, while there was an order in preparation, the administration's action "has been delayed by recent attempts by congressional supporters of RIO to prevent action against it by attaching a binding rider to Department's authorization Bill. As a result, we are proceeding carefully with issuance and timing ..."[202] Looking over its shoulders as its own diplomats dithered, the State Department was curious as to what actions the Australians were taking regarding the Rhodesian Information Centre in Sydney.[203] As it happened, the Australians were also dithering and were watching to see what the Americans did. Both the American and Australian governments were still very nervous about the powerful pro-Rhodesia domestic lobbies that

[197] *UN Yearbook*: vol. 31, 1977 (Department of Public Information, New York, 1980) p. 181.

[198] Transcript for "Rhodesia Blackout," *Firing Line* program on PBS, originally aired July 29, 1977; Rusher Papers, Box 169, Letter to President Carter from seventeen members of the media, June 3, 1977.

[199] "Rhodesia Lobbying Office Seems about to Close," *The Washington Post*, June 1, 1977. See also: S. Diamond, *Roads to Dominion: Right-Wing Movements and Political Power in the United States* (Guilford Press, New York, 1995) p. 136.

[200] "The Twilight Diplomats," *Washington Post*, July 27, 1977.

[201] State Department Telegram from Secretary of State, Washington, to Brussels, "Rhodesia Information Office," August 25, 1977, accessed via Wikileaks on June 9, 2017: wikileaks.org/plusd/cables/1977STATE202727_c.html.

[202] State Department Telegram from Secretary of State, Washington, to Brussels, "Rhodesian Information Office," August 25, 1977, accessed via Wikileaks on June 9, 2017: wikileaks.org/plusd/cables/1977STATE202727_c.html.

[203] State Department Telegram from Secretary of State, Washington, to Brussels, "Rhodesian Information Office," August 25, 1977, accessed via Wikileaks on June 9, 2017: wikileaks.org/plusd/cables/1977STATE202727_c.html.

opposed their governments' implementation of the resolution. State Department officials surmised that the Australian government was "concerned that it might place itself out on a political limb which US would then saw off by not implementing Resolution 409 ourselves."[204]

By July 1979, the RIO had still not been shut down, and indeed the Rhodesians seemed to be closer than ever to achieving normalized relations with the United States. The Carter administration felt a great deal of pressure from North Carolina Senator, Jesse Helms, and others to ease pressure on the new Zimbabwe Rhodesia government, and to increase the American presence in Salisbury, something they hoped would be signaled by a senior State Department appointee assigned to Rhodesia.[205] In sending an unofficial representative back to Rhodesia after several years with no official presence, the United States was following the lead of Britain, which had sent several Foreign and Commonwealth Office officials back to Marimba House.

The United States was very clear that the new appointment was as a First Secretary to the American Embassy in Pretoria, and would not be accredited in Rhodesia, and that his appointment did "not constitute recognition, de facto or otherwise."[206] In the State Department's press talking points regarding the appointment it was to be noted its pick, Jeffrey Davidow, was a "mid-level officer" and was less senior than the British envoy.[207] To the chagrin of Helms and others the administration purposely sent a relatively junior appointee in Davidow, and initially disallowed his family from joining him for fear that this might reinforce the notions of permanence to which the State Department was studiously trying to avoid.[208] As the *Rand Daily Mail* reported upon his arrival in Rhodesia, there was "no splash."[209] Under the terms of his appointment, Davidow would "spend a considerable proportion of his time in

---

[204] State Department Telegram from Washington to Canberra, "Closure of Rhodesia Information Office, Sydney," October 7, 1977, accessed via Wikileaks on June 9, 2017: wikileaks.org/plusd/cables/1977STATE242319_c.html.

[205] Interview with Ambassador Jeffrey Davidow, July 19, 2017. Notes with author.

[206] State Department Telegram from Christopher, Secretary of State, Washington, to London, "Press Guidance for Designated Representative to Rhodesia, Jeffrey Davidow," June 25, 1979, accessed via Wikileaks: wikileaks.org/plusd/cables/1979STATE163984_e.html.

[207] State Department Telegram from Christopher, Secretary of State, Washington, to London, "Press Guidance for Designated Representative to Rhodesia, Jeffrey Davidow" June 25, 1979, accessed via Wikileaks: wikileaks.org/plusd/cables/1979STATE163984_e.html.

[208] Interview with Ambassador Jeffrey Davidow, July 19, 2017. Notes with author.

[209] State Department Telegram from Pretoria to Secretary of State, "Rhodesia: Media Report on Davidow in Salisbury," July 7, 1979, accessed via Wikileaks: wikileaks.org/plusd/cables/1979PRETOR06138_e.html.

Salisbury," but would be officially posted in Pretoria.[210] At first he stayed at the Meikles Hotel, but after several weeks the State Department eventually gave in to his demands and his wife and kids joined him in Salisbury, and in August they all moved into a furnished house in the city.[211] The Rhodesian government recognized his presence as a step in the right direction of greater international connectedness, even with the State Department's careful handling of his status.[212] It was obvious to anyone paying attention to such things that the Americans were engaging with the Rhodesians more, not less. The RIO did not go away either, and the rebellion ended before it was even shut down.[213] Towsey did not leave the United States, and he does not leave this story.

Transkei

Unlike Katanga's and Rhodesia's missions in the United States, Transkei's and Bophuthatswana's missions were created with the blessing of the mother country. Transkei's Washington Bureau was to a large extent funded by the South African government, and South Africa maintained a role in guiding its messaging strategy even after independence. This was in sharp contrast to the stories relayed above, where the Congo actively tried to have the United States close down the KIS and deport Struelens, and Britain tried to do the same with the RIO and its representatives. In those cases, the mother countries' pressure was a prompting factor in the United States moving against Rhodesia's and Katanga's missions, albeit haltingly, while the mother country's friendliness toward Transkei and Bophuthatswana's was a prompting factor in the US government maintaining its quarantine of their missions.

In the buildup to Transkei's independence, Kaiser Matanzima's regime went on a recruiting drive to fill the higher echelons of the Bantustan government. Ironically, among those best suited for administrative roles, including foreign representative positions, were the anti-apartheid activists and freedom fighters who were living in exile abroad.

---

[210] State Department Telegram from Secretary of State, Washington, to Pretoria, "Rhodesia: Salisbury-Designated Officer and 'Reciprocal Arrangements," June 23, 1979, accessed via Wikileaks: wikileaks.org/plusd/cables/1979STATE163456_e.html.

[211] Interview with Ambassador Jeffrey Davidow, July 19, 2017. Notes with author.

[212] Interview with Ambassador Jeffrey Davidow, July 19, 2017. Notes with author.

[213] Surprisingly, Towsey was offered and agreed to take up a position as the new chief envoy of Robert Mugabe's Zimbabwean government in Washington. This arrangement was short-lived, however, and focused primarily upon efforts to secure an aid package. "Rhodesia's Lobbyist Back for Mugabe," *Washington Post*, June 26, 1980. He resigned his Zimbabwe appointment in 1981 after the new ambassador arrived. "Kenneth Towsey, Diplomat," *Washington Post*, September 3, 1993.

The first task of the nascent government was to sell these exiled freedom fighters on the idea of an independent Transkei before they could be asked to sell Transkei to others. Kaiser Matanzima had mixed feelings about the African National Congress (ANC) and PAC, or at least he sent mixed signals. At independence, he claimed that the PAC and ANC could use Transkei as a base from which to launch their "liberation struggle" against South Africa, but not to wage armed incursions.[214] Despite these apparent sympathies, the Transkei regime inherited its massive security apparatus directly from the apartheid state, and as it had been before October 1976, this apparatus was focused primarily on surveilling and harassing African liberation groups.[215] Yet it was among this very group that Matanzima tried to rally support for Transkeian independence when he visited London in early 1975.[216] As part of this effort, Matanzima invited several of these exiled Transkeians of the PAC and ANC to London's Hilton Hotel to make his pitch.

Tsepo "T.T." Letlaka, then a member of the PAC, was a part of this South African community living in exile in London at the time. The Letlakas had been living in exile for thirteen years, and their kids only spoke English.[217] He had served his law articles under George Matanzima, Kaiser's brother, and this personal connection formed the basis of Kaiser's appeal to Letlaka to join him in working for the new Transkei.[218] Letlaka's wife Pamela was the sister of Digby Koyana, who would go on to become Transkei's first Foreign Minister. None of the other London exiles at the gathering could be convinced by Matanzima's appeal, and they all opted to continue to fight for a liberated, unified South Africa. Before Matanzima left, however, he invited Letlaka and his wife back to his hotel room for a final, private appeal. In this private meeting Matanzima asked Letlaka to return to Transkei to serve in the first independent Cabinet in October 1976. He allegedly assured Letlaka that Transkei would be truly independent of South Africa with its own functioning parliament and government ministries.[219] According to his wife's memoir, Matanzima pledged to Letlaka that Transkei was going to be a stepping stone for the eventual liberation of all of South Africa, and

---

[214] Stultz, *Transkei's Half Loaf*, p. 105. By the 1970s, the PAC was already in terminal decline and was increasingly eclipsed by the ANC. Irwin describes the PAC in 1970 as being "a shadow of its former self." *Gordian Knot*, p. 174.

[215] See: Southall, *South Africa's Transkei*. See Gibbs, *Mandela's Kinsmen*.

[216] Koyana-Letlaka, *This Is My Life*, p. 187.

[217] Koyana-Letlaka, *This Is My Life*, p. 202.

[218] Koyana-Letlaka, *This Is My Life*, p. 187.

[219] Koyana-Letlaka, *This Is My Life*, p. 188.

apparently convinced by this, Letlaka agreed to serve.[220] In this way, a former liberation fighter became a Bantustan official, and a trainee under the apartheid regime's Department of Foreign Affairs (DFA). This ideological journey was the same distance from left to right as earlier traveled by Max Yergan and Marvin Liebman, who were both onetime Communists who became radical anti-communists, but in Letlaka's case it was traversed over the course of a single night.

The Letlakas' return from exile to South Africa was facilitated by Pretoria. As Pamela Koyana-Letlaka recalls, "we had left home being harassed refugees but had returned as heroes."[221] In July and August 1975, T. T. Letlaka, Digby Koyana, Mlahleni Njisane, and others were sent to Pretoria for diplomatic training in the DFA.[222] The trainees stayed near the Union Buildings on Meintjieskop at the all-white Union Hotel and for their training they were driven in DFA cars to the Union Buildings.[223] In August the trainees' wives joined them for further training in protocol, such as how to host cocktail parties and diplomatic dinner functions, and by September of 1975, South Africa arranged for all the Transkeian diplomatic trainees and their spouses to be posted abroad to various South African missions.[224]

The Letlakas and the Njisanes arrived in Washington on September 1, 1975 as trainee diplomats, with all their travel and housing expenses paid by Pretoria.[225] Letlaka's fellow trainee, Mlahleni Njisane, had been a sociology lecturer in the United States since the 1960s. Like Letlaka, he too was called back to Transkei on the request of Kaiser Matanzima to play a role in an independent Transkei.[226] In these early days, the South Africans guided their trainees through this new diplomatic world.[227] It is clear from Pamela Letlaka's memoir that for former exiles the experience of being in the South Africans' diplomatic inner circle was both mind-boggling and flattering.[228] But the trainees certainly understood that the reason for their special treatment had little to do with real changes in the South Africans' racial attitudes.[229]

---

[220] Koyana-Letlaka, *This Is My Life*, p. 188.
[221] Koyana-Letlaka, *This Is My Life*, p. 203.
[222] Koyana-Letlaka, *This Is My Life*, pp. 209–210.
[223] Koyana-Letlaka, *This Is My Life*, p. 210.
[224] Koyana-Letlaka, *This Is My Life*, p. 211.
[225] Koyana-Letlaka, *This Is My Life*, p. 216.
[226] Koyana-Letlaka, *This Is My Life*, p. 218.
[227] Koyana-Letlaka, *This Is My Life*, p. 218.
[228] See for example: "Tsepo and Professor Njisane were driven to our hotel for lunch with their families and were dying to tell us about their first morning experience at the Embassy." "[Tsepo] was so surprised to find that the white officials were kind and polite to them, treating them as equals, which they never did back in South Africa." Koyana-Letlaka, *This Is My Life*, pp. 217–218.
[229] Koyana-Letlaka, *This Is My Life*, p. 218.

Like Lot Senda, and as will be described below, Leslie Masimini of Transkei's Washington Bureau, the Letlakas were awkwardly situated between two worlds and did not fit entirely into either one. In New York City they called on the ANC representative at the UN who greeted them cordially, but most others ostracized them. The ANC and PAC leadership denounced Letlaka for joining the nascent Transkei government, and when the Letlakas returned to London briefly before Transkei independence, they did not even seek out their old exiled friends, who "bitterly disagreed with Tsepo's decision."[230] The South African Minister at the Embassy, Jeremy Shearer, wrote that Letlaka and Njisane have "[b]oth taken heart searching decisions to take up their present assignments." He noted that Letlaka in particular was adamant that Transkei was not a manifestation of apartheid, something Shearer thought was indicated by his prior involvement with the PAC, which "must complicate his position here, but also his credibility outside in respect of his present functions."[231] Njisane's reasons for working for the Transkei, as expressed by Shearer, was that he said he had witnessed racial discrimination all over the world and that he had "more to give, and more to gain, by working for the Transkei than by trying to isolate himself from his home country by living abroad."

After several months of training out of South Africa's Embassy, Ambassador Pik Botha suggested that the Transkeians open their own office in Washington early in 1976. In this new office, "they would be less inhibited in their activities ... [and] ... by the same token their functioning under their own auspices could have practical benefits for the Embassy."[232] This was a manifestation once again of the concern that South Africa hide its hand in Transkeian affairs. In the meantime, South Africa and Transkei exchanged foreign missions with one another as though they were two sovereign states. On November 12, 1976, two weeks after Transkei's independence, South Africa offered Transkeian diplomats in South Africa the privileges and immunities it afforded the diplomats of sovereign states.[233] Under the apartheid regime these diplomatic privileges mattered in a practical way, such as when one of the

---

[230] Koyana-Letlaka, *This Is My Life*, p. 245.

[231] SA National Archives, Box: Transkei: Independence Celebrations and Invitations, 1/226/1/1, "Transkei Diplomats" Letter from SA Ambassador the US, Shearer, to Secretary DFA, November 13, 1975.

[232] SA National Archives, Box: Transkei: Independence Celebrations and Invitations, 1/226/1/1, Letter from SA Ambassador the US, Shearer, to Secretary DFA, November 13, 1975.

[233] SA Department of Foreign Affairs Archives, Box 90/1/226, File: "Diplomatic Immunities with Transkei," telegram from A. M. Grobler, Secretary for Foreign Affairs, to SA Ambassador Umtata, November 12, 1976.

Transkeian diplomats in Cape Town tried to play tennis on one of Cape Town's whites-only municipal tennis courts but first had to prove his diplomatic status to be allowed to do so.[234]

Before they left Washington, the Letlakas met a black American couple at one of the Washington cocktail parties at Ambassador Botha's residence, Jay and Dorothy Parker. Soon the families became very close. The Parker's relationship with the Letlakas continued after the Letlakas returned to Transkei. They corresponded regularly and Parker and his family visited the Letlakas in Umtata in 1978, after Letlaka became the Transkei's first Minister of Justice.[235] Growing up in a poor area of South Philadelphia, Parker would rise to become a very influential black conservative in American politics.[236] He was the first black board member of the Young Americans for Freedom (YAF), a group founded by Marvin Liebman, and the same organization that had bestowed upon Tshombe the "defender of freedom" award. Both Liebman and Parker worked on the Barry Goldwater campaign in 1964, and Parker was a volunteer for Ronald Reagan's campaigns in 1968 and 1976.[237] In 1970, Parker founded his public relations firm, Jay Parker and Associates, Inc. in Washington, which specialized in representing conservative clients. Parker always identified Max Yergan as his mentor, someone who had worked closely with Liebman on several organizing projects, most notably heading ACKFF and the AAAA.

By the mid-1970s, Parker was trying to position himself to work as a public relations officer and lobbyist for the Bantustans, and Pretoria was willing to spend money for the promotion of these new states. Among other things, this meant South Africa paid for brochures, promotional materials, and large advertisements making the case for Transkei in major publications in the United States and Europe.[238] A little less than a year before Transkei's independence date, Jay Parker wrote to Njisane and Letlaka offering his services as a public relations expert.[239] In his pitch, Parker identified what he saw as the biggest obstacle to the grand goal of American recognition: "Above all, we would seek to inform and educate the American people (government and non-government) that

---

[234] SA Department of Foreign Affairs Archives, Box 90/1/226, File: "Diplomatic Immunities with Transkei," Letter from the Manager of Bathing Amenities, City of Cape Town, to Secretary of DFA, "Diplomatic Privilege," September 19, 1979.

[235] Koyana-Letlaka, *This Is My Life*, p. 221.

[236] Tyson, *Courage to Put Country above Color*.

[237] Dillard, *Guess Who's Coming to Dinner* p. 6, 185 fn. 10.

[238] John Burns, "Transkei Approaches Nationhood Helped, and Burdened, by Its Ties to South Africa," *New York Times*, October 22, 1976.

[239] SA National Archives, Box: Transkei: Independence Celebrations and Invitations, 1/226/1/1, Letter from Jay Parker to Letlaka and Njinsane, November 15, 1975.

the Transkei is not and will not be a 'tool' or 'puppet' of any other nation."[240] His pitch was right out of the Liebman playbook, creating his "Friends of __" organizations, the blue ribbon boards, the multi-media appeals, the full-page advertisement in newspapers, and the organization of canned fact-finding trips.[241]

As South Africa considered the proposal, Ambassador Botha wrote to Pretoria: "[Parker] is well known to the officers of all departments who have served recently in Washington."[242] Botha explained that Parker had twice visited South Africa, the last time in 1974, when he was the guest of the Department of Information. Botha wrote:

> He is a rarity in the United States, being a black American of marked conservative persuasion. Our experience of him confirms that this brand of conservatism is genuine, not simply cosmetic.... He has explained that his predilection for the Transkei and the progress of its people results from a close personal friendship with the late Max Yergan. Apart from the financial transactions, he views any role that he can play in this respect as his contribution to the memory of Dr. Yergan.[243]

In an attached memorandum to the DFA, Letlaka wrote that he personally was very impressed with Parker and vouched for his character.[244] Most importantly, perhaps, Letlaka thought that "[Parker] appears to have the expertise to project an image powerfully, and in the complex and intricate situation of American politics might well be the man to open doors which a foreigner, no matter how competent, might be unable to do."[245] Parker was finally hired by Transkei in April 1977, six months after independence, although he claimed he had already been working to

---

[240] SA National Archives, Box: Transkei: Independence Celebrations and Invitations, 1/226/1/1, Letter from James Parker to Letlaka and Njinsane, November 15, 1975.

[241] SA National Archives, Box: Transkei: Independence Celebrations and Invitations, 1/226/1/1, Letter from Jay Parker to Letlaka and Njinsane, November 15, 1975.

[242] SA National Archives, Box: Transkei: Independence Celebrations and Invitations, 1/226/1/1, "Investment in the Transkei: Mr J. A. Parker," Letter from SA Ambassador to the United States, Pik Botha, to Secretary for Foreign Affairs, Pretoria, December 11, 1975.

[243] SA National Archives, Box: Transkei: Independence Celebrations and Invitations, 1/226/1/1, "Investment in the Transkei: Mr J. A. Parker," Letter from SA Ambassador to the US, Pik Botha, to Secretary for Foreign Affairs, Pretoria, December 11, 1975.

[244] SA National Archives, Box: Transkei: Independence Celebrations and Invitations, 1/226/1/1, "Investment in the Transkei: Mr J. A. Parker," Memorandum on Parker by T. T. Letlaka attached as an addendum to letter from SA Ambassador to the United States, Pik Botha, to Secretary for Foreign Affairs, Pretoria, December 11, 1975.

[245] SA National Archives, Box: Transkei: Independence Celebrations and Invitations, 1/226/1/1, "Investment in the Transkei: Mr J. A. Parker," Letter from SA Ambassador to the United States, Pik Botha, to Secretary for Foreign Affairs, Pretoria, December 11, 1975.

promote Transkei for a year prior out of his own pocket motivated by his personal conviction.[246]

Parker overlapped briefly with another black American publicist working for Transkei, Andrew Hatcher, who had been hired in the early summer of 1976.[247] Hatcher had been an associate press secretary for President Kennedy, but he was later hired to run the new South Africa account in the mid-1970s. As the *New York Times* reported, the South African government explicitly "hired an American black publicist to try to counter the racism specter that the mention of South Africa raises for many Americans."[248] This was a well-known tactic. For instance, to gather support for Rhodesia's "internal settlement" several years later, Kenneth Towsey wrote to William Rusher to suggest "an association of Americans to generate support for and recognition of 'the internal solution,'" and he ended his letter: "P.S. We should have some blacks associated with the enterprise. I have one or two in mind – Rhodesians resident in the US."[249] There were messaging advantages for these aspirant states in having both American black men such as Yergan, Parker, and Hatcher out front, in addition to having men like Masangu, Senda, Masimini, or Letlaka who were Africans from the states in question. Having black representatives who were both American and African was in and of itself a powerful visual rhetoric, because it was a way to visually muddy the binaries of race associated with these independence bids. But even if the race of their spokespersons was at times employed cynically by these would-be states, it does not mean that these spokespersons did not also believe in these causes.[250] It could be both things at once.

Parker soon took over the work of Hatcher. Apart from direct lobbying and distributing propaganda, he also created a news digest which was very similar in style and substance to the RIO's "Viewpoint."[251] Parker would come to work closely with Ngqondi "Leslie" Masimini, a former PAC member who was living in the United States. While Parker remained associated with Transkei for some time, his public relations activities were most intense in the beginning of his term when Transkei's efforts at recognition were at their peak. They subsequently tapered off.[252] Despite the big promises during his pitch, Parker failed to break

[246] "US Black gets Paid to Boost Transkei," *Rand Daily Mail*, April 7, 1977.
[247] "US Black gets Paid to Boost Transkei," *Rand Daily Mail*, April 7, 1977.
[248] George Goodman, Jr, "Some US Blacks Visit South Africa on Business," *New York Times*, July 2, 1976.
[249] William Rusher Papers, Box 76, "RIO," Letter from Towsey to Rusher, March 3, 1978.
[250] Dillard, *Guess Who's Coming to Dinner*.   [251] 1978 FARA Report.
[252] Interview with Barbara Cannady-Masimini, widow of Ngqondi Masimini, July 25, 2017. Notes with author.

through the diplomatic quarantine. Telling the *Rand Daily Mail* that he was going to focus most of his efforts trying to educate American journalists, Parker commented: "People have been misled with bad information. I'm getting to those guys."[253] He added: "People don't even know where Transkei is. A lot don't even know where Africa is."[254] From 1981–1984 Jay Parker would be registered under FARA as a foreign agent working for the third Bantustan to emerge from South Africa, Venda, which celebrated its independence in 1979.[255]

Masimini had spent much of his youth in prison in South Africa for political activities.[256] He was jailed for his participation in the 1952 Defiance Campaign, again for the 1954 potato boycott, and again for the 1960 anti-pass law campaigns, and he was a founding member of PAC in 1959.[257] He would later move to Zambia to link up with the PAC in exile and was sent for a period of time to China and Soviet Union for training in military camps.[258] From Zambia he was then sent to Georgetown, Guyana, to be a PAC representative, and it was there that he met an American woman who would soon be his wife, Barbara Cannady.[259] They would later move to the United States. In a profile in the *New York Times*, Masimini said of his past: "Being a refugee, not belonging, not having a home, that's a great frustration."[260]

As former PAC colleagues in Zambia Masimini had known Letlaka, and it was likely during Letlaka's time in Washington as a diplomatic trainee over the fall and winter of 1975/1976 that Letlaka recruited Masimini into working for Transkei.[261] Like Letlaka, Masimini's former

---

[253] "US Black Gets Paid to Boost Transkei," *Rand Daily Mail*, April 7, 1977.

[254] "US Black Gets Paid to Boost Transkei," *Rand Daily Mail*, April 7, 1977.

[255] From 1985 onward, Parker would work directly for South Africa, alongside William Keyes, another black American, who, like Hatcher, was recruited by the republic to help stem the tide of black American opposition to South Africa. See: Ron Nixon, "The Anti-Mandela Lobby," *Politico Magazine*, December 8, 2013. In 1984, Parker and Keyes had worked together to create Black PAC, a political action committee which among other activities railed against the "terrorist outlaw" ANC, and worked to help reelect the North Carolina Senator Jesse Helms, a longtime vocal opponent of civil rights. Letter to the Editor, Edward S. Herman, "Judge Thomas's South Africa Connection Needs Clarification," *New York Times*, September 8, 1991.

[256] Jacqueline Trescott, "South Africa's American Dreams," *New York Times*, August 7, 1977.

[257] Streek and Wicksteed, *Render unto Kaiser*, p. 201.

[258] Interview with Barbara Cannady-Masimini, widow of Ngqondi Masimini, July 25, 2017. Notes with author.

[259] Interview with Barbara Cannady-Masimini, widow of Ngqondi Masimini, July 25, 2017. Notes with author.

[260] Jacqueline Trescott, "South Africa's American Dreams," *New York Times*, August 7, 1977.

[261] Interview with Barbara Cannady-Masimini, widow of Ngqondi Masimini, July 25, 2017. Notes with author. On Njisane's draft invitations to Transkei Independence

role as a PAC fighter, activist, and representative likely led Transkeian authorities to believe that he could have greater credibility as a Transkeian representative overseas.[262] In July 1977, he was called back to Transkei by Matanzima's regime and offered an appointment as "Minister at Large" representing Transkei in the North, Central, and South America.[263] A *Rand Daily Mail* article from July 9, 1977 stated that Masimini was leaving that day from Umtata to open a Transkei office "in the ambassadorial area of Washington."[264] Shortly after being hired, Masimini boasted: "I am not new in the diplomatic field. I have been a freedom fighter and a representative of the PAC in Zambia, Algeria, South America, and British [Guiana]."[265] Also, like Letlaka, Masimini would put himself on an island working for Transkei and in so doing isolated himself from his former activist friends in exile. This was something that bothered him, and he tried to maintain his old friendships and compartmentalize their political differences, even as he would at times have intense debates with them over the merits of Transkei's independence bid.[266]

After arriving back in the United States, Masimini registered under FARA as a foreign agent with the US Justice Department, just as Struelens, Hooper, Towsey, and Parker had done. But similar to Parker, who was a US citizen, Masimini had a legal right to reside in the United States because of his American wife and was not subject to threats of expulsion. Reports of Masimini's status as an agent of Transkei in Washington began to cause significant embarrassment for the American mission to the UN, especially since the controversy overlapped with the State Department's prevarications over shutting down the

Day celebrations it listed a "Mr. Leslie Maximini" at an address in Orenta, New York. Below Masimini's name on the invitation list, it said: "(Former P. A. C. Transkeian refugee – suggested for Foreign Service.)" SA National Archives, Pretoria, Box: Transkei 1/226/1/1, "Independence Celebrations and Invitations," "Invitations as of 27 July 1976." It is not clear if he actually attended the celebrations.

[262] Interview with Barbara Cannady-Masimini, widow of Ngqondi Masimini, July 25, 2017. Notes with author.

[263] "Off to Washington," *Rand Daily Mail*, July 9, 1977.

[264] See: US State Depart Telegram from United Nations mission, New York, to Washington, "Transkei's 'Representative' in America' Reportedly to Open Office in Washington" July 9, 1977, accessed via Wikileaks on June 9, 2017: wikileaks.org/plusd/cables/1977PRETOR03372_c.html.

[265] See: US State Department Telegram from Durban to Washington, "Further Information on Transkei Representative," July 27, 1977, accessed via Wikileaks on June 9, 2017: wikileaks.org/plusd/cables/1977DURBAN00499_c.html.

[266] Interview with Barbara Cannady-Masimini, widow of Ngqondi Masimini, July 25, 2017. Notes with author.

RIO.[267] In planning their reply, the American mission to the UN argued that Masimini's presence and apparent official status would cause messaging headaches for the State Department: "As in the case of Rhodesia Information Office, most UN representatives simply will not understand how Masimini's alleged actions can be tolerated in contradiction to US policy on Transkei."[268] A cable from the US mission to the UN argued for following Masimini's actions and prosecuting him were he to act outside of his agency mandate or if he had not properly registered.[269]

In August 1977, the State Department felt there was a need to publicly clarify the legal position of Masimini and American policy toward Transkei more generally.[270] A cable from Washington to the US embassy in South Africa advised:

Missions in South Africa should take appropriate occasion to let it be known publicly that Masimini is not in the United States as an official of the Government of Transkei. As the US does not recognize Transkei, Masimini is simply a registered foreign agent under the Foreign Agents Registration Act of 1938, and enjoys no, repeat, no official standing.[271]

This explanation was never wholly convincing for opponents of Transkei, just as it was never convincing for opponents of Katanga or Rhodesia. For their part, the Transkeians did not make matters easier for the Carter administration's defense of Masimini's FARA registration. In justifying the exorbitant spending the government dedicated to overseas missions, the Transkeian Foreign Minister, Digby Koyana, told his Parliament that one fruit of this spending was that the US government had granted de facto recognition to Transkei by virtue of them allowing Masimini to

[267] See: US State Department Telegram from United Nations Mission, New York, to Washington, "Transkei Representative's Activities in Washington" July 27, 1977, accessed via Wikileaks on June 9, 2017: wikileaks.org/plusd/cables/1977USUNN02382_c.html.

[268] See: US State Department Telegram from United Nations Mission, New York, to Washington, "Transkei Representative's Activities in Washington" July 27, 1977, accessed via Wikileaks on June 9, 2017: wikileaks.org/plusd/cables/1977USUNN02382_c.html.

[269] See: US State Department Telegram from United Nations mission, New York, to Washington, "Transkei Representative's Activities in Washington" July 27, 1977, accessed via Wikileaks on June 9, 2017: wikileaks.org/plusd/cables/1977USUNN02382_c.html.

[270] See: US State Department Telegram from Secretary of State, Washington, to Cape Town, "Transkei Representative, in Washington" August 2, 1977, accessed via Wikileaks on June 9, 2017: wikileaks.org/plusd/cables/1977STATE180432_c.html.

[271] See: US State Department Telegram from Secretary of State, Washington, to Cape Town, "Transkei Representative, in Washington" August 2, 1977, accessed via Wikileaks on June 9, 2017: wikileaks.org/plusd/cables/1977STATE180432_c.html.

open an office in Washington to register with the federal government as the "Republic of Transkei Washington Bureau."[272]

The controversy never fully died down, and over the years new officials in the State Department had to learn the meaning of FARA registration, and then had the task of defending the US government's registration of foreign agents in this manner. In 1979, some two years after he first registered, and after the State Department first explained this designation, the OAU became aware of the activities of Masimini in the United States and protested against the US government allowing him to represent Transkei on American soil.[273] The State Department's UN mission staff at that time was unfamiliar with FARA and forwarded on the OAU's concerns to Washington, citing the Security Council resolutions on the nonrecognition of the Bantustans.[274] With what one might imagine would be a collective eye roll and sigh, officials in Foggy Bottom explained to the UN mission that Masimini was acting in accordance with FARA, and his registration with the Justice Department did not imply any sort of endorsement or recognition by the US government, just as it had not done with Streulens and Towsey.[275]

While this storm raged around his presence in Washington, Masimini insouciantly went about his business, and as the *Rand Daily Mail* reported, he "has been in Washington telling as many people as he can his story of the birth of Transkei."[276] Masimini's work included distributing literature, giving speeches, being available for interviews by print and broadcast media, meeting with potential investors, and lobbying on Capitol Hill.[277] In June 1977, he said, "I'm going to make all sorts of contacts. Primarily we have to talk to lawmakers and also try to lobby the American people for support in getting the US government to recognise

---

[272] "Koyana Counts the Cost," *Rand Daily Mail*, June 5, 1980. Transkei's successive budget crises were typically resolved only by influxes of South Africa money. See, for instance Gibbs, *Mandela's Kinsmen*, p. 60.

[273] See: US State Department Telegram from United Nations mission, New York, to Washington, "OAU Concern about Representative of the Transkei in Washington" December 4, 1979, accessed via Wikileaks on June 9, 2017: wikileaks.org/plusd/cables/1979USUNN05825_e.html.

[274] See: US State Department Telegram from United Nations mission, New York, to Washington, "OAU Concern about Representative of the Transkei in Washington" December 4, 1979, accessed via Wikileaks on June 9, 2017: wikileaks.org/plusd/cables/1979USUNN05825_e.html.

[275] See: US State Department Telegram from Washington to Pretoria, "OAU Concern about Transkei Representative in Washington," December 12, 1979, accessed via Wikileaks on June 9, 2017: wikileaks.org/plusd/cables/1979STATE320159_e.htm.

[276] Guy Bernard, "Transkei in Search of Image," *Rand Daily Mail*, August 18, 1977.

[277] FARA Report 1978.

the Transkei."[278] One article from August 1977 described Masimini as being "cheerful about his present task of trying to convince the world in general, and US investors in particular, that Transkei is an independent country in its own right and was not created by South Africa."[279] Another *Rand Daily Mail* article likewise described Masimini as a man who "never loses his optimism."[280] But, as Masimini's wife remembers of his efforts to break out of Transkei's diplomatic quarantine, this was "not a popular thing."[281]

Masimini's Washington Bureau office was at first located out of the Masimini home in a wooded section of Northwest Washington, DC. According to Guy Bernard, the *Rand Daily Mail* correspondent, the bureau's reception room "was furnished in conservative, good taste, with handmade Transkei tapestry on the far wall and a carved wooden plaque in front of the fireplace to bring a touch of Africa to the upper middle-class American home."[282] He soon moved the bureau to the National Press Building and hired two employees, who were described in FARA filings as "foreign service employees."[283] According to the FARA filings, the Washington Bureau's operating expenses were covered 30 percent by the South African government and 70 percent by Transkei.[284]

While Masimini's activities followed closely with what his predecessors Struelens and Towsey had done in terms of public relations and lobbying, there were no similar governmental efforts to try to silence him. For the most part he was ignored. In June 1978, the UPI ran a story that was picked up across the country titled "Minister for Transkei: Loneliest Diplomat."[285] As this article notes, "Masimini is ignored by diplomats here [in Washington], even some black envoys who know he has fought for some of their causes."[286] Unlike both Struelens and Towsey, Masimini did not enjoy his own access to congressmen and opinion makers. While South Africa was itself growing more isolated in the late 1970s, its own diplomats could still get meetings with important political leaders, however Transkei's chief diplomat in America struggled to do so. One *New York Times* article from 1978 describes how Masimini had to corner congressmen and senators when he could find them and would

---

278 "Transkei's Agent Recognised," *Rand Daily Mail*, July 23, 1977.
279 Guy Bernard, "Transkei in Search of Image," *Rand Daily Mail*, August 18, 1977.
280 "Transkei Man to Chat with Young?" *Rand Daily Mail*, September 8, 1978.
281 Interview with Barbara Cannady-Masimini, widow of Ngqondi Masimini, July 25, 2017. Notes with author.
282 Guy Bernard, "Transkei in Search of Image," *Rand Daily Mail*, August 18, 1977.
283 FARA Report 1984.   284 FARA Report 1984.
285 "Minister for Transkei: Loneliest Diplomat," *Sarasota Herald-Tribune*, June 4, 1978.
286 "Transkei, Apartheid's Product, Struggles to Break Isolation," *New York Times*, August 12, 1978.

"recite the reasons why his country should be recognized by the US government, at times even pulling out old maps to display Transkei's pre-colonial credentials."[287] Yet, despite what a *New York Times* reporter called his "affable manner," Masimini's arguments failed to convince anyone and he "wander[ed] in a diplomatic wilderness, shunned by the international community."[288]

Masimini's efforts at times provoked some backlash in Southern Africa. On November 8, 1977, days after the UNSC passed a mandatory arms embargo against South Africa following the wave of detentions and the banning of several black organizations and newspapers in the republic, Masimini wrote a letter to the editor aligning himself with world opinion against South Africa.[289] Masimini's letter to the *New York Times* drew the attention of the South Africans. The *Rand Daily Mail*, published large parts of the letter under the title "Transkei Backs Anti-SA Sanctions."[290] The letter drew immediate criticism from Matanzima, who said that supporting sanctions against South Africa would be to "cut her own nose despite her face," and made an impossible defense of Masimini that "it is doubtful whether Mr. Masimini even made the statement."[291] This was an absurd argument to make in the face of the published article, with Masimini claiming authorship of the article.[292] The Foreign Minister, Digby Koyana, later clarified that he did in fact approve the Masimini letter, but pointed out that the wording of the letter was qualified such that Transkei would only support stronger sanctions if it were exempted and recognized, a policy Koyana said Transkei still stood behind.[293]

Though he regularly communicated via telex back and forth with Umtata, and occasionally by telephone, there seems to be evidence that Masimini was often still cut out from the goings-on back home.[294] When Matanzima announced his break with South Africa in April 1978, Masimini found out about it only when the rest of the world did – from the press. His rather embarrassed explanation for being out of the loop was that all communications with Umtata were conducted through South African cables and telephone exchanges, and these might have

---

[287] "Transkei, Apartheid's Product, Struggles to Break Isolation," *New York Times*, August 12, 1978.
[288] "Transkei, Apartheid's Product, Struggles to Break Isolation," *New York Times*, August 12, 1978.
[289] Ngqondi Masimini, *New York Times* letter to the editor, November 8, 1977.
[290] "Transkei Backs Anti-SA Sanctions," *Rand Daily Mail*, November 9, 1977.
[291] "Matanzima Denies Backing Sanctions," *Rand Daily Mail*, November 10, 1977.
[292] "Matanzima Denies Backing Sanctions," *Rand Daily Mail*, November 10, 1977.
[293] "Kei's Stand on Sanctions," *Rand Daily Mail*, December 5, 1977.
[294] Interview with Barbara Cannady-Masimini, widow of Ngqondi Masimini, July 25, 2017. Notes with author.

delayed him hearing of this major development.[295] Masimini was quick to embrace the move, however, remarking that "I think it is a good omen to show that Transkei was never the puppet of South Africa in the first place."[296] Like Matanzima, Masimini saw the break as an opportunity to make a final rush for recognition: "We are going to look at the world with interest now, to see if it is going to come to the aid of Transkei or if three million people will be allowed to go down the drain."[297]

From 1982 until he returned to Transkei in 1984, Masimini also worked alongside Kenneth Towsey, but their exact working relationship is unclear. In his FARA form from 1982, Towsey described his work for Transkei: "Registrant discussed with congressional staff members Transkei's distinct-ive constitutional position and its strategic significance to Western defense."[298] Towsey would remain a registered agent of Transkei until 1987, but judging from his annual payments, his role was gradually reduced from the mid-1980s on.[299] Transkei had several seemingly redundant public relations firms working for them in the United States simultaneously according to FARA filings, a treasury drain that was consistent with Transkei's loose spending in other regions in trying to purchase influence. In 1980 Koyana defended these expenditures by saying that Masimini had presented Transkei's case to both the Democratic and Republican parties, and had managed to change the views of black congressmen.[300] The most tangible achievement that he could claim, however, was that World Atlas Publishers had been convinced to show Transkei on their world map as a separate country with its own color and flag.[301] After seven years at his post, Masimini was eventually recalled to Transkei permanently in 1984 to work in the government in Umtata.[302]

Conclusion

What are the legacies of these foreign missions in the United States? None of them achieved the status of a bona fide diplomatic mission, and

[295] "Nobody Told Mr. Masimini," *Rand Daily Mail*, April 11, 1978.
[296] "Nobody Told Mr. Masimini," *Rand Daily Mail*, April 11, 1978.
[297] "Nobody Told Mr. Masimini," *Rand Daily Mail*, April 11, 1978.
[298] FARA Report 1982.
[299] For instance, in his last year working for Transkei, in 1987, he received $5,840.13 for his services, whereas he made $27,775.50 in his first full year in 1983. In 1985, Towsey's payments began to be reduced by a significant amount. FARA Reports 1985, 1987.
[300] "Koyana Counts the Cost," *Rand Daily Mail*, June 5, 1980.
[301] "Koyana Counts the Cost," *Rand Daily Mail*, June 5, 1980.
[302] Interview with Barbara Cannady-Masimini, widow of Ngqondi Masimini, July 25, 2017. Notes with author.

yet not one was fully closed down, and all continued to operate despite the pressures brought to bear on them. Among the representatives there were disparate outcomes in terms of their personal legal statuses: Struelens was forced to leave the country, but he eventually returned; Hooper was not deported, but his status was such that he could not leave and be expected to return; Towsey's application for permanent residency was granted, but just barely; Masimini had the legal right to live in the United States by virtue of his marriage; while Parker and Hatcher were both American citizens. Each of them had to register under FARA under the authority of the Justice Department, a designation that did not imply recognition, yet one that was consistently misunderstood by the enemies of the regimes, and it was a procedure that had to be defended year after year by the State Department. Once in the United States, all of the representatives benefited from the rights of free speech, moved around the country without restrictions, and wrote articles and made speeches out in the open. Ultimately, all the regimes they represented collapsed and the foreign policy apparatus of the United States supported the efforts to crush them. These offices and the domestic lobbies that supported them aligned themselves with powerful allies inside and outside Congress who supported their causes, and this ensured that American political support for the fall of Katanga, Rhodesia, and the isolation and eventual irrelevance of Transkei and Bophuthatswana, were all pyrrhic victories won by their opponents at considerable cost.

6   Establishing Foreign Missions in Europe
"La Délégation Permanente du Katanga" in Brussels, Rhodesia House, and "Bop House"

This chapter will look at the controversies related to the operations of Katanga's mission in Brussels, the installation of Rhodesia's mission in Lisbon, Rhodesia House in London, and the opening of "Bop House" in London.[1] The missions examined in this chapter were not all equally important. By any measure, Rhodesia House was the most significant overseas mission of any of these aspirant states, inside or outside Europe.[2] As will be described below, Katanga's European missions were primarily recruiting centers for various technicians and mercenaries, Rhodesia's Lisbon mission was mostly symbolic and was a foothold for illegal European arms purchases, and Bophuthatswana's mission in London assumed much more humble functions and rarely attracted much attention from the press or the general public. Nonetheless, all these missions were intended to be the tips of the camel's nose. These aspirant states took great pains to present these missions as practical and innocuous, and any domestic resistance to their establishments was characterized as mere pettiness. It will be shown that in the battles over these European missions the rhetorical exchanges were similar to those in the United States despite very different legal structures and political cultures. And like the fates of the American missions and their representatives after the domestic battles described in the last chapter, these missions and their staffs likewise often settled in a twilight zone between acceptance and rejection.

---

[1] Much of this chapter's section on Rhodesia House in London is substantially drawn from the author's article published in the *Journal of Imperial and Commonwealth History*: Brownell, "'A Sordid Tussle on the Strand'."

[2] Carl Watts makes the important point that Rhodesia House and the British Residual Mission in Salisbury "served as the main channels of communication between British and Rhodesia governments and there were no equivalent forms of bilateral representation between Rhodesia and any other state." Watts, *Rhodesia's Unilateral Declaration of Independence*, p. 140.

Katanga

Elisabethville had several foreign consulates which were officially attached to the central government in Leopoldville, but that designation was merely a legal artifice. It was through these foreign missions within Katanga that the regime conducted the bulk of its state-to-state engagements. These missions offered the sending states several advantages, most notably that they offered a way to directly communicate with the Katangese government without the risk of activating foreign or domestic backlash for granting legitimacy to the illegal secession. This was how most states communicated with Tshombe's illegal regime.

The Belgians set up a crucially important technical mission in Elisabethville (Mistebel) under Harold d'Aspremont Lynden, deputy chef du Cabinet of Prime Minister Gaston Eyskens. One author described Mistebel as the "nerve centre of the break-away province."[3] Out from Mistebel Belgian advisors were embedded in most Katangese ministries and the Belgian advisors and Katangese officials worked together on the ground, seemingly precluding the need for a potentially provocative pseudo-diplomatic mission in the European capital itself.[4] In terms of state-to-state communications, Britain routed all engagement with Tshombe's regime through the British Consulate in Elisabethville, which was officially subordinate to their Leopoldville Embassy. For example, when the Katangese regime through its resident minister in Brussels attempted to meet directly with Harold MacMillan it was shut down in a very direct way and instructed to communicate only through the British Consul in Elisabethville.[5] The British saw this Katangese attempt at direct, formal communication as violating the understood rules of the game.

Even so, Katanga did attempt to establish several foreign missions. Katanga's major missions outside of Michel Streulens' KIS in New York, were Dominique Diur's mission in Paris and the mission in Brussels, run by Jacques Masangu. The latter's position in Brussels was symbolically very important. Educated by Belgian missionaries through secondary school, Masangu was hired as a young man by an international shipping

---

[3] DeWitte, *The Assassination of Lumumba*, p. 44. DeWitte quotes Belgian Colonel Vandewalle as describing the Mistebel advisors as "string-pullers" and "Katanga's tutors," p. 64.

[4] Othen, *Katanga 1960–1963*, p. 57.

[5] Moise Tshombe Papers, Williams College, Letter from the British Ambassador to France, French Embassy, to J. Masangu and Diur, October 3, 1961.

company based out of Belgium.[6] He was soon granted a Belgian government scholarship to study at the Solvay Institute of the Free University of Brussels, and leaving his family behind in what was then the Belgian Congo, he moved to Brussels in 1958.[7] With the Congo's Independence in 1960, Masangu was elected as a senator in the new Congolese Senate, and was even made a vice president of the new body. Just two weeks later, on July 11, Tshombe declared Katanga's independence from the Congo. In a book by his son, Masangu was described both as "a grassroots militant of the Balubakat" and "an admirable champion of the Luba Katanga culture."[8] Despite the Balubakat leadership opposing an independent Katanga, several Balubakat members "crossed the aisle" to join the regime. Masangu's predicament, as described much later by his son, was that "my father unwillingly found himself at the bridge of two strong Katanga traditions, on the one hand, the local or regional particularities and, on the other hand, the loyalty to the Congolese nation."[9] It was four days after the declaration when Masangu threw his lot in with Tshombe.[10]

His recruitment was part of Tshombe's CONAKAT party's larger strategy of expanding the domestic base of support for the secession. Tshombe knew immediately that the contested state's legitimacy was threatened by its lack of support of other political parties in Katanga. The day after he declared independence, Tshombe told the assembly: "The most urgent question is that of broadening the government, to restore confidence by the introduction of representatives of the Cartel [an alliance of several parties – including Balubakat]."[11] Despite this, the Cartel leadership did not support Tshombe's declaration, a decision that undermined support for the secession not only in Katanga, but among

---

[6] Jean-Claude Masangu Mulongo, *Why I Believe in Africa's Progress: An African Banker's Creed* (Prestige Communication, Paris, 2011) p. 20.

[7] Masangu Mulongo, *Why I Believe in Africa's Progress*, p. 21.

[8] Masangu Mulongo, *Why I Believe in Africa's Progress*, p. 20.

[9] Masangu Mulongo, *Why I Believe in Africa's Progress*, pp. 24–25.

[10] According to his son's memoirs, Tshombe offered Masangu a job in the Ministry of Foreign Affairs of the breakaway state, but he turned it down "in the name of his allegiance to prime minister Patrice Emery Lumumba," and that he considered himself still to be the legitimate vice president of the Congolese Senate. Additionally, his son claimed that Masangu, even while serving as the Katangese representative in Brussels did his utmost to push for a confederal Congolese solution to the secession. Masangu Mulongo, *Why I Believe in Africa's Progress*, p. 22. See also: Gerard-Libois, *Katanga Secession*, p. 108.

[11] Quoted in Gerard-Libois, *Katanga Secession*, p. 183.

political groups in Belgium as well.[12] Jules Gerard-Libois makes the claim that because of its strong showing in the pre-independence elections, the lack of Cartel support for the secession weakened Katanga's position in the United Nations and in world opinion.[13] Tshombe went so far as to offer Balubakat leader, Jason Sendwe, the vice presidency and four ministerial posts, but Sendwe refused to support the secession.[14]

Tshombe quickly appointed Masangu the "Resident Minister" of Katanga's "Permanent Delegation" to the European Common Market in Brussels. Masangu's well-known party affiliation and his high-profile defection made his presence in Belgium that much more appealing from a political messaging perspective. That he was already studying international law and diplomacy in Belgium, and was from a country that infamously had only sixteen college graduates at the time of independence, meant his appointment made both strategic and tactical sense.[15]

There are also strong parallels between Tshombe's efforts to draw in Cartel members into his regime's foreign policy apparatus and Matanzima's and Mangope's efforts to bring former PAC and ANC members into their regimes' foreign policy apparatuses. In these cases, the regimes hoped these defections and their visibility overseas would convey a wider support for their causes and confer legitimacy, but none of these aisle crossings lead to any broader increase in support and the individual defectors were often stuck between the mistrust felt by their new allies and the feelings of betrayal felt by their old ones. Despite his public defection, Tshombe's government was initially skeptical of Masangu's loyalty because of his tribal ties, but these were evidently swayed by an investigation into his loyalty by Katanga's Intelligence services (SCCR) which ultimately concluded that he was in fact loyal to Tshombe and the secession.[16]

Masangu's was a pseudo-diplomatic post and his installation at 30 Rue Marie de Bourgogne was attended by representatives of the Belgian

[12] M. Larmer and E. Kennes, "Rethinking the Katangese Secession," *Journal of Imperial and Commonwealth History*, vol. 42, no. 4 (2014) p. 11. See also: Gerard-Libois, *Katanga Secession*, p. 107.

[13] Gerard-Libois, *Katanga Secession*, p. 107.   [14] Othen, *Katanga 1960–1963*, p. 72.

[15] Harry Gilroy, "Lumumba Assails Colonialism as Congo Is Freed," *New York Times*, July 1, 1960. Herbert Weiss makes the argument that even though this was the correct number of secular university graduates, that this low number ignores the much higher number of seminary graduates who were "intellectually trained individuals who did to some extent fill the need for 'modern' or 'Westernized' role models." "The Congo's Independence Struggle Viewed Fifty Years Later," *African Studies Review*, vol. 55, no. 1 (April 2012) p. 110.

[16] Moise Tshombe Papers, Williams College, Memorandum from Service de la Centralisation et de la Coordination de Renseignment (SCCR), December 14, 1961.

ministers of foreign affairs and African affairs, an event which inched very close toward formal recognition.[17] Prior to Masangu's delegation moving in, the building had been occupied by the Belgian Congo parastatal, Societe des Forces Hydro-Electriques de l'Est de la Colonie. In its title and protocol the "Delegation Permanente du Katanga" held itself out as an embassy, and in correspondences on official stationery, Masangu always held himself out as "Le Ministre Resident."[18] His son defended his father taking the position in the breakaway state by writing, "he was not offered the position of ambassador to Belgium from a country which was not recognized by international standards. It was rather an appointment as a resident minister of a Congolese autonomous entity to the European Common Market."[19] This was, of course, a distinction that likely did not serve as the justification for Masangu taking the position beforehand, and it was certainly a distinction which Masangu's mission actively sought to eliminate, since diplomatic recognition was a primary foreign policy goal of Tshombe's regime. However, the main purpose of the mission seemed to be to serve as a recruiting center for mercenaries.[20]

It did not take long for Katanga's mission in Brussels to run into controversy. His son incorrectly claimed both that Masangu's mission had "friendly ties with the Congolese delegation" and that they "shared premises on Marie-de-Bourgogne." The first claim might be a possible conflation of personal relationships Masangu may have had with some members of the Congo's delegation, but it was not true that their missions were officially on friendly terms. While the Congo later took over the premises as the site of the future Congo Embassy, they did not share the building at the same time as Masangu's mission.[21] Like other missions, controversies swirled around issues regarding official titles, nameplates, and the statuses of the representatives. The mission's nameplate had originally read: "Delegation Permanente du Katanga." But in late 1961, some left-of-center Belgian press and left-of-center politicians reacted angrily to what they saw as the Katangese mission holding itself

---

[17] This building at that time was owned by a Congolese parastatal organization. After the secession ended this building would house the Congolese Embassy. Gerard-Libois, *Katanga Secession*, p. 182.

[18] See generally correspondences to and from the Permanent Delegation: Moise Tshombe Papers, Williams College.

[19] Masangu Mulongo, *Why I Believe in Africa's Progress*, p. 22.

[20] Gerard-Libois, *Katanga Secession*, p. 182.

[21] It should be stated that after the secession ended there were strong incentives for both father and son to downplay Jacques' role in the secession.

out as an embassy.[22] The Leopoldville government also cited the shutting down of the mission as a condition of restoring diplomatic relations with Belgium, hardly an expression of friendliness. As a result of a compromise, the Katangese agreed to change the mission's name to "Office Culturel et Economique du Katanga."[23] Similarly, a year beforehand in November of 1960, the Belgian Foreign Ministry informed Jacques Masangu, the so-called Resident Minister of Katanga in Brussels, that he would not be able to put diplomatic plates on his car in Belgium, because he lacked official status.[24] Indeed, Masangu even ran into difficulties as to where he could park near the mission building since he did not have diplomatic tags.[25]

Rhodesia

Rhodesia House was the British colony's most visible representation over-seas, much more so than the small suburban house in Washington that was the RIO or Reedman's office in Lisbon, discussed below.[26] There was no exact parallel to Rhodesia House among the other missions discussed in the book, and not just because of its visibility and prominence.[27] Rhodesia House was a pseudo-diplomatic mission in the capital of the mother country which contested its independence. This would have been the equivalent of there being a Katangese mission, flying the Katangese flag, with its occupants enjoying diplomatic privileges and immunities, holding themselves out as diplomatic representatives of a sovereign Katangese state, and hosting cocktail parties right in the heart of Leopoldville.

[22] Moise Tshombe Papers, Williams College, photo 2, memorandum by SCCR, December 14, 1961.

[23] Moise Tshombe Papers, Williams College, photo 2, memorandum by SCCR, December 14, 1961.

[24] Moise Tshombe Papers, Williams College, photo 71, Letter from Josse Gits, Belgian Foreign Ministry, to Jacques Masangu, Ministre-Resident du Katanga, September 14, 1960; Letter from Joseph Gits, Belgian Ministere des Affaires Etrangeres et du Commerce Exterieur, to Masangu, Ministre Resident du Katanga, November 7, 1960.

[25] Moise Tshombe Papers, Williams College, Letter from A. De Gryse, Le Commissaire en chef de police, to Josse Gits, Belgian Foreign Ministry, September 13, 1960. These were hardly friendly relations. But as it would turn out, Masangu's rift with Leopoldville did not last long after the defeat of Katanga. This might have been less the result of his successful rehabilitation rather than an expression of the lack of qualified diplomats in the young state. In 1967, Masangu was appointed as Congolese ambassador to West Germany.

[26] This section of the chapter is derived largely from an article written by the author and published in the *Journal of Imperial and Commonwealth History*. "'A Sordid Tussle on the Strand'."

[27] For an examination of Rhodesian pseudo-diplomatic relations with the Old Commonwealth, see: Watts, *Rhodesia's Unilateral Declaration of Independence*, pp. 139–146.

Much like American policy toward the RIO, British policy toward Rhodesia House reflected the ambiguities and tensions of their broader policy concerning the Rhodesian rebellion.[28] Competing demands for either conciliation or stern action resulted in successive British governments of both parties adopting a muddled middle approach which was both ineffective and unpopular. Regarding Rhodesia House, British policymakers were similarly pulled between some sectors of international and domestic public opinion calling for harsh measures against the rebel mission and a countervailing deference to imperial legalisms, diplomatic niceties, and concerns about Rhodesia's retaliatory treatment of the British High Commission and Government House in Rhodesia. In addition, fears of domestic opposition to the government seizing Rhodesia House by force paralleled the government's fear of the potential reaction to a military invasion of Rhodesia to put down the rebellion. As a result, the British imperial practice of carving out new exceptions and allowing for legal anomalies led to Rhodesia House continuing to exist for four years as a quasi-consular office with quasi-diplomatic protections on a reciprocal basis with the British mission in Salisbury. In practice, however, the regime's representatives in London constantly probed the outer limits of their agreed-upon functions and often brazenly acted in a fashion well outside their consular activities, causing much embarrassment for the British government as the would-be state tried to push the camel's nose deeper into the tent.

While most white Rhodesians had likely never heard of the Washington-based RIO and certainly could not identify the building by sight, even if they vaguely knew that there was some sort of Rhodesian representation in the United States, Rhodesia House in London was widely known among white Rhodesians and held a great amount of symbolic value for white Rhodesians. Rhodesia House's closure and eventual evacuation in 1969 added to many settlers' sense of isolation in living in an African continent increasingly hostile to white settler colonialism. Its final closure also served as a physical expression of the shift in the Rhodesian state's international focus away from the British Commonwealth to a more localized and immediate, albeit officially unrecognized, alliance with the other white-dominated states of Southern Africa. It was thus in the physical space of 429 Strand that much larger imperial struggles were contested in microcosm.

After the passing of the British Diplomatic Immunities Act of 1952, Rhodesian envoys and the premises of Rhodesia House were granted

---

[28] For the classic text on Britain's policy toward Rhodesia, see: E. Windrich, *Britain and the Politics of Rhodesia Independence* (Groom Helm, London, 1978).

diplomatic privileges and immunities identical to those of the independent states of the Commonwealth. During its decade of existence, the federation took over Rhodesia House, but upon the federation's dissolution in 1963, the territory of Rhodesia regained control over the premises. In July 1964, the diplomatic privileges set forth in the Act were updated in accordance with the British ratification of the Vienna Convention on Diplomatic Relations and the dissolution of the federation, and it was inserted that "this Act shall be construed *as if* Southern Rhodesia were a state."[29] Accordingly, the Rhodesia high commissioner was placed in the official Foreign and Commonwealth Office Diplomatic List, a unique status for a representative of an imperial dependency. In the run-up to UDI, Rhodesia House occupied a legal space analogous to the old dominions' high commissions prior to the Statute of Westminster.

Rhodesia's first major effort to assert an international personality occurred not in London, but in Lisbon. On June 9, 1965, five months before UDI, the Rhodesians announced they were going to open a diplomatic mission in Lisbon, an announcement which apparently caught the British completely by surprise.[30] This was a new position, and the Rhodesians insisted that it not be attached to the British Embassy.[31] According to historian J. R. T. Wood, placing a Rhodesian representative in Lisbon was seen as important to the Rhodesians not just because of Rhodesia's proximity and closely aligned interests with Portuguese East Africa (Mozambique), but because Lisbon provided a foothold in Europe so as to break out of the informal arms embargo in anticipation of a UDI.[32] Some in the British parliament were concerned that if this appointment were allowed to go forward over British objections it would inadvertently grant de facto recognition to Rhodesia, which would be a case of "independence by the back door."[33] For its part, the South African government read Rhodesia's actions in the Lisbon affair as part of an effort by the Rhodesians to gradually erode British sovereignty, even before UDI.[34] Rhodesia's choice for this

---

[29] "Diplomatic Privileges Bill (Lords)," Parliamentary Debate, Hansard, July 1, 1964. (italics added).

[30] Wood, *So Far and No Further*, p. 319.   [31] Wood, *So Far and No Further*, p. 319.

[32] Wood, *So Far and No Further*, p. 319.

[33] "Rhodesia (Diplomatic Representative, Portugal)" HC Deb July 28, 1965, vol. 717, cc468–70.

[34] South African DFA Archives, Box 1/156/6, UDI External Representation, Letter from AJF Viljoen, SA Ambassador to Portugal to Secretary of Department of Foreign Affairs, "Rhodesiese Verteenwoordiging in Portugal," July 23, 1965.

diplomatically sensitive position was the undiplomatic, impulsive, and loose-lipped former Minister of Immigration and Tourism, Harry Reedman.[35]

The British told the Portuguese that if Reedman's appointment were accepted it could encourage the Rhodesians to make a declaration of independence, but the Portuguese maintained that they were neutral in the British/Rhodesian dispute. Pointedly, they cited past British policy regarding contacts with Tshombe's regime during the Katangese secession on the basis that it was necessary to maintain dealings with a nearby rebel territory.[36] Despite British continued pressure, the Portuguese remained coy about Reedman and after he arrived seemed to afford him and his office some diplomatic status. Never one to play humble or be quietly magnanimous, Harry Reedman's first public act in Lisbon was to deliver an explosive speech on Portuguese government-operated radio on September 24. In his speech he claimed that he was "the head of the Rhodesian diplomatic mission," sent to Lisbon to "to put our case for independence not only to the people of Portugal, in order to obtain your understanding and support of our just, proper claims, but to all those people who are interested in the cause of justice." Reedman went on to identify what he saw as the real threat of Chinese communists in Africa, and to denigrate what he called the "trash democracy of one man one vote."[37]

A frustrated Prime Minister, Harold Wilson, suggested in a meeting with his advisors on September 7 that the British should "rough it up" with Portugal.[38] Britain demanded that Portugal make a public statement clarifying Reedman's status instead of official equivocations voiced by the Portuguese. When this did not happen, in a dramatic diplomatic move, the British ambassador was recalled to London and was put on extended leave as a protest of Lisbon's actions regarding the Reedman

---

[35] Reedman was well-known in Rhodesia for making outlandish statements. He had a particular disdain for the Chinese whom Reedman feared were threatening to conquer and settle Southern Africa by the thousands. He did not change as a diplomat. In an interview on the record to the *Financial Times*, Reedman commented that the Chinese were "little yellow men, spawning like mice," perhaps unaware that Nogueira's wife was part Chinese. See: PRO, DO 183/885, Letter from NAI French, British High Commission, to JN Allen of the Rhodesia Department, January 13, 1965; Parliamentary Debates, vol. 63, "Motion: Family Planning," March 9, 1966; "Reedman Discusses His Latest Lisbon Diplomatic Coup," *Rhodesia Herald*, November 2, 1966.

[36] Wood, *So Far and No Further*, p. 347.

[37] Harry Reedman's Speech broadcast over Portuguese National Radio, September 24, 1965. SA DFA, Box 1/156/6, UDI External Representation, Letter and Annexures from W. Malan, First Secretary Lisbon Embassy to SA Ambassador in Lisbon, Annexure A, October 6, 1965. Earlier in his speech, Reedman expressed his fear that the Chinese would enslave Africans were the Europeans to leave.

[38] Wood, *So Far and No Further*, p. 345.

Figure 6.1 Harry Reedman being greeted by the acting head of protocol
in the Portuguese Foreign Ministry in Lisbon, September 1965.

appointment.[39] As part of the "rough it up" tactic, on September 14,
Britain, with the support of the United States and other Western
European delegates, took the Reedman issue to NATO Council.[40]
Infuriated, the Portuguese Foreign Ministry made the vague threat that
if Britain used NATO for these purposes Portugal would "use the
greatest firmness to repel any attempt to attribute particular responsi-
bilities or to make criticism of Portugal's position."[41] Portugal finally
replied formally to Britain's demand for clarification of Reedman's status
on September 29, 1965. Lisbon's note indicated that it recognized
Britain as the sovereign power over Rhodesia, but that the Portuguese
saw that they would benefit by close and direct communications with

[39] K. Fedorowich and M. Thomas, *International Diplomacy and Colonial Retreat* (Frank
   Cass, London, 2001) p. 187.
[40] Wood, *So Far and No Further*, p. 353.
[41] "Issue Raised at NATO Council," *The Glasgow Herald*, September 16, 1965.

Rhodesia since they shared many of the same concerns in Southern Africa.[42] The British waited one day before releasing the private Portuguese note to the public. This was a breach of protocol and the Portuguese responded that publishing the private note was "unpleasant, disagreeable, and discourteous," and gave a false impression of the Portuguese position.[43]

Wood makes the case that the choice of Reedman had little to do with diplomatic tact and everything to do with his perceived ability to covertly buy aircraft and weapons from European arms dealers. Before he was a businessman and later a politician, he had some experience in wartime as an RAF bomber research specialist.[44] Under this rationale the choice of Reedman made more sense since any arms and aircraft would be arriving via a port in Portuguese East Africa.[45] In Lisbon Reedman would be allowed access to Portuguese ministers on a ministry-to-ministry level, but neither he nor his successors were afforded a diplomatic title or full status.[46] Yet to Britain's great frustration, his presence in Lisbon was a done deal and British diplomats struggled with how to negotiate this embarrassing diplomatic predicament on the cocktail circuit.[47] On his end, Reedman grumbled that despite his claim that he was granted some diplomatic status by the Portuguese, he was still not invited to any of the diplomatic parties.[48]

Back in London, in the months leading up to a possible UDI, the British government struggled over what should happen to Rhodesia House and its staff if UDI were declared. In an October 2, 1965 meeting of the Overseas Policy and Defense Committee (OPD) it was decided

[42] Wood, *So Far and No Further*, p. 363.

[43] Wood, *So Far and No Further*, p. 363. The press in Portugal were highly critical of the breach of trust and protocol in Britain publishing the correspondence without prior consultation, and the Portuguese government then released the rest of the note. SA Department of Foreign Affairs Archives, Box 1/156/6, UDI: External Representation, Letter from W. Malan, SA First Secretary of Lisbon Embassy, to the Ambassador in Lisbon, October 6, 1965.

[44] Wood, *So Far and No Further*, p. 319.

[45] As it turned out, the first proposed arms purchase through Reedman and his Portuguese intermediaries had the Portuguese middlemen approach a British arms dealer with forged end-user certificates claiming they were buyers for Pakistan. After the dealer worked through this and another shopping list, the deal aroused too much suspicion from the seller who ended up reporting the deal in all its complexity to the British government. Wood, *A Matter of Weeks Rather than Months*, p. 73.

[46] Skeen, *Prelude*, p. 43.

[47] See for example: SA Department of Foreign Affairs Archives, Box 1/156/6, UDI: External Representation, Letter from W. Malan, SA First Secretary of Lisbon Embassy, to the Ambassador in Lisbon, October 6, 1965.

[48] "Reedman Discusses His Latest Lisbon Diplomatic Coup," *Rhodesia Herald*, November 2, 1966.

that in the event of a UDI, British authorities should occupy Rhodesia House, by force if necessary.[49] This ran contrary to Britain's larger policy stance on the use of force. On the legality and wisdom of seizing Rhodesia House, an October Commonwealth Relations Office (CRO) memorandum concluded, "it is considered on balance that if we are going to attract the criticism that will undoubtedly attach to the expulsion of Brigadier [Alexander] Skeen from Rhodesia House by any method ... we may as well make a virtue of necessity and choose the most dramatically effective method ..."[50] After weighing the advantages and disadvantages, CRO officials concluded that the British government should make "a dramatic gesture and, while it would not stop the pressures on us to use force [against Rhodesia in Africa], it would have political value in Africa ..."[51]

As the British moved forward with plans to seize Rhodesia House, there were concomitant plans to shut down their own high commission in Salisbury.[52] As the thinking within the CRO leaned toward a decisive seizure of Rhodesia House after UDI, there was resistance from the Home Office. The home secretary met with Secretary of State for Commonwealth Relations, Arthur Bottomley, on October 7, 1965, and informed him that he was opposed to the seizure option under which government agents would act prior to the legal authority to do so.[53] Asked for a legal opinion by Bottomley on the option of the Queen's agents seizing Rhodesia House under her residual executive authority, the attorney general concluded that "while I am inclined to think that such action would be lawful, I think it would be attended with some degree of risk."[54] The attorney general's concern centered on the possibility that the occupation would violate the Diplomatic Privileges Act of 1964, which expressly treated Rhodesia "as if" it was a state. He argued that a possible way around this would be to claim that in seizing the premises the Queen was acting in right of the sending state, Rhodesia,

---

[49] PRO, DO 183/596, "Action against Rhodesia House after UDI," Letter to Prime Minister, Harold Wilson, from Arthur Bottomley, Secretary of State for Commonwealth Relations, October 15, 1965.

[50] PRO, DO 183/596, "Occupation of Rhodesia House after a UDI," Draft memorandum by the CRO, October 7, 1965.

[51] PRO, DO 183/596, "Occupation of Rhodesia House after a UDI," Draft memorandum by the CRO, October 7, 1965.

[52] See for instance: PRO, DO 183/596, Cypher Telegram to JG Finland (DEDIP), Deputy HC, from JB Johnston, High Commissioner, October 4, 1965; Rhodes House Library, Oxford University, *Jack Johnston Memoirs*, p. 126.

[53] PRO, DO 183/596, Letter to A. Snelling, Deputy Undersecretary of State for Commonwealth Relations, from OG Forster, of the CRO, October 8, 1965.

[54] PRO, DO 183/596, Letter to A Bottomley, Secretary of State for Commonwealth Relations, from Elwyn Jones, Attorney General, October 12, 1965.

not the receiving state, Britain. In the event of an occupation, Skeen would obviously apply to the courts for an injunction, and the ensuing court battle, he feared, "would of course attract world-wide publicity and, if the injunction were eventually granted, Her Majesty's Government would have sustained a resounding defeat." He concluded that since "[o]ur case against Mr. Smith and his associates is based on legality. We should not, in my view, take the risk of being ourselves to have acted unlawfully."[55]

Two weeks after the OPD meeting recommending the occupation of Rhodesia House, Bottomley reversed course. He argued that British planning should proceed with possible action against the high commissioner, but no occupation of the premises.[56] After Bottomley's change of heart, government focus turned toward other methods of applying pressure on Rhodesia House if a UDI did occur. To monitor Rhodesian activities, it was agreed that in the event of a UDI there would be increased surveillance of the building and its occupants.[57] British officials would monitor and report on international and domestic phone calls to and from Rhodesia House, and Bottomley envisioned a small police detachment ringing the building.[58] Tellingly, Arthur Snelling, then the Deputy Undersecretary of State at the Foreign and Commonwealth Office, commented that "it is important that anything we do should be *seen* to be effective in order to satisfy the demands of public opinion at home and in the international sphere."[59]

The final policy was not a seizure of the sort advocated in the October 2 OPD meeting, nor did it include a police presence outside. Competing demands for a continued consular presence in Salisbury, nagging legal doubts concerning any forcible occupation, Home Office resistance to the police being used as propaganda tools, and the fear of offending public opinion all mitigated against bolder approaches to Rhodesia House. In the event, the police presence that was intended to be outside Rhodesia House to intimidate those inside was very clearly there to protect the building and those inside from protestors. The ruse fooled no one.

---

[55] PRO, DO 183/596, Letter to A Bottomley, Secretary of State for Commonwealth Relations, from Elwyn Jones, Attorney General, October 12, 1965.

[56] PRO, DO 183/596, "Action against Rhodesia House after UDI," Letter to Prime Minister, Harold Wilson, from Arthur Bottomley, Secretary of State for Commonwealth Relations, October 15, 1965.

[57] PRO, DO 183/596, "Note for the Record," by MB Chitty, October 25, 1965.

[58] PRO, DO 183/596, "Action against Rhodesia House's Communications in the Event of UDI," Letter to Mr. Costley-White from IFS Vincent of the DSAO, October 26, 1965.

[59] PRO, DO 183/596, "Action to Be Taken with Regard to Rhodesia House in the Event of UDI," Note of Meeting held in the CRO, October 28, 1965. (My emphasis).

With UDI on November 11, 1965, British Prime Minister, Wilson, moved against Rhodesia's international presence on multiple fronts. In Washington, DC, when Air Vice-Marshall, Bentley, refused to disavow UDI he was sent home. Wilson also withdrew the British exequaturs from the Rhodesian missions in Pretoria and Lisbon.[60] But in practical terms, if not in legal terms, the life and work in Rhodesia's Portuguese and South African missions went on as usual.

The Rhodesian regime suffered other setbacks in its quest to break out of international isolation. Simultaneous with Reedman's struggles to gain recognition in Portugal, the Rhodesian Deputy Minister of Information, P. K. Van der Byl, was traveling through Europe attempting to convince Western European governments to circumvent British sanctions, but after British pressure he was kicked out of Holland, then Germany and France, finally having to return to Rhodesia in defeat.[61] If the Rhodesians had managed to pull one over on the British regarding the Lisbon mission generally, in the particular sense Reedman still found that there were significant barriers to his diplomatic acceptance. He complained publicly that he was ostracized by all the other diplomats except the South African representative, and in early 1968, Reedman withdrew from the prestigious Lisbon Club after the management refused to waive his nondiplomatic fee.[62] The British Foreign Office was quite obviously delighted.[63] By February 1968, Reedman had banned his mission staff from speaking with any non-Portuguese journalists. Reportedly, he was embittered by the diplomatic slights he suffered and publicly claimed that the mission was wasting Rhodesians' tax money.[64] By May 1968, it was decided that Reedman would be replaced.[65]

---

[60] Wood, *A Matter of Weeks Rather than Months*, p. 5.
[61] "Van der Byl Is Told to Leave," *Rhodesia Herald*, December 1, 1966. Post-UDI Rhodesia's foreign affairs had several representatives abroad. These included a trade representative in Luanda, Angola; an information center in Sydney, Australia; a commercial consul and consul-general in Lourenco-Marques, Mozambique; a consul in Beira, Mozambique; a commercial counselor and senior information attaché in Lisbon, Portugal; a Rhodesian trade mission in Johannesburg; a senior information attache, a consul, and an accredited diplomatic representative in Cape Town; an accredited diplomatic representative and two senior information attaches in Pretoria; in addition to four Rhodesia National Tourism Board offices in South Africa, one in Lourenco-Marques, one in Basle, Switzerland, and another in New York City. Strack, "International Relations," chart, pp. 109–110.
[62] "Reedman Withdraws after Fee Dispute: Lisbon Club Row," *Rhodesia Herald*, January 9, 1968.
[63] "Reedman Withdraws after Fee Dispute: Lisbon Club Row," *Rhodesia Herald*, January 9, 1968.
[64] "Reedman Ban on Foreign Journalists," *Rhodesia Herald*, February 23, 1968.
[65] "Reedman Thanks Portugal," *Rhodesia Herald*, July 26, 1968; SA Department of Foreign Affairs Archives, Box 1/156/6, UDI: External Representation, Telegram from

In spite of his diplomatic shortcomings, Reedman's Lisbon model of ministry-to-ministry accreditation was to later be used for all other sub-diplomatic representation after UDI, for instance in Portuguese Mozambique.[66] The Rhodesians' diplomatic experiences in Portugal were therefore a mixed success, and any gains they did achieve, as with the establishment of the Lisbon office over the objections of the British, came at a high cost to the hosts. The Lisbon model was a legalistic way to maintain relations without overtly offering recognition and drawing the full ire of the international community, most especially from Britain. One of the many ways in which the Portuguese coup negatively affected Rhodesia, was that in 1975 the Rhodesians were finally forced to abandon the Lisbon mission after ten years.[67]

Rhodesia's representatives drew controversy in the republic as well. John Gaunt approached his position in Pretoria much in the same way as Sydney Brice did in London. They both pushed against the boundaries put in place by their hosts, then when confronted would retreat, wait, and continue again. The 1961 *Who's Who of Southern Africa* biography of Gaunt described him this way:

Mr. Gaunt is a colourful, outspoken and irrepressible politician who has a considerable following in this country ...He is a fighter, a strong protagonist of the maintenance of white civilization ...[68]

Gaunt's "colourful" statements had drawn criticism in the republic even before UDI. Gaunt had asked Verwoerd in September to publicly state that South Africa supported Rhodesia in its struggle with Britain, which Verwoerd said he would not do.[69] In October 1965, a month before UDI, Gaunt answered a question in a press interview about South Africa's possible attitude toward a UDI, that the relationship between South Africa and Rhodesia was akin to the Good Samaritan, elaborating "it is hardly likely that South Africa will adopt the attitude of the priest who walked down on the other side of the road claiming that this had nothing to do with him."[70] Verwoerd was furious. He saw it as a deliberate misrepresentation of South Africa's policy that Verwoerd had

---

R. J. Montgomery, SA Accredited Diplomatic Representative in Salisbury, to Secretary DFA, Cape Town, June 6, 1968.

[66] SA Department of Foreign Affairs Archives, Box 1/156/6, UDI: External Representation, "Rhodesian Consular Representation in Mocambique," Letter from SA Consul-General Lourenco Marques to Secretary DFA, Pretoria, October 26, 1967.

[67] "Rhodesians to Quit Lisbon," *The Glasgow Herald*, May 1, 1975.

[68] Wooten & Gibson (ed.), *Who's Who of Southern Africa* (Wooten & Gibson, Johannesburg, 1961) p. 940.

[69] de Meneses and McNamara, *White Redoubt*, p. 52.

[70] SA DFA Archives, Box 1/156/1/1/, UDI, "Vertroulik: Kantoornota" (undated, but October 1965).

himself communicated to Gaunt. In a message to Gaunt the DFA scolded:

it would be incorrect and unwise for the Representative of Rhodesia to say anything which could place the Republic and/or Rhodesia in a false position. Dr. Verwoerd had made it clear that 'the least said, the soonest mended' would be a wise course to adopt ... No outside authority can commit South Africa as to its policy and future actions – even by implication. The words attributed to you can be interpreted as propaganda and even as implied criticism. (Here I refer of course to your use of the analogy of the Good Samaritan).

The message concluded with the threat that statements like these might require Verwoerd to publicly repudiate Gaunt, "which could well have undesirable consequences for Rhodesia."[71]

Six months later, in April 1966, the DFA was again irritated with Gaunt, this time over a confrontational comment he made in the press about Britain. Gaunt's statements again put South Africa's delicate balance of "non-interference" in jeopardy, and again, the DFA called him in.[72] Gaunt's undiplomatic behavior appeared to be a well-known thing in Rhodesian government circles.[73] Certainly his comments about Rhodesian/South African relations ran counter to Ian Smith's expression of thanks to Verwoerd for South Africa's stance toward UDI. Nonetheless, Gaunt would remain in his position until 1969.

On November 11, 1965, Skeen was present in his capacity as high commissioner at an annual memorial ceremony beside Westminster Abbey in the Field of Remembrance. Immediately before leaving Rhodesia House to attend this event, Skeen had read on the telex machine the words: "UDI declared in Salisbury."[74] Skeen attended the ceremony with everyone else unaware of the rebellion of which the high commissioner was a part. By the time the ceremony had concluded, word had finally arrived in London and a crowd had gathered out in front of Rhodesia House. Immediately upon entering Rhodesia House, Skeen was instructed that Arthur Bottomley wished to see him. On his way to see Bottomley, he had to again pass through the large crowd in front of Rhodesia House and through yet another crowd in front of 10 Downing Street. Asked by Bottomley whether he wished to dissociate from the rebellion, Skeen, after what British officials described as "humming and

---

[71] SA DFA Archives, Box 1/156/1/1/, UDI, "Vertroulik: Kantoornota" (undated, but October 1965).

[72] SA DFA Archives, Box 1/156/1/1, UDI, Telegram from Donald Sole, DFA, to Montgomery, SA Accredited Diplomatic Representative in Salisbury, April 25, 1966.

[73] See for example: SA DFA Archives, Pretoria, Box 1/156/1/1, vols. 1, 2, 3 UDI, "Notes in Discussions between Mr. Dick Wetmore and Dr. Naude," December 9, 1965.

[74] Skeen, *Prelude*, p. 148.

hawing for some time," was given a letter.[75] He read it with, as he described, "bated breath," and "let out a sigh of relief" as he understood he "was to be treated with courtesy and compassion."[76] The letter said that Skeen was no longer acceptable to the British as high commissioner.[77] Only a month before, Skeen had reported to Smith's Cabinet that the British would surely occupy Rhodesia House in the event of a UDI, and he must have been surprised that this was not the case.[78]

In this meeting on the day of UDI, Bottomley told Skeen that the procedure applied to him would also apply to the senior members of Rhodesia House.[79] It was left for later how far down these undertakings of loyalty would be demanded. These oaths, as envisioned by the British, would allow for the expatriate staff to be divided into those who wished to adhere to the Smith regime and those who wished to adhere to the legal government of Rhodesia, at that point vested solely in the Governor of Southern Rhodesia, Sir Humphrey Gibbs.[80] Those wishing to adhere to the Smith regime would be deported immediately.[81]

Loyalty declarations were subsequently drafted by the British and distributed to Rhodesia House staff, seemingly requiring them to renounce UDI or face almost immediate deportation. They created a firestorm in the press and in parliament among those who believed the terms were unnecessarily harsh.[82] These criticisms prompted Harold Wilson to investigate whether or not British policy was in fact "pressing" Rhodesia House staffers too hard.[83] In an answer to a question in parliament several days later, the solicitor general insisted that such declarations were purely voluntary and it was not mandatory for the staff to affix their signatures: a clear retreat from the government's earlier stance, and contrary to the clear wording of the oath.[84]

---

[75] PRO, DO 207/112 ,"Rhodesia House," Letter to KJ Neale from AW Snelling, November 11, 1965.

[76] Skeen, *Prelude*, p. 150. According to the Head of Rhodesian Intelligence, Ken Flower, Skeen was as nervous as he was because, unlike anyone else in Rhodesia House, he was in the British Army and feared he could be hanged as a traitor. K. Flower, *Serving Secretly: An Intelligence Chief on Record* (John Murray, London, 1984) p. 49.

[77] Skeen, *Prelude*, p. 150.   [78] Flower, *Serving Secretly*, pp. 49–50.

[79] PRO, DO 207/112, "Rhodesia House," Letter to K. J. Neale from A. W. Snelling, November 11, 1965.

[80] PRO, DO 207/112, "Rhodesia House," Letter to K. J. Neale from A. W. Snelling, November 11, 1965.

[81] PRO, DO 207/112, "Rhodesia House," Letter to K. J. Neale from A. W. Snelling, November 11, 1965.

[82] "Southern Rhodesia Bill," *HL Deb*, November 15, 1965, vol. 270 cc413–38.

[83] PRO, DO 207/112, "Rhodesia House Residual Staff," Letter from D. Mitchell of the PM's Office to Oliver Forster of the CRO, November 14, 1965.

[84] "Southern Rhodesia Bill," *HL Deb*, November 15, 1965, vol. 270 cc413–38.

Ultimately, the relevant division determining the deportations of expatriate Rhodesia House staffers from Britain did not fall along the lines of loyalty or disloyalty to the constitutional Government of Rhodesia, but between those who were required for the reduced consular role of the mission and those who were not. Indeed, as a result of negotiations it was decided that the British would grant immunities and privileges to the Rhodesian staffers on a reciprocal basis to those afforded to the staff of the Residual Mission in Salisbury, regardless of their loyalty oaths and despite the possible legal conundrums this posed.[85] Throughout the rebellion, no member of the Rhodesia House staff was tried on charges of treason, though some in parliament did press for prosecutions of these individuals.[86] On the Rhodesian end, Smith magnanimously announced that no action would be taken against any Rhodesians overseas who signed oaths of non-allegiance to UDI, as many did in Zambia, as Smith claimed that these were not voluntary renunciations.[87] Skeen subsequently wrote that he considered the loyalty oaths an "act of crass folly" that "played right into our hands."[88] In terms of propaganda value, he was certainly right.

On the day of UDI, Duncan Watson of the CRO met with Rhodesia House officials and outlined the basis for Rhodesia House's status that would last until 1969.[89] He communicated to the Rhodesians that Britain would allow for a small staff to stay on at Rhodesia House "for the purpose of rendering 'quasi' consular services to Rhodesians in this country – subject of course to our being free to maintain consular services if we wished in Salisbury."[90] Despite protestations by the Rhodesians, the CRO rejected any immigration promotion staffers and employment recruiters, staffers involved in propaganda dissemination,

---

[85] See: PRO, DO 207/112, Telegram from Head of Mission, Mr. Fingland, in Salisbury to the CRO, November 19, 1965; PRO, DO 207/112, "Status of Rhodesian Residual Staff" from M. B. Chitty to K. J. Neale, November 26, 1965; PRO, DO 207/112, "Immunities and Privileges for Rhodesia House," Letter from M. B. Chitty to Mr. Burden of the Protocol Department, February 7, 1966.

[86] "Rhodesia House (Occupants)", *HC Deb*, March 14, 1968, vol. 760, c355W.

[87] See: US National Archives at College Park, MD, Central Files 1964–1967, RG 59, Box 2607, Telegram from American Consulate in Salisbury to State Department, December 3, 1965.

[88] Skeen, *Prelude*, p. 165.

[89] PRO, DO 207/112, "Staff at Rhodesia House," Letter from N. D. Watson, Assistant Undersecretary of State, to K. J. Neale, Head of Rhodesia Department, November 12, 1965.

[90] PRO, DO 207/112, "Staff at Rhodesia House," Letter from N. D. Watson, Assistant Undersecretary of State, to K. J. Neale, Head of Rhodesia Department, November 12, 1965.

and any involved in any trade-related activities.[91] The mission was explicitly forbidden from conducting any public relations or recruiting activities of any kind.[92] It was agreed that Rhodesia House would remain open only for the purposes normally associated with a consulate.[93]

From the outset, British officials realized that the options for their treatment of Rhodesia House were to a great extent limited by the vulnerable state of the Residual Mission. Skeen described these two vulnerable missions as, "both in a sense act[ing] as hostages for the other."[94] The reciprocal arrangement regarding Rhodesia House and the Residual Mission was hardly equal. Sydney Brice, the new Head of the Post at Rhodesia House, consistently tested the boundaries of the November 1965 agreements, while the staff at the Residual Mission found their latitude for extending these boundaries severely curtailed. Brice regularly wrote letters "putting the record straight" for British newspapers, clearly violating the public relations ban imposed on both missions in London and Salisbury. In April 1967, CRO officials were incensed by a string of Brice's articles published in the press. In one, Brice wrote a letter to the *Times* to correct a reporter's claim that John Gaunt was head of an "unofficial mission in Pretoria," whereas Brice asserted that Gaunt had been a fully accredited diplomat and Rhodesia's mission there was "accorded official recognition."[95] As one Rhodesia Department official in the CRO wrote in response: "Mr. Brice is getting very bold ..."[96] Even so, CRO officials concluded that he should not be called in to answer for the April articles, but should instead be called in for the next violation immediately after he "transgresses again (as he will undoubtedly do)."[97] Expressing obvious frustration with the unequal

[91] PRO, DO 207/112, "Proposals to Be Put to Mr. Heathcote about Staff to Remain at Rhodesia House," Memo by M. B. Chitty, November 18, 1965.

[92] It is unclear how aware the British government was of the public relations work already being conducted out of Rhodesia House, which had become an increasing priority in the buildup to a UDI. See, for example: Winston Field Papers, Rhodes House Library, Oxford University, MSS Afr. S. 2344, Letter from Even Campbell to Winston Field, February 21, 1964.

[93] This included looking after the welfare of the 400 Rhodesian students in Britain, pension distribution, and advising Rhodesians on whether and how to return to Rhodesia. "Agreement on Status of Rhodesia House," *Rhodesia Herald*, November 25, 1965. The final agreement left both Rhodesia House and the Salisbury Residual Mission with stripped-down staffs and reduced powers. In accordance with long-standing instructions from London, Johnston withdrew as the last High Commissioner in Salisbury. PRO, DO 207/112, "Rhodesia House," Letter from Chitty to Mr. Burltrop, February 15, 1966.

[94] Skeen, *Prelude*, p. 165.

[95] "Mission in Pretoria," Letter by S. F. Brice, *The Times*, May 3, 1967.

[96] PRO, FCO 36/93, Letter to K. J. Neale from M. B. Chitty, May 5, 1967.

[97] PRO, FCO 36/93, Letter to A. Bottomley from K. J. Neale, May 9, 1967.

latitude given to their respective mission staffs, the head of the Rhodesia Department wrote to Arthur Bottomley, "I am quite certain that the Rhodesians would not permit Mr. Hennings [Head of the Residual Mission] to do what Mr. Brice does. The latter is obviously probing how far he can go."[98]

Bottomley did have to wait long for another overstep by Brice. On August 24, 1967, Brice wrote a letter to the *Times* defending Rhodesia's policy of detentions and restrictions of African nationalists, claiming that Rhodesian policy was "no different from that of Britain in Aden."[99] In response, Bottomley called Brice in for a meeting. In the meeting, Bottomley told Brice that the letter was a clear violation of the November 1965 agreements on the functions of Rhodesia House. Continuing in this vein, Bottomley said to Brice that it was in deference to this agreement that the British "had never instructed Mr. Hennings to write letters of this kind to the press in Rhodesia correcting the many misrepresentations of British Government policies and actions." No warnings as to future ramifications if he violated the agreement again were made, but Bottomley seemed satisfied that he would not cross the line again.[100] Despite his apology for overstepping, Brice continued to probe the boundaries of the consular agreement.[101]

Contemporaneously with these controversies about the allowed functions of Rhodesia House, a quasi-diplomatic social life continued inside. On several occasions, cocktail parties were held on the premises. These included a March 10, 1966 reception at Rhodesia House hosted by Brice and his wife, with 100 invited guests, including many MPs.[102] A final cocktail party was held in Rhodesia House in July 1969, just days before the Rhodesian officials were ordered to evacuate the building after the severance of all diplomatic relations.[103] Embarrassingly for the British, these occasions often garnered wide press attention and intense criticism.

Both friends and enemies of the aspirant state were drawn to Rhodesia House as a protest venue. In the British government's ambivalent reaction to these protests, many of the tensions and contradictions of its Rhodesian policy can be discerned. Some of the more intense periods

---

[98] PRO, FCO 36/93, Letter to A. Bottomley from K. J. Neale, May 9, 1967.
[99] "Awaiting Execution," Letter from S. F. Brice, *The Times*, August 24, 1967.
[100] PRO, FCO 36/93, Letter to M. B. Chitty from A. Bottomley, August 24, 1967.
[101] PRO, FCO 36/93, "Rhodesia House," Letter to Mr. Faber from A. Bottomley, March 13, 1968; PRO, FCO 36/93, "Rhodesia House," Letter to Mr. Faber from A. Bottomley, March 13, 1968; PRO, FCO 36/93, Letter to Derek Marks from SF Brice, May 24, 1968.
[102] "Rhodesian Cocktails," *Daily Telegraph*, February 28, 1966.
[103] "... And Rhodesia House Stands Desolate," *Rhodesia Herald*, October 1979.

of protest activity in London corresponded with executions carried out in Rhodesia. The hanging of three Africans in defiance of the Queen's reprieve in March 1968 caused an international furor, especially in Britain. It was not merely the deaths of the Africans that seemingly activated the intensity of the London crowds, but the treasonous disregard of the Queen's royal order. It was ironically the British left who raised these patriotic calls the loudest, and the right, who traditionally were more jingoist in such Crown matters, was noticeably silent. Intense demonstrations and political violence followed outside of Rhodesia House. On March 6, wreaths were symbolically laid on the door of Rhodesia House on which were written "The Rule of Law."[104] These solemn displays were punctuated by a larger and more violent protest in front of Rhodesia House, in which one banner read: "Now Smith Defies Queen."[105] In separate incidents in March, four men were arrested and charged with planning to firebomb Rhodesia House, but ultimately only two men were convicted and charged fines. Another man smashed a plate glass window in Rhodesia House, insisting to police that the act was "purely political."[106] These acts of loyalist illegality outside Rhodesia House stand as an interesting corollary to the regime's purportedly loyalist rebellion occurring inside.

In the buildup to the Commonwealth Prime Ministers' Meeting in London in January 1969, the newer members, many of which had only recently wrested off imperial control, were expected to again attack Britain over its allegedly soft treatment of its rebel dependency. British officials prepared for the inevitable demonstrations in front of Rhodesia House.[107] Several days later, dozens of writers and London School of Economics students "occupied" the vestibule of Rhodesia House for more than four hours until police finally removed them.[108] When the major demonstration occurred on January 12, 4,000 demonstrators marched from Speaker's Corner to Downing Street, and finally on to Rhodesia House. In response to threats made against Rhodesia House, 500 police ringed Rhodesia House preventing the protesters from

---

[104] "Worldwide Dismay at Hangings," *The Times*, March 7, 1968.
[105] "Cabinet Meet Today to Consider Next Steps in Rhodesia Crisis: 'Cynicism' Charge by Smith," *The Times*, March 7, 1968.
[106] "Two Men Fined after Planning to Bomb Rhodesia House," *Rhodesia Herald*, March 27, 1968; "Bottle Hurled at Rhodesia House Window," *Rhodesia Herald*, March 30, 1968.
[107] "Scotland Yard to Protect Rhodesia House for PM's Commonwealth Conference," *Rhodesia Herald*, December 21, 1968.
[108] "Writers' Sit-in at Rhodesia House," *The Times*, January 8, 1969.

Figure 6.2 An image of the "Battle of the Strand" in front of Rhodesia House in January 1969. Several "rooftop raiders" can be seen on the roof of the building.

attacking the building.[109] Apparently frustrated with the security around Rhodesia House, 400 protesters broke off and charged west up the Strand and attacked unguarded South Africa House, smashing more than 100 windows and causing much damage before police could finally relieve the siege. The "Battle of the Strand," as it was called by some, attracted headlines across the world, and was heavily reported in Rhodesia.[110]

The controversies around the hoisting of the pseudo-state's new flag over Rhodesia House in January 1969 highlighted the importance to British policy of the projection of its continued legal authority over Rhodesia. Just hours after UDI, Rhodesia House officials inquired as to the continued flying of the old Rhodesian flag, which had a sky blue background with the colony's crest in the bottom right and the Union Jack in the upper left canton.[111] The British allowed the flag to remain flying, reasoning that "the Rhodesian flag is the properly approved flag of a part of Her Majesty's Dominions and not that of a rebel regime."[112] In November 1968, on the third anniversary of UDI, the regime introduced a new "independence" flag; a design which removed the Union Jack altogether and instead placed Rhodesia's crest against a white backdrop flanked by vertical green stripes on either side.[113] Many Rhodesians sputtered that the flag resembled Nigeria's flag, while others complained that the color choice was solely a product of the ministers' love for rugby.[114] Disregarding both the domestic controversy and British hostility, in October, Union Jacks were taken down from all Rhodesian government buildings and replaced by the new flag.[115] Rhodesia's Lisbon

---

[109] "Battle of the Strand in South Africa and Rhodesia Protest," *The Times*, January 13, 1969.

[110] See, for example, the front-page story: "Rhodesia House Attack Failed: London Demonstrators Turn on SA Embassy: Leaders of Mob Fight with Police," *Rhodesia Herald*, January 13, 1969.

[111] In 1964, the Rhodesians officially changed the background color from a blue ensign to a sky-blue ensign, but the design was the same as the original 1923 flag.

[112] PRO, DO 207/112, "Staff at Rhodesia House," Letter from N. D. Watson to K. J. Neale, November 12, 1965.

[113] For more on the politics behind development of Rhodesia's flag and its implications for Rhodesian's nation-building project, see: Kenrick, *Decolonisation, Identity and Nation in Rhodesia*; Berry, "Flag of Defiance."

[114] See, for example: US National Archives at College Park, MD, Central Files 1967–1969, RG 59, Box 2445, "The LBJ Flag, or the Case of Lardner-Burke's Jersey," Airgram from W. P. O'Neill, American Consulate, Salisbury, to State Department, August 16, 1968.

[115] US National Archives at College Park, MD, Central Files 1967–1969, RG 59, Box 2445, "Union Jack Replaced by New Rhodesian Flag," Airgram from W. P. O'Neill, American Consulate Salisbury, to State Department, October 11, 1968.

mission hoisted up the new Rhodesian flag immediately after its adoption on November 11, 1968.[116]

On December 9, Brice telephoned the Foreign and Commonwealth Office (FCO) to say that he had received "categorical instructions from Salisbury" to fly the new flag in London. Brice was informed that this was deemed unacceptable by the British and that were the flag to be flown, the government would find a means to bring it down. The British further warned that the flying of the flag jeopardized the prospects for settlement talks.[117] Following these warnings, Salisbury instructed Brice to hold off flying the flag for the time being, and Brice subsequently sent his flag pole away "for repair."[118] During this waiting period, the Special Branch kept watch over Rhodesia House for any flag-related developments.[119]

On New Year's eve, 1968, Rhodesia House raised the new flag.[120] Even though it was not easily seen from street level, the flag immediately caused a ruckus in the popular press and within Whitehall. Two days after it was hoisted, the British Cabinet held a meeting to discuss British policy regarding the new flag flying from Rhodesia House.[121] In the discussion which followed, it was agreed that the hoisting of the flag was timed to correspond with the eve of the Commonwealth Prime Ministers' Meeting from which Rhodesia was excluded, and was intended to be "highly provocative." In the meeting, George Thomson laid out what he considered to be the three courses of action open to the government. In his view, Britain could: (1) pay no attention to the event and treat the flag as "an insignificant 'piece of bunting'"; (2) seek parliamentary powers to have it removed, by force if necessary; or (3) arrange a compromise wherein the British Residual Mission in Salisbury would lower the Union Jack simultaneously with Rhodesia House lowering the new flag. Thomson offered the first course – that of ignoring the flag – as the best option available.[122]

---

[116] Berry, "Flag of Defiance," p. 16.

[117] PRO, PREM 13/2893, "Rhodesia: Flying the Flag," Memorandum by George Thomson, Minister without Portfolio, December 24, 1968.

[118] PRO, PREM 13/2893, "Rhodesia: Flying the Flag," Memorandum by George Thomson, Minister without Portfolio, December 24, 1968.

[119] PRO, PREM 13/2893, "Rhodesia: Flying the Flag," Memorandum by George Thomson, Minister without Portfolio, December 24, 1968.

[120] PRO, PREM 13/2893, "Rhodesia: Flying the Flag," Memorandum by George Thomson, Minister without Portfolio, December 24, 1968.

[121] PRO, CAB 130/410, "Rhodesia House Flag," British Cabinet Meeting Minutes, Misc 232 (69), January 2, 1969.

[122] PRO, CAB 130/410, "Rhodesia House Flag," British Cabinet Meeting Minutes, Misc 232 (69), January 2, 1969.

It was decided that removing the flag by force presented insurmountable problems. First, the flying of the flag contravened no law. Added to that, Rhodesia House was currently protected by certain diplomatic immunities, which would have to be legally removed before seizing the flag. It was feared that any bill to forcibly remove it would invite Tory opposition. In addition, a forceful removal would almost certainly invite reprisals in Rhodesia, which could include the closing down of the Residual Mission and the forced lowering of the Union Jack over Government House. In a handwritten note penned on the top of a Residual Mission telegram before the flag was raised, Harold Wilson suggested a nontraditional method to remove any new flag, asking, "Can't some husky youth take it down?"[123] This covert method of a private citizen removing the flag had the benefit of removing the flag while providing plausible deniability for the British government. It was decided, however, that even this surreptitious method of a contrived demonstration was fraught with unacceptable risks, including that similar acts of government-sponsored vigilantism would occur against the Residual Mission in Salisbury.[124]

In summing up the cabinet's conclusions, Harold Wilson said that everyone "agreed in disliking the compromise solution."[125] Indeed, Thomson had noted doing nothing "would seem to many to denote a measure of recognition of Rhodesian 'independence.'"[126] Yet despite these obvious shortcomings, it was agreed that the government would "swallow [its] warnings" and do nothing.[127]

The flag issue did not disappear as the cabinet had perhaps naively hoped it would: It was surely not an "insignificant piece of bunting." In parliament, a Labour MP threatened to "pull the ruddy thing down."[128] Individual "flag raiders" began to periodically climb up the flagpole of Rhodesia House and do just that, though without government connivance. On January 5, a member of the Young Communist League climbed to the top of Rhodesia House, ripped the new flag from the pole and

---

[123] PRO, PREM 13/2893, Handwritten Minute by Harold Wilson on Top of Telegram to FCO from Mr. Carter, Residual Mission, Telegram No. 1459, December 19, 1968.

[124] PRO, PREM 13/2893, "Rhodesia: Flying the Flag," Memorandum by George Thomson, Minister without Portfolio, December 24, 1968.

[125] PRO, CAB 130/410, "Rhodesia House Flag," British Cabinet Meeting Minutes, Misc 232 (69), January 2, 1969.

[126] PRO, PREM 13/2893, "Rhodesia: Flying the Flag," Memorandum by George Thomson, Minister without Portfolio, December 24, 1968.

[127] PRO, PREM 13/2893, "Rhodesia: Flying the Flag," Memorandum by George Thomson, Minister without Portfolio, December 24, 1968.

[128] "Smith Flag Survives Mauling," The Times, January 4, 1969.

launched it onto the street.[129] Several days later, another "rooftop raider" climbed the Rhodesia House flag pole and replaced the new Rhodesian flag with the Union Jack, which flew above Rhodesia House for seventeen hours.[130] Later in January, another "flag pole raider," this time a female University College London student, pulled down the Rhodesian flag and again replaced it with the Union Jack.[131] Throughout January 1969, British newspaper cartoonists had a field day with the entire illegal flag episode, especially poking fun at Wilson's powerlessness and the spectacle of the high-flying antics of the flagpole raiders.[132]

Flowing from these sporadic invasions and trespasses into and onto Rhodesia House, the government attracted criticisms from those on the right who complained that not enough was being done to protect diplomatic missions, and on the left who felt British resources should not be spent protecting the mission of the illegal rebel regime.[133] The flag-flying over Rhodesia House and the subsequent protests was also a great embarrassment to Britain internationally. The American Embassy in London reported to Washington that "everyone in London it appears has seen [the UDI flag above Rhodesia House] except [the] British Government."[134] Evidently surprised by the lack of a response, the embassy asked the British whether it planned to take the flag down, to which the Americans reported that the British official "smiled ruefully and said matter was 'under study'."[135] American Embassy officials remained unimpressed, and commented to Washington that "legalisms are unlikely to be persuasive with African Commonwealth members," concluding that "HMG's attitude toward flag-flying episode [is a] humiliating reminder of British impotence ..."[136] This smugness on

---

[129] "Smith Flag Survives Mauling," *The Times*, January 4, 1969.

[130] "Flag Pole Raiders Leave Their Perch," *Rhodesia Herald*, January 16, 1969.

[131] "Girl Climbs Flagpole in Rhodesia Protest," *Rhodesia Herald*, January 28, 1969.

[132] See, for example: M. Cummings, *Daily Express*, January 4, 1969; M. Cummings, *Daily Express*, January 5, 1969; W. Papas, *The Guardian*, January 13, 1969; J. Musgrave Wood "Emmwood," *Daily Mail*, January 14, 1969; R. Carl "Giles," *Daily Express*, January 14, 1969; K. Waite, *The Sun*, January 28, 1969. British Cartoon Archive, www.cartoons.ac.uk.

[133] See: "Rhodesia House (Flag)," *HC Deb*, January 23, 1969, vol. 776, cc161–2W.

[134] US National Archives at College Park, MD, Central Files 1967–1969, RG 59, Box 2445, "Oh Say Can You See?" Telegram from Bruce, American Embassy in London to State Department, January 7, 1969.

[135] US National Archives at College Park, MD, Central Files 1967–1969, RG 59, Box 2445, "Oh Say Can You See?" Telegram from Bruce, American Embassy in London to State Department, January 7, 1969.

[136] US National Archives at College Park, MD, Central Files 1967–1969, RG 59, Box 2445, "Oh Say Can You See?" Telegram from Bruce, American Embassy in London to State Department, January 7, 1969.

the part of the Americans conveniently ignored Washington's tolerance of the RIO and the work of Towsey and Hooper.

In June 1969, the Rhodesian electorate passed a referendum for a new republican constitution, ostensibly severing its connections with the Crown and Commonwealth. The British had initially planned on leaving the Residual Mission and Rhodesia House open and keeping Governor Gibbs installed in Government House even if the republican referendum was passed, so long as it did so by a relatively close margin.[137] The final "No" vote for the new republican constitution was a meager 27 percent.[138]

The Smith regime had hoped that its republic status would help in gaining international recognition and breaking out of its isolation: It did not have that effect.[139] Smith publicly stated that the new constitution need not affect the existence of the two missions.[140] But four days after the passage of the republican constitution in Rhodesia on June 20, 1969, Arthur Bottomley summoned Brice for the final time, and he instructed him and his staff to vacate Rhodesia House.[141] On the same day, the head of the Residual Mission in Salisbury informed the regime of Britain's intention to close down the Residual Mission.[142] The final telegram sent from the Residual Mission to London had the mournful feel of a funeral dirge: "Valedictory. All classified papers now destroyed and final search made. Office has distressed air. All affairs are left in order. We now consign them to God and to Lang [the residual caretaker of the property]. Flag has been lowered for last time. In the morning the last of us shall have gone."[143]

Republican status did not alter Gibbs' legal position as governor. Just as the 1965 UDI constitution was *ultra vires*, so too was the 1969 republican constitution. Nevertheless, days after the referendum vote the

---

[137] Gibbs stated that if Crown royalists could gain at least 40 percent of the vote he would stay. See: US National Archives at College Park, MD, Central Files 1967–1969, RG 59, Box 2445, "British Plans for Rhodesia," Telegram from W. P. O'Neill, American Consulate in Salisbury to State Department, April 15, 1969. See also: US National Archives at College Park, MD, Central Files 1967–1969, RG 59, Box 2445, "British Prepare for Break with Smith," Telegram from Annenberg, American Embassy in London to State Department, May 21, 1969.

[138] "Sweeping Victory for Ian Smith in Heavy Rhodesian Poll," *The Times*, June 21, 1969.

[139] Quentin-Baxter, *Rhodesia and the Law*, p. 18.

[140] PRO, FCO 36/93, "Funding of Rhodesia House," From Salisbury to CO, Telegram No. 113, January 31, 1967.

[141] PRO, FCO 36/579, Letter Handed to Brice from Bottomley, June 24, 1969.

[142] PRO, FCO 36/579, Telegram to Salisbury Residual Mission from Mr. Stewart of the Rhodesia Political Department, FCO, Telegram No. 541, June 23, 1969.

[143] PRO, FCO 36/584, Telegram from Mr. Lister, Residual Mission, Salisbury, to London, July 13, 1969.

British government finally relieved Gibbs of his post, ending the facade of a parallel, legal government in Rhodesia, though it continued to survive as a legal entity and the owner of Rhodesia House. On July 4, 1969, Gibbs held a final cocktail party at Government House, where guests toasted to the Queen's health.[144] On the next day, the Union Jack was taken down from the flagpole and Gibbs moved back to his farm in the Rhodesian countryside.

On July 14, 1969, Rhodesia House closed its doors and lowered the UDI flag from the pole.[145] The Rhodesia Pensions Office paid for a caretaker to live in the building and keep it in working order, ensuring that no water damage, or other problems developed.[146] Besides the lonely caretaker, Rhodesia House was empty for the entire decade of the 1970s.[147] Days after its closure, a cartoon in the *Sun* showed several bored policemen ringing the now empty building with one bobby plaintively asking, "Whatever will we do all day?"[148]

Wilson's decision to completely break relations with the illegal regime and close the missions was met with vigorous Conservative opposition.[149] It was attacked by the Tory leadership who argued that this would cut off those elements within Rhodesia amenable to a settlement, but also by backbenchers who pointed out the alleged unfairness in Britain's Rhodesia policy. For example, MP Cyril Osborne said, "If we can still keep a mission in Peking, why on Earth cannot we have one in Salisbury?"[150] So strongly did the Tories oppose the closing of the Salisbury Residual Mission, that opposition leader Edward Heath sent a secret message to President Nixon, whose American Consulate remained up and running, declaring that if the Conservatives won the 1970 general election, they would reopen the Residual Mission.[151] He did win, but he did not reopen it.[152]

With the exception of Belgium, which closed its consulate in Salisbury immediately after the referendum along with Britain, the other five countries with consulates in Salisbury took longer to close their doors. Portugal did not do so until the mid-1970s, and South Africa's never

---

[144] A. Megahey, *Humphrey Gibbs: Beleaguered Governor: Southern Rhodesia, 1929–1969* (MacMillan Press, London, 1998) pp. 168–169.

[145] "Rhodesians Strike Flag in London," *The Times*, July 15, 1969.

[146] "The Past Lingers: History Haunts the Silent Rooms of Rhodesia House," *Rhodesia Herald*, October 19, 1979.

[147] "The Past Lingers: History Haunts the Silent Rooms of Rhodesia House," *Rhodesia Herald*, October 19, 1979.

[148] K. Waite, *The Sun*, July 16, 1969. British Cartoon Archive, www.cartoons.ac.uk.

[149] See, for example: "MPs in Clash on Rhodesia Break," *The Times*, June 25, 1969.

[150] "Opposition to Resist Communications Ban," *The Times*, June 25, 1969.

[151] Lake, *"Tar Baby" Option*, p. 141.   [152] See: PRO, PREM 15/163.

closed. The British urged these remaining countries to close their Salisbury consulates, which most did only in March 1970, after the British threatened to withdraw the exequaturs from their consulates following Smith's formal declaration of Rhodesia's republican status.[153] In the interim, however, while the British were urging that the United States follow their lead and close their consulate, they were also anxious to hear the latest news as reported from the American Consulate in Salisbury since their own eyes and ears were sealed shut; an irony which was likely not missed by either side of the exchange.[154]

When the details of the Anglo-Rhodesian settlement proposals, which were negotiated by Edward Heath's Conservative government and the Smith regime, were announced on November 1971, the British Anti-Apartheid Movement (AAM) organized a demonstration against the settlement outside of the abandoned Rhodesia House.[155] On February 1, 1972, two firebombs were thrown at Rhodesia House by an unknown arsonist, setting fire to carpets and furniture, but apparently not harming the caretaker inside.[156] Two weeks after the firebombing, an enormous march, a half-mile long, descended on Rhodesia House from Trafalgar Square. The demonstration, which gathered over 10,000 people, was organized by the AAM to oppose the Anglo-Rhodesian settlement proposals.[157] The demonstrators placed a Zimbabwe flag outside the deserted Rhodesia House building and proclaimed it the property of all Rhodesians.[158] Soon thereafter, two bottles flew from the crowd smashing against the side of the building, and in response police reinforcements poured in from buses to thicken the wall encircling Rhodesia House.[159] As with the 1969 Battle of the Strand, this demonstration garnered overseas press, especially in Rhodesia.[160] Following the February 1972 demonstrations, there was no further violence directed against Rhodesia House.

---

[153] Lake, *"Tar Baby" Option*, pp. 142–143; US National Archives at College Park, MD, Central Files 1967–1969, RG 59, Box 2445, "Consular Representation in Rhodesia," Telegram from Ellsworth, US Mission to NATO to State Department, October 17, 1969.

[154] US National Archives at College Park, MD, Central Files 1967–1969, RG 59, Box 2445, "Rhodesia Matters," Memorandum of Conversation between W. P. O'Neill, James Bottomley, and Richard Faber, London, July 24, 1969.

[155] Roger Fieldhouse, *Anti-Apartheid: A History of the Movement in Britain, 1959–1994* (Merlin Press, London, 2005) p. 136.

[156] "Rhodesia House Bomb Attack," *Rhodesia Herald*, February 1, 1972.

[157] "43 Charged after Rhodesia Protest March in London," *The Times*, February 14, 1972.

[158] "Marchers Attack Rhodesia House," *Rhodesia Herald*, February 14, 1972.

[159] "43 Charged after Rhodesia Protest March in London," *The Times*, February 14, 1972.

[160] See, for example: "Anatomy of a Demonstration," *Rhodesia Herald*, February 15, 1972.

Bophuthatswana

In 1982, Bophuthatswana opened "Bop House" in London[161] Bop House was no Rhodesia House in terms of impact or visibility, but on a much smaller scale it followed along a similar path. Bop House was located on a quiet street in the posh Holland Park neighborhood of West London.[162] As described in a *Telegraph* article, the "Bantu Embassy" was a "lavishly decorated and restored" cream-colored Victorian home that was sheltered from the street by "heavy velvet curtains" in the front windows.[163] The stated purpose of Bop House was:

... to further the commercial, international, and tourist potential of Bophuthatswana and to encourage investment in this thriving and successful independently governed nation ... This should allow everyone to realise that Bophuthatswana is governed entirely independently of South Africa; that there is a fully integrated non-racial society, with a democratically elected President and Parliament; an independent judiciary; an economy that is able to stand on its own feet; a level of agricultural production which, unusual for most African states allows for an export of agricultural products; and an administration that is very strongly opposed to apartheid.[164]

Lucas Mangope was to come to London for the opening and while in London he and his family planned to stay at Bop House. As to be expected, the opening of the pseudo-embassy and Mangope's arrival

---

[161] Bophuthatswana's overseas presence was expressed primarily through the opening of "trade missions" in Paris, Frankfurt, Bremen, London, Rome, Washington, Hong Kong, and Taipei. Jones, "Etiquette of State-Building," p. 35. Mangope's overseas outreach had perhaps the greatest success with its mission in Tel Aviv, Israel. Mangope visited Israel in 1981 and met with General Moshe Dayan, among others. In Tel Aviv, the Bophuthatswanan mission was prominently located along the waterfront, and despite objections by the Israeli Foreign Office, the mission flew the Bophuthatswanan flag from a flagpole. Sasha Polakow-Suransky, *Unspoken Alliance: Israel's Secret Relationship with Apartheid South Africa* (Vintage, New York, 2011) p. 157. Bophuthatswana's representative who drove Mangope around was a man named Shabtai Kalmanovitz. Kalmanovitz could have easily been a character from a John Le Carre novel. He would be exposed as a KGB spy, serve time in an Israeli jail only to be traded in an intelligence deal back to Russia where he would go on to make a fortune and become a prominent sports team owner. He was murdered in Moscow in 2009. Andrew Osborn and Adrian Blomfield, "Former Israeli Double agent Shot Dead Near Putin's Office," *The Telegraph*, November 3, 2009; *Unspoken Alliance*, p. 157.

[162] Anti-Apartheid Movement Archive, Bodleian Library, Oxford, MSS AAM 981, Bophuthatswana, 1981–1994, Bophuthatswana National Commercial Organization memorandum, titled "Bophuthatswana House" (undated, but August 1982).

[163] AAM, Bodleian Library, Oxford, MSS AAM 981, Bophuthatswana, 1981–1994, "Demo at Bantu 'Embassy'," Telegraph, September 9, 1982.

[164] AAM, Bodleian Library, Oxford, MSS AAM 981, Bophuthatswana, 1981–1994, Bophuthatswana National Commercial Organization Memorandum, Titled "Bophuthatswana House" (undated, but August 1982).

immediately drew fire from the British Anti-Apartheid Movement.[165] Mangope arrived in London on September 6 and had traveled on special identity documents issued to him from the British Consulate in Johannesburg – a procedure the *Times* claimed had been used in the past for Bantustan citizens visiting Britain whose Bantustan passports were not recognized by Britain.[166] A spokesman for the FCO said, "[Mangope's visa] was not granted in his capacity as president or any other title but on the basis of his being a private visitor."[167] A routine condition was placed on the issuance of the travel document such that if Mangope acted "in an official or representative capacity" while in Britain, such documents would not be issued to him in the future.[168] The AAM Executive Director, Mike Terry, had fought hard to try to stop Lucas Mangope from coming to Britain to open the mission, but was unsuccessful.[169]

In addition to trying to block Mangope's visit, Terry wrote to the Royal Borough of Kensington and Chelsea arguing that the Bop House building was designated for residential use only and that it did not apply for a "change of use" from the Borough.[170] Expressing the big in the small, the letter stated that this was not simply a simple code violation but had international effects: "It is our view that Britain and the Royal Borough will be the subject of international opprobrium if Chief Mangope is permitted to continue with this adventure."[171] In response to the AAM letter, the council leader wrote that he viewed the council's concerns narrowly to just whether or not Bop House continued to be used as a residential property, something he promised the council would continue

[165] See for example: AAM, Bodleian Library, Oxford, MSS AAM 981, Bophuthatswana, 1981–1994 MSS AAM 981, Bophuthatswana, 1981–1994, Telegram containing press release from Mike Terry, September 4, 1982.

[166] AAM, Bodleian Library, Oxford, MSS AAM 981, Bophuthatswana, 1981–1994, Michael Hornsby, "Bantustan Opens London Mission," *The Times*, September 2, 1982.

[167] AAM, Bodleian Library, Oxford, MSS AAM 981, Bophuthatswana, 1981–1994, "Row over UK Visa for Mangope," *Sunday Times*, September 5, 1982.

[168] AAM, Bodleian Library, Oxford, MSS AAM 981, Bophuthatswana, 1981–1994, Michael Hornsby, "Bantustan Opens London Mission," *The Times*, September 2, 1982.

[169] AAM, Bodleian Library, Oxford, MSS AAM 981, Bophuthatswana, 1981–1994, Letter from Terry to Onslow, September 2, 1982.

[170] AAM, Bodleian Library, Oxford, MSS AAM 981, Bophuthatswana, 1981–1994, Letter form Terry to Nicholas Freeman, Leader of the Council, Royal Borough of Kensington and Chelsea, September 3, 1982.

[171] AAM, Bodleian Library, Oxford, MSS AAM 981, Bophuthatswana, 1981–1994, Letter from Terry to Nicholas Freeman, Leader of the Council, Royal Borough of Kensington and Chelsea, September 3, 1982.

to monitor.[172] For their part, the spokesman for Bop House wrote a letter to the editor to the *Kensington News and Post* to defend the Bophuthatswanan state broadly, but also the establishment of Bop House more specifically.

The facts concerning 60 Holland Park are that this is a residential property owned by a British Company and it will be kept as the Royal Borough of Kensington and Chelsea Council has been informed, for private residential use. Never has it even been suggested by Bophuthatswana or the owners of the house, that this is an Embassy or a mission.[173]

When asked later if the building was still being used a residence, Ruth Rees, the public relations representative for Bop House, said, "Do you want to see the bedrooms?"[174]

The FCO's arguments defending the presence of Bop House were similar to those the State Department used to defend the policy of allowing the existence of the KIS, RIO, and Bantustans' offices in the United States – that these offices did not constitute recognition, did not violate any law, and individuals working there were protected by the right of free speech.[175] This sort of response was likely expected by AAM campaigners, who also organized a direct-action campaign to draw a spotlight on Bop House. The AAM's fear that the opening of the Bop House and the corresponding visit by Mangope seemed to some to connote some degree of acceptance was not irrational. *The Times'* Johannesburg correspondent, Michael Hornsby, wrote of Bop House: "Although neither the House nor the officials who occupy it will have diplomatic status, its opening is considered to be the closest that any of South Africa's tribal Bantustans have yet come to achieving formal representation abroad. It seems bound to draw controversy."[176] A writer in the Johannesburg *Sunday Times* wrote that the opening of Bop House with Mangope in attendance was "likely to be seen as

---

[172] AAM, Bodleian Library, Oxford, MSS AAM 981, Bophuthatswana, 1981–1994, Letter from Freeman to Terry, September 7, 1982.

[173] AAM, Bodleian Library, Oxford, MSS AAM 981, Bophuthatswana, 1981–1994, Letter to the Editor from C. J. Guise, "Bophuthatswana Facts Misleading," *Kensington News and Post*, November 5, 1982.

[174] AAM, Bodleian Library, Oxford, MSS AAM 981, Bophuthatswana, 1981–1994, Draft Note by Richard Towden (undated, but September 9, 1982). See also: Michael Hornsby, "Bantustan Opens London Mission," *The Times*, September 2, 1982.

[175] AAM, Bodleian Library, Oxford, MSS AAM 981, Bophuthatswana, 1981–1994, Letter from Onslow to Terry, September 17, 1982.

[176] AAM, Bodleian Library, Oxford, MSS AAM 981, Bophuthatswana, 1981–1994, Michael Hornsby, "Bantustan Opens London Mission," *The Times*, September 2, 1982.

something of a public relations coup for Bophuthatswana."[177] Thus while the event was going on inside, outside there was a demonstration with a crowd of 100 banner-waving protestors out front chanting slogans and heckling and booing the guests.[178] It was an attempt to recreate the "Battle of the Strand" in W11. Two protestors were arrested for throwing eggs at the building.[179]

Inside the Bop House doors that night, it was estimated that there were 150 guests. The events that night included an introduction by Sir Peter Emery, MP; a talk by Bophuthatswana's director of information; two videos – one on Sun City; two tourist pitches; and closing remarks by Lucas Mangope.[180] The latter was described in the program as "His Excellency, President Lucas Mangope."[181] Reportedly at the reception, Mangope wore a lapel badge declaring him "President Lucas Mangope," but when reminded of the British Consul's warning that he could only visit in his private capacity, Mangope reportedly replied, "Ah, but it doesn't say President of anywhere. I am here as a private individual. When I am at home I am President."[182] Other Bophuthatswanan Cabinet officials present also had lapel badges announcing their titles.

According to an article in the *Independent* from 1994 Bop House "mostly employed former Rhodesians."[183] This was consistent with the former Rhodesian Cabinet official, Rowan Cronje, being Bophuthatswana's longtime Foreign Minister. In addition to Bop House, Bophuthatswana's interests were promoted by Ian Findlay and Anthony McCall-Judson from the Bophuthatswana International Affairs Office.[184] Findlay, who was also a Rhodesian, headed the office at Piccadilly House on Regent Street, which performed some

[177] AAM, Bodleian Library, Oxford, MSS AAM 981, Bophuthatswana, 1981–1994, "Row over UK Visa for Mangope," *Sunday Times*, September 5, 1982.

[178] AAM, Bodleian Library, Oxford, MSS AAM 981, Bophuthatswana, 1981–1994, "Demo at Bantu 'Embassy,'" *Telegraph*, September 9, 1982.

[179] "Bophuthatswana House Protest," Picture No. 8215, accessed on January 2, 2021: www.aamarchives.org.

[180] AAM, Bodleian Library, Oxford, MSS AAM 981, Bophuthatswana, 1981–1994, "Bophuthatswana Tourism Seminar Programme" (undated, but August or September 1982).

[181] AAM, Bodleian Library, Oxford, MSS AAM 981, Bophuthatswana, 1981–1994, "Bophuthatswana Tourism Seminar Programme" (undated, but August or September 1982).

[182] AAM, Bodleian Library, Oxford, MSS AAM 981, Bophuthatswana, 1981–1994, Draft Note by Richard Towden (undated, but September 9, 1982).

[183] Richard Dowden, "Toytown Image Hid Apartheid Tyranny: As White Right-Wingers Die at the Hands of Bophuthatswana Forces, Richard Dowden Examines the Racial Purpose of the 'Homeland'," *The Independent*, March 12, 1994.

[184] Nixon, *Selling Apartheid*, p. 104.

pseudo-diplomatic functions.[185] British friends of Bophuthatswana were able to lure several MPs to take an all-expense paid trip to visit their country, the so-called Bop Run.[186] Bop House facilitated these trips, similar to how the RIO had facilitated visits of friendly politicians, businessmen, journalists, and academics to visit Rhodesia. According to the *Independent*: "Most of them used it as an acceptable way of visiting South Africa (a free ticket from the South African embassy might have been embarrassing) and the Bop representatives frequently complained that the MPs would leave after one night in Sun City and take off to the coast for a holiday with their families."[187] Findlay appeared before the British parliament's Select Committee on Members' Interests in 1989 and was asked: "Are you satisfied that your government is getting good value for money from visits [to Bophuthatswana] by British MPs?" He replied: "Yes, very much so."[188]

Conclusion

Like the United States policy regarding the missions of these aspirant states, Britain's policy toward these missions was the result of compromises and accommodations, which similarly resulted in odd oscillations between conciliation and confrontation. Belgium too walked this tightrope in regard to the La Délégation Permanente du Katanga, balancing domestic pressures on both sides, as well as foreign diplomatic pressure. Pertaining to Rhodesia specifically, Britain asserted its continued legal authority over the colony, tried to isolate the regime internationally, and applied escalating economic pressure as attempts to coerce the regime back to legality. More aggressive measures to bring down the regime, including the use of force, were demanded from some members of the Commonwealth, many newer states in the UN, and the British left, as were calls for greater conciliation toward the regime from those on the British right, including the small but influential Rhodesia lobby. These

---

[185] Jones, "Mmabatho 'Mother of the People'," p. 270.

[186] Patricia Wynn Davies, Richard Dowden, and John Carlin, "The Attack on Sleaze: How Apartheid Regime Set Out to Woo Tories: Patricia Wynn Davies Tells the Story of the Firm Which Gave MPs a South African Perspective," *The Independent*, October 22, 1994.

[187] Richard Dowden, "Toytown Image Hid Apartheid Tyranny: As White Right-Wingers Die at the Hands of Bophuthatswana Forces, Richard Dowden Examines the Racial Purpose of the 'Homeland'," *The Independent*, March 12, 1994.

[188] Patricia Wynn Davies, Richard Dowden, and John Carlin, "The Attack on Sleaze: How Apartheid Regime Set Out to Woo Tories: Patricia Wynn Davies Tells the Story of the Firm Which Gave MPs a South African Perspective," *The Independent*, October 22, 1994.

demands were all resisted. Regarding the Lisbon office, the British were able to eventually, and only painfully, extract a statement from the Portuguese that the office was not a full diplomatic mission, but they were powerless to close it down. This broad policy path can be traced in microcosm in Britain's policy toward Rhodesia House. The mission was isolated, but was allowed to remain open in a limited capacity. Its functions were constrained, but violations of the agreements were never punished. Its illegal flag was condemned, but it was allowed to fly. The left thought the government's policy regarding Rhodesia House was too soft; the right thought it too severe. Prime Minister Wilson once said in reference to his cabinet's policy on the UDI flag, a statement which applied equally well to Britain's Rhodesia House policy, and more generally still, to its entire Rhodesian policy – that everyone "agreed in disliking" it.

Bop House reproduced many of the same familiar thematic contests that came up with Rhodesia House in Britain, and the KIS and RIO in the United States. In these cases, the statuses of the buildings and its inhabitants were attacked by opponents of the would-be states, and awkwardly defended by the host countries. In these battles Britain and Belgium, much like the United States, found itself in between the opposing sides, explaining to the opponents why they could not do more, and sometimes chastising the aspirant state for violating the terms of their presence in Britain. In all such cases, recognition was denied, but the lines between private individuals performing private acts protected by free speech and state officials performing state functions contrary to domestic and international law were blurred. The results in all cases were inglorious stalemates.

7   Putting Bop on the Map
Sun City and the Nonrecognition of Bophuthatswana

A mere 90-minute drive or a 30-minute flight from Johannesburg, was far and away the most famous site of interaction with the outside world for any of these four pseudo-states: Sun City Resort. One could hardly imagine a more different sort of node of international exchange than the resort casino popularly known as "Sin City." Unlike the other sites of foreign interaction examined in this book, the Sun City Resort was a private for-profit entity not operated by the government, and it did not purport to perform any official government services or house official government representatives. Sun City was a massive casino and entertainment complex sited inside one of the six enclaves of Bophuthatswana, with swimming pools; an 18-hole golf course designed by the resident professional Gary Player; tennis courts; discotheques; theaters playing soft-core pornographic films; and live, interracial, topless entertainment.[1] It was aesthetically and philosophically distinct from all the other foreign missions discussed in this book. In sharp contrast to these aspirant states' pseudo-embassies or pseudo-consulates, which were purposely made to appear sober and serious, Sun City was designed in a style that writer Aaron Latham once described as "Outer-space pueblo."[2] Despite its reputation as a hedonistic oasis, Sun City Resort became the most visible symbol of the Bophuthatswanan state, and the resort's early successes in attracting world-class entertainers and sports figures rendered it a crucially important venue for the battle over the recognition of Bophuthatswana and the whole Bantustan system of states. It was due to its fame and notoriety that one scholar wrote,

---

[1] Linda Ronstadt described Sun City's architecture as "Aztec-Dorito-Bauhaus." Aaron Latham, "Linda Ronstadt: Snow White in South Africa," *Rolling Stone*, August 18, 1983. *The New York Times* once described the 1992 addition of Lost City as "the most audacious and most deafeningly hyped theme resort in the Southern Hemisphere, at least." Alan Cowell, "Sol Kerzner, South African Casino Tycoon, Is Dead at 84," *The New York Times*, March 27, 2020.

[2] Aaron Latham, "Linda Ronstadt: Snow White in South Africa," *Rolling Stone*, August 18, 1983.

"the [Sun City] resort became the most notable, and certainly the most lucrative marker of the Bophuthatswanan nation."[3]

The resort was officially opened on December 7, 1979 by Solomon "Sol" Kerzner, the owner of Southern Sun Hotels, exactly two years after Bophuthatswana had declared independence. Kerzner was able to secure a monopoly casino license from the Mangope regime before independence, and his Mmabatho Sun casino hotel in the new capital opened in time for the Independence Day celebrations in 1977. The Sun City site was allegedly picked by Kerzner during a helicopter ride over the Bophuthatswanan countryside, when he found a spot against a dormant volcano where he decided to situate the mammoth resort.[4] In 1980, the people who had lived on what would be the new grounds of Sun City were relocated to a resettlement camp to allow for its construction.[5] From that spot the Sun City Resort quickly grew outward like a tumorous mass of costume jewelry.

Kerzer was a giant without equal in South Africa's tourist industry, leading many to call him "The Sun King."[6] In the Bantustans Kerzner saw a lucrative escape from apartheid South Africa's strict laws governing gambling, topless dancing, and interracial social mixing, offering more convenient access points from South Africa's major urban centers than did Lesotho and Swaziland, whose tourist trades had formerly served as the republic's "pleasure periphery." He would later go on to obtain exclusive casino licenses in all the other Bantustans taking advantage of their different legal and economic landscapes as well, but Sun City was always the flagship of Kerzner's Sun International empire. Sun City was on a different scale of ambition, and its political and cultural impact would dwarf the Mmabatho casino and his other Southern African properties, including Transkei's Wild Coast Sun. It was enormously successful, at least early on.[7] Kerzner boasted in the early 1980s that Southern Sun Hotels hosted three quarters of all foreign tourists to South

---

[3] T. Sannar, "Playing Sun City: The Politics of Entertainment at a South African Mega-Resort," PhD dissertation in Theater Studies, University of California, Santa Barbara (2011) p. 3. Sannar's study looks at Sun City as a venue for spectacle, and he adroitly analyzes the multiple meanings of the performances on Sun City's stages.

[4] Sannar, *Playing Sun City*, p. 58.

[5] Marietta Kesting and Aljoscha Weskott (eds.), *Sun Tropes: Sun City and (Post-) Apartheid Culture in South Africa* (August Verlag, Berlin, 2009) p. 29.

[6] *The New York Times* referred to him as the "Kubla Khan of southern Africa," with Sun City as his Xanadu. Joseph Lelyveld, "Bring a Bit of Vegas to South Africa's 'Homelands'," *New York Times*, July 19, 1981. Less impressively, he was also called the "Donald Trump of Africa." David Marlow, "Crowning Glory," *Chicago Tribune*, March 6, 1994.

[7] Jonathan Crush and Paul Wellings, "The Southern African Pleasure Periphery, 1966–83," *The Journal of Modern African Studies*, vol. 21, no. 4 (1983) p. 695.

Africa, and Sun City in particular generated $75 million of South Africa's total $400 million in tourist revenue.[8]

In the case of Sun City, Kerzner's and Lucas Mangope's interests aligned almost perfectly. Bophuthatswana's leaders saw in Sun International's casino hotels the potential for legitimate international attractions that could lure foreign visitors, foreign entertainers, and foreign athletes who could shore up claims to its separate existence. By visiting Sun City and acquiescing to Bophuthatswana's border control processes and taking advantage of legal and social systems different from those of South Africa, especially regarding racial segregation, tourists were implicitly acknowledging that they were entering a different sovereign space. As will be explained in detail below, for some entertainers who came to Sun City, most notably Frank Sinatra, this claim of Bophuthatswana's independence was made explicitly and forcefully, as a defense to charges that they were breaking the South African cultural boycott or their own ethical code of non-racialism. This chapter will explore the irony of the performative rejection of apartheid by the Bantustans and by the foreign entertainers who performed there, and the legitimation of Bantustans' independence which this distinction allowed.

Bophuthatswana's benefit from Sun City was less financial than political and symbolic. Journalist Alan Greenblo asserts that Kerzner's Sun International paid next to no taxes whatsoever in Bophuthatswana.[9] According to Greenblo, in addition to the near-zero tax load, Sun International received kickbacks from the Bophuthatswanan government from the taxes charged to foreign entertainers and athletes who performed in Sun City, such that of the 40 percent, and after 1987, 50 percent, taxes applied to the fees charged by visiting entertainers and athletes, the Bophuthatswana treasury would then give 90 percent of that amount back to Sun City.[10] One of the rationales behind Sun City tax breaks was that it was receiving tax deductions for every action undertook which publicized Bophuthatswana and put it in a positive light internationally, burnishing its image as a fully functioning independent state.

---

[8] Doris Klein Bacon, "For $2 Million, a South African 'Homeland' Gets Frank Sinatra – and Some Priceless Credibility," *People Magazine*, August 10, 1981.

[9] Alan Greenblo, a South African financial journalist, wrote an explosive exposé on Kerzner and Sun International titled *Kerzner: Unauthorized*, but Kerzner successfully blocked the publication of the book in a controversial court ruling in 1997. See for example: Donald G. McNeil Jr, "Casino Owner Stops South Africa Book," *New York Times*, November 8, 1997; "How Sol Got Off the Hook," *Mail & Guardian*, October 30, 1997. Despite the book being barred from publication, the *Noseweek* tabloid published parts of the book. "Sol: The Full Monty," *Noseweek*, issue 21, March 1998.

[10] "Sol: The Full Monty," *Noseweek*, issue 21, March 1998.

Figure 7.1 Lucas Mangope and Sol Kerzner at the Sun City Golf Classic in 1982.

Bophuthatswana's Finance Minister, Leslie Young, who was a British national, defended these expenditures to the Bophuthatswana Executive Council in a 1986 letter obtained by Greenblo, explaining: "The publicity generated overseas [by the entertainers] has been great. The country has obtained wide media coverage portraying it as a peaceful and prosperous African state."[11] Young was behind many of Sun International's kickbacks, and according to Greenblo's research, Mangope asked that Sun International directly augment Young's salary, an arrangement Sun willingly agreed to do.[12] The symbiotic relationship was therefore defined by money flowing from overseas into Bophuthatswana and to Sun City, and from Sun City back to individual ministers, in exchange for international legitimacy flowing from Sun City to Bophuthatswana.

Sun City resided in an ambiguous zone. It was both a supposedly politics-free "pleasure dome" and a stalking horse for the normalization of the Bantustan independence, and this allowed Sun City to serve as an effective node of international contact for the regime. It was one whose

---

[11] "Sol: The Full Monty," *Noseweek*, issue 21, March 1998.
[12] "Sol: The Full Monty," *Noseweek*, issue 21, March 1998.

significance could be simultaneously discounted as nonpolitical entertainment for some audiences – such as wary foreign performers – while simultaneously touted as proof of international acceptance to other audiences.[13]

The controversies over Sun City need to be viewed within the context of the broader efforts to culturally isolate white Southern Africa. Katanga's short secession came and went before any comprehensive cultural or sports boycott was put into place, and though it was certainly difficult for regime officials such as Tshombe and Struelens to travel internationally, the international rejection of Katangese passports did not have the same cultural bite that it would for the other three would-be states. Following UDI, Rhodesia faced international efforts to apply a cultural boycott, especially in the area of sports. Initially allowed to participate in the 1968 Summer Olympic Games in Mexico, Rhodesia's invitation was subsequently pulled under a threat of an Olympic boycott by African states. Four years later, Rhodesia sent athletes to Munich under a compromise agreement whereby the regime agreed that its athletes would hold themselves out as British subjects, compete as "Southern Rhodesia," fly the British flag, and be accompanied by the British national anthem. Nonetheless, it was still subsequently disallowed from participating after the delegation had already arrived in Germany due to resistance from African states and black athletes.[14] A year later, the settler state was formally banned from future Olympics.[15] Due to these efforts, Rhodesia's sporting and cultural world was increasingly southward facing, with a notable exception being the controversial British Lions rugby tour of Southern Africa in 1974 which featured a match between the Lions and the Rhodesian national squad in Salisbury.[16] It was only after Rhodesia had already fallen when the cultural boycott targeting South Africa and the Bantustans increased in intensity and moved beyond sports.

---

[13] In his doctoral dissertation on the politics of performance and spectacle in Sun City, Torsten Sannar describes this tension between the purportedly nonpolitical and the inherently political nature of Sun City. Sannar, "Playing Sun City," p. 77.

[14] Neil Amdur, "Rhodesia out of Olympics after Dispute on Racism," *New York Times*, August 23, 1972.

[15] See: Charles Little, "The Sports Boycott against Rhodesia Reconsidered," *Sport in Society*, vol. 12, no. 2 (March 2011); Andrew Novak, "Rhodesia's 'Rebel and Racist' Olympic Team: Athletic Glory, National Legitimacy and the Clash of Politics and Sport," *The International Journal of the History of Sport*, vol. 23, bo. 8 (December 2006).

[16] John Reason, *The Unbeaten Lions: 1974 Tour of South Africa* (Rugby Books, London, 1974).

Anti-apartheid activists inside and outside South Africa saw the cultural boycott as a vital part of the isolation and degradation of the apartheid regime.[17] In 1968, the UN General Assembly passed resolution 2396 urging all member states to "suspend cultural, educational, sporting, and other exchanges" with South Africa.[18] Over the course of the 1970s the knot around South Africa tightened further, perhaps most visibly in the realm of international sports. This isolation led the South African press in the late 1970s to refer to their country as "the polecat of the world."[19] In 1981, the UN Special Committee Against Apartheid announced it would "initiate a register of cultural contacts with South Africa in order to promote an effective boycott."[20] Two years later, the committee published its first annual "Register of Entertainers, Actors And Others Who Have Performed in Apartheid South Africa" (listing all those who performed since January 1981). The intention of the register was to name and shame the artists in a public way. The register was seen by some entertainers to be a form of a McCarthyite "blacklist."[21] Nonetheless, it came to have a discernable impact on performers' decision-making as to whether or not it was worth it to break the boycott.[22] The *Chicago Tribune* noted in the spring of 1985 that the number of prominent white performers going to South Africa and Sun City was still high in 1983 and 1984, but "the number appears to be dwindling dramatically, replaced by lesser-knowns. Significantly, the number of prominent blacks listed for visits since 1982 has decreased to zero from previous years."[23] Overall, the cultural boycott was largely successful

---

[17] Ronnie Kasrils, "Boycott, Bricks and the Four Pillars of the South African Struggle," in Rich Wiles (ed.), *Voices from the Boycott, Divestment and Sanctions Movement* (Pluto Press, London, 2013).

[18] UNGA Resolution 2396 (December 2, 1968).

[19] See for example: "'Polecat of the World'," *Washington Post*, June 17, 1979. The sports boycott was effective where other aspects of the international effort to isolate South Africa became jumbled because, as Rob Nixon argued it, had a "narrow focus and strategic clarity." Rob Nixon, *Homelands, Harlem and Hollywood: South African Culture and the World Beyond* (Routledge, New York, 1994) p. 156.

[20] Michael Beaubien, "The Cultural Boycott of South Africa," *Africa Today*, vol. 29, no. 4 (4th Qtr., 1982) p. 7.

[21] Sean Jacobs, "The Legacy of the Cultural Boycott Against South Africa," in Kareem Estefan, Karen Cuoni, and Laura Raicovich (eds.), *Assuming Boycott: Resistance Agency and Cultural Production* (OR Books, New York, 2017) p. 25.

[22] Among those stars who appealed to the committee to have their names removed via this process were Kenny Rogers and Tina Turner. John M. Wilson, "UN's 'Register' of Performers Raises Blacklist Specter in S. Africa Boycott," *Chicago Tribune*, May 19, 1985.

[23] John M. Wilson, "UN's 'Register' of Performers Raises Blacklist Specter in S. Africa Boycott," *Chicago Tribune*, May 19, 1985.

because it struck at the core of white South Africans global identity as an outpost of Western civilization, and cutting them off from the rest of Western culture greatly damaged white morale.[24]

The public relations impact of breaking the boycott to perform or play in South Africa was known to be formidable for Western entertainers and sports figures. Some entertainers continued to tour South Africa in spite of the public relations fallout, judging perhaps that the financial rewards were worth the reputational harms and/or perhaps that their artistic message was such that they could plausibly contend that their performances were subversive of apartheid in their own way.[25] Others seemed to dispense completely with any attempt at righteous justifications. Singer Millie Jackson reportedly said in an interview during her 1980 tour of South Africa: "I am not a politician and I am not going to mix my career with politics. All I want is the money."[26] Nonetheless, there were high walls of entry to climb even if the monetary rewards were high. Jackson would later publicly express regret for playing in South Africa and struggled for years to remove this public relations stain from her name.[27]

It was upon this Southern African cultural landscape that Sun City emerged as an oasis, and as a portal to the outside world. Performing at Sun City Resort in Bophuthatswana was different than performing in South Africa proper, at least at first. Sun City Resort was able to capitalize on the widespread ignorance of African geography and politics among the performers and entertainment agents, especially American ones. Allies of the regime described Bophuthatswana as a new and independent African country, under black African leadership, without any of the visible racial segregation or markers of apartheid that would have been impossible to miss within the republic itself. Its name was hard to pronounce perhaps, but to unfamiliar ears it was not too dissimilar from Botswana, or perhaps Lesotho, both legal states. Dr. Nthato Motlana, a prominent South African anti-apartheid activist claimed that foreign stars pretended that in coming to Sun City they were not performing in South Africa when they played in what he joked was

---

[24] Jacobs, "Legacy of the Cultural Boycott," p. 26.

[25] For instance, Gerry Beckley from the band "America" made this argument. Christopher Connelly, "Apartheid Rock," *Rolling Stone*, June 10, 1982.

[26] Jackson later said her statements were intentionally twisted. Michael Beaubien, "The Cultural Boycott of South Africa," *Africa Today*, vol. 29, no. 4 (4th Qtr., 1982) p. 5.

[27] Michael Beaubien, "The Cultural Boycott of South Africa," *Africa Today*, vol. 29, no. 4 (4th Qtr., 1982).

"Bophuta-something."[28] There was good reason then that the *Chicago Tribune* referred to Sun City as "the most tempting bait to ignore the [cultural] boycott."[29]

Anti-apartheid activists tried hard to attach the same stigma to performing in Sun City as attached to South Africa. In the UN Register the pseudo-independent Bantustans were collapsed into the republic, with no distinction made between those who toured South Africa from those who only toured Sun City. Michael Beaubien makes the case that it was Millie Jackson's 1980 tour and the response it elicited within South Africa, and Sinatra's 1981 concerts in Sun City that were the major catalysts for the publication of the UN Register.[30] Ghana's permanent representative to the UN and the supervisor of the register, Victor Gbeho, said, "To be listed in a United Nations document as a collaborator with a racist regime is not an easy load to bear. Those with conscience must struggle with that."[31] But the generalized American unfamiliarity with African politics and the plausible deniability provided by the trappings of Bophuthatswanan statehood offered enough of an excuse for many marquee names to distinguish between Sun City tours and South African tours, in spite of the UN Register. In its first six years Sun City's booking agents were tremendously successful in attracting world-class performers to Bophuthatswana in contravention of the cultural boycott of South Africa.

In being a draw for foreign talent Sun City provided another function for the apartheid regime besides aiding Bophuthatswana's struggle for recognition. As one article in the *New York Times* described it: Sun City was South Africa's "window on the world."[32] This window was a way for the world to see Bophuthatswana as an independent state, but also as a way for white South Africans to escape their cultural isolation and see the world. The South African writer, Ivan Vladislavic, said the appeal of Sun City outside of its allowance of many of the taboos of the republic was that it allowed for a break from their isolation and that it "created a kind of fantasy of internationalism."[33] A well-known white South African

---

[28] Joseph Lelyfeld, "Why Bophuthatswana Needs American Stars," *New York Times*, October 12, 1982.

[29] John M. Wilson, "UN's 'Register' of Performers Raises Blacklist Specter in S. Africa Boycott," *Chicago Tribune*, May 19, 1985.

[30] Michael Beaubien, "The Cultural Boycott of South Africa," *Africa Today*, vol. 29, no. 4 (4th Qtr., 1982) p. 5.

[31] John M. Wilson, "UN's 'Register' of Performers Raises Blacklist Specter in S. Africa Boycott," *Chicago Tribune*, May 19, 1985.

[32] Joseph Lelyfeld, "Why Bophuthatswana Needs American Stars," *New York Times*, October 12, 1982.

[33] Kesting and Weskott, *Sun Tropes*, p. 41.

columnist said, "Sun City, in some ways, was something that gave us the feeling that we were connected to the outside world. But it was not true."[34] It was "a fantasy of freedom."[35]

As in many other ways detailed in this book, the Bantustans' relationship with the former High Commission Territories was formative. It was partially the Freudian "narcissism of small differences" which can explain the great hostility the HCTs felt toward the Bantustans, that the idea of equating them rendered not only the Bantustans as more legitimate but rendered the HCTs less legitimate. There were also practical financial reasons why the HCTs wanted the Bantustan project to fail.[36] Both countries were almost completely dependent upon the South African tourist market, but because they lacked a competitive advantage over South Africa in terms of "orthodox tourist attractions," this quickly led to a search for alternative angles to exploit in the tourism sector, namely in the so-called forbidden fruit genre of tourism.[37] In 1963, Swaziland legalized gambling, and the Royal Swazi Spa opened in 1965 and the Holiday Inn complex following that in 1969. These operations were immediately successful and South African capital very quickly looked to Lesotho to do something similar.[38] In 1970, Lesotho opened its first casino. Throughout the 1970s "forbidden fruit" tourism from the republic to these countries boomed, and both Swaziland and Lesotho added more casinos, with Lesotho constructing a Hilton Hotel casino in Maseru in 1979-80.

This early increase in tourism money for Lesotho and Swaziland began to decline for reasons that Crush and Wellings attributed to other developments in the region – namely the emergence of rivals in the forbidden fruit tourist destinations. Upon assuming their purported independence, all the Bantustans legalized gambling. Jeffrey Sallaz explains that the laws in all four Bantustans that legalized gambling were "identical," suggesting the guiding hand of Pretoria.[39] In all the Bantustans, gambling was structured in the same way, with the head of each Bantustan given personal discretion over the distribution of property rights, and casino operators granted monopoly licenses.[40] The Bantustans offered several competitive advantages over Lesotho and Swaziland. One of these was the perception of the unfriendliness of the local populations toward

---

[34] Kesting and Weskott, *Sun Tropes*, p. 125.   [35] Kesting and Weskott, *Sun Tropes*, p. 27.
[36] Crush and Wellings, "Southern African Pleasure Periphery."
[37] Crush and Wellings, "Southern African Pleasure Periphery."
[38] Crush and Wellings, "Southern African Pleasure Periphery," p. 677.
[39] Jeffrey Sallaz, *The Labor of Luck: Casino Capitalism in the United States and South Africa* (University of California Press, Berkeley, 2009) p. 144.
[40] Sallaz, *The Labor of Luck*, p. 144.

apartheid among the HCTs. White South Africans became increasingly convinced that while the Lesotho government may have wanted them there the Basuto people certainly did not. Acts of political violence within these countries only added to this feeling, such as when the Lesotho Liberation Army bombed the Hilton Hotel in 1981.[41] To counter this perception, both Swaziland and Lesotho performed public relations campaigns to reassure their people wanted visitors from the republic.[42] The Bantustans did not have similar problems keeping their population quiescent.

There was also a convenience factor. Most tourists who visited the Basuto and Swazi casinos were from the affluent and highly populated Witwatersrand region. With the emergence of Bophuthatswana, as a new legal and economic region, its proximity to this region undercut the dominance of Lesotho and Swaziland. There were no border formalities to complicate travel, and many of the Bantustans were accessible for day-trips that were shorter than the former HCTs. Unlike Lesotho and Swaziland, the Bantustans also had the full financial backing of Pretoria, and had created economic environments with tight labor controls all designed to facilitate the flow of South African capital. Faced with the challenge of the Bantustans, Lesotho and Swaziland responded with more forbidden fruit, and explicitly marketed themselves as being more open to violating the republic's taboos, being more "salacious." This took the form of more explicit live shows and forthrightly making prostitution more accessible. Crush and Welling write: "Gambling, pornographic films (with brazen titles or, in the cases of doubt, the sub-title 'Banned in South Africa') and more informally, prostitution across the colour line, became the cornerstone of Lesotho and Swaziland's tourist attractions."[43]

Southern Africa's hotel industry had been dominated from the 1970s until the 1980s by two massive hotel chains: the Holiday Inn Group and the Southern Sun Group.[44] Before 1976, the Holiday Inn Group had a

---

[41] Crush and Wellings, "Southern African Pleasure Periphery."

[42] Crush and Wellings, "Southern African Pleasure Periphery," p. 685.

[43] Crush and Wellings, "Southern African Pleasure Periphery," p. 685. The cultural boycott of the Bantustans at times helped the former HCTs since it did not necessarily mean foreign performers did not still tour Southern African for predominantly white South African crowds. For example, the Commodores had signed to play in Sun City in 1989 but backed out when anti-apartheid groups caught wind of it. The Commodores then rescheduled to play in Botswana and Lesotho, to crowds which were reportedly mostly white South Africans anyway, who were then at least spending their money in the former HCTs. Scott Kraft, "Boycott Sounds a Sour Note: Economic Sanctions May Have More Teeth, but for Middle-Class South Africans the Cultural Curbs Have More Bite," *Los Angeles Times*, February 24, 1990.

[44] For a good overview of the casino wars, see: Crush and Wellings, "Southern African Pleasure Periphery."

monopoly on all gambling in Southern Africa. This Holiday Inn monopoly was broken by Southern Sun building two massive complexes in Bophuthatswana: Mmabatho Sun, in the newly built capital city, and Sun City. It should be recalled that the Holiday Inn was the major hotel in Umtata that played such a large role in Transkei's Independence Day planning, and that it was that same Holiday Inn where Berkeley was abducted on that strange night in 1979. In response to Sun City, Holiday Inn opened a casino resort on Transkei's Wild Coast in December 1981 in an effort to draw South Africans from Durban and surrounding areas.[45] Holiday Inn then began plans for a new complex in the KwaNdebele homeland. Southern Sun next opened a complex in Ciskei, and planned another in a Bophuthatswanan exclave near Lesotho. However, the so-called Casino Wars ended in 1983 with the Southern Sun Hotels and Holiday Inn Group merger, the new entity being renamed Sun International. The cannibalistic competition ended and the KwaNdebele and Thaba Nchu projects were shelved. Following the merger, Sun International owned every casino in Southern Africa with the exception of the Hilton Hotel casino in Maseru, Lesotho.[46] That lone casino would soon be absorbed as well, and by 1984 Sun International included eighteen hotels, twelve casinos, located in four legal states in Southern Africa – Lesotho, Swaziland, Botswana, Mauritius, as well as in all four Bantustans – Bophuthatswana, Transkei, Ciskei, and Venda. The Sun International merger left Kerzner at the apex of the Southern African tourist industry, and the jewel in the Sun King's crown remained Sun City.

Kerzer's ambitions did not end with him rising to the top of the hotel casino business in Southern Africa: He wanted to make Sun City a world-class entertainment venue. To do so he built a new 7,000-seat entertainment venue, the "Superbowl," in 1981. To inaugurate it, he boldly went straight to the Chairman of the Board, Frank Sinatra, who was paid somewhere between $1.6 million and $2 million for a nine-night stand.[47] Sinatra opening the Superbowl at Sun City was momentous for both Kerzner and for Mangope. Coming after three and a half years of

---

[45] C. M. Rogerson, "Sun International: The Making of a South African Tourismus Multinational," *GeoJournal*, vol. 22, no. 3, A New South Africa – A New South African Geography? (November 1990) p. 349.

[46] Rogerson, "Sun International," p. 349.

[47] Relaying the figure reported in the Johannesburg press, the *New York Times* reported a $1.6m payout, while *People Magazine* claimed $2m. Torsten Sannar claimed, without citation that it was a $1.79 million fee. See: Joseph Lelyveld, "Bring a Bit of Vegas to South Africa's 'Homelands'," *New York Times*, July 19, 1981; Doris Klein Bacon, "For $2 Million, a South African 'Homeland' Gets Frank Sinatra – and Some Priceless Credibility," *People Magazine*, August 10, 1981; Sannar, "Playing Sun City."

constant and universal international rejection, Sinatra's arrival was a much-needed win for the pseudo-state in terms of international exposure and legitimacy. Booking Sinatra was, as *Rolling Stone Magazine* stated, "a stunning propaganda coup."[48] *The Sunday Times* exclaimed that his concerts "put Bophuthatswana on the map in the US like nothing before."[49] Sun City's resident golf pro, Gary Player, said, "When Sol signed Frank Sinatra to come way down here, it was the biggest thing to hit this part of the world since Cecil Rhodes."[50]

Instead of running from the politics of the cultural boycott, Sinatra ran directly toward them at full speed. In playing the tour dates, Sinatra and his team had to support the Bantustan system of independence in order to back his claim that he would never play to an apartheid audience, as to deny Bophuthatswana's independence would be an acknowledgment that he violated his own publicly expressed views on performing in apartheid South Africa. Sinatra's lawyer, Mickey Rudin, affirmed that Sinatra had "always rejected South African offers" because of apartheid.[51] Sinatra himself insisted: "I wouldn't have any part of segregation. That was part of the deal here, part of the contract. I play to all – any color, any creed, drunk, sober."[52] Lee Solters, his press agent, explained:

Sinatra is playing there because we were in the Republic of Bophuthatswana and were entirely satisfied with the condition of civil rights, integration and the like. It is not a question of defending Frank Sinatra going there, but an effort to make know to the world, especially those concerned with civil rights, the importance of the independence of Bophuthatswana. We think that the establishment of Bophuthatswana as an independent country is the right step for their future development.[53]

That the Bantustan system furthered the larger aims of the apartheid state was said to be beyond the responsibility of Sinatra's people. On this point, Rudin said, "I know that whatever the motives of South Africa were in establishing this country, the result is right."[54]

---

[48] Christopher Connelly, "Apartheid Rock," *Rolling Stone*, June 10, 1982.

[49] Quoted in Jones, PhD dissertation for Loughborough University, "Mmabatho, 'Mother of the People'," p. 285.

[50] Doris Klein Bacon, "For $2 Million, a South African 'Homeland' Gets Frank Sinatra – and Some Priceless Credibility," *People Magazine*, August 10, 1981.

[51] Quoted in Joe Hamill, "Sinatra Sings for Apartheid," *American Committee on Africa* (August 1981).

[52] Doris Klein Bacon, "For $2 Million, a South African 'Homeland' Gets Frank Sinatra – and Some Priceless Credibility," *People Magazine*, August 10, 1981.

[53] Quoted in Joe Hamill, "Sinatra Sings for Apartheid," *American Committee on Africa*, August 1981.

[54] Quoted in Joe Hamill, "Sinatra Sings for Apartheid," *American Committee on Africa*, August 1981.

The Sinatra camp was clear that they hoped that their assessment of the political situation would be adopted by other artists. When first announcing the concerts, Solters said, "Sinatra's appearance at Sun City could strongly influence other entertainers who may be reluctant to perform there because they assume that Bophuthatswana is in South Africa."[55] His lawyer, Rudin, continued on this theme: "My investigations have shown that there is no reason why Frank should not come here, and I hope it will encourage other performers to come. I'm sure it will."[56] And Sinatra's arrival did open the door for others to follow.[57] Some such as Shirley Bassey and Liza Minelli specifically cited Sinatra's acceptance as allaying their concerns over playing in the controversial venue. Singer Helen Reddy, for one, admitted that Sinatra's decision cleared the way for her to perform. Her husband-manager was quoted as saying: "I knew Frank would never consent to going down there if there was any segregation at all."[58]

Anti-apartheid organizations understood the dangers posed by Sinatra breaking the boycott, and endeavored to reject Bophuthatswana's independence and maintain that the Bantustans were properly within the cultural boycott, regardless of any pronouncements from Pretoria, Mmabatho, or Sinatra. Victor Mashabela of the ANC responded to the concert announcement:

He is trying to pretend that he's going into a separate state, which it is not. We don't recognize Bophuthatswana as a separate state from South Africa, and our policy is the same as if he had agreed to perform in South Africa. Therefore we will continue to protest against such behavior.[59]

Having made their determination, the Sinatra team was not interested in what the anti-apartheid critics had to say. When asked about the objections to the tour coming from anti-apartheid organizations, Solters replied, "I couldn't give a shit about the African organizations' opinions."[60]

---

[55] Quoted in Joe Hamill, "Sinatra Sings for Apartheid," *American Committee on Africa*, August 1981.

[56] Quoted in Joe Hamill, "Sinatra Sings for Apartheid," *American Committee on Africa*, August 1981.

[57] See for example: Kitty Kelley, *His Way: The Unauthorized Biography of Frank Sinatra* (Bantam Books, New York, 2015) p. 543.

[58] Doris Klein Bacon, "For $2 Million, a South African 'Homeland' Gets Frank Sinatra – and Some Priceless Credibility," *People Magazine*, August 10, 1981.

[59] Quoted in Joe Hamill, "Sinatra Sings for Apartheid," *American Committee on Africa*, August 1981.

[60] Quoted in Joe Hamill, "Sinatra Sings for Apartheid," *American Committee on Africa*, August 1981.

While in Bophuthatswana, Sinatra was attended by a large Bophuthatswanan security force, and during the second performance, Lucas Mangope himself attended.[61] In addition, Sinatra was asked to address the Bophuthatswana parliament, and Mangope awarded him the state's highest honor, the Order of the Leopard. He was also made an honorary tribal chief, which elevated his appearance as almost equating with a visit by a head of state.[62] Mangope was effusive about the concert afterward, exclaiming: "It was the greatest performance I've ever seen."[63] While Mangope no doubt meant "performance" in the literal entertainment sense, Sinatra's concert and the spectacle it provided was also one of the greatest performative acts of statehood that Mangope could have reasonably hoped for. So it was not simply empty flattery when Mangope told Sinatra: "We consider you a king," the President told Sinatra, "King of the entertainment world."[64]

Just as Mangope's regime had hoped, Sinatra's opening of the Superbowl initially worked to "pierce the curtain of isolation and boycotts" which covered apartheid South Africa, and indeed as Joseph Lelyfeld wrote in the *New York Times*, Sinatra's concerts "has torn a gaping hole in that curtain."[65] Kerzner was quoted in the *New York Times* as saying: "If we get lucky, we may make a little money out of the Sinatra appearances but it won't be exciting money." "[But] [t]he point is that we now have a facility where we can put up superstars and do it on a straight, reasonable economic basis ... this place could be an additional draw for foreign visitors."[66] One scholar studying Sun City during the apartheid era referred to this as the "Sinatra Effect."[67] The high-water mark of Sun City as a world-class venue began with Sinatra's opening concert in 1981.[68] During this brief time in the early 1980s,

---

[61] Doris Klein Bacon, "For $2 Million, a South African 'Homeland' Gets Frank Sinatra – and Some Priceless Credibility," *People Magazine*, August 10, 1981.

[62] Doris Klein Bacon, "For $2 Million, a South African 'Homeland' Gets Frank Sinatra – and Some Priceless Credibility," *People Magazine*, August 10, 1981.

[63] Doris Klein Bacon, "For $2 Million, a South African 'Homeland' Gets Frank Sinatra – and Some Priceless Credibility," *People Magazine*, August 10, 1981.

[64] Doris Klein Bacon, "For $2 Million, a South African 'Homeland' Gets Frank Sinatra – and Some Priceless Credibility," *People Magazine*, August 10, 1981.

[65] Joseph Lelyveld, "Why Bophuthatswana Needs American Stars," *New York Times*, October 12, 1982.

[66] Joseph Lelyveld, "Bring a Bit of Vegas to South Africa's 'Homelands'," *New York Times*, July 19, 1981.

[67] Sannar, "Playing Sun City," p. 171.

[68] On one such occasion, Elton John, who was on his way out of town, sat down to play piano for his friend Rod Stewart who was just then arriving for his run at the Superbowl. Scott Kraft, "Boycott Sounds a Sour Note: Economic Sanctions May Have More Teeth, but for Middle-Class South Africans the Cultural Curbs Have More Bite," *Los Angeles Times*, February 24, 1990.

the theater operations manager remembered "it was like Vegas in the old days."[69]

Rivaling Sinatra as far as impact, both because of the different fan base and because it came several years afterward was the performance by the group Queen in 1984. *Billboard* magazine referred to its booking as "unprecedented" and "The Queen 'coup'."[70] Queen would play eleven concerts in the Superbowl over a three-week stay. Hazel Feldman, Sun City's entertainment manager, positioned Queen as part of the resort's new "policy of attracting younger audiences by bringing in more contemporary acts in addition to the traditional Las Vegas-styled artists."[71] In response to criticism for the tour, Queen's business manager responded with the same response as did most artists: "Our whole philosophy is that music transcends all else. The group has always been unpolitical, believing only in music as an international unifying medium."[72] But within a year, Sun City, which was seemingly poised to continue to attract high quality acts, became a pariah venue for foreign performers. Sinatra's concerts in 1981 and Queen's stand in 1984 formed the two bridge towers spanning between Sun City's golden years.

Kerzner's monetary ambitions and South Africa's racial ambitions interacted in complicated ways. In defending Sun City from accusations that it helped the apartheid regime, Kerzner repeatedly claimed that the experiences of an integrated Sun City undermined apartheid philosophy by normalizing desegregated public spaces for visiting white South Africans. It was argued that this demystification of interracial mixing would change minds that would never have had the opportunity to experience it beforehand. Bophuthatswana was not legally segregated, and blacks and whites were free to interact socially, which would have been difficult in most of South Africa. Overseas, Sun City explicitly marketed itself as being nonracial. For instance, British Airways' *Highlife* magazine encouraged passengers to visit Sun City because regardless of race, people at Sun City "have an equal right to lose their money on the slot machines and at the roulette tables. The races mix on the dance floor, in the restaurants and at the shows."[73] Some apartheid

---

[69] Scott Kraft, "Boycott Sounds a Sour Note: Economic Sanctions May Have More Teeth, but for Middle-Class South Africans the Cultural Curbs Have More Bite," *Los Angeles Times*, February 24, 1990.

[70] John Miller, "Queen Makes South Africa News," *Billboard*, October 13, 1984.

[71] John Miller, "Queen Makes South Africa News," *Billboard*, October 13, 1984.

[72] John Miller, "Queen Makes South Africa News," *Billboard*, October 13, 1984.

[73] Quoted in Sannar, "Playing Sun City," p. 83.

hardliners argued that Sun City was the corrupting influence that Kerzner insisted it would be.[74] To the *New York Times*, Kerzner said:

I know for a fact that there are many strong right-wing Afrikaner people that do come to this place. I think a lot of people must be learning that on this question of apartheid, it's got to be looking like change isn't too bad because they're experiencing that change right here, even down at the swimming pool. So many people come just for the day, every weekend we have 15,000 to 20,000 people and the spread is crazy. Afrikaners, English, Indians, Chinese, black people. You go to Vegas, you go to Disney, I don't think you'll find that spread of people.[75]

The question of whether Sun City's overall effect tended to bolster or undermine the apartheid project yielded complicated, and uneven answers. Some scholars argue that the experience of desegregation did not destabilize apartheid's racial ideologies as Kerzner postulated, but instead offered a steam valve that released pent-up desires of white South Africans in such a way that push for real internal reform was made less urgent. This view disregards the effects of experiencing desegregation in Sun City as merely a vacation parenthetical that could be easily compartmentalized as part of the wider Sun City fantasy world.[76] Neither was Sun City blind to race. While there were no legal color bars in the casinos, Jeffrey Sallaz describes how Sun City in particular still found ways to limit the patronage of local blacks through the banning of loitering, the use of dress codes, and fees for entering the casino on foot.[77] As it was, blacks mostly came as day-trippers while the hotel was overwhelmingly white.[78] In his examination of the casino industry, Sallaz shows that while many local blacks from the Bantustans were hired to work at these various hotel casinos, with a preference for Tswanas in Sun City, the hiring was still such that blacks tended to be employed in "back of house jobs," and never in a position of authority over whites, while the dealer and croupier jobs, those that were higher paying and more prestigious, were all for whites, and often expats hired directly from England.[79] One of Sallaz's informers, who was a casino manager from

---

[74] A Dutch Reformed minister in the Cape gave a sermon in which he said that recent deaths from flooding were directly attributable to the sinfulness happening in Sun City. Joseph Lelyveld, "Bring a Bit of Vegas to South Africa's 'Homelands'," *New York Times*, July 19, 1981.

[75] Joseph Lelyveld, "Bring a Bit of Vegas to South Africa's 'Homelands'," *New York Times*, July 19, 1981.

[76] Crush and Wellings, "Southern African Pleasure Periphery."

[77] Sallaz, *The Labor of Luck*, p. 147.

[78] Joseph Lelyveld, "Bring a Bit of Vegas to South Africa's 'Homelands'," *New York Times*, July 19, 1981.

[79] Sallaz, *The Labor of Luck*, p. 157. This began to change with a top-down effort to hire "local labor" for the casino jobs in the late 1980s (pp. 179–184).

South Africa, said, "As a rule, blacks were never to touch a [gambling] chip."[80]

Sun City understood the propaganda advantages of foreign black performers coming to Bophuthatswana, and were willing to pay above market, sometimes for performers past their prime in the West. American singer Millie Jackson, who herself performed in Sun City, flatly said, "American blacks who are forgotten here [in the United States] have the chance to go there and make some money. Brook Benton was over there when I was. When was the last time you heard from him? Brook Benton's not going to South Africa isn't going to solve any problems."[81] Black performers who visited Sun City were the targets of "especially harsh judgements" from anti-apartheid activists, presumably because their positionality ought to have made them even more aware of the inequities of the apartheid system and even more motivated not to give South Africa any succor or comfort.[82] For example, in response to an invitation for the Harlem Globetrotters to play in Sun City, a well-known white anti-apartheid activist, Richard Lapchick, then an advisor to the UN Special Committee Against Apartheid, said of blacks touring South Africa: "It's one thing for the South Africans to bring a series of white entertainers there because one might expect you could get whites who don't care about the racial issue, but when you get black athletes it's another thing."[83] Black South Africans also targeted black American artists for touring South Africa, particularly for what some black South Africans claimed was either political naivety or downright greed.[84] One columnist in the *Sowetan* paper wrote in the early 1980s: "We are just about getting disgusted with the same stories given by various black American artists who perform here, particularly those who profess an astonishment that blacks are living under dubious conditions. It would be much more honest for artists from abroad to come out straight with the truth. They have come for the money."[85] This created

---

[80] Sallaz, *The Labor of Luck*, p. 134.

[81] Christopher Connelly, "Apartheid Rock," *Rolling Stone*, June 10, 1982.

[82] Sannar, "Playing Sun City," p. 203.

[83] Quoted in Ronald Jackson II, "African American Athletes, Actors, Singers, Performers, and the Anti-Apartheid Movement, 1948–1994," PhD dissertation, Michigan State University (2018) p. 207.

[84] Ronald Jackson, who studied the histories of black American entertainers and the anti-apartheid movement, divided black American artists and entertainers' responses to the South African cultural boycott into four groups: the leaders of the movement; the "staunch adherents" of the boycott; those who broke the boycott but recanted; and finally those who were unapologetic about breaking the ban. Jackson, "African American Athletes, Actors, Singers, Performers, and the Anti-Apartheid Movement," p. 7.

[85] Quoted in Michael Beaubien, "The Cultural Boycott of South Africa," *Africa Today*, vol. 29, no. 4 (4th Qtr., 1982) p. 15.

for many a heightened responsibility for blacks to abide by the boycott, something not necessarily even expected of foreign whites. Being discriminated against at home and now burdened with a heightened duty to fight discrimination abroad therefore put black performers and artists in a double-bind.

Some black foreign entertainers opposed the boycott. Singer Sharon Redd, who was booked on a South African tour to replace Millie Jackson, pushed back against the backlash and specifically the UN Register. Redd was quoted in *Billboard* magazine as saying: "I am a blacklist. Being black is a blacklist itself."[86] Shirley Bassey also lashed out at her UN critics: "I'll go to Africa if I want to."[87] She pointed to Sinatra as part of her defense: "I did nine shows in Sun City in Bophuthatswana in southern Africa, where Frank Sinatra appeared in August. I think he's going to be on the blacklist too. Now I'm a singer, not a politician, but Bophuthatswana is a separate state with its own president and king. I think the UN owes me an apology." It would be too tempting to attribute the motivations of the singer of "Diamonds are Forever" to simple material greed, as she asserted that she was truly convinced that Bophuthatswana was a separate entity from South Africa and she was entitled to perform.

Adding to this tension was that some white artists were more progressive on anti-apartheid policies and more abiding of the boycott than some black artists. This inversion complicated the seemingly clear racial lines of the apartheid conflict. "Little Steven" Van Zandt, who organized the "Sun City" project discussed below, was interviewed by the associate editor of *Jet*, a magazine with a focus on black American culture: "What's a nice New Jersey White boy like you doing orchestrating what TV's Phil Donahue described as 'the most politically aggressive movement in rock n' roll' with your anti-apartheid anthem, Sun City?" Van Zandt replied, "Well, I guess my mama taught me a lot of things when I was growing up, but she forgot to teach me that I was White. She didn't spend a lot of time on that part of the education."[88] There are several layers of possible meaning behind Van Zandt's reply, even to what extent it should be taken as anything more than breezy persiflage, but at the very least it speaks to the idea that unlike blacks, whites had no special obligation to

---

[86] Suzanne Brenner, "Blacklist: Despite Threats, Artists Continue to Accept South African Bookings," *Billboard*, March 5, 1983.

[87] "Shirley Bassey Blasts UN's Blacklisting Her for Date in So. Africa," *Jet*, December 17, 1981.

[88] Robert E. Jackson, "Rock Star Says, 'Mama Forgot to Teach Me That I Was White;' Helped Raise Millions to Fight Racism," *Jet*, March 17, 1986.

prioritize racism as a problem to address, and those who did were exceptional.

Sports were another site of contest in the struggle over Bophuthatswanan sovereignty. The major boycott-busting sport associated with Sun City was boxing. Boxing had long been associated with gambling and the casino venues of Las Vegas and Atlantic City. With its notoriously shady promoters, competing regulatory bodies, and massive one-time payouts, the sport was naturally more amenable to breaking any sort of boycott because of the cash incentives offered from someone like Kerzner. But it was not the only high-profile sporting event pursued by Sun City.[89] A million-dollar tennis match was scheduled to be played in Sun City on December 6, 1980 between Bjorn Borg and John McEnroe. The appeal of the Sun City match to tennis fans and the wider sports world was obvious, and the potential payout to the players was described by Arthur Ashe as being "gargantuan."[90] In the United States, NBC-TV was going to televise the match. Both Borg and McEnroe were guaranteed $600,000 to play and the winner would get an additional $150,000, in addition to a share in the television rights money.[91] Several prominent black Americans, including fellow professional tennis player and activist Arthur Ashe, reached out to McEnroe urging him not to play.[92] On his end, Borg was greeted with a front-page picture on Sweden's most influential evening paper, the *Express*, with a headline reading: "Don't Do It."[93] Nonetheless, Borg was apparently still willing to go ahead with it. According to his business manager, Borg "… was ready to do it, flak or no flak. Bjorn believes that politics should not enter into sport and is not involved in politics in any way. He just wants to play tennis. Hell, he can't even pronounce Bophuthatswana."[94] But at the last minute, McEnroe bowed out.[95] Ashe, who had been a vocal critic of apartheid for a number of years, praised the decision to cancel the match, writing a column for the *Washington Post* afterward titled: "Morality triumphs over money."[96]

---

[89] Professional golf events provided another potential hole in the cultural boycott. Over the New Year's holiday in 1981/1982, Sun City hosted the "Sun City Million Dollar Challenge," a 72-hole event that was at the time the richest payout in golf history. The event became a regularized stop on the golf circuit. Glenne Currie, "Record $1 Million Purse," UPI wire, December 29, 1981.

[90] Arthur Ashe, "Morality Triumphs over Money," *Washington Post*, October 26, 1980.

[91] Arthur Ashe, "Morality Triumphs over Money," *Washington Post*, October 26, 1980.

[92] Neil Amdur, "South Africa Is out for Borg-McEnroe," *New York Times*, October 17, 1980.

[93] Arthur Ashe, "Morality Triumphs over Money," *Washington Post*, October 26, 1980.

[94] Arthur Ashe, "Morality Triumphs over Money," *Washington Post*, October 26, 1980.

[95] Neil Amdur, "South Africa Is out for Borg-McEnroe," *New York Times*, October 17, 1980.

[96] Arthur Ashe, "Morality Triumphs over Money," *Washington Post*, October 26, 1980.

In the article he described Bophuthatswana as "one of two phony independent nation-states that have been forced upon unwilling black South Africans ..."[97] He added that "the other phony mini-state is the Transkei." This comment prompted Leslie Masimini, Transkei's pseudo ambassador to the Americas, to pen a letter to the editor defending the authenticity of Transkei against Ashe's attack (Masimini was silent as to the phoniness of Bophuthatswana).[98]

Two years before the ill-fated Borg/McEnroe match, Kerzner very nearly landed the biggest name in boxing history. In 1978, Leon Spinks announced he was going to fight Muhammed Ali in a rematch for the heavyweight title. There were early plans to locate the fight in Sun City. Using the sport of boxing, and especially the towering figure of Muhammed Ali, to legitimize the contested state is not too dissimilar to the use of the Muhammed Ali versus George Foreman fight, the legendary "Rumble in the Jungle," to legitimate Mobutu Sese Seko's controversial regime in the Congo in 1974. In response to the Sun City proposal, many black American political leaders loudly denounced the plan, with Reverend Jesse Jackson declaring: "Louis fought Schmelling to free us from the midst of inferiority and this fight would declare us to be inferior all over again."[99] Due to pressure from activists, the fight's location was changed to New Orleans. Afterward, Butch Lewis, the boxing promoter behind the Spinks/Ali fight, said that Bophuthatswana was presented to Top Rank Inc. as an independent country, having nothing to do with South Africa, but "as soon as I saw the political situation, we changed."[100]

The racial politics were more murky with a series of fights between two South African Afrikaner heavyweight fighters and their black American opponents. Together these brought international attention to Bophuthatswana and temporarily centered Sun City as a world-recognized boxing venue. Just as the big Superbowl concerts no doubt helped to legitimize the Bantustan system in the broad sense, and thereby further the goals of apartheid, so too did these high-profile boxing matches. But in these raw spectacles of physical combat, they also

---

[97] Arthur Ashe, "Morality Triumphs over Money," *Washington Post*, October 26, 1980.

[98] Ngqondi Masimini, "There's Nothing Phony in Transkei," op-ed, *Washington Post*, October 26, 1980.

[99] Quoted in Jackson II, "African American Athletes, Actors, Singers, Performers, and the Anti-Apartheid Movement," p. 190.

[100] In May 1982, Sun City invited the Harlem Globetrotters to come, and they agreed to play four games at the resort. Under pressure from anti-apartheid organizations the Globetrotters eventually canceled the tour. Jackson II, "African American Athletes, Actors, Singers, Performers, and the Anti-Apartheid Movement," p. 191.

provided opportunities for black Americans and black South Africans to confront and do battle with white Afrikaners in a metaphorical sense. The symbolism of these fights again invoked the symbolism of the famous Joe Louis versus Max Schmeling fights in the 1930s in a way quite different from the way Jesse Jackson referenced them.

The first Bophuthatswanan heavyweight fight was held in Mmabatho between a black American, "Big John" Tate and a former South African policeman, Kallie Knoetze. The fight took place in June 1979 in Mmabatho's makeshift open-air Independence Stadium in front of a mostly black crowd of over 50,000.[101] It was reported that the boxing crowd was bigger than the country's Independence Day celebrations held only a year and half before.[102] Kerzner apparently paid promoter Bob Arum, who would later be behind several high-profile fights in South Africa, $675,000 for the rights.[103] His quote as to the rationale for organizing the fight was quite telling: "We expect to lose $250,000, but it will be worth it to put the place on the map."[104] It is worth noting that Sinatra's visit to Bophuthatswana two years later was also celebrated in those exact terms, for "putting Bophuthatswana on the map." Many years later in an interview, a columnist for the *Sunday Times*, Gwen Gill, said of Kerzner: "Look, I can't remember that anybody was turning around and saying Sol Kerzner is a good guy. Sol was always a hero in this country. I mean, whatever he did, he put South Africa on the map of the entertainment world ... [Kerzner] built what became an Entertainment Centre known worldwide."[105]

Having the Tate/Knoetze fight in Mmabatho was a promotional boon to Mangope's fledgling regime and a commemorative postage stamp was created to memorialize the event. After Tate won, the streets of Mmabatho were reportedly filled with celebrating Bophuthatwanans. Tate's manager addressed the controversy of fighting in the contested state: "John loves his color and loves his people, but he went over there just to whip one guy, Knoetze, because he was ranked No. 1. He did it, against the worst kind of psychological warfare."[106]

Even before the Superbowl was built, Sol Kerzner was successful in securing Sun City as a Las Vegas-style boxing venue. On October 25, 1980, he arranged a heavyweight title fight between Mike Weaver, a black American Vietnam veteran, and Coetzee to take place in Sun City.

---

[101] Dave Brady, "A Loss for Apartheid," *Washington Post*, June 8, 1979.
[102] Pat Putnam, "It was One Giant Win for Big John," *Sports Illustrated*, June 9, 1979.
[103] Pat Putnam, "It was One Giant Win for Big John," *Sports Illustrated*, June 9, 1979.
[104] Pat Putnam, "It was One Giant Win for Big John," *Sports Illustrated*, June 9, 1979.
[105] Kesting and Weskott, *Sun Tropes*, p. 120.
[106] Dave Brady, "A Loss for Apartheid," *Washington Post*, June 8, 1979.

The Weaver/Coetzee fight was in front of a predominately white crowd of 17,000 in a newly constructed open-air pavilion on the grounds of Sun City.[107] Coetzee, the overwhelming favorite of the crowd, was led into the ring by a chorus girl from the "Sun City Extravaganza" carrying a South African flag and donning headdress of orange feathers, "a pair of net stockings, some sequins, and very little else."[108] After the introductions, the crowd reportedly stood respectfully for the Bophuthatswanan national anthem.[109] In the United States, CBS aired the Weaver/Coetzee fight on 6-hour delay.[110] Weaver would go on to win the fight by knockout in the 13th round and retain his title. Like Tate, Weaver was denounced for fighting in contravention of the boycott. When asked about the anti-apartheid activists who criticized his decision to go fight in Sun City, he replied, "They weren't with me when I was down."[111]

Sun City would play host to another heavyweight boxing match in 1984, again with Coetzee, again against a black American, and again ending with Coetzee being knocked out. Unlike the Weaver/Coetzee bout, the fight against Greg Page was in the Superbowl. Boxing promoter Don King was behind this fight. Only two years before, Ashe and King had been among the charter signatories of the Artists and Athletes Against Apartheid, and King had even labeled his promoting rival Bob Arum, who had been behind the Weaver fight and other bouts in South Africa, the "Apostle of Apartheid."[112] Yet King had arranged for the then World Boxing Association heavyweight champion Gerrie Coetzee to fight Greg Page in Sun City. Arthur Ashe said that Don King had been "the most influential signatory to our [organization's] position, since boxers are the most likely athletes to be invited to South Africa, boxers and tennis players."[113] Publicly, Ashe lamented that their successes in

---

[107] Joseph Lelyveld, "Weaver Retains Title on Knockout," *New York Times*, October 26, 1980.

[108] Joseph Lelyveld, "Weaver Retains Title on Knockout," *New York Times*, October 26, 1980.

[109] Joseph Lelyveld, "Weaver Retains Title on Knockout," *New York Times*, October 26, 1980.

[110] "Stadium Construction Continues as Weaver-Coetzee Title Fight Nears," *Austin American Statesman*, October 23, 1980.

[111] Joseph Lelyveld, "Weaver Retains Title on Knockout," *New York Times*, October 26, 1980. Weaver was also defended by one of Bophuthatswana's hired public relations firms in an op-ed in the *New York Times*. Adrienne Strelzin, "On Bophuthatswana," *New York Times*, op-ed, December 20, 1980.

[112] Michael Katz, "King Angers Ashe on South Africa Deal," *New York Times*, November 8, 1984.

[113] This would presumably be because they were individual sports amenable to one-off exhibitions and matches and not subject to any governing sports league. Michael Katz, "King Angers Ashe on South Africa Deal," *New York Times*, November 8, 1984.

convincing black athletes not to go to South Africa were going to be undermined by the fight: "As far as I know, Page is the only one who slipped through in the last 12 months." But for Don King, Ashe was convinced that Page would not have agreed to fight in South Africa.[114] Muhammed Ali, Larry Holmes, and Sugar Ray Leonard had all been offered large sums to fight in South Africa, but had refused, Ashe relayed. Never one to apologize, Don King replied, "I'm against apartheid today, and I was against apartheid yesterday. I'm not going to South Africa. All I did was sell my rights [promotional rights to the bout to Sol Kerzner]." Former heavyweight champion, Larry Holmes, said in response: "I think King should be ashamed of himself. He's always talking about his principles. It seems he sold 'em. If a man's got principles, you can't buy 'em."[115]

The major downturn in Sun City's ability to attract foreign talent came in 1985 after the successful release by Steven Van Zandt's Artists United Against Apartheid (AUAA) of the "Sun City" song and music video, which was accompanied by a full album and educational booklet.[116] The project brought together fifty-four musicians across the spectrum of genres from hip-hop to jazz to reggae to folk to rock and roll in what music writer David Marsh described as "probably the most diverse group of musicians ever assembled for any purpose."[117] Thereafter, musicians could no longer plead ignorance as to the applicability of the cultural boycott on apartheid applying equally to Sun City in Bophuthatswana as it did to South Africa. As the fourth verse of the AUAA lyrics attest:

> Bophuthatswana is far away
> But we know it's in South Africa no matter what they say
> (no matter what they say)
> You can't buy me, I don't care what you pay
> Don't ask me, Sun City, because I ain't gonna play

To Lucas Mangope, Kerzner, and the apartheid state's great annoyance, most big name acts took their cues from the chorus of the song: "I ain't gonna play Sun City!"

[114] Michael Katz, "King Angers Ashe on South Africa Deal," *New York Times*, November 8, 1984.

[115] Michael Katz, "King Angers Ashe on South Africa Deal," *New York Times*, November 8, 1984.

[116] See: Jennifer Bratyanski, "Mainstreaming Movements: The US Anti-apartheid Movement and Civil Rights Memory," PhD dissertation, University of North Carolina at Greensboro (2012).

[117] David Marsh, *Sun City by Artists United Against Apartheid: The Making of the Record* (Penguin Books, New York, 1985) p. 16.

The brainchild behind "Sun City" was "Little Steven" Van Zandt, most famously of Bruce Springsteen's E Street Band. Initially, Van Zandt had been among those who questioned the need for the cultural boycott of South Africa, and had visited the country in 1984 after one of his solo albums was released. However, Van Zandt returned to South Africa shortly thereafter and was able to speak with some anti-apartheid leaders. The most consequential part of this return trip for Little Steven was his short side-trip to the Sun City resort in what was ostensibly Bophuthatswana. The disparity between the glamour and the glitz of the Las Vegas-style resort so close to the shanty towns and poverty just miles away was reportedly too much for him to bear. Describing the impact of the visit, Van Zandt later said, "The mind-boggling aspects of it really got me there. I got sick, as sick as I've ever gotten in my life. The doctor said it was not something I ate or drank, it was just psychological – the old tourist-in-hell syndrome."[118] It was when he was down in South Africa, with the experiences of apartheid still fresh in his mind, when Little Steven began writing what would become the "Sun City" album.[119] "Sun City" was so effective because it was not only a catchy single, but because of its provocative use of the then still relatively new medium of Music Television (MTV) to promote its political message. The visually arresting video debuted on October 31, 1985, and entered twenty-six million homes across the United States.[120] Unlike the other star-studded charity benefits of the mid-1980s, this was more a call for political action than a fundraiser, and its intention was to educate the public and other artists about the Bantustans and the cultural boycott, and to discourage future tours to Sun City.[121]

The effectiveness of the "Sun City" project obviously angered Kerzner and had the effect of unraveling the normalizing effect of Sinatra and the performers who followed him. By and large, the big names stopped coming. The casino magnate's luck began to run out in other ways. His corrupt dealings that had served him so well in Bophuthatswana ended with his getting caught in a serious bribery scandal over the summer of 1986–1987 involving Sun International illegally transferring large sums of money to Transkeian officials, in particular the Matanzima brothers,

[118] Marsh, *Sun City by Artists United Against Apartheid*, p. 25.
[119] Marsh, *Sun City by Artists United Against Apartheid*, p. 25.
[120] Bratyanski, "Mainstreaming Movements," p. 168.
[121] Bratyanski, "Mainstreaming Movements," pp. 154–155.

to secure monopoly casino rights in Transkei. This Transkeian bribery scandal forced Kerzner into exile from South Africa for a number of years.[122] Asked about Sun City thirty years after its founding (and after the Transkeian bribery charges were finally dropped), Kerzner was defensive and returned back to the effect of the "Sun City" song.

[Sun City] was a place all South Africans could enjoy irrespective of their race. "Sun City" [the anti-apartheid song] was a cheap shot. I met Nelson Mandela after he was released and asked him what he thought of Sun City. He said: "I thought creating thousands of jobs would be very useful and would help when I get released." I'd do it all again.[123]

Some years after the boycott really began to bite in Sun City, a melancholy picture was painted by the *Los Angeles Times*: "The bright stars have disappeared from the Superbowl marquee."[124] The article's author observed that the massive stage with its expensive sound system which had formerly boasted big name entertainment, was then preparing for a Tupperware convention and later a dog show. Hazel Feldman, the booking agent for Sun City said of the downturn: "We're treated like a leper with AIDS."[125]

---

[122] The corruption charges were finally dropped under controversial circumstances in 1997, the very same year Kerzner also managed to block the publication of Greenblo's biography of him which alleged extensive corruption beyond that which occurred in Transkei. Even so, the dark cloud of these scandals continued to follow him as Sun International expanded outward from Southern Africa. See for example: Mary Braid, "Sun King of Sin City Rises above Bribery Charge," *The Independent*, April 19, 1997; "How Sol Got Off the Hook," *Mail & Guardian*, October 30, 1997; Greg Myre, "Corruption Scandal," AP wire, January 18, 1989; "The Great Casino Cash-in: The Sun King (and His Shady Past)," *The Independent*, February 1, 2007; Research Staff, South African Institute of Race Relations, Race Relations Survey 1988/1989 (Johannesburg, 1989); "Nel Tells Why He Dropped Kerzner Prosecution," *Mail & Guardian*, May 6, 1997; David Cohen, "The Man after Our Casinos," *London Evening Standard*, September 24, 2002; Hennie Van Vuuren, "Apartheid Grand Corruption: Assessing the Scale of Crimes of Profit in South Africa from 1976 to 1994," Report prepared by civil society at the request of the Second National Anti-Corruption Summit, May, 2006.

[123] Ray Charles, "20 Questions: Sol Kerzner, Kerzner International," *Financial Times*, May 6, 2010.

[124] Scott Kraft, "Boycott Sounds a Sour Note: Economic Sanctions May Have More Teeth, but for Middle-Class South Africans the Cultural Curbs Have More Bite," *Los Angeles Times*, February 24, 1990.

[125] Scott Kraft, "Boycott Sounds a Sour Note: Economic Sanctions May Have More Teeth, but for Middle-Class South Africans the Cultural Curbs Have More Bite," *Los Angeles Times*, February 24, 1990.

8   Conclusion

Reactionary Statehood in Africa

Looking back from a vantage point of more than twenty-five years after
the end of apartheid, it can be seen that the individual struggles for
sovereignty of Katanga, Rhodesia, Transkei, and Bophuthatswana can
be usefully read together as individual chapters in a larger story.
Combined, they tell of a two-and-a-half-decade long ideological project
undertaken by various opponents of pan-ethnic African nationalism
within these territories themselves, each one driven in part by its own
local concerns and parochial logics, but each one also relying upon the
support of certain political and economic forces in Southern Africa and
networks of individuals and organizations in the West. In retrospect, this
common project takes the shape of a scramble to try to preserve what
could be preserved of the old order in Southern Africa, economically,
socially, culturally, and politically. Constrained by the radically changed
circumstances of postcolonial Africa, these enemies of African nationalism were forced to acknowledge at least some of the changed international dynamics, namely, the triumph of the nation-state in Africa.
As a result, these four reactionary movements each adopted and coopted the language and aesthetics of decolonization in an attempt to
obscure the nature of this project. All those with a stake in the African
state system succeeding or failing, from inside and outside Africa, recognized at the time the significance of these challenges and this raised the
stakes of their struggles for sovereignty to regional and even global
concerns.

The larger story of these four reactionary independence bids has been
told in this book through a series of small, seemingly unconnected, flash
points. But it was in these flash points where the claims and counterclaims, representations and counter representations, and performances
and counter performances over their sovereignty were contested. When
these contests are plotted out, they form an identifiable shape of the
reactionary ideological project behind these four individual struggles
for legal statehood. One site of contest in these battles over claims to
statehood was in the details over the aesthetics and performances of their

independence days and subsequent commemorations. As explained in Chapter 3, each of the four used the occasions of their independence days and commemorations to establish the trappings, symbols, and rituals of statehood and nationhood to project to various audiences inside their territories, across Africa, and overseas that these would-be states were legitimate and popular expressions of self-determination, that they were fully functioning states, and that their cases for sovereignty were justified and sympathetic. To further these goals, these regimes purposely attached themselves to recognizable aesthetico-ideological lineages: this included mimicking the midnight flag-swapping of the Indian and Ghanaian models; holding martial parades and military reviews; for Transkei and Bophuthatswana this also meant fiery Lumumba-inspired independence day speeches in front of the mother state's representatives; and for Rhodesia, the mirroring of American Revolutionary imagery and symbols.

Beyond the inventions and performances of their new national rites, all four aspirant states actively sought diplomatic recognition through every available means, as described in Chapter 4. All four were met with international policies of nonrecognition at the state level and international organization level, and for Rhodesia and the Bantustans this nonrecognition was even preemptive. Each case of rejection had the effect of making subsequent rejections easier and more formulaic for the international community to put into place. All four also faced quarantines blocking them from most formal channels of communication to directly make their cases for statehood. Against this unwelcoming international environment each fruitlessly pursued nontraditional means to win acceptance, end arounds through unofficial contacts, which often resulted in scams and frauds that embarrassed the regimes in power. Nonetheless, they were forced to continue to search for acceptance even as it became clear that this was a futile exercise.

The most visible of flash points overseas were the battles over the establishment of foreign missions and the legal statuses of their representatives, outlined in Chapters 5 and 6. There was a remarkable amount of similarity between how these four established their missions, the domestic controversies they caused in the host countries, and the American, Belgian, British, Portuguese, and South African governments' uneasy accommodations of them. These foreign missions were allowed to function within certain constrained circumstances and were a source of constant political friction within the host state between proponents and opponents of these regimes. Ultimately the host governments negotiated their presence through a series of finely calibrated compromises that balanced competing domestic political demands from the right and the left while complying with domestic constitutional and legal restrictions and maintaining the framework of the diplomatic quarantine.

Chapter 7 shifted the focus slightly to analyze the most famous of all these contested states' nodes of international interaction: Sun City Resort. The resort was an ostensibly nongovernmental private enterprise explicitly dedicated to exploiting the economic benefits of being on the "pleasure periphery" of apartheid South Africa. But it was also in practice and by design a primary means of legitimating the independence of the Bophuthatswanan state. Though the names and events were no doubt splashier than in the other sites of contest, Bophuthatswana used Sun City as a means to break out of its international quarantine and achieve recognition as an independent entity much as these four used their official foreign missions. Despite its early successes, the cultural boycott of South Africa and the collective nonrecognition of the Bantustans combined to choke off even this final node of the state by the mid-1980s. While it was never completely shuttered and moth-balled like Rhodesia House was in the 1970s, after the mid-1980s Sun City moved out of the international limelight and ceased to attract the international attention it once enjoyed. The setting of Sun City in the mid-1980s marks the chronological end of the book.

The commonalities of Katanga, Rhodesia, Transkei, and Bophuthatswana are only partially attributable to the participants recognizing that their individual movements were like some and unlike others in fundamental respects or the same individuals involved supporting or opposing multiple of these movements. As argued in Chapter 2, it is more significant that the discourses around these four states create a distinct discursive web, the shape of which can be discerned clearly from a wider historical view. If the flash points described above can be envisioned as plotting out the perimeters of Katanga, Rhodesia, Transkei, and Bophuthatswana's sovereign expressions, then this discursive web filled out this shared ideological shape. All four aspirant states rested their legitimacy in part on a conception of African authenticity that ran completely counter to that professed by most African nationalists and postcolonial African leaders, one that privileged ethnicity, tribal linkages, and traditional patriarchal authorities over that of civic patriotism and pan-ethnic loyalties. All four also expressed their natural affinities with the West, economically, ideologically, and culturally, even though out of frustration with the West's denial of recognition Katanga and Transkei at times suggested they might turn to the Eastern Bloc for help.

These four pseudo-states all made arguments asserting that independent Africa under African nationalist rule had been almost universally a disaster, and that their claims for statehood were objectively superior to the rest of the legal states of postcolonial Africa. Their collective attacks on postcolonial African governance had the effect of gathering and generalizing disparate stories across time and space about the failings of various postcolonial African states and knitting them together into a wider narrative of continental failure, something that tapped into the already growing Western disillusionment with postcolonial Africa.[1] While these would-be states and their friends abroad did not invent these bad African stories, in their packaging and combining of decontextualized individual examples they played a role in helping to create the dominant story in the West of the failure of African governance as a continental paradigm.[2]

That these four were related movements pursuing a common ideological project does not imply that they were completely artificial creations, with no internal logic, and directed from abroad by a single guiding hand or hands.[3] There was no conspiracy guiding them, no smoky map-filled room from which these movements were all orchestrated. Apartheid South Africa, which strongly supported the Bantustans, only cautiously lent its support to Katanga and Rhodesia, always weighing the benefits of supporting these aspirant states and the underlying reactionary project they each were manifestations of, against the potential dangers this support posed for the republic itself. As explained in previous chapters, each of these four was unique and they emerged out of their own particular contexts, with their own parochial concerns, and could rely on some degree of internal support. Neither does it imply that all who supported these aspirant states identified their individual independence movement as being part of a larger project. Individuals who supported these pseudo-states inside and outside Africa numbered in the thousands, were spaced out over several decades, and were distributed across the globe. Many did know each other, many more did not, and could not have.

Supporters of these regimes within the territories themselves often had their own reasons to throw their lot in with the secessionist regime having nothing to do with the furtherance of a larger ideological project – and they very well might have opposed the aims of the larger project. This

---

[1] See Staniland, *American Intellectuals*, chapter 4.

[2] Staniland made a similar point: "A fashion for gloom had replaced the earlier fashion for high optimism." *American Intellectuals*, p. 266. Noer makes the argument that a pessimism about the future of Africa was already affecting liberals even before Kennedy's assassination. Noer, *Soapy*, p. 273.

[3] There were efforts at military coordination between South Africa, Rhodesia, and Portugal, but this was a separate issue from the reactionary ideological project described in this book. See: de Meneses and McNamara, *White Redoubt*.

would include men such as Masangu, Letlaka, and Masimini. For their part, Tshombe, Matanzima, and Mangope all endeavored to have their self-determination claims evaluated on their own merits and not be seen as part of any larger project, and for Matanzima and Mangope this meant even distancing themselves from each other and the other Bantustans. Smith was alone among the four in publicly positioning Rhodesia as part of a larger reactionary project, a worldview consistent with Luise White's observation that Rhodesia was perhaps always "more of a cause than a country."[4] This was also demonstrated in the number of active functionaries across these four regimes who were white Rhodesians, men such as Towsey, Reid-Daly, Cronje, Findlay, as well as the many unnamed mercenaries and uniformed military who identified these regimes as allied causes.

In the West, the ad hoc institutions and organizations formed to defend these would-be states typically did identify these specific independence movements as being parts of a larger project. This can be shown through the literature they produced and disseminated linking these individual movements to a larger anti-African nationalist project, as well as by the matching up of the same names that appear in the leadership of the various lobbying organizations, men such as Yergan, Rusher, and Liebman. Here, the cases of the Bantustans differ slightly. Some overseas supporters of the Bantustans were attracted to their causes because they recognized that their survival was crucial to the larger reactionary ideological project, this included men such as J. A. Parker. But other supporters, most famously Frank Sinatra, backed Bantustan independence precisely because they were *opposed* to apartheid and the wider reactionary project. Overseas opponents of these regimes typically did frame their opposition to each one in terms of their relationship to the larger reactionary project, men such as Nkrumah, Kaunda, Williams, Rowan, and Terry.

But how much did the self-conceptualization and self-identification of the historical actors involved matter? Whether or not certain individuals and groups who supported the independence of Katanga, Rhodesia, Transkei, and Bophuthatswana located their support as part of a larger project, or even supported that project, is not necessarily determinative. Historical actors at the time might think of their actions very differently than do subsequent generations. Like the parable of the blind men and the elephant, with the benefit of hindsight it is sometimes possible to

---

[4] White, *Unpopular Sovereignty*, p. 28.

discern the entire shape of the elephant unseen by historical contemporaries, who identified only the parts immediately in front of them.

In the end, the political project failed. It failed in every instance and it failed collectively. But this does not mean it did not leave an impact. In different ways, all four pseudo-states never really died. Each continue to linger on in memories or imaginations or in the ether of cyberspace among supporters inside and outside Africa. In fact, their nonexistence actually strengthens their emotive powers as lost alternatives, counter-examples, and critiques of African nationalism and postcolonial African statehood, and their appeal extended then, as now, outside their territories and in some cases outside Africa, and sometimes long after they collapsed. In their book on the history of the Katangese Gendarmes, Larmer and Kennes trace the resilience of the idea of restoring the lost Katanga nation among many Katangese as lasting long after Tshombe's Katangese secession failed in 1963.[5] Rhodesia has always had the most robust presence on the Internet among these four, energized by ex-Rhodesian emigrants and supporters of Rhodesia in the West who viewed the Smith regime as a great Lost Cause. The continued appeal of Rhodesia as a martyr continues to gather adherents, especially among white supremacists, including some who were born long after it collapsed.[6] In the past ten years, the Bantustans have themselves been the subject of an explosion of new studies that look at both the role of the Bantustans in the larger apartheid project, but also reexaminations of the Bantustans on their own merits.[7] Various essays in recent volumes have looked at the recent resurgence of nostalgia among certain populations for the era of pseudo-independence of the Bantustans, and have reexamined the degrees of popular support and legitimacy of these regimes.[8] As such, these four dead states all offer "usable pasts" that continue to be employed to further present-day political agendas.

---

[5] Kennes and Larmer, *Katangese Gendarmes*.

[6] See chapters 7 and 9 in Geary, Sutton, and Schofield, *Global White Nationalism*.

[7] This renewed interest began with the "Let's Talk About the Bantustans" Conference at the Witswatersrand University in April 2011. That conference led to a special issue in the *Southern African Historical Journal* in 2012 and an edited volume: Shireen Ally and Arianna Lissoni (eds.), *New Histories of South Africa's Apartheid-Era Bantustans* (Routledge, London, 2017). In a parallel effort there was a special issue of the *Journal of Southern African Studies* in 2015, which was made into an edited volume: Stefen Jensen and Olaf Zenker (eds.), *South African Homelands as Frontiers: Apartheid's Loose Ends in the Postcolonial Era* (Routledge, Abingdon, 2017).

[8] Leslie Bank and Clifford Mabhena, "Bring Back Kaiser Matanzima? Communal Land, Traditional Leaders and the Politics of Nostalgia," in John Daniel, Prishani Naidoo, Devan Pillay, and Roger Southall (eds.), *New South African Review 2: New Paths, Old Compromises?* (Wits University Press, Johannesburg, 2011).

The concept of state sovereignty is in part predicated on the idea that state units are the primary containers of the global system, and it is within these state units where the sharing and redistribution of certain burdens and resources can be mandated.[9] This burden and resource redistribution inevitably brings out conflicts even in the most cohesive states with highly consensual political cultures, and in less consensual political cultures with less national cohesion these inequalities of distribution can lead to political and social unrest, and possibly civil war or secession. At its core, the primary claim of all secessionists is that their region should form its own container, and the re-formed state's moral and political obligations for redistributions of burdens and resources should only extend to those within that new unit. Tshombe, for instance, vehemently disagreed with Lumumba's assertion that "the riches of the Congo [were] a common patrimony" to be shared throughout the whole country: for the Katangese, their riches were theirs alone.[10] Secessionists such as Tshombe hold that any forced redistributions outside of their region was a form of theft. Similarly, apartheid supporters saw that separating the white republic from the Bantustans saved it from the economic, political, and moral burdens of its black population.

Successful secessionist movements are rare, and since African independence, only a few alterations to Africa's borders have ever been accepted by the world community.[11] While nearly all states in the world are potentially vulnerable to secessionist or irredentist claims, the generalized antipathy toward secession globally is particularly acute among the states of sub-Saharan Africa, as the centrifugal forces pulling away from the center in African states are uniquely strong compared to other world regions.[12] One of the primary claims of this book is that exploring these

---

[9] For the origins of the state as container idea, see: Anthony Giddens, *The Nation-State and Violence* (University of California Press, Berkeley, 1987). See also: Peter J. Taylor, "The State as Container: Territoriality in the Modern World System," *Progress in Human Geography*, vol. 18, no. 2 (1994).

[10] Quoted in Irwin, "Sovereignty in the Congo Crisis," p. 206.

[11] These were dissolution of the short-lived Mali Federation in 1960, the merger of Somaliland and Somalia in 1960, the merger of Tanganyika and Zanzibar in 1964, and most recently, the creation of Eritrea in 1993 and South Sudan in 2011.

[12] Crawford Young writes: "Partly because separatism is one latent political option for cultural segments in every plural state, there is an instinctive reaction against fragmentation. The potential for splintering is highest in Africa, and here official diplomatic doctrine is most firmly set against secession." Young, *Politics of Cultural Pluralism*, p. 82. Barry Bartmann concurs, writing that the "sacred principle of territorial integrity [is] a principle particularly and frantically held by African states ..." "Political Realities and Legal Anomalies," p. 14. See also: C. Clapham, *Africa and the International System: The Politics of State Survival* (Cambridge University Press, Cambridge, 1996); J. Castellino, *International Law and Self-Determination: The Inter-*

important examples of what self-determination in Africa *was not* can be an effective way of understanding what *it was* – an outline seen through the negative spaces of what was left out, like Henri Matisse's famous paper cutouts.[13] Analyzing these four breakaway states' efforts to establish external sovereignty therefore has wider implications for studying the relationship between the parts and the whole of the African state system, between individual aspirant states' claims to sovereignty and the effects of secession on the mother country, as well as the effects of such a precedent on the stability of the whole African state system.[14] Ripping apart African states for their valuable scraps and tossing off the rest was an end feared by all those interested in preserving African independence as it was then constituted across the continent.

The corollary to the process of salvaging the valuable parts of Southern Africa was the discarding of those regions and peoples considered to be an economic, social, or political burden. It would be disingenuous to claim that it was entirely the failures of African governance that sparked this common reactionary project. Tshombe famously declared that Katanga was "seceding from chaos," but as outlined above, Katangese separatist plans long preceded Congolese independence and the chaos of those first days in July 1960. It was argued, and not without some truth behind it, that Katanga's secession was actually a cause of much of the chaos in the Congo that the secession purportedly was escaping from. Pulling apart African states in furtherance of this reactionary project held the potential to mortally wound the remainders of the states left behind. For instance, the South Africans summarized the American State Department's fear regarding Katanga's secession: "By itself Katanga would be economically viable, but not so Congo without it."[15] This same logic was flipped around in the case of the Bantustans, in which the international community saw that South Africa kept to itself all the most viable and productive parts of the country and left the Bantustans as unviable and dependent scraps. This Congolese argument was

---

play of the Politics of Territorial Possession with Formulations of Postcolonial "National" Identity (Nijhoff Publishers, The Hague, 2000) p. 189.

[13] For a legal and political analysis of the African paradigm of statehood, see: S. N. Grovogui, *Sovereigns, Quasi-sovereigns, and Africans: Race and Self-determination in International Law* (University of Minnesota Press, Minneapolis, 1996).

[14] Linda Bishai writes of secessionist movements generally as having "the potential to cause tremendous rifts in the geopolitical fabric." *Forgetting Ourselves*, p. 8.

[15] See for example: SA National Archives, Box 1/112/3/1, "Secession of Katanga," Telegram from SA Embassy in Washington to Secretary for External Affairs, July 15, 1960. The British Foreign Office felt the same: SA National Archives, Box 1/112/3/1, "Secession of Katanga," Telegram from SA High Commission to Secretary External Affairs, July 16, 1960.

extrapolated out to the rest of Africa – that it was the dual threats of ethno-regional secessionism and Western interference that were behind much of the supposed failures of African governance, both in its chaotic and repressive forms, and that these movements and the forces behind them in some ways exacerbated the very conditions upon which these aspirant states rested their moral and political claims to independent statehood. Viewed in this way, the process of salvaging actually contributed to the supposed wreckage that justified the salvaging in the first place.

The leaders of Katanga, Rhodesia, and South Africa (minus the Bantustans) argued that they owed no special duty to raise up other regions or peoples outside their own. Since the forces of the old order could no longer rule all of Southern Africa outright, there were efforts made to seize the most productive parts, leaving the rest behind to shrivel and die.

And the Lord said unto Cain, "Where *is* Abel thy brother?" He said, "I know not. *Am* I my brother's keeper?

In the rejection of these aspirant reactionary states' sovereignty, the international community held that they *were* their brothers' keepers, and the curse that the Lord put on Cain was the very same punishment as the international community put on each of Katanga, Rhodesia, Transkei, and Bophuthatswana, that they were each accursed to be:

A fugitive and a vagabond shalt thou be in the earth.[16]

---

[16] *King James Bible*, Genesis 4:9–12.

Bibliography

Primary Sources

Archives

Anti-Apartheid Movement Archives, Weston Library, Oxford University, Oxford, UK
British National Archives, Kew, UK
Gerald Ford Presidential Library, Ann Arbor, MI
Group Research Inc. Archives, Columbia University, New York, NY
Ian D. Smith Papers, Rhodes University, Grahamstown, South Africa
J. Wayne Fredericks Papers, Schomburg Center, New York, NY
James O. Eastland Papers, University of Mississippi, Oxford, MS
John F. Kennedy Presidential Library, Boston, MA
Lyndon B. Johnson Presidential Library, Austin, TX
Marvin Liebman Papers, Stanford University, Stanford, CA
Moise Tshombe Papers, Williams College, Williamstown, MA
Schomburg Center for Research in Black Culture, New York Public Library, New York, NY
Sir Roy Welensky Papers, Weston Library, Oxford University, Oxford, UK
South African Department of Foreign Affairs Archive, Pretoria, South Africa
South African National Archives, Pretoria, South Africa
Thomas J. Dodd Papers, University of Connecticut, Storrs, CT
United Nations Archive, New York, NY
United States National Archives, College Park, MD
William A. Rusher Papers, Library of Congress, Washington, DC
Winston Field Papers, Rhodes House Library, Oxford University, Oxford, UK

Media Sources

South Africa

Daily Dispatch
Mail & Guardian

Noseweek
Rand Daily Mail
Sechaba

Rhodesia/Zimbabwe

The Chronicle
Rhodesia Herald

United Kingdom

Daily Telegraph
Financial Times
The Glasgow Herald
The Guardian
The Independent
London Evening Standard
Reuters
The Spectator
The Times

United States

Associated Press
Austin American Statesman
Billboard
Chicago Tribune
The Evening Star
Jet
Lincoln Review
Los Angeles Times
Newsweek
New York Times
People Magazine
Rolling Stone
Sarasota Herald-Tribune
Sports Illustrated
United Press International
Washington Notes on Africa
Washington Post
The Week

Government Publications

"Anatomy of Terror," Rhodesian Ministry of Information (January 1974)

Foreign Relations of the United States (FRUS) (Office of the Historian in the United States State Department)

"Implications for US International Legal Obligations of the Presence of the RIO in the US," subcommittee on Africa, Foreign Affairs Committee US House of Representatives, May 15, 17, 1973

Katanga Calling

"The Murder of Missionaries in Rhodesia," Zimbabwe Rhodesia Ministry of Information (January 1978)

Reports of the Attorney General to the Congress of the United States on the Administration of the Foreign Agents Registration Act (FARA)

Rhodesia Commentary

Rhodesia Viewpoint

Rhodesian Broadcasting Corporation (RBC) "Making for Midnight," November 11, 1977. www.rhodesia.me.uk

"Visa Procedures of Department of State: The Struelens Case," *Report of the Subcommittee to Investigate the Administration of the Internal Security Act and Other Internal Security Laws to the Senate Committee on the Judiciary* (Washington: U.S. Government Printing Office, August 6, 1962)

Interviews

Ambassador Jeffrey Davidow
Barbara Cannady-Masimini
P. B. Gemma

Secondary Sources

Allman, Jean Marie, *Quills of the Porcupine: Asante Nationalism in an Emergent Ghana* (University of Wisconsin Press, Madison, 1993)

Ally, Shireen and Arianna Lissoni (eds.), *New Histories of South Africa's Apartheid-Era Bantustans* (Routledge, London, 2017)

Andereggen, Anton, *France's Relationship with Subsaharan Africa* (Praeger, Westport, 1994)

Anderson, B., *Imagined Communities: Reflections of the Origin and Spread of Nationalism* (Verso, London, 1983)

Anthony III, D. H., *Max Yergan: Race Man, Internationalist, Cold Warrior* (New York University Press, New York, 2006)

Armitage, D., *The Declaration of Independence: A Global History* (Harvard University Press, Cambridge, MA, 2007)

Arsenault, R., "White on Chrome: Southern Congressmen and Rhodesia, 1962–1971," *Issue: A Journal of Opinion*, vol. 2, no. 4 (Winter 1972)

Bank, Leslie and Clifford Mabhena, "Bring Back Kaiser Matanzima? Communal Land, Traditional Leaders and the Politics of Nostalgia," in John Daniel, Prishani Naidoo, Devan Pillay, and Roger Southall (eds.), *New South African Review 2: New Paths, Old Compromises?* (Wits University Press, Johannesburg, 2011)

Bartmann, Barry, "Political Realities and Legal Anomalies: Revisiting the Politics of International Recognition," in Tozun Bahcheli, Barry Bartmann, and Henry Srebrnik (eds.), *De Facto States: The Quest for Sovereignty* (Routledge, Oxfordshire, 2016)

Beaubien, Michael, "The Cultural Boycott of South Africa," *Africa Today*, vol. 29, no. 4 (4th Qtr., 1982)

Bereketeab, R., *Self-Determination and Secession in Africa: The Postcolonial State* (Routledge, Abingdon, 2016)

Berry, Bruce, "Flag of Defiance: The International Use of the Rhodesian Flag Following UDI," *South African Historical Journal*, vol. 71, no. 3 (2019)

Biney, Ama, *The Political and Social Thought of Kwame Nkrumah* (Palgrave Macmillan, New York, 2011)

Bishai, Linda, *Forgetting Ourselves: Secession and the (Im)possibility of Territorial Identity* (Lexington Books, Lanham, 2006)

Blake, R., *A History of Rhodesia* (Knopf, New York, 1978)

Borstelmann, T., *The Cold War and the Color Line: American Race Relations in the Global Arena* (Harvard University Press, Cambridge, MA, 2001)

Botwe-Asamoah, Kwame, *Kwame Nkrumah's Politico-Cultural Thought and Policies* (Routledge, New York, 2005)

Bratyanski, Jennifer, "Mainstreaming Movements: The US Anti-Apartheid Movement and Civil Rights Memory," PhD dissertation, University of North Carolina at Greensboro (2012)

Brewer, David, *The Greek War of Independence: The Struggle for Freedom and the Birth of Modern Greece* (Overlook Press, New York, 2011)

Briggs, H. W., "Relations Officieuses and Intent to Recognize: British Recognition of Franco," *The American Journal of International Law*, vol. 34, no. 1 (January 1940)

Brinkley, D., *Dean Acheson: The Cold War Years, 1953–71* (Yale University Press, New Haven, 1992)

Brownell, J., "Book Review: Eric Kennes and Miles Larmer, *The Katangese Gendarmes and War in Central Africa*," *Journal of Modern African History*, vol. 55, no. 3 (2017)

Collapse of Rhodesia: Population Demographics and the Politics of Race (I. B. Tauris, London, 2010)

"Diplomatic Lepers: The Katangan and Rhodesian Foreign Missions in the United States and the Politics of Nonrecognition," *International Journal of African Historical Studies*, vol. 47, no. 2 (2014)

"The Hole in Rhodesia's Bucket: White Emigration and the End of Settler Rule," *The Journal of Southern African Studies*, vol. 34, no. 3 (September 2008)

"'The Magical Hour of Midnight': The Annual Commemorations of Rhodesia's and Transkei's Independence Days," in Toyin Falola and Kenneth Kalu (eds.), *Exploitation and Misrule in Colonial and Postcolonial Africa* (Palgrave Macmillan, New York, 2018)

"Out of Time: Global Settlerism, Nostalgia, and the Selling of the Rhodesian Rebellion Overseas," *The Journal of Southern African Studies*, vol. 43, no. 4 (Fall 2016)

"'A Sordid Tussle on the Strand': Rhodesia House during the UDI Rebellion (1965–1980)," *The Journal of Imperial and Commonwealth History*, vol. 38, no. 3 (September 2010)

"The Visual Rhetoric of Settler Stamps: Rhodesia's Rebellion and the Projection of Sovereignty (1965–80)," in Yu-Ting Huang and Rebecca Weaver-Hightower (eds.), *Archiving Settler Colonialism: Culture, Space and Race (Empires and the Making of the Modern World, 1650–2000)* (Routledge, New York, 2018)

Bustin, Edouard, "Remembrance of Sins Past: Unraveling the Murder of Patrice Lumumba," *Review of African Political Economy*, vol. 29, no. 93/94, State Failure in the Congo: Perceptions and Realities (September–December 2002)

Butler, Jeffrey, Robert Rotberg, and John Adams, *The Black Homelands of South Africa: The Political and Economic Development of Bophuthatswana and KwaZulu* (University of California Press, Berkeley, 1977)

Cannadine, David, *Ornamentalism: How the British Saw Their Empire* (Oxford University Press, Oxford, 2001)

Carr, E. H., *The Twenty Years' Crisis* (Macmillan, London, 1946)

Caspersen, N., *Unrecognized States* (Polity Press, Cambridge, UK, 2012)

Castellino, J., *International Law and Self-Determination: The Inter-play of the Politics of Territorial Possession with Formulations of Postcolonial "National" Identity* (Nijhoff Publishers, The Hague, 2000)

Charumbira, R., *Imagining a Nation: History and Memory in Making Zimbabwe* (University of Virginia Press, Charlottesville, 2015)

Clapham, C., *Africa and the International System: The Politics of State Survival* (Cambridge University Press, Cambridge, 1996)

Collins, Michael, "Nation, State and Agency: Evolving Historiographies of African Decolonization" in Andrew W. M. Smith and Chris Jeppensen (eds.), *Britain, France and the Decolonization of Africa: Future Imperfect?* (University College London Press, London, 2017)

Cooke, Alistair, *Alistair Cooke's America* (Basic Books, New York, 2009)

Cooper, Frederick, *Citizenship between Empire and Nation: Remaking France and French Africa, 1945–1960* (Princeton University Press, Princeton, 2016)

Colonialism in Question: Theory, Knowledge, History (University of California Press, Berkeley, 2005)

Crawford, J., *The Creation of States in International Law* (Oxford University Press, Oxford, 2006)

Crush, Jonathan and Paul Wellings, "The Southern African Pleasure Periphery, 1966–83," *The Journal of Modern African Studies*, vol. 21, no. 4 (1983)

Davis, Morris, *Interpreters for Nigeria: The Third World and International Public Relations* (University of Illinois Press, Urbana, 1977)

DeRoche, A., *Black, White and Chrome: The United States and Zimbabwe, 1953–1998* (Africa World Press, Trenton, 2001)

De Waal, Thomas, *Uncertain Ground: Engaging with Europe's De Facto States and Breakaway Territories* (Carnegie Endowment for International Peace, Washington, DC, 2018)

DeWitte, L., *The Assassination of Lumumba* (Verso, London, 2001)

Diamond, S., *Roads to Dominion: Right-Wing Movements and Political Power in the United States* (Guilford Press, New York, 1995)

Dillard, A. D., *Guess Who's Coming to Dinner Now? Multicultural Conservatism in America* (New York University Press, New York, 2001)

Drummond, J., "Reincorporating the Bantustans into South Africa: The Question of Bophuthatswana," *Geography*, vol. 76 (1991)

Drummond, J. and A. H. Manson, "The Evolution and Contemporary Significance of the Bophuthatswana-Botswana Border," in D. Rumley and J. V. Minghi (eds.), *The Geography of Border Landscapes* (Routledge, London, 1991)

Ellis, Joseph J., *Revolutionary Summer: The Birth of American Independence* (Vintage Press, New York, 2014)

Emerson, Rupert, "The New Higher Law of Anti-Colonialism," in Karl Deutsch and Stanley Hoffmann (eds.), *The Relevance of International Law* (Schenkman Publishing, Cambridge, 1968)

Fabry, M., *Recognizing States: International Society and the Establishment of New States since 1776* (Oxford University Press, Oxford, 2010)

Falola, T., *Nationalism and African Intellectuals* (University of Rochester Press, Rochester, 2001)

Fanon, F., *Wretched of the Earth* (Grove Press, New York, 2005)

Fatton, Jr, Robert, "The African National Congress of South Africa: The Limitations of a Revolutionary Strategy," *Canadian Journal of African Studies / Revue Canadienne des Études Africaines*, vol. 18, no. 3 (1984)

Fedorowich, K. and M. Thomas, *International Diplomacy and Colonial Retreat* (Frank Cass, London, 2001)

Ferguson, James, *Global Shadows: Africa in the Neoliberal World Order* (Duke University Press, Durham, NC, 2006)

Fieldhouse, Roger, *Anti-Apartheid: A History of the Movement in Britain, 1959–1994* (Merlin Press, London, 2005)

Flower, K., *Serving Secretly: An Intelligence Chief on Record* (John Murray, London, 1984)

Geary, Daniel, Jennie Sutton, and Camilla Schofield (eds.), *Global White Nationalism: From Apartheid to Trump* (Manchester University Press, Manchester, 2020)

Geisler, M. E., "The Calendar Conundrum: National Days as Unstable Signifiers," in D. McCrone and G. MacPherson (eds.), *National Days: Constructing and Mobilising National Identity* (Palgrave Macmillan, London, 2009)

Geldenhuys, D., "International Attitudes on the Recognition of Transkei," *occasional paper given to the South African Institute of International Affairs (October 1979)*

  Isolated States: A Comparative Analysis (Cambridge University Press, Cambridge, 1990)

  Contested States in World Politics (Palgrave Macmillan, New York, 2009)

Gerard-Libois, J., *Katanga Secession* (University of Wisconsin, Madison, 1966)

Getachew, Adom, *Worldmaking after Empire: The Rise and Fall of Self-Determination* (Princeton University Press, Princeton, 2019)

Gibbs, D. N., *The Political Economy of Third World Intervention: Mines, Money, and US Policy in the Congo Crisis* (University of Chicago Press, Chicago, 1991)

Gibbs, Timothy, *Mandela's Kinsmen: Nationalist Elites and Apartheid's First Bantustan* (James Currey, London, 2017)

Giddens, Anthony, *The Nation-State and Violence* (University of California Press, Berkeley, 1987)

Gillis, J. (ed.) *Commemorations: The Politics of National Identity* (Princeton University Press, Princeton, 1996)

Godwin, P. and I. Hancock, *Rhodesians Never Die* (Oxford University Press, Oxford, 1993)

Gould, Michael, *The Biafran War: The Struggle for Modern Nigeria* (I. B. Tauris, London, 2013)

Gournay, I. and J. C. Loeffler, "Washington and Ottawa: A Tale of Two Embassies," *The Journal of the Society of Architectural Historians*, vol. 61, no. 4 (December 2002)

Grant, Thomas, *Admission to the United Nations: Charter Article 4 and the Rise of Universal Organization* (Martinus Nijhoff Publishers, Leiden, 2009)

Grovogui, S. N., *Sovereigns, Quasi-sovereigns, and Africans: Race and Self-determination in International Law* (University of Minnesota Press, Minneapolis, 1996)

Hamill, Joe, "Sinatra Sings for Apartheid," (American Committee on Africa, August 1981) JSTOR, jstor.org/stable/10.2307/al.sff.document.acoa000557

Heller, Joseph, *The Birth of Israel: 1945–1949: Ben-Gurion and His Critics* (University Press of Florida, Gainesville, 2003)

Heraclides, Alexis, *The Self-Determination of Minorities in International Politics* (Taylor & Francis, New York, 1991)

Hempstone, S., *Rebels, Mercenaries, and Dividends: The Katanga Story* (Praeger, Westport, 1962)

Heydt, Donald A., "Nonrecognition of the Independence of Transkei," *Case Western Reserve Journal of International Law*, vol. 10, no. 167 (1978)

Hillgruber, C., "The Admission of New States to the International Community," *European Journal of International Law*, vol. 9 (1998)

Hobsbawm, E. and T. Ranger (eds.), *The Invention of Tradition* (Cambridge University Press, Cambridge, 1983)

Holland, R., S. Williams, and T. Barringer (eds.), *The Iconography of Independence: "Freedoms at Midnight"* (Routledge, London, 2010)

Horne, Gerald, *From the Barrel of a Gun: The United States and the War against Zimbabwe, 1965–1980* (University of North Carolina Press, Chapel Hill, 2015)

Hoskyns, C., *The Congo Since Independence* (Oxford University Press, Oxford, 1965)

Howe, Russell Warren and Sarah Hays Trott, *The Power Peddlers: How Lobbyists Mold American Foreign Policy* (Doubleday, Garden City, NY, 1977)

Hughes, M., "Fighting for White Rule in Africa: The Central African Federation, Katanga, and the Congo Crisis, 1958–1965," *International History Review*, vol. 25, no. 3 (September 2003)

Irwin, Ryan, *Gordian Knot: Apartheid and the Unmaking of the Liberal World Order* (Oxford University Press, Oxford, 2012)

"Sovereignty in the Congo Crisis," in Leslie James and Elisabeth Leake (eds.), *Decolonization and the Cold War: Negotiating Independence* (Bloomsbury, London, 2015)

Jackson, R., *Quasi-States: Sovereignty, International Relations, and the Third World* (Cambridge University Press, Cambridge, 1991)

Jackson II, R., "African American Athletes, Actors, Singers, Performers, and the Anti-Apartheid Movement, 1948–1994," PhD dissertation, Michigan State University (2018)

Jacobs, Sean, "The Legacy of the Cultural Boycott against South Africa," in Kareem Estefan, Karen Cuoni, and Laura Raicovich (eds.), *Assuming Boycott: Resistance Agency and Cultural Production* (OR Books, New York, 2017)

James, A., *Britain and the Congo Crisis, 1960–63* (MacMillan Press, London, 1996)

Jensen, Stefen and Olaf Zenker (eds.), *South African Homelands as Frontiers: Apartheid's Loose Ends in the Postcolonial Era* (Routledge, Abingdon, 2017)

Jones, Peris Sean, "'To Come Together for Progress': Modernization and Nation-Building in South Africa's Bantustan Periphery – The Case of Bophuthatswana," *Journal of Southern African Studies*, vol. 25, no. 4 (1999)

"The Etiquette of State-Building and Modernisation in Dependent States: Performing Stateness and the Normalisation of Separate Development in South Africa," *Geoforum*, vol. 33, no. 1 (February 2002)

"Mmabatho, 'Mother of the People': Identity and Development in an 'Independent' Bantustan, Bophuthatswana, 1975–1994," PhD dissertation, Loughborough University (1997)

"From 'Nationhood' to Regionalism to the North West Province: 'Bophuthatswananess' and the Birth of the 'New' South Africa," *African Affairs*, vol. 98, no. 393 (October 1999)

Kaplan, L., "The United States, Belgium, and the Congo Crisis of 1960," *The Review of Politics*, vol. 29, no. 2 (April 1967)

Kasrils, Ronnie, "Boycott, Bricks and the Four Pillars of the South African Struggle," in Rich Wiles (ed.), *Voices from the Boycott, Divestment and Sanctions Movement* (Pluto Press, London, 2013)

Keesing's Record of World Events (formerly Keesing's Contemporary Archives), vol. 6, November 1960, Congo Republic, Belgian.

Kelley, Kitty, *His Way: The Unauthorized Biography of Frank Sinatra* (Bantam Books, New York, 2015)

Kennes, Erik and Larmer, Miles, *Katangese Gendarmes and War in Central Africa: Fighting Their Way Home* (Indiana University Press, Bloomington, 2016)

Kenrick, David, *Decolonisation, Identity and Nation in Rhodesia, 1964–1979: A Race against Time* (Palgrave, London, 2019)

Ker Lindsay, J., "Engagement without Recognition: The Limits of Diplomatic Interaction with Contested States," *International Affairs*, vol. 91, no. 2 (2015)

Kertzer, D., *Ritual, Politics, and Power* (Yale University Press, New Haven, 1988)

Kesting, Marietta and Aljoscha Weskott (eds.), *Sun Tropes: Sun City and (Post-) Apartheid Culture in South Africa* (August Verlag, Berlin, 2009)

Kohen, M. G. (ed.), *Secession: International Law Perspectives* (Cambridge University, Cambridge, 2006)

Koops, J., N. MacQueen, T. Tardy, and P. D. Williams (eds.), *Oxford Handbook of UN Peacekeeping Operations* (Oxford University Press, Oxford, 2015)

Koskoff, D., *The Senator from Central Casting* (New American Political Press, New Haven, 2011)

Koyana-Letlaka, P., *This Is My Life: A South African Journey* (Xlibris, Bloomington, 2014)

Lake, A., *The "Tar Baby" Option: American Policy toward Southern Rhodesia* (Columbia University Press, New York, 1976)

Larmer, M. and E. Kennes, "Rethinking the Katangese Secession," *Journal of Imperial and Commonwealth History*, vol. 42, no. 4 (2014)

Lawrence, Michael and Andrew Manson, "The 'Dog of the Boers': The Rise and Fall of Mangope in Bophuthatswana," *Journal of Southern African Studies*, vol. 20, no. 3, Special Issue: Ethnicity and Identity in Southern Africa (September 1994)

Liebman, Marvin, *Coming Out Conservative: An Autobiography* (Chronicle Books, San Francisco, 1992)

Little, Charles, "The Sports Boycott against Rhodesia Reconsidered," *Sport in Society*, vol. 12, no. 2 (March 2011)

Louis, Wm. Rogers, *The Ends of British Imperialism: The Scramble for Empire, Suez, and Decolonization* (I. B. Tauris, London, 2007)

Lowry, D., "The Impact of Anti-communism on White Rhodesian Political Culture, ca.1920s–1980," *Cold War History*, vol. 7, no. 2 (2007)

"The Queen of Rhodesia versus the Queen of the United Kingdom: Conflicts of Allegiance in Rhodesia's Unilateral Declaration of Independence," in H. Kumarasingham (ed.), *Viceregalism: The Crown as Head of State in Political Crises in the Postwar Commonwealth* (Palgrave MacMillan, London, 2020)

"The Ulster of South Africa," *Southern African-Irish Studies*, vol. 1 (1991)

Lupant, Michel, *Emblems of the State of Katanga, 1960–1963* (Belgian-European Flags Studies Centre (CEBED), Ottignies, Belgium, July 2004)

Mahoney, R. D., *JFK: Ordeal in Africa* (Oxford University Press, Oxford, 1983)

Mamdani, M., *Citizen and Subject: Contemporary Africa and the Legacy of Late Colonialism* (Princeton University Press, Princeton, 1996)

Manela, E., *The Wilsonian Moment: Self-Determination and the International Origins of Anticolonial Nationalism* (Oxford University Press, Oxford, 2007)

Marsh, David, *Sun City by Artists United against Apartheid: The Making of the Record* (Penguin Books, New York, 1985)

Masangu Mulongo, Jean-Claude, *Why I Believe in Africa's Progress: An African Banker's Creed* (Prestige Communication, Paris, 2011)

Mazrui, A., *Towards a Pax Africana: A Study of Ideology and Ambition* (University of Chicago Press, Chicago, 1967)

McCrone, D. and G. MacPherson (eds.), *National Days: Constructing and Mobilising National Identity* (Palgrave Macmillan, London, 2009)

McDermott Hughes, D., *Whiteness in Zimbabwe: Race, Landscape and the Problem of Belonging* (Palgrave Macmillan, New York, 2010)

McKay, V., "The Domino Theory of the Rhodesian Lobby," *Africa Report*, vol. 12, no. 6 (June 1967)

McNeil, Brian, "'And Starvation Is the Grim Reaper': The American Committee to Keep Biafra Alive and the Genocide Question during the Nigerian Civil War, 1968–70," *Journal of Genocide Research*, vol. 16, nos. 2–3 (2014)

Megahey, A., *Humphrey Gibbs: Beleaguered Governor: Southern Rhodesia, 1929–1969* (MacMillan Press, London, 1998)

de Meneses, Filipe Ribeiro and Robert McNamara, "The Last Throw of the Dice: Portugal, Rhodesia and South Africa, 1970–74," *Portuguese Studies*, vol. 28, no. 2 (2012)

    The White Redoubt, the Great Powers and the Struggle for Southern Africa (Palgrave MacMillan, London, 2018)

Michel, Eddie, "Those Bothersome Rho-dents: Lyndon B. Johnson and the Rhodesian Information Office," *Safundi*, vol. 19, no. 2 (2018)

    "'This Outcome Gives Me No Pleasure. It Is Extremely Painful for Me to Be the Instrument of Their Fate': White House Policy on Rhodesia during the UDI Era (1965–1979)," *South African Historical Journal*, vol. 71, no. 3 (2018)

Miller, J., *An African Volk: The Apartheid Regime and Its Search for Survival* (Oxford University Press, Oxford, 2016)

Minter, W., *King Solomon's Mines Revisited* (Basic Books, New York, 1986)

Mwakikagile, Godfrey, *Nyerere and Africa: End of an Era* (New Africa Press, Pretoria, 2010)

Nelson, Craig, *Thomas Paine: Enlightenment, Revolution, and the Birth of Modern Nations* (Penguin Books, New York, 2007)

Nixon, Rob, *Homelands, Harlem and Hollywood: South African Culture and the World Beyond* (Routledge, New York, 1994)

Nixon, Ron, *"The Anti-Mandela Lobby,"* *Politico Magazine* (December 8, 2013)

    Selling Apartheid: South Africa's Global Propaganda War (Pluto Press, London, 2016)

Nkala, J., *The United Nations, International Law, and the Rhodesian Independence Crisis* (Oxford: Clarendon Press, 1985) chapter 4

Nkrumah, Kwame, *Challenge of the Congo: A Case Study of Foreign Pressures in an Independent State* (Panaf Books, London, 2002)

Noer, T., *Cold War and Black Liberation: The United States and White Rule in Africa, 1948–1968* (University of Missouri Press, Columbia, 1985)

    "New Frontiers and Old Priorities in Africa," in Thomas G. Paterson (ed.), *Kennedy's Quest for Victory, American Foreign Policy, 1961–1963* (Oxford University Press, Oxford, 1989)

    Soapy: A Biography of G. Mennen Williams (University of Michigan Press, Ann Arbor, 2006)

Novak, Andrew, "Rhodesia's 'Rebel and Racist' Olympic Team: Athletic Glory, National Legitimacy and the Clash of Politics and Sport," *The International Journal of the History of Sport*, vol. 23, no. 8 (December 2006)

O'Mahoney, J., "Proclaiming Principles: The Logic of the Nonrecognition of the Spoils of War," *Journal of Global Security Studies*, vol. 2, no. 3 (July 2017)

O'Meara, Patrick, *Rhodesia: Racial Conflict or Coexistence?* (Cornell University Press, Ithaca, 1975)

Othen, C., *Katanga 1960–1963: Mercenaries, Spies, and the African Nation that Waged War on the World* (The History Press, Gloucestershire, 2015)

Parnell, Susan, "From Mafeking to Mafikeng: The Transformation of a South African Town," *GeoJournal*, vol. 12, no. 2, South Africa: Geography in a State of Emergency (March 1986)

Passemiers, Lazlo, "Safeguarding White Minority Power: The South African Government and the Secession of Katanga, 1960–1963," *South African History Journal*, vol. 68, no. 1 (2016)

Pfister, R., *Apartheid South Africa and African States: From Pariah to Middle Power, 1961–1994* (I. B. Tauris, London, 2005)

Pieres, J. B., "The Implosion of Transkei and Ciskei," *African Affairs*, vol. 91, no. 364 (July 1992)

Polakow-Suransky, Sasha, *Unspoken Alliance: Israel's Secret Relationship with Apartheid South Africa* (Vintage, New York, 2011)

Price, R. M., *Apartheid State in Crisis: Political Transformation in South Africa, 1975–1990* (Oxford University Press, Oxford, 1991)

Quentin-Baxter, A., *Rhodesia and the Law: A Commentary on the Constitutional and International Law Aspects of the Rhodesian Situation* (New Zealand Institute of International Affairs, Wellington, 1970)

Quigley, P., "Independence Day Dilemmas in the American South, 1848–1865," *Journal of Southern History*, vol. 75, no. 2 (2009)

Rafiqul Islam, M., "Secessionist Self-Determination: Some Lessons from Katanga, Biafra, and Bangladesh," *Journal of Peace Research*, vol. 22, no. 3 (September 1985)

Ranger, Terence, "Missionaries, Migrants, and the Manyika: The Invention of Ethnicity in Zimbabwe," in Leroy Vail (ed.), *The Creation of Tribalism in Southern Africa* (James Currey, London, 1989)

Reason, John, *The Unbeaten Lions: 1974 Tour of South Africa* (Rugby Books, London, 1974)

Research Staff, *South African Institute of Race Relations, Race Relations Survey 1988/89 (Johannesburg, 1989)*

Rogerson, C. M., "Sun International: The Making of a South African Tourismus Multinational," *GeoJournal*, vol. 22, no. 3, A New South Africa – A New South African Geography? (November 1990)

Rushdie, Salman, *Midnight's Children* (Random House, New York, 1981)

Ryan, J., George Dunford, and Simon Sellars, *Micro-nations: The Lonely Planet Guide to Home-Made Nations* (Lonely Planet, London, 2006)

Sack, John, *Report from Practically Nowhere: An Uproarious Account of Thirteen No-Account Countries – From Sark to Sikkim to Swat* (Harper & Bros., New York, 1955)

Sallaz, Jeffrey, *The Labor of Luck: Casino Capitalism in the United States and South Africa* (University of California Press, Berkeley, 2009)

Sannar, T., "Playing Sun City: The Politics of Entertainment at a South African Mega-Resort," PhD dissertation in Theater Studies, University of California, Santa Barbara (2011)

Scarnecchia, T., "The Congo Crisis, the United Nations, and Zimbabwean Nationalism, 1960–1963," *African Journal of Conflict Resolution*, vol. 11, no. 1 (2011)

Schofield, Camilla, *Enoch Powell and the Making of Postcolonial Britain* (Cambridge University Press, Cambridge, 2013)

Simmonds, R., *Legal Problems Arising from the United Nations Military Operations in the Congo* (Martinus Nijhoff, Leiden, 1968)

Skeen, A., *Prelude to Independence: Skeen's 115 Days* (Nasionale Boekhandel, Cape Town, 1966)

Skey, M., "'We Wanna Show 'Em Who We Are' National Events in England," D. McCrone and G. MacPherson (eds.), *National Days: Constructing and Mobilising National Identity* (Palgrave Macmillan, London, 2009)

Smith, Andrew W. M. and Chris Jeppensen (eds.), *Britain, France and the Decolonization of Africa: Future Imperfect?* (University College London Press, London, 2017)

Smith, I., *Bitter Harvest: The Great Betrayal* (Blake, London, 2001)

Southall, R., *South Africa's Transkei* (Monthly Review Press, New York, 1983)

Staniland, Martin, *American Intellectuals and African Nationalists, 1955–1970* (Yale University Press, New Haven, 1991)

Starke, J. G., *Introduction to International Law*, 5th ed. (Butterworths, London, 1963)

Strack, H., "The International Relations of Rhodesia Under Sanctions" PhD dissertation, University of Iowa (1974)

Streek, B. and R. Wicksteed, *Render unto Kaiser: A Transkei Dossier* (Ravan Press, Johannesburg, 1981)

Stremlau, John L., *The International Politics of the Nigerian Civil War, 1967–1970* (Princeton University Press, Princeton, 1977)

Struelens, M., *ONUC (United Nations in the Congo) and International Politics* (American University Press, Washington, 1968)

Stultz, N. M., *Transkei's Half Loaf: Race Separatism in South Africa* (Yale University Press, New Haven, 1981)

Talmon, Stefan, "The Constitutive versus the Declaratory Theory of Recognition: Tertium Non Datur?" *British Yearbook of International Law*, vol. 75, no. 1 (2004)

Taylor, Peter J., "The State as Container: Territoriality in the Modern World System," *Progress in Human Geography*, vol. 18, no. 2 (1994)

Tyson, D. W., *Courage to put Country above Color: The J.A. Parker Story* (unknown publisher, 2009)

Urquhart, B., *A Life in Peace and War* (W. W. Norton, New York, 1987)

Vail, Leroy, *The Creation of Tribalism in Southern Africa* (James Currey, London, 1989)

Van Vuuren, Hennie, "Apartheid Grand Corruption: Assessing the Scale of Crimes of Profit in South Africa from 1976 to 1994," *Report prepared by civil society at the request of the Second National Anti-Corruption Summit* (May 2006)

Waddy, N., "The Strange Death of 'Zimbabwe–Rhodesia': The Question of British Recognition of the Muzorewa Regime in Rhodesian Public Opinion, 1979," *South African Historical Journal* vol. 66, no. 2 (2013)

Walker, Lydia, "Decolonization in the 1960s: On Legitimate and Illegitimate Nationalist Claims-Making," *Past & Present*, vol. 242, no. 1 (February 2019)

Watts, C., "Killing Kith and Kin: The Viability of British Military Intervention in Rhodesia, 1964–5," *Twentieth Century British History* vol. 16, no. 4 (January 2005)

Rhodesia's Unilateral Declaration of Independence: An International History (Palgrave Macmillan, New York, 2012)

Weiss, Herbert, "The Congo's Independence Struggle Viewed Fifty Years Later," *African Studies Review*, vol. 55, no. 1 (April 2012)

Weissman, S., *American Foreign Policy in the Congo, 1960–1964* (Cornell University Press, Ithaca, NY, 1974)

White, L., "'Normal Political Activities': Rhodesia, the Pearce Commission, and the African National Council," *The Journal of African History*, vol. 52, no. 3 (2011)

Unpopular Sovereignty: Rhodesian Independence and African Decolonization (University of Chicago Press, Chicago, 2015)

Williams, S., *Who Killed Hammarskjold? The UN, The Cold War, and White Supremacy* (Hurst, London, 2011)

Windrich, E., *Britain and the Politics of Rhodesia Independence* (Groom Helm, London, 1978)

Witz, L., *Apartheid's Festival: Contesting South Africa's National Pasts* (Indiana University Press, Bloomington, 2003)

Wooten & Gibson (ed.), *Who's Who of Southern Africa* (Wooten & Gibson, Johannesburg, 1961)

Wood, J. R. T., *A Matter of Weeks Rather than Months: The Impasse between Harold Wilson and Ian Smith: Sanctions, Aborted Settlements and War 1965–1969* (Trafford, Victoria, 2008)

So Far and No Further: Rhodesia's Bid for Independence during the Retreat from Empire (Trafford, Victoria, 2005)

Young, C., *Politics in the Congo: Decolonization and Independence* (Oxford University Press, Oxford, 1965)

The Politics of Cultural Pluralism (University of Wisconsin Press, Madison, 1976)

Zoppi, Marco, "The OAU and the Question of Borders," *Journal of African Union Studies*, vol. 2, nos. 1–2 (2013)

Index

Lightning Source UK Ltd.
Milton Keynes UK
UKHW021840100122
396936UK00003B/368